AF608008

MARRIAGE IN EUROPE, 1400–1800

Marriage in Europe, 1400–1800

EDITED BY SILVANA SEIDEL MENCHI
with the collaboration of Emlyn Eisenach

UNIVERSITY OF TORONTO PRESS
Toronto Buffalo London

Toronto Buffalo London
www.utppublishing.com

ISBN 978-1-4426-3750-4

Library and Archives Canada Cataloguing in Publication

Marriage in Europe, 1400–1800 / edited by Silvana Seidel Menchi ; with the collaboration of Emlyn Eisenach.

Includes bibliographical references.
ISBN 978-1-4426-3750-4 (bound)

1. Marriage – Europe – History. 2. Marriage – Social aspects – Europe – History. I. Seidel Menchi, Silvana, editor II. Eisenach, Emlyn, 1967–, contributor

HQ515.M38 2016 306.81094'0903 C2016-900870-3

University of Toronto Press acknowledges the financial assistance to its publishing program of the Canada Council for the Arts and the Ontario Arts Council, an agency of the Government of Ontario.

Canada Council for the Arts
Conseil des Arts du Canada

Funded by the Government of Canada
Financé par le gouvernement du Canada

Contents

Editor's Note

The phenomena analysed in this volume belong to a politico-geographic unit comprising eight European countries plus the Roman curia, the regulator of mixed marriages.

In order to delineate this overall panorama, the authors of the 11 chapters have made use of documents, normative texts, and secondary literature in nine different languages. Such linguistic and archival diversity poses a challenge to the reader. The present note is intended to guide the reader in the use of the notes and of the complex bibliography to which the notes refer.

The archival sources used in some of the chapters are listed, together with the appropriate abbreviations, in the first note of each chapter that makes direct use of such sources. In those cases in which an archive is mentioned only once, however, that archive is cited only in the note that refers to the specific information contained in the text. Because of this editorial choice, the bibliography contains only printed sources.

Printed works listed in the bibliography are divided into three distinct sections: (1) primary sources, (2) works of reference, and (3) secondary literature. The primary sources – including classics of juridical literature – and the works of reference are indicated in the notes by their abbreviated titles or initials; the secondary literature is indicated simply by the name of the author and the publication date of the book or article cited. This distinction allows the reader to identify immediately whether a piece of information in the text is based on a primary source (or more rarely on a work of reference) or is taken from the secondary scholarly literature. An appreciable amount of the primary sources used in this book is available online, so the system of abbreviating sources that we have adopted will assist the interested reader in verifying the information contained in the text.

The subject treated in this book places particular emphasis on certain categories of sources that the reader will find cited in several chapters, especially the *Corpus Iuris Civilis* and the *Corpus Iuris Canonici*. Of similar importance are the acts of Parliament under various British sovereigns. All of these well-known sources are cited according to the internationally agreed conventions. In particular, British statutes and laws – indicated by the abbreviated name of the reigning sovereign, preceded by one or two numerals identifying the years of his or her reign – are not cited in a specific edition, because the many existing ones have been superseded by digital versions. These may be consulted on the website of the UK Statute Law Database (www.legislation.gov.uk/).

The numerals that the reader will find in brackets, or in the notes, without further indication, refer to the pages of this book.

—S.S.M.

Preface

SILVANA SEIDEL MENCHI

This volume is the culmination of a long journey. The process of bringing together a comparative history of marriage in Europe and of securing the participation of specialists for particular European countries developed in three seminars held over the course of four years (in 2004, 2006, and 2008) and in the exchange of ideas that these meetings fostered. The 11 chapters that resulted were written by authors who are internationally recognized for their explorations of archives of marriage documents and for their analyses of encounters and clashes within couples, both married and otherwise. Some of these authors are true pioneers who have opened up to research archival series that had previously been unexplored or nearly so. The volume's first chapter and last two chapters have a multinational orientation in accord with the research experiences of their authors; the eight central chapters delineate as many pictures of marriage within particular national contexts: England, France, Spain, the Holy Roman Empire of the German Nation, the Netherlands, Italy, Germany/Switzerland, and Sweden.

The realization of such a large-scale project would not have been possible without the substantial support of many institutions and individuals. The initial financing for the three seminars where the seeds of this volume germinated came from the Italian Ministero dell'Università e della Ricerca scientifica e tecnologica, which gave its support to three national research projects that I directed. The first of the international seminars was held in 2004 in the Archivio Patriarcale di Venezia, thanks to the cooperation of Francesca Cavazzana Romanelli, the archive director, who also organized on that occasion an exhibit of the impressive marriage-related materials held there. Also thanks to her intercession, we enjoyed an exquisite dinner in the princely setting of Palazzo

Vendramin Calergi. In 2006, the director of the Harvard University Center for Italian Renaissance Studies, Joseph Connors, bountifully hosted the second seminar in Fiesole at the stupendous Villa I Tatti. We will forever remember the discussion of the papers in the *limonaia*, as well as the meals served us in the villa's garden and the September air redolent with *olea fragrans*. The concluding meeting of that seminar took place in the conference hall of the Museo del Bargello in Florence and included the participation of the museum's director, Beatrice Strozzi. The final seminar, in 2008, was held in the great hall of the Biblioteca Universitaria di Pisa, with the support of the chair of the university's History Department, Giuseppe Petralia, and the library director, Alessandra Pesante. Charles Donahue's book, *Law, Marriage, and Society in the Later Middle Ages* (2007), which had recently been published, was one of the primary focuses of that meeting, illuminated by the presentations of David d'Avray, Richard Helmholz, and Ludwig Schmugge.

Among the scholars who participated in these seminars and enriched them with their contributions, questions, and comments, I would like particularly to thank Andrea Addobbati, Renata Ago, Giorgia Alessi, Georgia Arrivo, Urs Baumann, Marco Bellabarba, Paola Benussi, Elena Brambilla, Francesca Cavazzana Romanelli, Valeria Chilese, Francine Daenens, Ida Fazio, Lucia Ferrante, Anne Jacobson Schutte, Chiara La Rocca, Reinier Leushuis, Sara Luperini, Gherardo Ortalli, Marina Poian, Kirsi Salonen, Ulrike Strasser, Christina Strunck, Francesca Terraccia, and Roni Weinstein.

The success of such a work of many hands depends on the professionalism of its authors. This book is a monument not only to the professionalism of its 10 authors but also to their generosity. The requests and suggestions to which I ceaselessly subjected the authors in the course of this work – suggestions to clarify or to modify, to shorten or to expand, and in some cases to rewrite and rewrite again an entire chapter – were met with patient courtesy and put into action with lucidity. The dialogue with this group of colleagues taught me that concern for others, flexibility, and geniality are companions of scholarly excellence.

I cannot leave this work without remembering my friend and colleague Diego Quaglioni, with whom many years ago I undertook a research project on marriage litigation records held in Italian ecclesiastical archives, which ultimately led to the present volume. I am deeply grateful to him and to the entire group of scholars who helped us to complete that Italian project. Among them I would like to remember with special warmth Stanley Chojnacki, Giovanni Ciappelli, as well as

Valeria Chilese, Cecilia Cristellon, Oscar Di Simplicio, Anna Esposito, Luca Faoro, Joanne Ferraro, Irene Fosi, Cristina Galasso, Daniela Hacke, Anke Hufschmidt, Anna Maria Lazzeri, Giuliano Marchetto, Andrea Marchisello, Christine Meek, Giovanni Minnucci, Dea Moscarda, Ermanno Orlando, Elena Papagna, Beatrice Paolozzi Strozzi, Ulderico Parente, Marina Poian, Angelo Rigo, Pierroberto Scaramella, Kim Siebenhüner, Laura Turchi, and the publisher of the four volumes that were the fruit of the project, Chiara Zorzi. I am grateful to the late Alessandra Contini, who strongly encouraged our work. The other co-authors of these volumes will find their names repeatedly mentioned in the pages that follow.

Without the unobtrusive yet sustained encouragement that Richard Helmholz has given to research into Italian marriage court records, the international dialogue of which this book is the product would never have begun.

In 2010 a group of French historians organized a colloquium entitled *Les officialités dans l'Europe médiévale et moderne: Des tribunaux pour une société chrétienne* (Troyes, 27–9 May). Véronique Beaulande-Barraud and Martine Charageat deserve the gratitude of all historians of ecclesiastical courts for publishing the proceedings of that conference in 2014.

I owe to my friends Therese and Tapan Bhattacharya Stettler the privilege of publishing for the first time in a high-resolution reproduction Vittore Belliniano's painting *The Bashful Bride* (ca. 1520), which appears as Figure 2 in this volume. For the excellent reproduction of the painting by Titian known as the *Venus of Urbino* (1538), published here as Figure 1, I am indebted to the Florentine photographer Antonio Quattrone.

In the editorial standardization of all chapters and in the compilation of the bibliography and index, I have benefited from the assistance of Chiara Mandosso. I was extremely fortunate to find in the later stages of the project a collaborator of such great skill, care, and flexibility.

Particular thanks are due to my colleagues Giovanni Cossa and Marco Ventura, both of the University of Siena, for their advice on the compilation of the bibliography.

Chapters 2 and 6 were expertly translated from the German by Pamela Selwyn.

I am profoundly grateful to Mark Adrian Roberts for translating the introduction and the conclusion of this book and for providing moral support at some very difficult turning points in my professional life. My gratitude to him is deeper than I can express. The loyal friendship of my colleague Anne Jacobson Schutte never fails to support me.

In Suzanne Rancourt, Executive Editor at the University of Toronto Press, in Barbie Halaby of Monocle Editing, and in their associates I was exceptionally fortunate to find the collaborators that every author or editor dreams of. I am deeply grateful for their enthusiasm, their accuracy, and their efficiency.

Emlyn Eisenach has been my literary conscience and intercultural advisor for this work. In addition to this preface, she translated chapters 3, 7, 9 (with Lydia Cochrane), 10, and 11; but other parts of the manuscript too were submitted to the scrutiny of her relentless perfectionism. Her sense of the language, her intellectual rigour, and the warmth of her friendship have been among the gifts of my life as a scholar.

Florence, 30 July 2014

MARRIAGE IN EUROPE, 1400–1800

Introduction

SILVANA SEIDEL MENCHI

Wife or Concubine?

There is no consensus as to exactly what a marriage was in early modern society. In the conventional and still prevalent interpretation, eroticism and passion are aspects that are alien to the traditional marriage. The famous painting with which I open this introduction will supply a context for this statement.

In Titian's *Venus of Urbino* the artist speaks in a clear and perspicuous iconographic language (Figure 1). The myrtle bush adorning the sill of the window which lights the scene is an unequivocal nuptial symbol (the *Venus Pronuba*, the divine protectress of conjugal love, is crowned with myrtle); the twin cassoni in the background are a necessary part of the trousseau of any well-dowered bride;[1] the lapdog curled up at the young woman's feet promises domestic fidelity and docility; with the roses she holds in her hand, the protagonist will shortly decorate the corsage of the dress which her handmaidens are extracting for her from one of the two cassoni. The painting shows a bride about to be dressed to take part in the rite known in Venice as *il toccamano*, that is, to express her consent to the marriage *per parole di presente* (*per verba de presenti*) and to perform the gesture that confirmed this consent, touching the hand of the groom: a domestic and not an ecclesiastical rite, which signalled the irreversible passage from the promise to the union – also, and indeed primarily, the sexual union – of the couple.[2]

An even more evident clue to the event that the painter intended to represent is the dress that the two handmaidens, one standing and the other kneeling, have just taken from the open cassone: a gown of yellow silk, with transverse appliqué in dark green. The painter has

Figure 1. Tiziano Vecellio, called Titian (ca. 1488–1576), *Venus of Urbino*, 1538. Galleria degli Uffizi, Florence. Courtesy of Galleria degli Uffizi and Antonio Quattrone. © Antonio Quattrone, Florence.

taken great pains to describe it. The especially detailed account of a noble Venetian marriage (September 1515) informs us, in fact, that yellow was one of the privileged colours for the bridal dress of a Venetian patrician: the bride in question, a member of the Bollani family, made her appearance on the scene of the *toccamano* gowned in yellow to recite her part in a domestic rite on which the Bollani family wished to confer especial emphasis.[3] That green stripes applied onto a yellow base, moreover, conferred particular sumptuosity on a bridal gown appears from a painting attributed to Giovanni Busi (known as Giovanni Cariani) or, more recently, to Vittore Belliniano (Figure 2, ca. 1520).[4] The painting shows a patrician bride adorned for the rite of the *toccamano*, but timorous and hesitant about appearing on the festive scene. Virginal modesty, which Renaissance courtesy stressed, enjoined the well-born

Figure 2. Vittore Belliniano (ca. 1456–1529), *The Bashful Bride* (ca. 1520). Private collection.
Image courtesy of the owner.

maiden not to fling herself into the arms of her husband: a bride should be reluctant, she should weep, and she should suffer the question about her consent to be thrice repeated before proffering her "I do."[5] In Belliniano's painting two female figures – the myrtle crown that adorns the head of one of them suggests Venus Pronuba, while the other might be the mother of the bride – support the reluctant girl and encourage her to make her entrance into the room where the bridegroom and wedding guests await her. The painter minutely describes the sumptuous gown of the young woman who occupies the centre of the scene, a gown of yellow silk with appliqué of dark green (now darkened and made brown by time): it is the same type of gown as the one that the handmaiden in the *Venus of Urbino* has just taken out of the cassone to clothe Titian's damsel. Taken together with the other iconographic clues, this concordance of the dresses sanctions the interpretation of the *Venus of Urbino* as a nuptial scene.

Despite these multiple signs, art critics are reluctant to read Titian's painting in nuptial terms. They prefer to fantasize about a "lascivious painting" that is intended to unleash "extreme erotic fantasies," they discover in the painting a "new erotic tension," they read it as a "philosophical manifesto of a new sexuality" – and other variations on this theme.[6] Not even well-founded scholarly interpretations such as the one published on the occasion of the exhibition at the Metropolitan Museum *Art and Love in Renaissance Italy* (New York, 2008) can resist referring – even though locating the picture in a nuptial context – to the "erotic charge ... not entirely innocent or domestic" of this painting.[7]

But what Venetian father or husband – so the objection goes – would have wanted to see his own daughter or wife portrayed in the pose of the Venus of Urbino, where virginal modesty is far from emphasized? To this objection I reply that the reading of Titian's painting as a nuptial image does not postulate the figure of a patron who was personally involved. Whereas Belliniano's virginal bride presents all the physiognomic traits of a portrait – and could for this reason have been painted on commission – Titian's bride is an emblematic figure.[8] Everyday Venetian life in this period offered the painter abundant instances capable of unleashing fantasies of matrimonial eroticism. These were not personal fantasies but public and political ones.

The Venice in which Titian spent his youth debated fiercely and legislated vigorously on amorous disorder – i.e., on "shameful, base, and indecent" marriages – insisting on the "shame" of these mésalliances, which subverted the social order and intruded *bastardi* into the ruling class of the Republic. Young women of great beauty, initially installed in respectable houses as concubines and later promoted to the rank of patrician wives, were the bait that gave rise to genuine scandals. In a state ruled by a restricted number of families, where government office was handed down from father to son, family scandals became political scandals. In 1526 – the *Venus of Urbino* is dated to the 1530s – a scandalous marriage, which a few years previously had sowed hatred and war in a family of Doges, the Dandolo di San Moisé, contributed to the promotion of a series of laws framed to mitigate the problem of brides of *vile condizione* (base status) and, by implication, of doubtful chastity.[9] The laws of 1526 failed in their purpose, just as the laws promulgated for the same purpose in earlier decades had all failed.

The reluctance of art critics to accept the *Venus of Urbino* as a nuptial poem or fantasy is a reflection of the tardiness with which the humanities have come to terms with the state of research on the formation and character of marriage in the age of the Renaissance and in the early modern period. As a result of this tardiness, eroticism is tenaciously perceived as a transgressive element, and amorous rapture is considered incompatible with the "conventionally arranged Renaissance marriage." One of the aims of this book is to put an end to such misconceptions, tracing an updated picture of marriage not only in its norms but in the concrete terms of individual human experience.

Marriage: Regulated or Unregulated?

The tension between the model of the disciplined marriage and the particularity of individual choices was a constant of European social history from the waning of the Middle Ages until the early nineteenth century. The tendentiously uniform model recommended by the ecclesiastical and secular authorities is counterpoised by a plurality of individual conjugal initiatives. A lively nuptial experimentation paralleled and challenged the norm. The model of a disciplined, regulated, socially conforming marriage, as formulated by jurists and theologians, found itself in competition with a variegated and undisciplined category of marriage, obeying individual impulses and emotions. The decision-making centres of the Christian world – the churches, the states – elaborated the first type of marriage and promoted it, later imposing it from above. On the other hand, the undisciplined marriage, which belonged to the dimension of lived experience, was actuated from below, as it were, and sought – and occasionally obtained – recognition from above. The history of marriage in Europe is the history of this dichotomy between two levels of marriage.

The 10 scholars who have accepted my invitation to trace in this volume the lineaments of a comparative history of marriage in Europe in the early modern period have scholarly backgrounds that are very different one from the other. They come from eight different historiographic cultures, and they practise research methods that cannot be forced into a single academic constituency. One feature, however, they have in common: they are all, by scholarly *habitus*, crossers of frontiers. The principal frontier they cross daily is the one that separates the sphere of the norms, doctrines, and laws from the sphere of the day-to-day experience of individuals. The ordered marriage belongs to the first sphere, is relatively uniform, and as such lends itself to serial data collection. The individual experience, an improvisation that breaks the rules (we are now in the second sphere), constitutes a single case and requires the kind of analytical and empirical language that belongs to singularity. Unlike traditional historiography, which considered the individual case as marginal and deviant, tending to exclude it from the historian's area of observation, the authors of the following pages are equally at home in both spheres, but they pay particular attention to the singular case, which challenges the norm and which – precisely on account of this challenge – illuminates it.[10]

The book opens with a chapter that delineates the normative framework within which our discourse is located: we owe it to the scholar who, among all the authors involved in our project, has the widest experience of comparativist research at a European level (Charles Donahue Jr.). It is counterbalanced by a final chapter, centred on the matrimonial experimenting that flourished in parallel with institutionalized marriage, preparing the way for the present-day variety of conjugal or paraconjugal understandings (Silvana Seidel Menchi).

In the central chapters of this book, nine authors illustrate the theme of marriage within the politico-cultural context that each one has studied in depth:

The Holy Roman Empire (Heide Wunder),
Italy (Daniela Lombardi),
England (Richard H. Helmholz),
The Netherlands and especially Holland (Manon van der Heijden),
Germany and Switzerland (Susanna Burghartz),
Spain (Jesús M. Usunáriz),
Sweden (Mia Korpiola),
France (Anne Lefebvre-Teillard), and finally
European trans-confessional (i.e., mixed) marriages (Cecilia Cristellon).

That the collaboration of these scholars might give rise to a comparative history of marriage in Europe was, when I began, a hypothesis still to be verified. The result of the experiment was all the more uncertain in as much as the authors had complete liberty to structure their discourse in accordance with their own concrete research experience and to advance their own personal interpretation of the theme. The variety of structures, the multiplicity of accents, and the plurality of timescales which the reader will encounter in passing from chapter to chapter are the result of this autonomy granted to the individual authors; but they are also imposed by the various trajectories of the national histories.

The final result of the collaboration begun in 2004 does demonstrate the validity of the comparativist hypothesis that was our point of departure. At the end of our study, European marriage appears as a many-sided phenomenon held together by strong connective threads. Despite the decision to favour case-by-case and chapter-by-chapter particularity, these connective threads clearly emerge. I will mention three.

First, one of the most visible of these transverse links may be summarized as the principle enunciated by a Venetian priest: "marriages must be free" (*i matrimoni devono essere liberi*, 1532).[11] That priest was commenting on a particular problem he had been called upon to unravel; but he knew that he was touching on the most delicate point of his office as judge. Christian marriage was basically free: it could be stipulated by a simple agreement between the parties. The validity of the act did not depend on any external condition. That the expression of consent was public or private, solemn or secret, approved or opposed by the families, blessed or not blessed by a cleric, was neither here nor there. Provided it was free and voluntary, it bound the two parties for life (Donahue 34, 35, Wunder 65–6, Lombardi 99, 101, Helmholz 134–5). They were bound even if, immediately after expressing their consent, they separated from one another permanently. Contested, evaded, circumvented, never entirely obliterated, constantly invoked, the principle that marriage is free re-emerges in all the matrimonial cultures of Europe in the passage from the Middle Ages to the modern period.

Second, such freedom was dangerous. The marriage managed by the two parties, freely, could resolve itself into an undisturbed cohabitation that was socially accepted – especially if the spouses were simple tradespeople or poor peasants and if patrimonies involved in the union were of modest entity[12] – but it could also be a precipitate or ephemeral arrangement, a socially scandalous union, a strategy of seduction, an imposture, a deception. What if a man who had once privately said to a young girl, "I take thee for my wife," and had thus been accepted by her as her husband – and this would be a legitimate form of marriage, even though disapproved of by the authorities – what if such a man should then deny that he had contracted a marriage?[13] Thus, freedom could give rise to disorder, discord, vendetta (Wunder 62, Lombardi 99, 100, van der Heijden 164–5, 166, Usunáriz 205, 207). Churches, states, and families all had an interest in disciplining and controlling an institution that had such important effects on the life of the community and that influenced the distribution of wealth. Since the principle of freedom had produced multiplicity and disorder, the control of marriage passed through the imposition of a regime of uniformity. All the various Christian bodies, the Protestant churches no less than the Catholic Church, strove to transfer marriage from a multiform to a uniform regime. This is another link that connects all the central chapters of this book together (Donahue 35–8, Wunder 71–3, 75–6, Lombardi 102–3, van der Heijden 162–3, 165, Burghartz 177–9, Usunáriz 203, Lefebvre-Teillard 261–2). Marriage had to become, and did become, an obligatory and uniform procedure in its basic stages.

Third, Christian ethics locates marriage in close proximity to sin. Every union duly celebrated is a barrier erected against evil. Secular and ecclesiastical authorities waged a centuries-long struggle to contain sexuality within the bounds of holy matrimony (Burghartz 187–9, Lefebvre-Teillard 271–2). It was of paramount importance, therefore, to fix in unequivocal fashion the point of no return in stipulating the conjugal bond (Donahue 34, Wunder 72, Korpiola 225–7). The reader will discover that this became an obsession shared by secular and ecclesiastical authorities without distinction of denomination. The crucial figure in this struggle to repress sin (extramarital sexuality) was the woman. In Venice, where incomparable documentation from the fifteenth century onwards has been analysed, the key role of the woman as the instrument of sexual control is clearly demonstrated: it is she, the woman (or sometimes the girl child), who is the preferred interlocutrix of the matrimonial judge. But also in the Holy Roman Empire, in the Swiss cantons, in France, the figure of the woman advances in the sixteenth and seventeenth century to the centre of attention (Burghartz 191–2, Lefebvre-Teillard 277–8, 281–2). It is she who is the guardian of the sanctity of marriage and who bears responsibility for the community shame associated with the inopportune exercise of sexuality. Expiation falls upon her (Wunder 80, van der Heijden 170–2, Burghartz 192–3, Lefebvre-Teillard 282).

To what degree these tendencies, which are found widespread and over a long period in European matrimonial culture, and of which I have mentioned only three, were the distant result of the monogamy, which is the informing principle of Christian conjugal morality, is a question that for the moment must remain open. Experiments in polygamy – by which I mean legalized polygamy – were not completely unknown in Europe. We find a clear rejection of them (Seidel Menchi 329).

I conclude this section with a glance at the privileged sources of our group. The authors of this book, I believe, have more easily found common ground because they share a predilection for a particular category of sources. All of them, myself included, have devoted years of research to documents that are widely present all over Christian Europe but are not everywhere studied: the records of matrimonial trials preserved in ecclesiastical or secular archives (Helmholz 123–4, 125–8).[14] The matrimonial trials provide a training in hermeneutic flexibility: to study them on a daily basis means learning how to disentangle marriage in all its many configurations, in the irreducibility *ad unum* of the social and emotional needs to which it responded and still responds.

The volume is organized in three sections. Section I gathers the chapters that stress the alternative "Continuity and Change" in the norms and praxis of marriage; Section II brings together four chapters that emphasize the alternative "Licit and Illicit"; Section III is entitled "Uniformity and Singularity." This arrangement is intended to help the reader to access the work in an organic fashion and to make a comparison between the component parts, juxtaposing chapters linked by transverse analogies, by similarities of structure or by affinities of emphasis.

Section I: Continuity and Change

Chapter 1: The Legal Background

In the first chapter Charles Donahue Jr. introduces the reader to the heart of the argument, with magisterial lucidity and a penetrating power of synthesis. Disciplined marriage is here presented in its three principal variants:

a) as a model elaborated by the theologians of the Catholic Church, one that remained in force throughout Christendom until the sixteenth century;
b) as a counter-model elaborated by the Lutheran and Calvinist theologians, one that was introduced – with a few denominational variants – and put into effect in Protestant Europe;
c) as a model subjected to the strict control of the Catholic Church, one that prevailed – not without resistance and exceptions – in those countries that adopted the decrees of the Council of Trent (1545–63) and imposed them by state legislation.

Already in this first chapter, however, disciplined marriage begins to resemble a besieged castle. The besiegers are the aspirant spouses. For 300 years, from the sixteenth to the eighteenth century – Donahue informs us – European jurists continued to debate the norms that regulated the various matrimonial models and to re-propose these norms in ever differing formulations: this investment of intellectual energy was imposed by the tenacious permanence of unions not conforming to the rules. There resulted a "conversation about marriage across confessional lines" (Donahue 42), in which two topics constantly recurred: the requirements that rendered a marriage perfectly contracted (and therefore indissoluble) and the conditions needed for dissolution of the bond. Particular aspects and features of this debate, which is incisively sketched for the reader in the first chapter, reappear in all the later chapters.

Chapter 2: The Holy Roman Empire of the German Nation

In the second chapter, the normative discourse opened by Donahue is tested in the concrete reality of a particular political and social landscape: the Holy Roman Empire of the German nation. What in the first chapter was juridical doctrine here becomes interdenominational coexistence, plurality of political constitutions, cultural dialogue. The outline delineated by Heide Wunder covers in systematic fashion the four centuries that form the chronological framework of this book. The many-sided viewpoint she adopts brings together individual cases with quantitative data, theological arguments with elements from criminal history, and literary sources with details taken from the history of legislation, foreshadowing the plurality of expositive registers employed by the authors of the successive chapters.

The basic political function ascribed to marriage in early modern Europe receives emphasis precisely from the versatile arrangement of this chapter: in the succession of epochs and cultures, marriage is constantly defined as the ordering principle of society, both the matrix and the banner of the well-ordered community. What applies to the politically composite panorama of the Holy Roman Empire applies also to the politico-cultural entities discussed in the following chapters: "The purity of society was based on the gender relations integrated into matrimony" (Wunder 75). What we have here is one of the lynchpins of European matrimonial discourse in the modern period. Wherever the state takes over from the church as the authority regulating marriage, as happened in France from the sixteenth century, this situation increases rather than reduces pressure tending to impose regulated marriage on the couple (Lefebvre-Teillard 262–8).

Chapter 3: Italy

In the third chapter, Daniela Lombardi has taken on the task of delineating the institution of marriage in Italy. The juxtaposition of Italy and Germany is one of analogy and of contrast. A country with a single religious denomination is compared to one with several; a uniformly Catholic people is compared to one that gave birth to the Reformation; a culture that treats marriage as a sacrament is compared to one that denies it sacramental status; a legislation that considers matrimony an indissoluble bond is compared to a legislation in which divorce is possible, at least in theory. The analogies that Lombardi emphasizes are, however, deeper than these contrasts. Thus, in Italy too we see matrimony pass from a regime of multiformity to a regime of uniformity, transformed from a process managed from below (by the spouses or by their families) into a single event controlled from above (in this case, by ecclesiastical authority). In Italy too we see the age of the Enlightenment signal a radical change in mentality and the triumph of a culture of sensibility.

Compared with the previous chapter, however, the chapter on Italy inaugurates a more discontinuous strategic narrative and presents a less compact structure. The overall picture seems fragmented, religious and social control is questioned, the contradictions within the system appear more glaring. This change is the result of the viewpoint of the concrete case which, introduced in the previous chapter, rises here to a privileged epistemological resource. Lombardi deals with the crucial elements of the discourse, illustrating them by specific cases and focusing on concrete examples: she does this, for instance, for the "clandestine marriage" and its contradictory interpretations (Lombardi 99–101), for the binding or non-binding character of the promise (105–7), for the freedom of choice of sons and daughters (104–5), for the transformation of the "presumed marriage" from a legitimate form of partnership into a crime – an effect of the implementation of the decrees of the Council of Trent (109–10).[15]

Chapter 4: England

The privileged position assigned to the individual case constitutes the link between the chapter on Italy and the chapter on England. Here Richard Helmholz opens his discourse by illustrating the nature, potential, and limits of that category of sources in which individual cases are most fully documented: the matrimonial court records. For this reason, the chapter on England turns out to be – from the heuristic viewpoint – of fundamental importance in our volume, even though it is the shortest as regards the period of time covered by the reconstruction.[16] Two arguments militate in favour of England as the framework for a systematic discourse on the sources privileged by the authors of this book: the pre-eminent position of the English matrimonial causes in the framework of international research (for England has preserved these kinds of sources in a more complete and more articulated form than any other European country), and the role that Helmholz himself has played in evaluating these sources and in training historians of marriage in the use of the individual case.[17]

Some unexpected – in fact very surprising – features of marriage in England are highlighted thanks to the comparison with Italy. I will mention only one of the most obvious. In England the medieval regulations on matrimony remained in force for five centuries and more, without the Reformation modifying in substantial fashion the stipulation of the bond, as did happen in Italy as the result of the decrees of the Council of Trent. The paradoxical result of this was that the medieval marriage, in which the simple exchange of consent by words of present assent (*per verba de presenti*), even in the absence of any solemnization, was the performative element of the bond – the matrimonial model that the Catholic Church had formalized in the thirteenth century and continued to recognize as valid until the sixteenth century – remained valid in Anglican England until the eighteenth century, whereas it had been abrogated, and condemned as "clandestine marriage," in Catholic Italy, just as it had in France and in Spain.[18]

In the animated and varied scene that appears before our eyes in the chapter on England, many features will arouse the reader's curiosity and will suggest possible avenues for future research. Among those that arouse my own curiosity, I will mention two: the cunning and ingenious expedients, sometimes amounting to genuine impostures, orchestrated to entice a man or a woman to enter into a marriage or to leave open a means of escape after having married (Helmholz 129, 134–5, 139); and the multiplicity of forms which could be assumed by the amorous disorder that the English courts prosecuted by right of office (*ex officio*) – for example, the insidious crime of soliciting the chastity of a maiden, a phenomenon that was by no means restricted to Catholic confessionals in the age of the Counter-Reformation (*sollicitatio castitatis*, Helmholz 145).

Section II: Licit and Illicit

The amorous disorder that in the first part of this volume appears as a danger to be combatted, or as an instinct to be controlled, moves to the centre of the stage in the second part. It is the protagonist of the chapter on Germany and Switzerland (6) and it permeates – through the multiplication of concrete cases – the other three chapters in this part: those on the Netherlands (5), Spain (7), and Sweden (8).

But was it really a disorder that the churches and states of the early modern era denounced in such intransigent terms and combatted with such drastic measures? Or has the historian – in this case the editor of the present volume – been deceived by the vocabulary and by the values system absorbed from her sources? The variegated matrimonial experiences we find in our contemporary society would seem to counsel extreme caution in the use of the kind of disparaging terminology that our esteemed masters employed without reserve. Perhaps those who a few decades ago appeared to be subverters of conjugal order were in fact precursors of a new order.

Chapter 5: The Netherlands

In this part of the volume, the effects of the Protestant Reformation take concrete form in the society of the Netherlands, a predominantly Calvinist state. Manon van der Heijden contrasts on the one hand holy matrimony, exalted by Protestant theologians as having been ordained by God and as the "morally normative centre of society" (Wunder 68), and on the other hand "fornication" – i.e., sexual intercourse outside wedlock – which was liable to sanctions both ecclesiastical and secular. The control of this delicate matter was exercised by the town councils and the church councils, with a harmony that was undoubtedly favoured by the denominationally uniform character of the Calvinist Netherlands: whereas the secular authorities were responsible for making and enforcing laws, the church assemblies (in particular the consistory courts) controlled the actual behaviour of the believers. The mass of particular cases – some described individually here – handled by this double discipline throws light on two principles often emphasized by the new matrimonial order: the prerequisite of parental consent (unavoidable for those who had not reached the statutory age) and the penalization of any kind of sexual activity outside of wedlock. These are the same principles which in chapter 6 Susanna Burghartz defines, respectively, as the social order and the sexual order.

The means of enforcement for this discipline were of penal nature when applied by the secular authority (imprisonment, banishment) and of symbolic nature when applied by the ecclesiastical authority (exclusion from the Lord's Supper). But also in the Netherlands – as in the Holy Roman Empire (Wunder 74) – denunciation of transgressors depended on the cooperation of the local population: this meant involving the entire society in the disciplinary process and promoting the interiorization, on the part of the individual believer, of the notion of belonging to a community of saints.

The quantitative data that van der Heijden has gathered during her archival researches demonstrate that the Dutch ecclesiastical and secular authorities won the war against social disorder in matrimonial matters – because marriages stipulated without parental consent form only a small percentage of contested unions – but lost the war against sexual disorder. In van der Heijden's evocation, this latter phenomenon assumes varied forms: we find it as the anticipation of marital relations (sexual activity on the part of the betrothed); as the result of being inveigled into making a promise of marriage, immediately renounced; as stable though not formalized paraconjugal cohabitation; as an act of occasional promiscuity; and as long-lasting concubinage (van der Heijden 163–9). According to the law, all these kinds of behaviour were crimes and "fornicators" were liable to social ostracism and other punitive measures.

But how rigid were these rules in actual practice?

Chapter 6: Germany and Switzerland

This question forms the link between the chapter on the Netherlands and the one on Switzerland and Germany (paying particular attention to southern Germany). The leitmotif of this chapter is the struggle against illicit sexuality. In Susanna Burghartz's spirited reconstruction, the aspiration to construct a society of saints becomes the matrix that produces a regime of sharp demarcation between the sphere of the licit (marriage sanctioned by churchgoing) and the sphere of the illicit (all other forms of sexuality). Burghartz illuminates both in fine detail and in sweeping generality the full scale of the human drama aroused by such rigour: prohibition of marriage for couples with insufficient income (to bring up children), ostracism of unmarried mothers, infanticide.

Burghartz states that the severe and occasionally draconian laws that governed illicit sexuality should be regarded not as the effect of "fornication" (*Unzucht*) but rather as its cause: "by adopting an increasingly repressive morals policy," the ecclesiastical and secular authorities in South Germany and Switzerland achieved "the paradoxical effect ... of continually recreating the very evil [they were] supposed to combat" (182). The reader is tempted to recall St Paul's principle that it is the law that gives rise to sin (1 Corinthians 15:56) and to interpret it as a reproof to Protestant rigorism. But once again the similarities prevail over the dissimilarities: in Catholic Italy, indeed, the demonization of the female body that characterizes post-Tridentine morality had a similar effect of "eroticizing the language of the body and accentuating its sensuality" (Lombardi 108).

One of the more drastic consequences of the regime of sharp and non-nuanced demarcation between decency (*Zucht*) and licentiousness (*Unzucht*) was the creation of the crime known as "premature intercourse": initiating sexual relations before the celebration of marriage. Rigorist communities kept under control not only the betrothed but even the married. Whenever a premature pregnancy gave rise to the suspicion that a couple's sexual relations had begun prior to the nuptial blessing, the woman was liable to be summoned before a matrimonial court for the crime of fornication (with her present husband, Burghartz 187–8). The principle that "matrimony purges all that has gone before" (*matrimonium omnia precedentia purgat*, Helmholz 144), applied in similar cases by judges both in Italy and in Sweden, cut no ice in a society that aspired to impose total restraint on all amorous impulses. In this respect, Protestant Basel resembled the Calvinist Netherlands and Anglican England.[19]

In Switzerland too, however, the intransigent position was a losing one. Nocturnal visits by young men to the bedchambers of young women – a form of ritualized courting, organized by groups of young bachelors, with the agreement of the families and of the community – were an erotic initiation that could easily result in a pregnancy. The prevailing sexual discipline never called this rite into question, and rural society took full responsibility for its results. As appears from the outline delineated here, premarital sexual experimentation was a widespread and accepted custom in the rural areas of the Protestant Swiss cantons. More complex and differentiated was the situation in Bavaria, for which there exist precise quantitative data (Burghartz 186, 190).

Comparison of the chapter on Germany and Switzerland with the one on the Netherlands favours a parallel reading that may stimulate critical reflection. Although the two matrimonial cultures have many features in common, both general and particular,[20] the tone of the two chapters is nevertheless very different. Regarding the harshness of the punishments and the severity of the repression, the overall historical judgment diverges. Van der Heijden emphasizes the conciliatory attitude of the Protestant consistory courts (in the matter of parental consent) and the mildness of the secular tribunals (when the "fornicating" couple had made a promise of marriage).[21] In Switzerland and in the nearby principality of Württemberg, on the other hand, the culture of "purity" elaborated a language "of sin and contamination" that entered the legislation – and perhaps influenced the collective mentality (Burghartz 179–80).

Chapter 7: Spain

In the chapter on Spain, the comparativist project that has inspired this volume enters very promising territory for future studies. A landscape of uniformly Catholic composition is once again compared with two landscapes of mixed (though predominantly Protestant) denomination, the Netherlands and Switzerland. This comparison, one that we have already encountered in the first part of the book, has so far revealed more analogies than differences. What can we learn about this dichotomy from Jesús M. Usunáriz, an explorer who investigates a documentary territory that is still relatively unknown?[22]

The insertion of Spain into our framework of observation enriches with additional colour the theme of premarital and extramarital sexuality that forms the principal link between the first two chapters in this second part. The fornicators, the scandalous young women whose profligacy necessitated draconian laws from the legislations of Württemberg and Basel – here they are, confiding in us in their own words. Their love letters, their promises of marriage, are genuine archival treasures. The documents that Usunáriz has unearthed during his researches in Pamplona (Navarre) convey fragments of an amorous discourse of great emotional power, one that would be difficult to parallel anywhere else in Europe.

From his rich documentation, Usunáriz has selected particularly eloquent testimonies regarding the significance of the promise to marry. It is certain that the young women of Navarre and their lovers who appear in this chapter considered the promise to marry as the signal for the commencement of sexual relations, which were perceived by the betrothed themselves as licit. The young women in these accounts regarded themselves as legitimate wives, addressing their beloved as "*esposo mio*" and regularly sharing with him the conjugal bed; they could rely on the solidarity of a social context that at least in part shared their convictions and defended their rights. Although we must try to avoid the error of excessive generalizing from data that are taken exclusively from documents in the archive of Pamplona and that refer to a very small minority, the Spanish experience nevertheless expresses with especial vigour an attitude that the reader will find ramified in various parts of Europe, especially in the countryside but also among the urban middle classes: the promise to marry signalled the start of progressively intimate relations between the betrothed spouses. The authors of this volume record this conviction in the Netherlands as in the Holy Roman Empire, in Italy as in Sweden.[23]

The Spanish betrothed spouses who engaged in premarital relations, thus violating the sexual order imposed by the Catholic Church in the wake of the Council of Trent, also violated the social order, in as much as they chose on their own initiative a bride or a groom who had not been selected by the strategies of family advancement. Parental consent, which in Protestant countries was an indispensable precondition for the stipulation of marriage between underage persons, was not a prerequisite for matrimonial candidates in Catholic countries, even though – as we learn from the Spanish cases – this freedom of the children was perhaps more apparent in theory than in practice. The importance for Spanish society of the principle of social homogamy – a principle guaranteed and safeguarded by parental authority – is expressed in the first part of the chapter, where Usunáriz deals with "clandestine matrimony," that is to say socially nonconformist matrimony, and the struggle waged against it in the legislation both ecclesiastical and secular. While in the second part of the chapter on Spain the theme of sexual order prevails, the first part is concerned with social order. The interaction of these two principles, social and sexual order, is the transverse link relating the discourse on Spain to the previous two chapters.

Chapter 8: Sweden

The chapter that concludes the second part of the volume transports us once again from the south to the north of Europe. Mia Korpiola has treated the theme of marriage in Sweden in a systematic yet polyhedric fashion: the chapter's many facets include elements from the history of private law, of criminal history, and of historical anthropology. Special attention is paid to ritual.

In an agrarian economy such as that of Sweden, where riches consisted essentially of real estate, marriage was closely associated with the distribution and transmission of landed property (see the case of Elin Tönnesdotter, 241). Korpiola devotes considerable space to a theme that in the immediately preceding chapters was left somewhat in the background: property relations between the spouses. Further aspects of economic and legal history, discontinuously addressed in the previous chapters, are addressed in the chapter on Sweden, such as the sumptuary laws (242).

The reader will discover interesting points of intersection between the Swedish matrimonial experience and the experiences traced in the preceding chapters. It is the particular features of Scandinavian society and culture that confer special significance on such intersections.

An example: in 1571 the Swedish Lutheran Church ruled that a betrothal celebrated in the presence of witnesses and respectful of the customary rites, if sexually consummated, is a performative act of matrimony; children born from such a union are to be considered legitimate, even though their parents have omitted to formalize the marriage. In this way the Swedish Church evidently provided its own solution to the problem of premarital sexuality, a problem common to all cultures in early modern Europe (225–6, 230–1).

Another example: the notion of matrimony as a succession of stages, requiring considerable time (Lombardi 94), posed the Swedish ecclesiastical authorities with a problem crucial to European juridical culture: how to establish "the precise moment when an indissoluble marriage was created" (Korpiola 245) and how to make it coincide with the church ceremony. One of the solutions excogitated in Sweden was so radical as to be judged outrageous – the bedding of the spouses ought to take place in church – but the problem per se was the same one that for centuries had exercised the canonists of Europe (Korpiola 244).

The transverse correspondences that link Sweden to Europe are striking when they refer to well-defined rites and customs. In addition to the morning gift and the bedding (232–5) we may mention the virginal crown and the loosened hair of the bride: both of these were forbidden to non-virgin young women who presented themselves at church to be married. Ignoring this prohibition was regarded as an indictable offence (a crown offence, Wunder 80 and Korpiola 249–50).

Section III: Uniformity and Singularity

The third part of this volume has its focus on France. Compared to the outline of Europe delineated in the previous chapters, the Kingdom of France represents an exception. From the sixteenth century, in fact, controlling and disciplining the formation of the couple was an objective inscribed in capital letters in the program of the government of the French crown. To attain this objective – which responded to a basic orientation of the country's political culture – the Kingdom of France took a peculiar path, one that diverged in method and in timing from that taken by other European matrimonial cultures, where the marriage rules were laid down by the churches. The peculiarity of this path is the first of two reasons why France has been accorded the last place among the countries here treated. The second reason is opposed and complementary: while from the viewpoint of political culture, and of time for development, France is an exception, from the viewpoint of social history and of the history of emotions, it represents on the contrary a point of arrival and of verification of two alternatives that permeate all the earlier chapters: the alternative between socially conformist and nonconformist marriage and the alternative between the sexually disciplined and the sexually undisciplined couple.

Chapter 9: The Kingdom of France

In the sixteenth and seventeenth centuries the formation of matrimony passed, in France, from the control of the church to the control of the state. This took place with the consent of the bishops and without disturbing relations between the Most Christian King and the papacy. It was a process in stages, and its political refinement and juridical subtlety are well illustrated by Anne Lefebvre-Teillard.

The taking control of the formation of the couple did not come about through negotiation between the French crown and the papacy in Rome but was the result of royal edicts and ordinances. In three successive moments (1556, 1579, 1639), French jurisprudence managed to achieve the aim which the bishops of the kingdom did not succeed in reaching during the Council of Trent: assuring to parents or guardians the legal instruments for preventing children of family (*enfants de famille*) from marrying without their – the parents' or guardians' – permission or against their will. The conceptual sophistication of this procedure is expertly analysed by Lefebvre-Teillard.

Thus we see how a sophisticated juridical construction, the "abduction by seduction" (*rapt de séduction*), allowed the royal courts to threaten severe penalties, potentially even capital punishment, for the man or woman responsible for having "abducted" his or her partner – not by violence but by "seduction" – and for having induced her or him to enter into a mésalliance (Lefebvre-Teillard 266–8). These kinds of expedient also illuminate the emotional features of the phenomenon which Lefebvre-Teillard analyses primarily in its political and juridical aspects. The two marriages within the royal entourage that Lefebvre-Teillard links respectively to the edict of 1556 and the ordinance of 1639 – in as much as the court cases were affected by them – reveal how "clandestine marriages" (i.e., without parental consent) could effectively shipwreck the strategies of family advancement devised by the aristocracy, even by the royal family. The danger was so palpable and far-reaching, the fear so pressing, that it became necessary to mobilize the most sophisticated intellectual resources of jurisprudence to circumvent the difficulty. Evidently the young French aristocracy was far from docile in its amorous proclivities.

If "clandestine marriage" offers a key to understanding the first part of the chapter on France, the key to understanding the second part is provided by "presumed marriage." The church has formalized the "presumed marriage" as far back as the thirteenth century. In order to remedy the phenomenon of premarital sexuality, canon law declared as a "marriage" valid in the forum of conscience (*in foro conscientiae*) – but valid also, if proved, in the judicial forum – the bond established between a man and a woman when their sexual relations had been preceded by a promise to marry in the future. This was evidently an expedient to regularize behaviour that the church condemned but could not prevent. After the Council of Trent, this type of union was branded as sexual disorder ("fornication") and was prosecuted both in Catholic countries and, even more severely, in Protestant ones. Despite this, the idea that a young virgin, or a woman of good reputation, could make a claim against the man who had deflowered or "seduced" her and could demand to be recognized as his wife, or at least compel him to pay her a dowry – in other words, could avail herself of the institution of "presumed marriage" – took deep root in the collective understanding in all countries of Europe and continued to be evoked centuries after that ancient institution, "presumed marriage," had been abrogated and its surviving forms had been criminalized.

In the second part of the chapter on France, Lefebvre-Teillard analyses the possibilities for compensation which – after the abolition of "presumed marriage" as a legal concept – the law made available to a seduced woman, and in particular to an unmarried mother. The theme of the unmarried mother, which emerges in four chapters in this book, is here treated in analytical fashion. The tragedies that sound such sorrowful notes in the chapters on the Holy Roman Empire, on England, on the Netherlands, and on Germany and Switzerland assume in the chapter on France concrete identities (Marie-Thérèse Douchet, Marion la Brune).[24]

Exactly what space French jurisprudence allowed for the "seduced" woman is a question that Lefebvre-Teillard answers in detail. The evolution she reconstructs for France reveals in the rigour of its juridical discourse an evolution that the reader of this volume already knows: the moral, social, and indeed penal responsibility for premarital and extramarital sexuality and its consequences (the illegitimate child) is progressively loaded onto the female partner (Wunder 79–80, Lombardi 111–12, Burghartz 192). In the eighteenth century a young woman, who in earlier times could have relied on the protection of the law and on the solidarity of the social network, became a scapegoat heaped with responsibility for her bastard, who was seen as a drain on the public resources and as polluting the honour of the community.

The legislation on infanticide, a crime of which the unmarried mother was always suspected, marked the climax of this evolution. The effects of this legislation made themselves felt especially in Germany, where women who committed infanticide were condemned to death, and in the Netherlands, where the exposure of the infanticide mother to public shame on a platform was aggravated by a pitiless symbolism (Burghartz 193–4, van der Heijden 170–1). In France, the laws passed by the Parlement of Paris tended to attenuate – as Lefebvre-Teillard explains – certain inhumane measures, abolishing for example the interrogation that an unmarried mother had been obliged by law to undergo during childbed, being questioned by the midwife concerning the paternity of the baby she was about to deliver; but not even in France was an unmarried pregnant woman spared suspicion as a potential child-killer (Lefebvre-Teillard 277–8).

Chapter 10: European Mixed Marriages

The chapter on France, which concludes our overview of Europe, is followed by the only chapter, apart from the opening and the last one, that emerges from a national or culturally unified setting in order to address a plurinational and interdenominational problem – that of the "mixed marriage," or marriage between spouses of different religious denominations. This chapter, based on hitherto-unexplored documentation conserved in the Roman archive of the Congregation for the Doctrine of the Faith (formerly the Holy Office of the Inquisition), anticipates some of the results due to emerge from an immense research project on which one of our authors, Cecilia Cristellon, is currently engaged. It is intended as a contribution that our group of historians wishes to make towards the prospects of future research.

One motif that, declaredly or implicitly, runs throughout this volume is directly examined by Cristellon: the transgressive marriage. Whereas in the previous chapter by Lefebvre-Teillard the regulated union is the standard against which the transgressive one is measured, in this chapter the transgressive union becomes the protagonist. Conjugal union between persons of differing religions or denominations is, in fact, transgressive *par excellence*. All religions and denominations oppose it, forbid it, hinder it; and all of them are obliged to give in and to enact, for this purpose, regulations which are the admission of a historical defeat. The mechanism by which couples were brought together was not, in the last analysis, controllable by the authorities. In this way chapter 10 anticipates one of the principal conclusions of our comparative study.

Chapter 11: Conjugal Experiments in Europe

The study of marriage in history has long coincided with the study of the laws that regulated it. In the historiographical lexicon of our most authoritative masters, therefore, the key substantive appears in the singular: their books deal with "marriage."[25] Among today's historians there is a tendency to pass from the use of the singular to that of the plural.[26] The passage from singular to plural was not an objective explicitly enunciated in the plan for this book or in the meetings that prepared for it. But the emphasis placed from the outset on the records of matrimonial trials as a privileged source for the history of marriage – i.e., on concreteness, on multiplicity, on the inventiveness of lived experience – made that result inevitable. In the chapters of this book, "marriage" ramifies into a plurality of variants: "clandestine marriage," "presumed marriage," "morganatic marriage," "surprise marriage," "marriage of conscience," "secret marriage," marriage with the addition of the cicisbeo, "bigamy." These formulas, which the reader will encounter in the pages that follow, refer to conjugal experiences that aspired to be recognized as legitimate unions and that did in fact obtain such recognition, even though they violated the existing norms in varying degrees of gravity. Not even homosexual marriage is completely absent from the documentation used by the authors of this volume.[27]

In the last chapter I gave narrative form to five concrete examples of matrimonial variants, which we find mentioned but not described in one or more chapters of this book. In this respect chapter 11 performs an integrative function, responding to the foreseeable requirements of a reader attentive to the concreteness of the individual case. At the same time it has a recapitulatory function, because it proclaims the heuristic and hermeneutic choices that have oriented my approach. From the epistemological viewpoint, in effect, the chief emphasis of this book falls on the individual case as a heuristic resource capable of setting up a new framework of reasoning, and on the narrative dimension that is a constitutive part of it.

Reading Exercises

So far we have leafed through the book systematically, chapter by chapter and state by state. But these 11 chapters also lend themselves to a diagonal reading. Crucial themes in the matrimonial debate and practice run through more than one chapter and lend themselves to being recomposed through an operation of aggregation. To the patient reader this book offers a greater number of chapters than are listed in the contents. Here I can do no more than indicate the existence of these potential extra chapters and to recommend such reading exercises as a useful training, for students, in the interpretation of texts. I restrict myself to listing five possible themes.

a) *The metamorphoses of the promise.* Whether or not betrothal constitutes a legally binding commitment, what were its canonical forms, what was its contractual weight, what was its evolution – these are matters to which each chapter devotes ample space. It was not always, to be sure, but predominantly the female contracting party who insisted on the binding nature of the promise.[28] For this reason the metamorphosis of the promise from officially recognized quasi-matrimony (*matrimonium per verba de futuro*) to private agreement, liable at any moment to be unilaterally dissolved, is a significant stage in the passage of the female subject from a condition of weakness, requiring the protection of the law (*infirmitas sexus*), to the assumption of increasing responsibility for the planning and management of her own life. This passage, undoubtedly marked by terrible suffering, has nevertheless contributed to that still incomplete process of the development of female autonomy, which is one of the basic hallmarks of Western societies.

b) *Marriage as sacrament or marriage as contract?* The interlocutors whose words we shall hear in the following pages reassume the path followed by the Western institution of matrimony in the early modern centuries as the passage from sacrament to civil contract. The Marriage Patent of the emperor Joseph II (1783), the *code Napoléon* (1804), and the Prussian code enacted in the time of Bismarck (1874) are some of the codifications that sanctioned this passage: together with other nineteenth-century legislative codes, they represent the culminating point of a parabola that was launched in the sixteenth century (Wunder 87–8, Lombardi 116). Other co-authors of the present volume, however, object that the two notions of sacrament and contract are not mutually exclusive and indeed have coexisted side by side in Christian marriage since the Middle Ages. These historians prefer to use the term "secularization" to define the parabola performed by marriage in the early modern period (Donahue 38–9, 41–3, Lefebvre-Teillard 262). This preference, at first sight merely a matter of terminology, might indicate an interpretative divergence. On the process of secularization all the authors of the present volume are in agreement; but they diverge in identifying the prime mover in this process. Was it a *movens* of a religious nature, or the effect of a change in political culture? In other words, might the priority accorded by nineteenth-century codifications to the contractual aspects of matrimony be a distant reflection of Protestant theology, which denies the sacramental nature of marriage (Donahue 41), or might it rather be a consequence of the fact that "the secular interests of the early modern state ... gained ascendency" in the age of the Enlightenment and that "jurisprudence ... , together with the law of reason, relegated theology to second place as a central normative authority" (Wunder 76)? Might it even have been the Council Fathers assembled at Trent, with their insistence on the term "contract," who set in motion the "secularization" of matrimony (Lefebvre-Teillard 268)?

c) *Indissoluble or dissoluble matrimony?* Between societies of Catholic and of Protestant culture, the institution of divorce signals a clean break: impossible in the former, admissible in the latter (Donahue 40, 43). The comparativist viewpoint adopted in this volume teaches us, however, that such a frontier was more apparent than real. Separation from bed and board (*divortium quod ad mensam et thorum*) opened to Catholic spouses an escape route from miserable cohabitation (Lombardi 112–14); a declaration of nullity, by which an ecclesiastical tribunal could pass sentence that a particular marriage bond had never existed in the first place – even though children had been born – made it possible for Catholic parties to re-stipulate a new and fully legitimate union (Lombardi 112, Helmholz 135). If we bear in mind the extreme reluctance with which Protestant consistory courts conceded divorce, at least in the first two centuries following the Reformation, we may well wonder whether the similarities between the European matrimonial cultures were not stronger than the differences, including those regarding the dissolubility of the bond.[29] In this territory the reader will find ample scope for comparison and discernment.

d) *Ritual as an instrument of social control.* Although ritual is not one of the themes most treated by the authors of this volume, the reader will nevertheless encounter it often in the following pages as a sign of inclusion or exclusion, of approbation or rejection. This instrument was especially effective when used on young women. Ritual language was employed with great awareness in Germany, Italy, Holland, Switzerland, and France. Whether in a mild form (placing the newborn child of an unmarried mother on the doorstep of the presumed father's house) or in pitiless one (exposing a woman convicted of infanticide to public shame, with a doll in her arms), ritual operated at the imaginative level and had for this reason a greater deterrent power, being subtler and more pervasive, than the penal measures (Lefebvre-Teillard 276, van der Heijden 171).

e) *Periodization.* As regards marriage and the control of marriage, are there period breaks common to all European countries? Despite the fractures and gaps that mark the political panorama of Europe and make it impossible to unify the histories of individual nations, the formation of the couple and its politics of control evinces a surprising synchronicity from country to country. For the heart of the Continent – the Holy Roman Empire of the German nation – Heide Wunder proposes a periodization in three phases, which can be paralleled in Italy, are recognizable in the Low Countries, and apply (albeit with a century of delay) to an eccentric conjugal culture such as that of Sweden. From the fifteenth to the late sixteenth century, the institution of marriage has a flexible character, which in some places is prolonged into the seventeenth century: in this phase the marriage arranged from below, including the improvised kind, enjoys public recognition and chrism of legality, even though deviating from the model recommended by civic and ecclesiastical authority, and involving various degrees of penalization in countries like France. Between the late sixteenth and the seventeenth century, this plurality gave way to a phase of ever more rigorous discipline: the churches and states strengthened their grip on marriage, imposing uniform rites, criminalizing behaviour previously regarded as legitimate, and creating a lexicon of opprobrium with which to condemn impulsive unions or ones dictated by emotion ("clandestine marriage," "*matrimonium turpe*," "prenuptial fornication," "concubinage"). The politics of rigour was a failure everywhere, even though this failure manifested itself at very different times[30] and in very different ways (one of the clues of this failure is the percentage of premarital pregnancies, Burghartz 190). The third phase – which corresponds with the age of Enlightenment, of tolerance, of natural rights – saw the affirmation of that culture of sensibility which the authors of this book trace in its ramifications from the Kingdom of Prussia to the Republic of Venice, from Geneva to England (Wunder 83, 87; Lombardi 114–16). The culture of sensibility crowning in the ideal of conjugal felicity generates a new model of marriage: the marriage of inclination, a product of that emotion or emotion-complex that literature would soon define as "love."[31] It was in this context that there came into being – albeit with emphases that varied from culture to culture – the notion of conjugal happiness as a program for life.[32]

NOTES

1 Seidel 2003, 427–8.
2 Cristellon 2010, 195–7.
3 Seidel Menchi 2001, 46–51.
4 For the convincing attribution to Belliniano, see Fossaluzza 2012, 84; for the earlier attribution to Cariani, see Straussman-Pflanzer 2008, 319–21.
5 Bertling Biaggini, 2002–2003; Seidel Menchi 2006, 676–8.
6 Calabrese 2003, 29; Paolucci 2003, 59, 62, 63.
7 Bayer 2008, 230–2, esp. 232. Also for other famous Italian Renaissance paintings the interpretation in epithalamic or nuptial terms has been affirmed late and – despite the weight of evidence in its favour – has been accepted with reluctance. This is the case with Giorgione's *Sleeping Venus*, now in the Gemäldegalerie, Dresden, and with the so-called *Sacred and Profane Love* by Titian, now in the Borghese Gallery, Rome.
8 Everything we know about the origin of the painting points to the year 1538: in early March the Duke of Urbino, Guidobaldo della Rovere, saw

the canvas in Titian's studio in Venice, was fascinated by it and wanted it for his collection. He did not at the time have to hand the – evidently very large – sum of money that the artist was asking for: the information that we have about the painting therefore comes from the duke's later correspondence with his Venetian emissary Gian Giacomo Leonardi, who was instructed to guarantee payment to the artist and to ensure that the painting was not sold to anyone else. See Agostini 1978, 125–35. We have no information about a possible patron.

9 Seidel Menchi 2009.

10 Passeron and Revel 2005, 9–27.

11 Cristellon 2010, 146: *"I matrimoni, per giungere a buon fine, devono essere liberi."*

12 Paolin 1984, 203.

13 Seidel Menchi and Cristellon 2011, 276–8.

14 Some countries, such as Portugal and Poland, do not figure in this book because the sources privileged here – the matrimonial trial records – were not yet accessible to researchers when the present comparative book was planned.

15 For "presumed marriage," see 34, 98, 261–2.

16 The author himself explains this choice; see his Introduction, esp. 122.

17 Helmholz 1974 and 2004, supported by Lefebvre-Teillard 1973.

18 Helmholz 134; Lefebvre-Teillard 261–2; Usunáriz 202–3.

19 Wunder 78–9; van der Heijden 172; Helmholz 144. For Italy, Lombardi 110; for Sweden, Korpiola 235–6.

20 See Burghartz 177, 179; van der Heijden 159–61.

21 "Judges saw to it that … clandestine marriage promises were … solemnized in church or at city hall," so as to avoid "premature intercourse" (van der Heijden 165).

22 Barahona 2003; Charageat 2011.

23 Van der Heijden 163–5, 169–70; Burghartz 187–8; Lombardi 98–9; Korpiola 225–6, 231. For France, see 271.

24 Wunder 80; Helmholz 145–6; van der Heijden 170–2; Burghartz 193–4; Lefebvre-Teillard 271, 273–4.

25 Gaudemet 1987.

26 Mazo Karras 2012.

27 Alfieri 2011.

28 Beaulande-Barraud and Charageat 2014, 249; Oïffer-Bomsel 2014, 265; see also Seidel Menchi and Quaglioni 2006, 139, 159, 185.

29 Wunder 73; Helmholz 134; van der Heijden 160–1; Korpiola 237–40.

30 Wunder 79; Lombardi 108, 110–11; van der Heijden 169–70; Burghartz 190–1, 192–3. In Sweden the rigorist line endured considerably longer than in Germany (Korpiola 248).

31 The influence of Samuel Richardson's novel *Pamela* (1740) as a formative element moulding European sensibility has generally been undervalued by historians but is rightly emphasized by Hunt 2007.

32 Coontz 2006.

SECTION I

Continuity and Change

Chapter 1

The Legal Background: European Marriage Law from the Sixteenth to the Nineteenth Century*

CHARLES DONAHUE JR.

What Came Before

We must begin with a few basic principles of the classical medieval canon law of marriage. This law was also the law of marriage of the *ius commune*, the mixture of Roman and canon law that was taught in the universities and that served in many, if not quite all, places in Europe as a law in default of specific local law. Also, throughout medieval western Europe the ecclesiastical courts had, in most places, exclusive jurisdiction over cases concerning the formation and dissolution of marriage, and these courts applied the general canon law with some local additions.[1]

The rules of the classical canon law of marriage are largely the creation of an extraordinary outpouring of canonistic activity that took place roughly between the years 1150 and 1250. While legal, moral, and theological principles about marriage are found in Christianity before this time, the canon law in this period created a comprehensive law of marriage, whereas in the preceding centuries Christian principles had been grafted onto whatever the law and custom of marriage was in the areas in which Christians found themselves. In particular, four characteristics of Christian marriage law were assumed when the twelfth- and thirteenth-century canonists began their work.

First, marriage is between a man and a woman and is monogamous. The notion of marriage as binding a man and a woman is common to the Jewish, Greek, and Roman worlds in which Christianity began; monogamy was, as far as we can tell, Jewish practice in the time of Jesus and was also the practice – and, to a large extent, the law – of the Greco-Roman world.

Second, a Christian marriage once fully formed was indissoluble while both of the parties were living. This principle was derived from the teaching of Jesus in the New Testament, and it received a powerful reinforcement in the reform movement of the eleventh century.

Third, close relatives could not validly marry. This prohibition had its origins in both Jewish and Roman law, but it had been greatly expanded in the early Middle Ages. The extent of the prohibition had been debated in the eleventh and twelfth centuries, and traces of these debates, and their resolution, can be found in the canonistic activity in the second half of the twelfth and the first half of the thirteenth centuries.

Fourth, marriage between Christians, once fully formed, was a sacrament of the church. This idea was not fully articulated until the twelfth century, but it was accepted without comment by the later canonists.

What is missing from this collection of principles is any clear notion of when a valid marriage is fully formed. That notion is critical in any law that attaches legal consequences to marriage and is particularly important in one that declares a valid and fully formed marriage to be indissoluble. Subordinate to this basic question but potentially of vital importance are the following questions: (1) What is meant by "indissoluble"? The sayings in the New Testament seem to condemn divorce and remarriage, but what of divorce without remarriage (separation)?[2] (2) What kin are included within the notion of "close relatives" with whom marriage is forbidden? (3) What are the legal consequences, if any, of the sacramentality of marriage?

After approximately a century of debate, the following rules emerged in the early thirteenth century. (1) Present consent freely exchanged between a man and a woman capable of marriage – *matrimonium per verba de presenti* – makes a marriage that is indissoluble so long as both of them lived, unless, prior to the consummation of the marriage, one of them chooses to enter the religious life. (2) Future consent freely exchanged between a man and a woman capable of marriage – *matrimonium per verba de futuro* – makes an absolutely indissoluble marriage so long as both of them live, if subsequent to the exchange of future consent and prior to the formation of another marriage, the couple who has exchanged future consent has sexual intercourse with each other. (3) Any Christian man is capable of marrying any Christian woman so long as: (a) both are over the age of puberty and capable of sexual intercourse; (b) neither was previously married to someone who is still alive; (c) neither has taken a solemn vow of chastity, and the man is not in major orders, and (d) they are not too closely related to each other.[3]

This last requirement was, indeed, complicated, but recent work suggests that it was not so important socially as it used to be – and to some extent still is – thought to be. In 1215, the Fourth Lateran Council under the auspices of Pope Innocent III reduced the prohibited degrees of consanguinity and affinity from six or seven to four in the canonic computation (third cousins) but insisted on strict observance of the rules as modified.[4] The principle, however, that the prohibition of intermarriage in the more remote degrees of consanguinity and affinity was a matter of human, not divine, law meant that parties could be dispensed to marry within these degrees. After the council, popes continued to employ dispensing power in the more remote degrees of consanguinity and affinity (fourth and third). A baroque variation on the concept of affinity, known as "spiritual affinity," prohibited the marriage of godparent and godchild, godparent and the natural parent of his or her godchild, and a godchild with the natural children of his or her godparent. Dispensation could also be obtained for this impediment.[5]

The striking thing about Alexander's rules on the formation of marriage is not what they require but what they do not require. Although the church strongly encouraged couples to solemnize their marriages, no solemnity or ceremony of any sort was necessary to contract a valid marriage.[6] There did not even have to be witnesses to the exchange of consent if both parties admitted that it took place and the rights of third parties were not involved. Further, in an age characterized by arranged marriages and elaborate provisions in the secular law for feudal consents to be given to marriages, it is striking to find that Alexander required the consent of no one other than the parties themselves for the validity of the marriage.[7] Finally, in an age also characterized by class consciousness, it is surprising to discover that the only significant restrictions on the capacity of persons to choose marriage partners were the rules prohibiting the marriage of close relatives.[8]

Legislation in the Sixteenth Century and Beyond

By the sixteenth century the medieval canonical rules about the formation of marriage were in trouble. There was, to begin with, the difficulty of proof of informal marriages, something that is amply illustrated in the works of those who have studied medieval marriage litigation.[9] Partially in response to this problem, the Fourth Lateran Council in 1215 had required couples to have banns of marriage proclaimed publicly before they married, but the council had not invalidated marriages that simply complied with the rules as just stated. Second, the rules encountered opposition in those portions of society where marital property was important. In particular, the Roman lawyers kept alive the tradition that parental consent was necessary for the validity of a marriage, and the Roman rules on dowry and customary rules about community property affected – adversely it would seem, particularly with women – the equality that seems to lie at the root of the canonical rules.[10] As we shall see, opposition to recognizing marriages formed by consent alone is a feature common to many European legal systems in this period (Wunder 72–3, Lombardi 99–100, Helmholz 137, Lefebvre-Teillard 264–5).

It would seem that the French proved particularly resistant to the canonical rules. There was nothing that the French could do about the law of the universal church that said that informal marriages were valid, but French local councils throughout the Middle Ages proclaimed that those who married without the usual ecclesiastical solemnities were automatically excommunicated. The Protestant reformers were quick to attack the medieval canonical rules. For both Luther and Calvin they violated the fundamental principle of the authority of fathers in managing the affairs of their families, including the authority to determine whom their children were going to marry.[11] When the Council of Trent came to consider marriage in 1563, an intense debate ensued.[12] The delegates from France pressed for two changes in the law: no marriage was to be valid unless publicly solemnized in the church after promulgation of banns, and no marriage of a son or daughter subject to paternal power was to be valid without parental consent. The Italians, however, suggested that the validity of non-solemnized marriages was a matter of doctrine, like the Trinity, that could not be changed. To change the rules, they also argued, would be to concede too much to the Protestant reformers. The result, the council's decree *Tametsi*, was a compromise. It had four important elements.[13]

First, the medieval rules were confirmed and anathemas proclaimed against those who held that they had been invalid.

Second, the medieval rules were changed for the future. Marriages not solemnized before the parish priest and at least two witnesses were thereafter declared to be invalid.[14]

Third, marriages of minors without parental consent were condemned but were expressly declared to be valid. Indeed, the parish priest was authorized to dispense with the promulgation of banns if he feared that force might be applied to the couple.

Fourth, because the general promulgation of these rules in countries that were no longer Catholic would have led to the invalidation of Protestant marriages, at least in the eyes of Catholics, the Tridentine rules were declared to take effect only when they were promulgated in the parish.

The French were furious.[15] They refused to promulgate *Tametsi* in their country, and the Tridentine rules, it can be argued, did not come into effect in France until early in the twentieth century.[16] They promulgated instead their own ordinance, the *Ordonnance* of Blois of 1579, similar to Trent but stricter.[17]

First, the promulgation of banns was made a condition of the validity of the marriage (something that Trent had not required). A priest who married a child in the power of its parents without parental consent was to be held guilty of misprision of rape.

Second, those who suborned the consent of the child in power were to be punished capitally for rape, the consent of the child being irrelevant.

The *ordonnance* raised more problems than it solved. First, the sanctions were draconian, and draconian sanctions have a tendency not to be enforced. There is one example that I know of capital punishment being imposed for abduction, but such punishments were certainly not common.[18] Second, by refusing to promulgate the decrees of the council, the French, in fact, left the medieval rules in effect. The possibility was raised of canonically valid marriages that were not valid secularly. Third, the statute was unclear as to just what conditions were necessary for validity. It needed to be amended in 1639 by another *ordonnance* that required parental consent as a condition of the validity of the proclamation of the banns.[19]

The decrees of the Council of Trent were not promulgated in England either, where the monarch was, by this time, a Protestant. The English Church continued to condemn informal marriages, as had the medieval church, but it did not invalidate them. In 1753, 190 years after the decree *Tametsi*, Parliament, in Lord Hardwicke's Act, finally invalidated, in most cases, informal marriages not performed by an authorized Anglican clergyman.[20] The sanctions of the act are less severe than those of the *Ordonnance* of Blois. It is hard not to see in the contrast in both the timing and the contents of the *Ordonnance* of Blois, on the one hand, and Lord Hardwicke's Act, on the other, a fundamentally different attitude towards marriage, at least among those who had the power to make statutes.

In those areas in which *Tametsi* was promulgated it had, as we shall see, the immediate effect of invalidating *de presenti* marriages that were not performed in the presence of the parish priest and at least two witnesses (Wunder 75; Lombardi 102–3, 105, 109–10). It had another effect, less often noted. The second branch of the medieval rules, the formation of a marriage by consent *de futuro* followed by sexual intercourse, also disappeared. While this does not follow ineluctably from the words of the decree, the practical difficulties of completing this form of contract in the presence of the parish priest and two witnesses achieved this effect (Lefebvre-Teillard 261–2). Hence, two of the major sources of matrimonial litigation in the Middle Ages – marriages alleged to have been formed by informal exchange of present consent and marriages alleged to have been formed by exchanges of future consent followed by intercourse – disappeared from those courts that were situated in areas in which the decree *Tametsi* was promulgated. More in the state of our current knowledge we cannot say. The comparative study of post-Tridentine marriage litigation in England, France, Germany, and Italy that we undertake in this book should be enlightening.

Both the English non-development and the French development clearly reflect the rise of the nation-state and its importance. The French development may also reflect the growing importance of Roman law, which unambiguously required the consent of fathers to the marriage of their children.

One would have thought that these decisions would have put an end to the discussion, but it did not. Parental consent remained a matter for discussion until the adoption of the nineteenth-century legal codes, which had a tendency to require parental consent but to reduce the age at which that consent was required.[21] A solemnity requirement remained a matter of discussion in England until the passage of Lord Hardwicke's Act.[22] Elsewhere, the focus of discussion about solemnities shifted. The issue now became not whether solemnities would be required but what solemnities would be required, and that, in turn, raised the issue of whether they were to be religious (and, if so, what religion) or secular. This debate broke out most notably in the 1870s in Germany, when the issue was raised of adopting a civil form of marriage like that of the *code Napoléon*,[23] but it also can be seen in England somewhat earlier, when increasing religious toleration raised the issue about whether the solemnity before a Church of England clergyman required by the 1753 statute would also be required of Protestants who were not members of the Church of England and Catholics.[24]

As is well known, the *code Napoléon* of 1804 adopted a radically secularized version of the formation of marriage; it also authorized divorce, in limited circumstances. What is less well known is how much of the pre-code law remained. Banns, consent of the parents, consent of the couple themselves, and a somewhat reduced incest prohibition all feature in the code. What changed was that what had formerly taken place before the parish priest now took place before a "civil officer," traditionally, in France, the mayor of the town. Because of the influence of the *code Napoléon*, this model was widely adopted. Napoleon brought his code to the Low Countries, the Rhineland of Germany, and a number of Italian states. After Napoleon's fall from power, it remained in effect, with some modification, in Belgium, the Netherlands, the Rhineland, and in the Italian states in which it had been adopted. In 1865, it was adopted, again with modifications, in the civil code that followed the unification of the country. A secularized form of marriage was adopted in Germany at the time of unification and was retained in the civil code of 1900.

Radical secularization was not, however, the only possibility in nineteenth-century Europe. England retained a religious form of marriage and accommodated religious pluralism by authorizing more and more religious officers to perform marriages that would be recognized by the state. A similar solution was adopted in the Austro-Hungarian Empire by the code of 1811.[25] The Spanish Civil Code of 1889 incorporated the canon law for Catholics and a secular form of marriage for all others. Hence, while the tendency in the nineteenth century was definitely in the direction of a secularization of marriage, secularization was by no means complete in that century, nor is it today. Our concern in this chapter is with the pre-code law and with the centuries before the nineteenth, but the story is not heading to a fixed ending point. Methodologically, the codes represented a radical change; in some cases they represented a radical substantive change as well, but these latter changes were not all in the same direction.

The Role of Juristic Discussion

As we have seen, the legislation of the early modern nation-state plays an important role in the case of marriage, more important than it does, to take another example, in the development of the law of contract and delict.[26] Even in the area of marriage, however, it would be a mistake to see the law solely as a creature of the nascent nation-states. The Tridentine legislation was not authoritative in Protestant Europe (and not in all of Catholic Europe), but it had an effect well beyond the boundaries of the area in which it was officially in force, among other reasons, because of the work of legal scholars.

The generalization I will suggest in what follows is that in terms of their relation to the nation-state the intellectual movements in law in the sixteenth, seventeenth, and eighteenth centuries, insofar as they are concerned with private law, share with the *ius commune* of the fourteenth and fifteenth centuries the feature that they are not particularly dependent on the nation-state. The French humanists, the second scholastic, elegant jurisprudence, the natural law school, and the *usus modernus pandectarum* – all, with the exception of the natural law school – are quite firmly associated with what was or what was to become one nation-state. But the writers in these traditions all based their discussions largely on texts from the ancient world, with particular emphasis on Roman law, and with few exceptions they wrote in Latin. Thus, I think it is possible to speak of a European conversation about private law that survived the rise of the nation-state and came to end, if it did come to an end, only with the codifications of the nineteenth century.

The Role of the Protestant Reformers

But on what basis would this conversation be held when it came to the topic of marriage? The Protestant reformers had much to say about marriage, and much of what they said challenged the assumptions that lay behind the canonical rules and the rules themselves. At the risk of oversimplification, we may reduce these challenges to five.[27] First, the reformers tended to deny the sacramentality of marriage. As they read the Bible, Jesus had introduced only two sacraments, baptism and the Eucharist, and not seven, within which marriage was included. Second, they tended to cut back on the degrees of prohibited kin. Here, too, the argument was scriptural. The divine prohibitions on marriage with close kin were those found in the eighteenth chapter of the book of Leviticus. Third, they questioned the absoluteness of the prohibition against divorce, here relying on the "except" clauses in Matthew 5:32 and 19:9 and what they took to be St Paul's ruling in 1 Corinthians 7. Fourth, as we have already noted, they tended to require parental consent for marriage, a requirement not so much founded on Scripture (though the commandment to honour one's father and mother was frequently cited) as on their understanding of the religious role of fathers of families. Fifth, they were uniformly opposed to anything that smacked of papal power. Hence, anything that was dependent on papal legislation or gave authority to the pope to control, whether by prohibiting or dispensing, relations among the faithful would have to be eliminated, or at least questioned if it was to be continued by another authority.

These challenges were so sweeping that one might get the impression that everything about marriage law changed as a result of them, at least in Protestant Europe. That was not the case, however. Changes there were, and some of them proceeded along confessional lines, but the amount of continuity with the past was substantial, and as we have just seen, many of the same changes occurred in both Catholic countries and Protestant, despite the confessional differences.

The effect, then, of the reformers' views on marriage law was more subtle than what we might expect. Protestant countries did not go off in an entirely different direction, and Catholic countries did change. The effect, however, was, at least in my view, profound; it made possible the ultimate secularization of marriage law that occurred in most of the nineteenth-century codes. This effect is easiest to see in the transnational conversation about marriage law that continued after the break-up of Europe into separate sovereign nation-states in the sixteenth century. If one is writing with a sense, however vague, that one is engaged in conversation across national and religious lines, one will tend to rest on principles and sources that transcend the national and the confessional. There is always a tension in this type of writing, because most lawyers also imagine that their works will be used to solve real disputes among real people. Hence, local legislation, be it secular or religious, and local decisions will be cited, but even these will be interpreted in the light of what are thought to be general principles.

But, in the case of marriage law, where those principles are found will change as a result of the fact that one can no longer count on everyone's accepting the unquestioned authority of the pre-Tridentine canon law found in the *Corpus Iuris Canonici*. Even here, the change is subtle. Despite the fact that some of the early Protestant reformers seemed to urge the abolition of canon law entirely, that did not happen in most places. Ultimately, for example, both Lutheran Germany and Calvinist England accepted the authority of the *Corpus Iuris Canonici* with the substantial qualification that it had to be stripped of its papal excrescences. Questions, however, about the authority of the *Corpus Iuris Canonici* did have an effect. In the area of marriage law, as in many other areas of law, questioning the authority of the *Corpus Iuris Canonici* enhanced the authority of the *Corpus Iuris Civilis*. If an acceptable principle could be found in Roman law, that is the authority that would be used in preference to support for the same principle in canon law.

But there is much in the Roman law of marriage that was unacceptable in early modern Europe. A substantial portion of the texts on marriage in the *Corpus Iuris Civilis* are from pagan sources. They reflect a slave-holding society, in which slaves could not lawfully marry. In pagan Rome, divorce was common and legally quite unproblematical. Another source has to be added to Roman law in order to have a conversation about marriage across confessional lines in early modern Europe, and the most obvious one is the Bible. To these we may add, with qualifications, the philosophers of the ancient world, the fathers of the church, and the practices of ancient peoples, particularly the Romans and the Jews. One might even form an amalgam of all these sources and call it "natural law."

Before we look more specifically at what happened, let us return to the five areas in which the Protestant reformers challenged the traditional teaching of the church on the topic of marriage. Denial of the sacramentality of marriage is certainly the most important theologically. It may be the most important legally. That proposition, however, should be examined more closely. It has been argued that the denial of the sacramentality of marriage produced a shift that ultimately allowed the law to view marriage in more contractual terms than it had before.[28] There is certainly something to the argument, though one might question the extent to which it is the denial of sacramentality that produced this shift. If one is going to turn from canonic to Roman legal sources in one's search for rules about marriage, one is turning to sources that undeniably viewed betrothal in contractual terms, and which can be made to view marriage itself in contractual terms if one focuses on the importance that these sources place on consent. The problem is that both of these foci are quite apparent in the pre-Tridentine law. Betrothal (espousals of the future tense) was viewed in quite strictly contractual terms, and much of the doctrine surrounding present consent (e.g., the age requirements and the doctrine of force and fear) was understood as derived from similar doctrines about contractual consent. Indeed, there is relatively little in the pre-Tridentine law of marriage that can be confidently attributed to the sacramentality of marriage.[29]

Hence, I am inclined to think that we should look elsewhere for the effect of the Protestant denial of the sacramentality of marriage.

What it did was remove the principal argument for ecclesiastical jurisdiction over marriage. The removal of ecclesiastical jurisdiction over marriage did not happen in all Protestant countries. England retained it, at least nominally, until the nineteenth century. Nor did it remain in all Catholic countries. In France jurisdiction over marriage cases came largely into the hands of the secular courts in the sixteenth century. But in most Protestant areas jurisdiction over marriage cases fell largely into the hands of the secular courts relatively soon after the Reformation,[30] and in most Catholic areas it remained largely in the hands of the church courts until the nineteenth century.

Other effects of the Reformation can be treated more briefly. In Catholic countries the pre-Tridentine rules about marriage with close kin remained, as did the possibility of papal dispensation from all but the closest relations. In Protestant countries, there were changes. The Protestant principle was relatively clear: a prohibition that could be dispensed was abolished, and those prohibitions that remained could not be dispensed. There was not complete agreement, however, on what prohibitions remained.

Divorce of a validly formed marriage became possible in at least some Protestant areas, but the grounds tended to be quite narrow and the instances of it quite rare. In England, for example, divorce was available only by means of a private bill in Parliament.

Parental consent appeared as a requirement in a number of Protestant areas. As we have seen, however, it also appeared in secular legislation in France. The introduction of a solemnity requirement of some sort for the validity of marriage (a requirement, at least in the view of many, closely related to parental consent) appeared in many areas both Protestant and Catholic. Here it was England that was exceptional.

A final problem is not so much the result of what the reformers said as it is of the fact of the Reformation: What of marriage between Christians of different confession, what today is sometimes called "mixed marriage"? The Council of Trent had introduced, in effect, what came to be known as the "impediment of mixed religion" – the impediment, however, was dispensable.[31]

Because the varying requirements for the formation of marriage and its dissolution did not neatly divide along confessional or national lines, juristic conversation across those lines remained possible. Let us look at some examples from various periods.

The Humanists

The most difficult period to characterize is the sixteenth century. No single work on the topic of marriage stands out. Let me generalize about humanist work on the topic on the basis of a number of works.[32]

In a world in which theological differences were provoking wars and massacres, the humanists largely avoided theology. In this, however, they were no different from their predecessors who followed the *mos italicus* (a method of studying and teaching the *Corpus Iuris Civilis* that originated in Italy). Where they do differ from the practitioners of the *mos italicus*, and differ markedly, is in their sense of history. Their admiration for the ancient world led them to study the ancient sources with the tools of philology and a new sense of history. Roman marriage was not the same as marriage in sixteenth-century Europe, and the humanists' mastery of the ancient sources allowed them to show just how different it was. But they also believed that this fact did not make the experience and writings of the ancients irrelevant to their own day; the relevance consisted in finding fundamental principles that could operate across the long gap of time and place. Antonius Guibertus Costanus, for example, attempts to argue for a basic consistency across time on the question of parental consent.[33] His attempt is not true to his Roman sources but may be seen as an argument against those who wanted to introduce such a requirement. Costanus accepts the ruling of Council of Trent on solemnity, but he makes it clear that the default rule (where Trent is not in effect, though he does not say this) is that clandestine marriages are valid. None of the humanist authors I have examined deals expressly with the question of secular power to make law about marriage, though their emphasis on classical Roman sources makes it quite clear that there was a time in which the church was not the sole source of law about marriage.

Protestants

It might be objected that the humanists are a bad example if I am trying to maintain that a conversation about marriage continued across national and confessional lines. The nature of the humanist enterprise was to try to unite not divide. Let us examine, therefore, the work by an author not writing in the humanist tradition, who was undeniably Protestant.

Joachim von Beust (1522–97) studied in Bologna, where he received his doctorate in law. He returned to Germany and became a professor of civil law at the University of Wittenberg. He held numerous judicial, conciliar, and academic appointments in various Protestant areas. His best-known legal works are his treatises *De sponsalibus, de matrimoniis et de dotibus*, which were combined in an edition that appeared the year of his death.[34] He also wrote various theological and catechetical works and delivered some orations that were ultimately published.

Von Beust writes a consciously practical treatise. The work contains numerous forms for use in the courts, and the author in many places slipped in the German equivalents of the Latin terms that he used. It is probably for this reason that the treatise was never, so far as I am aware, published outside of Germany.

What is remarkable about von Beust's treatise is that despite the undeniably Protestant and German bias of the author, much of it is consistent with the *ius commune* that can be found in Catholic and Romance Europe in the same period. Von Beust's first problem is that Luther had argued for abolishing the distinction between present and future consent to marry. If von Beust cannot make that distinction, then much of the *ius commune* on the topic of marriage will have to go by the boards. Luther had acknowledged, however, that if a marriage was subject to a condition, then the distinction between present and future consent made some sense. But he had argued that one could not distinguish between present and future consent in the German language simply by the words used to express the consent. What von Beust does is to show all the ways in which one can distinguish between present and future in the German of his day, while conceding Luther's point that the distinction between *accipio* – I take (you) – and *accipiam* – I will take (you) – cannot be made in so many words. Having established that the distinction between present and future can be made, he goes on to argue that where the words used are ambiguous, present consent should be presumed.[35]

Once von Beust is over this hurdle, what follows is not at all surprising, though it is not quite what we would find in Catholic writers in the same period. Espousals of the future tense (*per verba de futuro*) are just promises; they may be dissolved by mutual dissent, or even unilateral dissent. Espousals of the present tense (*per verba de presenti*) are a marriage, and what God has united man should not divide. Espousals of the future tense followed by intercourse also make a marriage. In Catholic areas, unconsummated espousals of the present tense could be dissolved by papal dispensation. That recourse was obviously unacceptable in Protestant Saxony, and von Beust struggles with a number of questions as to the dissolubility of such espousals. He seems to allow it in situations where fraud has been committed, such that the marital consent has been vitiated, in situations of supervenient incurable illness, such as leprosy, and in situations where one of the parties has been unfaithful. These conclusions involve some twisting of his pre-Tridentine sources, but not much. That unconsummated present consent marriages were not absolutely indissoluble was a commonplace among the pre-Tridentine doctors.[36]

The same may be said of von Beust's treatment of clandestine espousals of the present tense. He seems to accept Luther's conclusion that no matter how many witnesses are present, all espousals made without parental consent are clandestine, but his conclusion that public espousals take precedence over clandestine ones except where the latter have been consummated, although contrary to the thrust of pre-Tridentine canon law, is not, at least as I read them, one that would shock the pre-Tridentine doctors. (After Trent, of course, all clandestine espousals of the present tense were invalid, so the problem cannot arise.)[37]

A Spanish Scholastic

Among Catholics, the work of the Spanish scholastic Tomás Sánchez (1550–1610) stands out.[38] Sánchez's *Disputationum de sancto matrimonii sacramento tomi tres* is a truly massive work. The edition published in Antwerp in 1626 contains 1,311 closely packed folio pages of text, not including front and back matter for each of the volumes and some 34 pages of indices. The work is divided into 10 *libri*. Each *liber* is divided into numerous scholastic *disputationes*, ranging in number from 114 (*De impedimentis*) to 19 (*De consensu conditionato*).

There is much in this work that would be quite familiar to an author in the pre-Tridentine Italian style. There are, however, changes in emphasis that reflect both what had happened at Trent and the rise of the nation-state. The fact that Trent had invalidated the exchange of marital consent that did not take place before the priest of the parish to which at least one of the members of the couple belongs and before two witnesses gives rise to a separate book on clandestine consent that requires 54 disputations. That requirement and the concomitant emphasis on the authority of parents may also account for the separate book on the topic of coerced consent (admittedly, with only 27 disputations). Dispensations, which have been shown to have become increasingly important in the fifteenth century, now are given a separate book (36 disputations).

More emphasis is placed on the life of the couple after the formation of the marriage, with separate books on marital property (41 disputations) and the rendering of the "conjugal debt" (the obligation of the parties to respond to each other's sexual needs, 47 disputations).

The emphasis of Sánchez's book on the Tridentine decrees on marriage might make one think that its use would be confined to those who accepted the authority of, and were concerned with applying, Roman Catholic canon law. It certainly was of use to such people; it remained a primary authority on the Catholic canon law of marriage well into the eighteenth century. But Sánchez's range is broader. He is a Spanish scholastic and as such he is prepared to give considerable scope to the nation-state. He has also not forgotten the *ius commune*, and the solutions of the *ius commune* of various problems are presented first even where they have been changed by Trent and without qualification where they have not.

The range of citations to Castilian law in the work is quite broad. The *Siete Partidas* are cited more often than the decrees of the Council of Trent (36 versus 25) and *Nueva Recopilación* of Castile almost as often (20 versus 25).[39] Sánchez's own views about the permissible range of secular law about marriage are cautious. The fullest treatment is found in *disputatio* 3 of *liber* 7, where he asks whether a secular prince, be he faithful (i.e., a Christian) or unfaithful, can establish diriment impediments to marriage.[40] His answer is that a Christian prince cannot, because the church has reserved the topic to itself. Were it not for this reservation, however, a secular prince could do so. Citing Thomas Aquinas, Sánchez holds that marriage, insofar as it is a civil contract, is subject to the ordination of civil law. The fact that it is also a sacrament does not block the power of the secular prince. "Because its matter is civil contract, for this reason he [the prince] can invalidate it as if it were not a sacrament." But the church can forbid Christian princes from exercising this power, because this secular contract has spiritual things annexed to it, and in Sánchez's view, as in that of many doctors, the church has done so, though he recognizes that Pedro de Soto held to the contrary. Also, a non-Christian prince is free to legislate about this contract for non-Christians as he will.

A statute in Castile punished those who participated in clandestine marriages with confiscation of goods and exile and authorized disinheritance of a daughter who married without paternal consent.[41] The interpretation of this law raised numerous questions that Sánchez deals with systematically. He leaves what he regards as the hardest question to the end: Is this law "corrected" by canon law? While he recognizes that there are contrary opinions, in his view the civil law is valid when it adds penalties to something that is already forbidden by canon law (and his view here is not dependent on the Council of Trent). The civil laws are here "coadjutors" of the canon law. Such is not the case, however, with the part of the statute that authorizes the disinheritance of daughters who marry without paternal consent. That is not punishable but permissible in canon law, and therefore the secular laws cannot punish it.

In both his general opinion that the church had withdrawn from the Christian prince the power that he would otherwise have to create diriment impediments to marriage and in his specific opinion that the Castilian law penalizing marriages without parental consent was invalid, Sánchez's own views were contrary to those being developed in Protestant Europe and even, in some places, Catholic Europe. The form, however, of his work is that of disputation; he gives the other side of virtually every argument. His work, then, could be used by those who did not agree with him. That the work was widely available is clear from its publication history. Not only were there many editions, but most of them come from major publishing centres, though admittedly all in what was at least nominally Catholic Europe: Antwerp, Lyon, Venice.[42]

The Natural Law School

After the Spanish Scholastics, the centre of legal learning moved north, first to the northern Low Countries and then, increasingly, to Germany.

Selection here becomes painful, but let us focus on Samuel von Pufendorf (1632–94) and his *De iure naturae et gentium libri octo*, first published in 1672, a work clearly in the natural law tradition. Pufendorf taught briefly at Heidelberg, but the greater part of his career was spent in Sweden, where he enjoyed the patronage of the Swedish crown. The *De iure naturae* was of great influence. In addition to numerous reprintings in Latin, it was translated into both German (1712) and English (1749).[43]

In the course of dealing with the institution of marriage (6.1) and of paternal power (6.2), Pufendorf deals with two of the topics that had troubled marriage law in the West at least since the twelfth century. In considering the formation of marriage,[44] Pufendorf says, "At this point we must explain the common maxim of the lawyers, that 'consent and not cohabitation consummate marriage' [D.35.1.15], or, as is stated in Quintilian, *Declamations* 247: 'Copulation and intercourse that are unsanctioned by law do not make a woman a wife.'"[45] As Pufendorf's citation of Gratian's *Concordance of Discordant Canons* shows, this was not the first time since the ancient world that these texts had been used. Like Gratian, Pufendorf immediately draws the distinction between necessary and sufficient conditions. Of course, cohabitation (or sexual intercourse) without more does not make a marriage. It makes fornication or adultery or worse. The question is not whether consent is a necessary condition for a marriage; the question is whether it is a sufficient condition. Like Gratian, Pufendorf holds that it is not. Unlike Gratian, what he holds is not that there must be consummation to perfect the marriage but that there must be a *deductio in domum*, a leading of the bride to the house of groom. (He puts it more broadly by saying that the bride "must have come, as it were, into the hands of the man in such a way that he may treat her as a wife."[46])

Where does this idea come from? The *deductio* plays a considerable role in the Roman texts and continued to play a role in the secular law about marriage, even after the medieval canonical rules were formed.[47] But Pufendorf does not cite Roman or medieval sources. Rather, he cites biblical examples that seem a bit strained. The obviousness of the argument comes from what he has said before, an argument that the power of the husband over the wife is required by natural law.[48] The requirement of the *deductio* follows from Pufendorf's argument that natural law requires some subordination of the wife to the husband, though the amount of it is a matter of positive law or agreement.

If Pufendorf follows a basically Roman-law solution when dealing with the moment of the formation of marriage, he emphatically rejects it where he asks whether as a matter of natural law a father may dictate the marriage choice of his children.[49] He recognizes the institution of paternal power but holds that it is only for the purpose of ensuring the care and education of the offspring. Once the function ceases, the natural law power ceases. He does, however, recognize the power of the state to condition the validity of marriages on obtaining parental consent.

Again, this is not the first time that the question had been asked since the Romans. Justinian had held that natural reason (which may not be the same thing as natural law) required that fathers consent to the marriage of their children.[50] The medieval canonists had emphatically denied it, while the medieval Romanists had emphatically maintained it.[51] So long as the canonists controlled the question of the validity of marriage, their view prevailed, but as we have seen, by Pufendorf's time many secular states, particularly in the Protestant areas, had taken over the determination of the validity of marriage. For Pufendorf to maintain that parental consent to the marriage of their children was not a matter of natural law required considerable courage.

We can make sense of what Pufendorf does with two long-standing issues about marriage in the light of what we know about his enterprise. Pufendorf was living in a world in which legal pluralism was a fact. Not only was Europe divided into nation-states each with its own law, but travellers were coming back with stories that showed even greater variety in other parts of the world. Pufendorf thinks it is possible to get down to the basics, to devise a set of basic norms. What he seems to be looking for is a simple, secular principle that will hold together a coherent scheme of natural law and accommodate most of the diversity.

Marriage, Pufendorf tells us, is constituent of the state.[52] No one that I know of had made much of that point before Jean Bodin.[53] Medieval people did not because they had a very different idea of the state. In order for the family to constitute the state it is necessary to know whose children are whose. Hence, the necessity of marriage, with the possibility of polygyny but not polyandry. Husbands play a different role from that which wives play. The amount of power that the husband has varies, but the wife cannot rule her husband. The Amazons' practices are "irregular."[54] In order for the husband's power (however great it may be) to be exercised, the wife must come into his house. Fathers must have power over their children but only for purposes of nurture and education. When children leave the household (as they do when they marry), fathers have no natural law right to dictate the marriage choice, though they put their children out of the house if they marry against their wishes.

The *Usus Modernus Pandectarum*

Recently, attention has been turned to the writers of the *usus modernus pandectarum*. Putting it crudely, it is they, more than the humanists or the natural lawyers, who integrated Roman law with case law, at least in Germany, in such a way that the nineteenth-century codes could be as much based on Roman law as they were. The phrase *usus modernus pandectarum* was first brought into prominence by Samuel Stryk (1640–1710), professor of Roman law at the universities of Frankfurt (Oder),

Wittenberg, and Halle, successively, who published in 1690 the beginning of a work entitled *Specimen usus moderni pandectarum*. The entire work, in five volumes, was not completely published until shortly after his death, an act of pietas by his son Johann Samuel.[55]

Stryk's *Usus modernus* is a massive work, arranged in the order of the titles of the *Digest*. Each section begins with an exposition of the Roman law on the topic, with notes as to what extent it is adopted in Protestant Germany, followed by questions about the law. In both cases the current law is illustrated by statutes and decisions of the courts, the professors, and the universities. The effect of the Roman law, however, is more than comparative. Putting the local law under the headings of the Roman law forces it into the structural mould of Roman law, and Stryk does his best to reconcile the specifics of the Roman law with what is found in the cases; in more cases the local law is brought closer to the Roman law than vice versa.

In the case of marriage, Stryk has to deal not only with Roman law but also with canon law and with local practices and statutes that differ quite widely from his basic Roman model. He is quite free in acknowledging how widely contemporary practice differs from Roman law, but his doing so should not make us ignore the fact that the basic principles of Roman law, and still more so those of the *ius commune*, are affecting the pattern that he is imposing on his material.[56]

The effect of the Roman material can be seen on the very first pages of Digest 23.1, *De sponsalibus*. Florentinus at the beginning of title *De sponsalibus* defines *sponsalia* as the *mentio et repromissio futurarum nuptiarum*, or, as an Anglo-American lawyer without too much distortion might say, "the offer and acceptance of a future marriage." The point is that we are dealing here with what is, in effect, a consensual contract; there must be, once more to use Anglo-American terminology, a "meeting of the minds." This is illustrated by a case in which a man's proposal of marriage was followed by a delay, when the father of the girl to whom the proposal was made asked for some time to think about it. Before the father accepted, the suitor changed his mind. Stryk had rendered an opinion that the suitor was not bound; absent the acceptance no obligation was formed.[57]

Civil (i.e., Roman) law, Stryk tells us, freely allows the parties to break *sponsalia*. Penalties added to the contract cannot be enforced. Canon law does the same (where the *sponsalia* are *de futuro*, citing Sánchez). But the principles of the two, Stryk argues, ought to be different. Canon law, unlike civil, leans in favour of the consummation of the contract.

Therefore, canon law is inconsistent in not allowing penalties to be added to the contract, and the German consistories that enforce such penalties and even impose penalties *ex officio* for frivolous breaking of marriage contacts are more consistent.

In Roman law, Stryk continues, all *sponsalia* are *de futuro*, but canon law has introduced the distinction between *sponsalia de presenti* and those *de futuro*. He then refers to Luther's opposition to the distinction and states that all the consistories and Protestant jurists hold that all consents are *de presenti* except for those that are expressly made conditional. Stryk, however, urges a return to the distinction, as had von Beust. He holds that *sponsalia de presenti* are the same thing as marriage and that by sexual intercourse *sponsalia* [*de futuro*] become marriage.[58] He urges more adherence to the Roman practice that simple *sponsalia de futuro* could be dissolved by mutual agreement.[59]

Having established these basic propositions, Stryk can concede much to statute and practice. In Roman law *sponsalia* were made by consent alone; in Germany in many places they must by statute be made before witnesses.[60] In Roman law only the consent of the father was required for *sponsalia*; in Germany the consent of both parents is generally required for unemancipated children.[61] In Roman law a daughter could not dissent from her father's choice of a marriage partner, but in both canon law and in German law, the daughter must consent.[62] One may put conditions on espousals, so long as the conditions are honest and possible, citing, among other authors, Sánchez, but also German cases.[63]

Once More, France

Robert Joseph Pothier (1699–1772) was *conseiller au présidal* of Orléans, a judge of an important local court, for 52 years. He published the *Pandectae Justinianeae in novum ordinem digestae* in 1748. The *Pandectae* was a very successful work that earned Pothier the attention of the chancellor, d'Aguesseau. Under d'Aguesseau's patronage, Pothier became a professor of French law at Orléans in 1749. Starting in 1761, at the age of 62, he published 19 treatises on specific topics of law, including one on marriage and two on marital property. He was also interested in theology, and in this regard, he was orthodox, though in church government he has decided Gallican tendencies. The natural law in Pothier owes as much to Thomas Aquinas as it does to the natural law school, although Pothier knew the work of Pufendorf, Christian Thomasius, and Christian Wolff.

Pothier's early discussion of the Roman rules on marriage in the *Pandectae* owes much to elegant jurisprudence and to the humanists. He is much more aware than many authors in the tradition of practical law how much the Roman texts are formed by a Roman context that is no longer applicable. Hence his discussion of Modestinus's famous definition of marriage – "marriage is the joining of man and woman and *consortium* for life, involving both human and divine laws" – is informed by an understanding of the archaic Roman institution of marriage with *manus*, something that had really not been known until the sixteenth century. He also, like many Romanists before him, notices how strong the Romans are on the necessity of parental consent, and there is no reason that he can see why this rule should not be applicable in his own day.[64]

In Pothier's treatise on marriage, this concern with parental consent comes to the fore. But first he must deal with the problem of religious and secular. Marriage is divine in origin. By beginning his treatise with Adam and Eve, Pothier reminds us of the medieval theologians and canonists; similar reminiscences are found in his emphasis on the unity of spirits rather than the unity of bodies.[65] He also separates the property consequences of marriage from the marriage itself. Indeed, he devotes two separate treatises to the former. When he comes to the issue of secular power, however, he unites the two laws in a most medieval way. Law is law, whether it proceeds from secular or religious power, and while the positive law cannot change the essence of marriage, it can prescribe the formalities and dictate who is and who is not capable of marriage. He even quotes Sánchez to this effect, conveniently forgetting that Sánchez had held that the church had withdrawn from secular princes the power that they would otherwise have to establish the terms of the contract.[66] Pothier's reading of the *Ordonnance* of Blois is broad. The sanctions of the statute do not apply where publicity has been had, even if the solemnities are not quite what the statute calls for. On the other hand, when the *ordonnance* of 1639 that required parental consent for the promulgation of banns is read together with the *Ordonnance* of Blois, Pothier has no doubts that marriages without parental consent are void.[67]

The conclusion that French law requires parental consent for the validity of a marriage needs to be reconciled with the decrees of the Council of Trent.[68] Pothier recognizes that the council anathematized those who say that the marriage of children of families (*enfants de famille*) contracted without the consent of their parents is null, but he argues that thereby the council intended only to condemn the opinion of certain Protestants who pretend that by natural law parents have on their own the power to validate or annul the marriages of their children contracted without their consent.[69]

> [T]he council did not, nor could it, decide that in the case of civil law that requires the consent of their parents on pain of nullity, their marriages contracted without the consent of their parents are nonetheless valid. The power that secular authority has to prescribe for the contract of marriage, just like all the other contracts, such laws that it judges appropriate, the non-observance of which renders the contract null, is a power which is essentially attached to it, which it holds from God, and of which the church has never wanted to deprive it ...[70]
>
> According to Roman law, the marriages of children of families were not valid without the consent in advance of him who had them in their power ... Never has the church opposed these laws; never has she regarded as valid marriages contracted contrary to their disposition. On the contrary she has regarded them as fornications. This is what we find in the second canonical letter of St. Basil to Amphilochus, canon 42, where this father says that the marriages of slaves and those of children of families, contracted without the consent of him in whose power they are, are fornications rather than marriages until their consent intervenes ... [71] This was the doctrine of the church on this topic at the time of Isidorus Mercator, because in the decretal that he falsely attributes to Pope Evaristus and which is reported in the *Decretum* of Gratian[72] he calls "marriages made without the consent of parents" "adulteries, concubinages, lusts or fornications."

The council thought that marriages contracted without the consent of parents were valid only so long as there was no positive law to the contrary. That can be seen in the fact that the council said that such marriages were valid "so long as the church has not declared them invalid." "Hence," Pothier continues,

> the spirit of the council is that the church could render them null if at length it thought it appropriate to make a diriment impediment the lack of consent of the parents. The proposal was even made to the council by the French bishops ... to make a decree declaring such marriages null. It did not pass. But if the church has this right, even more so ought the secular power have it, since the contract of marriage belongs just like all other

contracts to the political order. The right to prescribe laws that it judges appropriate to establish the validity of this contract belongs principally to the secular authority.

A generation after Pothier wrote, the "secular authority" in France would assert this right to the exclusion of that of the church.

Conclusion

By the nature of their discipline lawyers are conservative. They would prefer to manipulate an authority to make it fit with a result that they want to achieve rather than simply discard it. Change occurs when the overall framework of ideas within which the system is embedded changes or when the social stuff to which the system must be applied changes, but the internal system of ideas that make up the law strives to accommodate those changes within the existing system, so that social and intellectual changes tend to be blunted when they encounter an existing legal system. The accommodations that the legal system makes then tend to feed back into the world of ideas and the world of practice and to change them. Both the changes within the legal system and the feedback to the wider world occur slowly, however, and they are frequently more difficult to see than the intellectual and social changes that began the process in the first place.

However universal these generalizations may be,[73] they are certainly illustrated by the story of marriage law in the sixteenth through the eighteenth century. Three changes occurred in the wider world in the sixteenth century: one emphatically intellectual, the attack of the Protestant reformers on the existing system; one emphatically social (and more controversial), the shift from what Lawrence Stone has called the open lineage family of the Middle Ages to the restricted patriarchal family of the Renaissance; and the third both intellectual and social, the rise of the nation-state. Legal changes did occur in this period, some of them quite dramatic: the decree *Tametsi* of the Council of Trent, the *Ordonnance* of Blois in France, and the introduction of some form of solemnity requirement almost everywhere; the reduction of the prohibited degrees of consanguinity in most if not all Protestant areas and more widespread dispensation from the more remote degrees in Catholic areas; the introduction of the possibility of divorce of a fully formed marriage in at least some Protestant areas. Even in these cases we can question how radical these changes were from what had existed in the fifteenth century. The most radical was the introduction of the possibility of divorce, but having introduced the possibility most Protestants made relatively little use of it.

In the face of these changes, lawyers scrambled to make sense of them and in the process brought back the elements of the old system in a somewhat different form. Indeed, the English Protestant Henry Swinburne, confining himself to espousals, is able to argue that virtually nothing had changed. The humanists in nominally Catholic France are more radical in their use of sources than are the Protestants von Beust and Swinburne. Sánchez will recognize the changes wrought both by the new church legislation and the nation-state of Castile, but he will put the whole in a framework of the *ius commune* so that the Protestant Stryk and the Gallican Pothier can make use of his work. If one accepts a fixed solemnity for the formation of a marriage, as did those who accepted the Council of Trent, one can then focus on espousals as the contractual obligation to marry and return to Roman-law sources. If one does not accept a fixed solemnity, then one has to maintain the distinction between present and future consent, as did von Beust, Swinburne, and Stryk. Brooding over the whole development are those who attempt to use the materials from the past and from travellers' reports to find a coherent set of principles that are independent of both church and state. Pufendorf is the most successful in doing so, though ultimately his set of principles reminds one of a somewhat sanitized version of Roman law. Pothier will have a quite similar set of principles with more scope given to the state to enforce and modify them.

As we suggested before, the adoption of the codes did not end the conversation, but it made it more difficult because it removed the authority of the materials from the past. Methodologically, the codes were meant to be exclusive. Two centuries later some Europeans are seeking to revive that conversation. Whether that effort is wise or is likely to succeed is not for an American historian to say.

NOTES

* A version of this paper has been published as "The Role of the Humanists and the Second Scholastic in the Development of European Marriage Law from the Sixteenth to the Nineteenth Centuries," in *Law and Religion: The Legal Teachings of the Protestant and Catholic Reformations*, Refo500 Academic Studies 20, edited by Wim Decock, Jordan J. Ballor, Michael Germann, and Laurent Waelkens (Göttingen: Vandenhoeck and Ruprecht, 2014).

Although the detail in that paper is substantially different, the overall argument is the same.

1 Donahue 2007, ch. 1. Briefer surveys along the lines undertaken here may be found in Donahue 2006, 3, 15–22, and Donahue 2008b, both with references. Good general accounts of the medieval developments may be found in Brundage 1987. Gaudemet 1987 is a masterly account of the whole story. Witte 2012 is particularly useful for developments in Protestant thought and countries.

2 Donahue 2007, ch. 1.

3 Donahue 2007, ch. 11.

4 4 Lateran (1215), constitutio 50, in *Decrees of the Ecumenical Councils*, 1:257–8.

5 On dispensation practice in the later Middle Ages, see Schmugge 2008.

6 Donahue 1976, 259–60.

7 Donahue 1976, 256–7, and sources cited.

8 The closest that the developed classical law came to an impediment on cross-class marriages was the impediment of error of person, and this was not a prohibition of cross-class marriage but a rule designed to ensure that one knew what one was doing. See Donahue 2007, 22–3.

9 E.g., Donahue 2007, ch. 2, and, in this volume, Wunder 72–3, Lombardi 94–5, Helmholz 129, 134–5, 138–9.

10 See Donahue 1978.

11 See Ozment 1983, 25–49, for a somewhat different and more nuanced story. For a broader view of the Protestant context, see Witte 2012.

12 Esmein 1929–35, 2:161–215, 483–9, tells the story fully with copious references to the *acta* of the council. See also Jedin 1951–75, vol. 4, pt. 2, 96–121, references at 277–81.

13 Council of Trent, sess. 24, *Canones super reformatione circa matrimonium*, caput 1 (*Tametsi*).

14 The parish priest was also to proclaim the banns and keep a marriage register, but these were not made elements of validity.

15 See, in this volume, Lefebvre-Teillard 261, 264. A full account of the French legislation on this topic in the sixteenth century may be found in Diefendorf 1983, 156–70. See also Gottlieb 1974, 143–6, with references. On the general legal development, see Ourliac and Malafosse 1961–8, 3:525.

16 Esmein 1929–35, 2:229–35, argues that the civil legislation of the sixteenth and seventeenth centuries made them, as a practical matter, in effect. *Tametsi* was, of course, not the only reason why the French refused to promulgate the decrees. For a nice account of the whole story, albeit from a somewhat ultramontane point of view, see Martin 1975.

17 *Ordonnance* of Blois (1579), arts. 40–1, in *Recueil des ordonnances des rois de France*, 173–4. See, in this volume, Lefebvre-Teillard 265–6.
18 Diefendorf 1983, 165–6, has one example.
19 Ibid., 167. The subject is discussed at greater length by Lefebvre-Teillard in this volume, 263–70.
20 See Outhwaite 1995, 75–144. In this volume, Helmholz 149, esp. n39.
21 E.g., Montesquieu, *De l'esprit des lois*, 4.23.7–8 (2:107–8).
22 Outhwaite 1995; see also Giesen 1973.
23 Klusmeyer 1989 reviews the debate with extensive references to prior literature. See also Fuhrmann 1998.
24 Quakers and Jews had been exempted from the statute from the beginning. For the gradual accommodation of other Protestants, Unitarians, and Catholics, see Outhwaite 1995, 145–67.
25 Ultimately England added civil marriage to the possibilities, a feature not present in the Austrian code. Outhwaite 1995, 164–5.
26 The latter has recently been given a magisterial account that can tell the story largely without reference to legislation between that of Romans and the nineteenth-century codes: Zimmermann 1996. Even in Zimmermann's account, the key developments in the early modern period take place largely within the confines of one *Sprachraum*, among the practitioners of the *usus modernus pandectarum* in what is now Germany.
27 Witte 2012 has a much more comprehensive account.
28 This is a main thrust of Witte 2012, but we should emphasize "ultimately." In Witte's view this shift to a contractual understanding was not fully realized until the eighteenth century.
29 I explore this topic in a bit more depth in Donahue 2008a.
30 At least that is the way that the generalization is normally put. My own work and that of other participants in this volume would suggest a greater importance for the Protestant consistories than is normally attributed to them. See in particular, in this volume, van der Heijden 159, 166–70.
31 See Esmein 1929–35, 2:225–37. This topic is treated at greater length in chapter 10 of this book.
32 In 1584, Francesco Ziletti published a massive collection of treatises on law, the ninth volume of which was devoted to marriage and dowry, with the first 185 folios of the volume being dedicated to the former topic. Some 20 treatises are here printed, and they probably illustrate well what was of interest about marriage to lawyers, at least in Romance-speaking Europe. The collection is called *Tractatus universi iuris, Index authorum*, fol. 1v.
33 Costanus, *De sponsalibus et matrimoniis*.

34 The prior publication history is complicated. What is called the first edition of *De sponsalibus et matrimoniis* appeared in Wittenberg in 1586. Three years previously a *Tractatus connubiorum* had appeared in Leipzig. Both treatises were published independently until the 1597 edition, which is said, perhaps correctly, to have been revised by the author. That is the edition that I have used.

35 Beust, *De sponsalibus* 8–9, ed. 1597, 11–13.

36 See Donahue 1995 and sources cited.

37 Beust, *De sponsalibus* 14, ed. 1597, 24.

38 The earliest editions of which I am aware of the complete work are Venice and Antwerp, 1606–7. I have used the edition of Antwerp published by Apud Haeredes Martini Nuti & Ioannem Meursium, 1626. I know of 13 other editions, well into the eighteenth century (the last edition that I know of is Venice 1754), with Lyon joining the other two major publishing centres in 1637.

39 Derived from the *Index locorum iuris* at the end of vol. 3.

40 Sánchez, *De sancto matrimonii sacramento* 7.3, ed. 1626, 2:9–11.

41 Ibid. 3.47, ed. 1626, 1:313–14. See, in this volume, Usunáriz 206–7.

42 A summary, entitled *Aphorismi reverendi patris Thomae Sánchez de matrimonio*, though itself of considerable length (887 pp.), published by decree of the Sacred Congregation of the Index and dated in 1627, was republished in Frankfurt in 1712.

43 I have used the reprint of the 1688 edition (the last to appear in Pufendorf's lifetime) and the translation into English by C.H. and W.S. Oldfather in the Classics of International Law series first published under the auspices of the Carnegie Endowment for International Peace.

44 Pufendorf, *De iure naturae* 6.1.14, trans. 863–4.

45 Ibid., trans. 863, C.27 q.2 c.5: Ambrose, "The deflowering of virginity does not make a marriage but the conjugal pact" [C. (causa), q. (quaestio), c. (chapter or canon)].

46 Pufendorf, *De iure naturae* 6.1.14, trans. 864.

47 See Donahue 1978, 34–53.

48 Pufendorf, *De iure naturae* 6.1.9–13, trans. 853–63. The argument is convoluted and much on these pages is devoted to refuting the authors who support more extreme versions of the power of the husband over the wife.

49 Ibid., 6.2.14, trans. 931–3.

50 Inst. 1.10.pr.

51 See Donahue 1978, 34–53.

52 Pufendorf, *De iure naturae* 6.1.1, trans. 839–40.

53 For Bodin, the point can be found in the first five chapters of book 1 of *Les six livres de la République*, in any of the numerous editions and translations. See Lefebvre-Teillard 263.

54 Pufendorf, *De iure naturae* 6.1.9, trans. 854.

55 Stryk, *Usus modernus*. I have used what is called the second edition (Halle and Magdeburg, 1713). It was many times reprinted. The last printing that I know of is 1780.

56 This effect, however, antedates Stryk. Many of the cases that he reproduces cite both Roman law and material from the general *ius commune*. Stryk's contribution is to tie this material into an overall Romanist framework.

57 This is probably one of Stryk's own *consilia*. He does not cite a source, as he normally does when he is reporting cases, and he says *respondimus*. The *consilium*, however, if such it was, was written in German.

58 Stryk, *Usus modernus* 23.1.5, 22, ed. 1713, 5, 43.

59 Ibid. 23.1.23, ed. 1713, 43–7.

60 Ibid. 23.1.6–9, ed. 1713, 5–12.

61 Ibid. 23.1.15–17, ed. 1713, 19–33.

62 Ibid. 23.1.18, ed. 1713, 33–8.

63 Ibid. 23.1.20–1, ed. 1713, 39–42.

64 *Pandectae Justinianeae* D.23.2, *De ritu nuptiarum*, 2:367–87.

65 Pothier, *Contrat de mariage*, par. 1–2 (prelim. 1–2), ed. 1768, 1:1–3, 11, 67, 69, 321–6.

66 Ibid., 11–14 (1.3.1), ed. 1768, 1:14–17.

67 Ibid., 67–9 (2.2.1), ed. 1768, 1:73–6; 322–6 (4.1.2.1.1), ed. 1768, 1:382–94. See, in this volume, Lefebvre-Teillard 265–9.

68 Pothier, *Contrat de mariage*, 321–2 (4.1.2.1.1), ed. 1768, 1:377–81. See, in this volume, 36, 102–4.

69 Pothier refers here to Jacques Boileau (1636–1716), *Traité des empêchemens du mariage*, c. 9, no. 7.

70 Pothier, *Contrat de mariage*, 321 (4.1.2.1.1), ed. 1768, 1:378–9. The quotations that follow come from 322, ed. 1768, 1:379–81.

71 This canon, attributed to St Basil, is found in a number of canonical collections of the Eastern Church. I have not found it in any Western canonical collections. Basil's *Opera omnia* were published in Paris by J. Garnier and P. Maran in 1721–30. That is probably the source of Pothier's Latin translation of the extract.

72 C.30 q.5 c.1. The first of Pothier's two quotations is not exact.

73 The implication, for example, that the pressure for change always comes from the outside probably should be resisted.

Chapter 2

Marriage in the Holy Roman Empire of the German Nation from the Fifteenth to the Eighteenth Century: Moral, Legal, and Political Order

HEIDE WUNDER

Introduction

In the history of the Holy Roman Empire of the German nation, the religious schism (Reformation) is generally considered a significant indicator of the beginning of a new era, along with the Imperial Reform of Maximilian I (1495). The institution of marriage long belonged to the important distinctions between the old church and the Protestant churches. In the early Reformation, priests who married and thus broke the vow of celibacy indeed understood it as a visible sign of turning away from the Roman Church. Recent scholarship[1] has modified this view, emphasizing that the Reformation continued the developments observable in the preceding centuries in many respects, albeit with different consequences than in the Catholic reform, which completed medieval Roman Catholic teachings and at the same time represented the response to the Reformation concept.[2]

A glance at the shared pre-history of the renewed Catholic Church and the Protestant churches has shown that monogamy, the voluntary, mutual consent of the betrothed, and the indissolubility of marriage were characteristic of the Christian church.[3] In distinction to Judaism, it insisted on monogamous marriage, although in the early and high Middle Ages it encountered polygyny among both the Germanic and Slavic tribes, at least among men of higher status.[4] The marital behaviour of those able to enter into legitimate marriage followed political and social objectives, so that ending a marriage was possible, and the coexistence of formal marriage, concubinage, and love affairs was a matter of course for (free) men. In the late Middle Ages the church had enforced monogamous matrimony and its indissolubility on principle, but this did not prevent many

German princes from maintaining concubines in addition to their legitimate marriages.[5] Moreover, differing secular and ecclesiastical notions of marriage continued to coexist, cooperate, and clash.[6] Church and laity agreed, however, on a patriarchal understanding of matrimony based on the hierarchy of husband and wife within marriage.[7] We have seen in the previous chapter how the church took responsibility for using its law, canon law, and its courts to watch over marital matters (the validity of marriage, impediments to marriage, marital age, annulment, legal separation, and suits for breach of promises to marry) to the extent that they touched on the spiritual symbolicity of marriage. The principle of mutual consent without witnesses, however, led to problems when one of the parties denied that there had been a promise to marry and the case came to court. This is one of the reasons why the church called for the publicity of matrimonial intent.[8] Although marriage symbolized Christ's connection with his church, in the eyes of the church the celibate way of life was deemed more desirable, so that marriage became a criterion separating the clergy from the laity. Although God instituted marriage in paradise and gave the commandment to be fruitful and multiply, marriage was regarded merely as a remedy for the weakness of the laity needed to prevent fornication (*Hurerei*).

The church's jurisdiction in matrimonial law is affirmed by town charters, which explicitly point to it or do not mention this aspect at all.[9] The church did not succeed in mandating a wedding ceremony conducted by a priest as essential for establishing marriage. Instead, the couple only had to seek the church's blessing at the church door: it was betrothal that continued to establish a marriage. Betrothal, marriage, and *Bettsetzung* (the ritual of setting the couple on the bed before witnesses after the wedding) took place in the circle of parents and kin and followed the regulations of matrimonial law codified in the statutory town charters, customary law, and feudal law, which often also contained detailed stipulations on marital age, impediments to marriage (such as existing promises to marry or inequality of rank), marital property law, and inheritance law, as well as the status of illegitimate children. Marital age by no means always coincided with canon law and was influenced above all by the economic implications of a given marriage and the concomitant founding of a household. If parents did not consent to their daughter's marriage, which was then construed as "abduction," the marriage was still valid, but the daughter could be disinherited.[10] A number of cities were not satisfied with a betrothal in the presence of parents and kin as witnesses, demanding a public espousal before the town council. Such regulations only applied to the minority of townspeople whose marriages were associated with the transfer of a dowry. Other towns were increasingly satisfied with written marriage contracts. Questions of matrimonial law with implications for marriage property law, for example legal separation, were accordingly dealt with before ecclesiastical and municipal courts. Adultery, in contrast, was both an ecclesiastical and a secular offence, since the temporal legal order was orientated towards the Ten Commandments.[11] The ecclesiastical courts were also entitled to execute their sentences.[12] The complainants could use the competing courts to their own ends, since they pursued different aims. Thus, for example, when hearing suits for breach of promise to marry, the ecclesiastical courts (*Offizialatsgerichte*) were concerned with the spiritual aspects of marriage, while the municipal courts treated such complaints from the perspective of order. Women suing for breach of promise to marry tended to have better chances before ecclesiastical than secular courts.[13] From the late fourteenth century, some imperial cities acquired portions of the jurisdiction of the synodal courts (*Sendgerichtsbarkeit*): thus, for example, as early as 1411 the archbishop of Mainz Johann von Nassau ceded the archdiocesan jurisdiction in cases of adultery, fornication, and incest to the town council of Frankfurt am Main, which rounded out the council's legal sovereignty and oversight of good order (*Policey und gute Ordnung*) in the territory under its authority.[14]

My account of marriage in the early modern period begins in the fifteenth century, the century of imperial and ecclesiastical reform, in which, particularly in the towns, laity and clergy alike revised older notions of marriage and took new paths towards a Christianization of the world, in which marriage would play a central role. The second section will treat theological, social, and political aspects of marriage in the age of Reformation, Catholic reform, and confessionalization. In a third section I outline new concepts of marriage as influenced by natural law and the Enlightenment, the marriage policies of the early modern state up to the codifications around 1800, and society's tendency towards independence from the church and theology, formulated in the "message of virtue" (*Botschaft der Tugend*) with its consequences for shaping the conditions of marriage.

Part I: The Fifteenth Century

In the third book of his chronicle, in which he recounts "how I, Burkhart Zingg [*sic*], have lived since the days of my childhood, what I aspired to and what my lot has been," the Augsburg citizen Burkart Zink (1396–1474 or 1475) gives an impression of what marriage meant to burghers of a large fifteenth-century imperial city.[15] In contrast to marriage contracts and wills, which regulated the aspects of marital property and inheritance,[16] it affords better insights into personal circumstances and attitudes in the narrower sense. Unlike the letters exchanged between spouses, between parents and children, and between children, also beginning in the fifteenth century,[17] the "self-written life story" (as Hans-Rudolf Velten called it) offered not detailed information and judgments but rather the overall outline of a life at the time of writing.[18] We need to read critically, however, in order to discover the author's overt and hidden intentions. Zink's account is all the more valuable for having been written by a man who came not from the rich merchant class, patriciate, or nobility but from the middle class in the imperial city of Memmingen, and later made his career in the great imperial city of Augsburg.

In 1420, Zink, son of a Memmingen artisan and originally destined for the clergy, married Margarete Störklerin, who served with him in the house of the weaver and merchant Jos Kramer. Ten children were born during their 20 years of marriage. The second marriage of Zink, now a wealthy man, was to the (poor) noble widow Dorothea Kuehlinbeckin, who brought two children with her. When she died in 1449 after seven years of childless marriage, he lived out of wedlock for four and a half years with the *freulein* (wench) Margret Segesserin; they had two children. In 1454, at the age of 58, Zink was married for a third time to the shopkeeper's daughter Dorothea Münstelerin, who died in 1459 giving birth to her fifth child. We know of two daughters from his fourth marriage to Anna (1460). He died in 1474 or 1475.

Zink does not mention a church ceremony for any of his marriages. In his story, the church's importance for marriage became apparent only when the *freulein* sued him for breach of promise to marry before the Augsburg synodal court.[19] The Hildesheim patrician Henning Brandis (1471–1528),[20] however, described the procedures accompanying his first marriage in minute detail: from his first approach to the bride's family to negotiations over the dowry and betrothal, the marriage ceremony performed by a priest friend as the bride's *Muntwalt* (a sort of guardian) in the house of his father and the subsequent lavish festivities, *Bettsetzung*, going to church, and *Beilager* (the ritual in which the couple got into bed and were covered up), culminating in the young couple moving into their own house. The priest's presence at the wedding was not rooted in canon law and thus did not constitute the marriage; when the couple went to church, it was merely to ask God's blessing.

In contrast to Henning Brandis's, Zink's first marriage was not an arranged one. Rather, Burkart and Margarete had decided to marry and "thus took each other in amicable concord" (*gute freuntschaft*). The bride's mother, a (poor) widow, approved of their union, for she provided her daughter with a small dowry. In this way they observed a number of formalities for the conclusion of a valid marriage: the mutual consent of the betrothed and of the bride's mother. Zink had no living parents, siblings, or close kin with any say in the matter, as was generally the case for couples from well-to-do circles. Zink does not even mention any wedding festivities. The public informed of this marriage was doubtless very small, for the event took the young couple's employer by surprise. He was annoyed that the 24-year-old Zink, who lived as a dependent in his household, had not asked his advice, and dismissed both Zink and his wife without notice. Apparently he had expected Zink to ask for his consent as head of household. Zink had not anticipated this outcome, believing himself dear to his master, since he had proven himself a good servant. Except for Margarete's small dowry, the young couple were virtually penniless. Zink had only his clothes and a little money. The couple lived in rented lodgings and had to earn their keep with wage labour. Working tirelessly, they soon succeeded, a fact that Zink attributed to the symbolic capital of "honour and virtuousness" (*er und frumkait*).[21]

Zink's subsequent weddings were "publicly" contracted "proper marriages." Before he married the impoverished noble widow Dorothea Kuehlinbeckin, Zink negotiated the conditions. She brought even less dowry with her than Zink's first wife and also had two children to educate and provide for. In exchange, Dorothea promised to be submissive and obedient to him and to make no demands. Although Zink acquired social prestige with a wife of aristocratic birth, he observed her closely at their first meeting, fearing that she would make much of her noble estate and challenge his authority within the marriage, a misgiving generally cited in opposition to marrying widows.[22] The shopkeeper's daughter presumably brought the dowry usual in Augsburg. Zink mentions no marriage in which the couple's property was regulated in terms beyond the stipulations of the town charter, as was common for the nobility, patrician couples, and spouses from the upper middle class.[23]

During his four marriages Zink was not involved in any conflicts that compelled him to turn to an ecclesiastical court. Such a conflict did arise, however, when Margret Segesser, who lived with Zink for four and a half years and was his "beloved," sued him – albeit unsuccessfully – before an Augsburg synodal court (*Korgericht*, i.e., the responsible ecclesiastical court) for not keeping his promise to marry. In fact, concubinage lasting several years – that is, cohabitation without marriage such as that between Zink and his *freulein* or that of Lukas Rem in Nuremberg[24] – was extremely difficult to distinguish from a marriage that had been concluded without formalities.[25] The fluidity of conjugal status, even the uncertainty of the two people directly involved, is a phenomenon amply documented in other parts of late medieval and early modern Europe as well.[26]

Zink's four marriages and his relationship with the *freulein* cast a telling light on marital conditions in the fifteenth century and how they were viewed. They illuminate the legal, economic, and social dimensions of marriage, but also the emotions Zink associated with it.[27] His first marriage was clearly a love match, and he also loved the *freulein*. In his second marriage to the noble widow, the striving for social prestige was probably paramount, but the fact that she was also a "beautiful, slender woman" of modest demeanour played a role as well: "She pleased me still better than before and I took her."[28] The decision to marry for a third time at the age of 58 doubtless had much to do with his loneliness now that most of his children had died or moved far away, so that he wished to marry a young woman and start a new family. When she died he needed a wife quickly to care for his small children. When describing this last relationship, he paints a picture of an "ill-matched couple": the young wife tyrannized her elderly husband, a fate he shared with his father, of whom he had rhymed,

als noch oft und dick alten mannen
junge weib wol gevallen

("For old men are often fond of young women.")[29]

At first glance, Zink's portrayals of marriage leave a highly personal impression, though they are shot through with stereotypical patterns of interpretation concerning gender relations. Thus he juxtaposes the image of the "ill-matched couple" with that of the obedient, hard-working, and virtuous wife whom he rewards in a gesture of patriarchal magnanimity. At the same time, the importance Zink placed in the moral notions of his age is striking. Honour and virtuousness (*frumkeit*) were central values for him, and he characterized his four wives as virtuous (*frum*). For him, honour and virtuousness were the preconditions for "good fortune and happiness" (*glück und heil*), that is, for personal well-being, economic success, posterity, and reputation in the world. For that reason, he realized in retrospect that living "in sin" with the *freulein* could only have ended in lies and deception. Among the laity, moral notions of purity and impurity were particularly widespread in the cities, doubtless in the wake of experiences of the Plague. From the late fourteenth century, some guilds (e.g., the goldsmiths) refused to accept apprentices born not of a "pure marriage bed" but rather of concubinage.[30] The greatest proportion of lawsuits concerning marriage before the ecclesiastical and secular courts,[31] as well as those concerning adultery and fornication, were heard in the name of moralizing gender relations.[32] At the same time, the town councils began to adopt a new policy of order (*gute Policey*) towards prostitutes (*freie Frauen*), by setting up brothels (*Frauenhäuser*) just inside the city walls, mandating that the women wear certain clothing and marking them with symbols as "common women" in order to separate them clearly and visibly from honourable women.[33]

This morals policy was accompanied by a broad didactics of Christian tenets and the Ten Commandments in words and images. St Mary's Church in Danzig has a panel painting of the Ten Commandments (1486). The tomb of the Frankfurt cleric Johann Lupi (ca. 1470) has representations of the Ten Commandments and the number of each commandment chiselled into the stone in finger symbols. Printed versions of the Ten Commandments were directed more at a literate audience, such as nuns.[34] In contrast, an unknown painter in St Lambert's in Hildesheim wrote the Lord's Prayer, the Hail Mary, the Apostles' Creed, and the Ten Commandments on a wooden catechism panel of 1451, all of which – with the exception of the Hail Mary – also belonged to the five main sections of the Small Catechism of Luther or Brenz.[35] As religious lay movements of the late Middle Ages saw it, this catechesis was intended to bolster the faithful in their beliefs and facilitate their spiritual participation in religion.

The morals movement took hold in the clerical estate as well and was not limited to reforming the religious orders and secular clergy. Members of the university who lived in concubinage also began to marry, as did jurists and medical doctors whose occupational fields were in lay society.[36] An expression of this reorientation may be found in humanist debates on whether or not one should marry.[37] The most prominent among them is Erasmus's *Praise of Marriage*.[38]

Part II: The Reformation and Catholic Reform: The Christianization of Life and "Good Order"

When it comes to marriage, there are many similarities between the Reformation and Catholic reform as well as Protestant and Catholic confessionalization, especially in regard to fornication, so it makes sense to treat them together.

Reformation: Matrimony as the "First Order of God"

The efforts of the laity and clergy, secular authorities, and the official church to purify society and the church sketched here first came together in the Reformation, which elevated wedlock to the morally normative centre of society. The "normative centring"[39] of clerical and secular reform movements was, however, accompanied by an institutional focus, which explains why the reform demands could be implemented. The monastic reforms of the fifteenth century had already been instituted by temporal territorial rulers, since the ecclesiastical institutions had failed; they oversaw church property and church discipline. In the large cities, the town councils had taken control of morality, anticipating and paving the way for their leadership role as "Christian authorities" in the Reformation.[40]

These reforms were joined, however, by a new theological understanding of the "Christian (individual)," a Christian anthropology that emerged from the renewal of faith. Martin Luther's anthropology, which he developed on the basis of the revealed Creation story, proved path-breaking here: God had created the first pair of humans as sexual beings, so the chastity privileged by the official church was contrary to human nature. Instead, the "holy matrimony" instituted by God in paradise was the site of true chastity. It should be made accessible to all Christians in order to prevent "unchastity" and create a *res publica christiana*. Luther thus discarded canon law impediments to marriage, to the extent that they exceeded those revealed in the Old Testament, as transitory works of man (Donahue 34–5, 43, Helmholz 141–3). Other reformers went still further. They questioned not merely canon law but also the sole jurisdiction of Mosaic law, as in the case of Johannes Brenz, the reformer of the imperial city of Schwäbisch Hall, and when it came to the "forbidden degrees" (of consanguinity) fell back upon Roman law.[41] Ultimately, the ideas of the Zurich reformer Heinrich Bullinger, who drew the circle of prohibited spouses more broadly than Luther, asserted themselves.[42] Godparenthood remained as an impediment to marriage, since it was treated like the forbidden degrees of consanguinity and considered incest. This restriction was (unsuccessfully) challenged with the argument that all Christians became brothers and sisters in baptism, and thus "spiritual kinship" could no longer represent an impediment to marriage. Dispensations remained, however, which now became the sole province of town councils and territorial rulers.

No matter how important the theological impediments to marriage were, social and economic impediments weighed far heavier. First marriages were to be contracted only between persons of equal rank, for example between a master, or a journeyman who was soon to become a master, and the daughter or widow of a master; between a merchant and the daughter of a merchant or the heir to a farm and a farmer's daughter, but never to a maid or servant of sub-peasant origin. Parents, relatives, and guardians exercised decisive influence, based on the commandment to honour one's mother and father.[43] In France, in the Netherlands, and in Scandinavia, parental authority would legitimize its own control over children's conjugal choices in accordance with the same principle (Donahue 40, van der Heijden 160, 167–8, Lefebvre-Teillard 263, 264–5). In many towns the age of marriage was set high to keep children in minor status and thus under parental authority as long as possible.[44] In the case of second and third marriages, equality of rank was no longer central if the first marriage had produced offspring; this applied not just to the nobility, particularly the high nobility,[45] but also to artisans: thus in Schwäbisch Hall, for example, widowed craftsmen married their maids.[46] The social relevance of parental consent extended in principle to all rural and urban propertied strata.[47] Farm servants, in contrast, who moved to town from the country, often had to work and save for decades for their dowries and married late, by which time many of them had already lost one or both parents.[48]

In the course of confessionalization, marriages between partners of different confessions were prohibited. In the sixteenth century, however, such marriages were not uncommon, and many brides demanded a guarantee of their right to practise their religion freely in the marriage contract, although the husband's authority did not apply in matters of conscience.[49] In the seventeenth and eighteenth centuries, too, mixed marriages were no exception, but they were under the surveillance of the respective authorities, which were especially concerned with the children of these marriages and their instruction in the "proper" faith.[50]

While developed in the theological controversies around clerical marriage[51] and propagated in the figure of the model clerical couple,[52] the new positive view of matrimony was generalized for all Christians ritually and legally in Protestant marriage and church ordinances. Wedlock advanced to the way of life most pleasing to God, the central institution for the Christianization of the world, the normative heart of gender relations and the gender order.

The notion of matrimony as an estate pleasing to God implied an understanding of "conjugal love" as *charitas*, the mutual support of spouses in channelling their desire as God intended, that is, performing the sexual act not as an end in itself and for their own pleasure but as a "marital act" (*eheliches Werk*) to conceive children. The spouses' reciprocal responsibilities also included the duty to help each other cope with everyday life, for which there was more than simply a theological basis. Thus the Zurich reformer Heinrich Bullinger explicitly demanded that couples should share "joy and sorrow,"[53] a principle of urban society documented in characterizations of economic relations between married couples since the fifteenth century.[54] Married people's duties included producing children as well as raising those children to be Christians, a task by no means relegated to the church. Rather, the "home church" was the first site of religious instruction and daily piety, the responsibility of the parents, particularly the mother of the household. A prerequisite was the spiritual equality of man and woman: in the sacrament of baptism, both were freed from original sin and both could hope for redemption as a result of Christ's death on the cross. Spouses were not merely "one flesh" but should also "become friends in the spirit,"[55] for only in their common striving did it seem possible to "bring faith into life" and thus effect a Christianization of the world by moralizing everyday life.

As a form of association, marriage represented the epitome of love, friendship, and (domestic) peace.[56] At the same time, marriage was understood as the "first order of God," the proper order of the sexes, prefiguring the hierarchical organization of society.[57] Adultery thus not only violated divine law but also imperilled the order of the society of estates as a whole, which was based on inequality. The new anthropology of the reformers thus did not affect gender relations "in the world": the husband remained the head of his wife, who owed him obedience.[58]

The form of rule in marriage was monarchy and was therefore defined in terms of contemporary political theory. It became "tyranny" when the husband abused his legitimate disciplinary powers. This association between morality and the hierarchical gender order made marriage a fundamental institution of early modern society, through which key social, economic (property and labour), and power positions were distributed; the founding of a household, legitimate parenthood, and inheritance rights depended on it, as did not least – in all estates – the status of widow and widower.[59] For that reason, marriage was a worthwhile aspiration for men and women of all estates. Although matrimony was described in writings and sermons on marriage as "the yoke of wedlock" (*Ehejoch*),[60] "a grievous estate" (*Wehestand*),[61] and in funeral sermons as "the cross of marriage," and although wives were restricted in their legal and economic activities, many of them appear to have found this state more bearable than spinsterhood, which meant lifelong dependency. Matrimony bestowed a privileged social status on both spouses, giving them authority and respectability, as elaborately displayed in the portraits of reigning couples, in the quartered coats of arms of noble couples, and in the inscriptions on the façades of town and village houses containing the names of those who built them.[62] While wives occupied second place in the marital hierarchy, they nevertheless knew the value of their status and defended it when challenged by other wives' unwomanly conduct, as the women's tribunal of Breitenbach (near Kassel) demonstrates.[63] Here in 1653 it was the village wives, not the church or the village court, who penalized in formal proceedings the misdeeds of a wife who had been seen beating her husband and thus violating the marital gender hierarchy. Many wives went so far as to request the release of or a more lenient sentence for their criminal husbands, whose absence threatened the women's own social status.[64]

Matrimonial Law, Marital and Moral Discipline

The reformers shared Luther's conviction that marriage was not a sacrament but rather a "secular matter" (*res politica*) because it had not been instituted by Jesus.[65] As a *res politica*, marriage was transferred to the jurisdiction of the secular Christian authorities, which assumed the status of a corporative *summus episcopus* in the large towns and of a monarchical *summus episcopus* in the territorial states. They did not submit matrimonial matters to the secular judiciary. Instead, after the introduction of the Reformation, they began setting up new church agencies, which were, however, subordinate to the town council or the territorial ruler and therefore did not attain the autonomy of the old ecclesiastical courts.[66] This is particularly evident in the personnel of these institutions, in which theologians made up only a minority. The consistory in the royal part of Holstein, whose members were all pastors, appears to have been the exception to the rule.[67]

The marriage courts were not coincidentally accorded a leading role in this institutionalization of church government (*Kirchenregiment*), for a particular need for action had arisen: on the one hand, the old ecclesiastical jurisdiction over marriage based on canon law and its institutions no longer applied, so that new regulations for valid marriage and its ritual sanctification had to be found and implemented.[68] On the other, the loss of the sacramental nature of marriage and the consequence of its possible dissolution opened up new perspectives for divorce suits. Finally, Protestant marital theology led to a ban on all pre- and extramarital sexual relations, a prohibition that applied not just to adultery but also to prostitution and concubinage, which was henceforth defined as "fornication" (*Unzucht*) and subject to ecclesiastical jurisdiction, and which represented the majority of cases treated by the courts. We shall see later how the Netherlandish urban courts and the Swiss matrimonial courts applied similarly strict criteria in judging extramarital sexuality (van der Heijden 164, 166, 168, Burghartz 187–8). The prohibition of "fornication" was closely related to the new forms of contracting marriage and greatly expanded the spectrum of the marriage courts' tasks.

(1) In order for a marriage to be valid, it became essential not merely that the espoused couple agree but also that they obtain the consent of parents or guardians, as was already stipulated in late medieval town charters, if the couple did not wish to risk losing the dowry. Now, however, the validity of parents' objections was examined, since people also had a right to marry.[69] The public nature of betrothal was increased on the one hand by the obligatory presence of witnesses and on the other by the announcement of the intention to marry in the local church before the assembled congregation in order to explore potential impediments to marriage. Finally, the public ceremony by the pastor at the altar became the official date when the marriage began. This abolished the distinctions between *sponsalia de presenti* and *sponsalia de futuro*, so that the "clandestine marriage," which rested solely on the reciprocal vows of

bride and groom and thus could not be proven in cases of doubt, was no longer deemed valid.[70] The church had been pursuing this aim since the thirteenth century, but it could only be tackled in the wake of the Reformation and the jurisdiction of the temporal Christian authorities. The old call for church registers to record baptisms, marriages, and burials was also implemented; in the period that followed, they became important instruments for controlling the moral behaviour of members of the congregation.

(2) The marriage courts heard suits for marriage as well as for divorce. Marriages were no longer indissoluble; they could be ended on serious grounds, and the innocent party was allowed to remarry. In this area, the broad differences between reformers on matters of matrimony become apparent. While the stricter reformers (Calvin) recognized only adultery, impotence, and "malicious abandonment" as grounds, the "more lenient" tendency (Zwingli, Luther, Brenz) admitted further grounds such as severe maltreatment (*saevitia*) and murderous persecution (*insidia*).[71] Others, like Erasmus Sarcerius and Martin Bucer, went still further but were unable to assert their positions. Church ordinances rarely incorporated the more lenient interpretations, but specific circumstances were certainly taken into account when treating individual cases.[72] In practice, however, the Protestant marriage courts made every effort to reconcile the quarrelling couple. Luther in particular propagated mediation as a means of resolving disputes between spouses. In Hesse-Kassel, such mediation, in which the local pastor participated, played an important role into the seventeenth century: only when it had failed was the way clear to a costly suit before the regular courts.[73] This helps to explain why divorces were rarely decreed before the eighteenth century;[74] frequently, the couple only separated temporarily.[75] Many divorce suits brought by women were rejected because the judges, for example in cases of physical violence, referred to the husband's right to discipline his wife, in order not to call his patriarchal authority into question, although violent husbands in particular were clearly lacking in authority.

The new marriage courts were quickly institutionalized in the course of the Reformation in large cities such as Nuremberg (1525), Zurich (1525), Basel (1529), and Augsburg (1534). In the territorial states, in contrast, this process frequently took many decades. Even Electoral Saxony, which introduced the Reformation in 1525, had only ad hoc commissions for matrimonial matters until a marriage court was set up in the late 1520s, out of which emerged the consistory as the central church authority.[76] The landgravate of Hesse, too, initially did without a central church authority.[77] One reason was that Lutheran marital theology developed in stages, so that its consequences for church discipline and the cases to be dealt with before the church courts emerged only gradually. Another was doubtless that moral discipline, which encompassed a number of new offences in marital affairs such as prostitution and concubinage, was already a subject of the local and customary police ordinances (*Policey- und Landesordnungen*) and ultimately the imperial police ordinances (*Reichspoliceyordnungen*),[78] with their orientation towards the Ten Commandments, and was a matter for the lower courts (*Niedergerichte*). Adultery, along with fornication, incest, abduction, rape, bigamy, and procuring, belonged not least to the crimes regulated by the Carolina, the criminal code that Charles V introduced for the empire in 1532, which was adopted by the city-states and territories.

The institutionalization of the church authorities sketched here was very important for implementing the new marital discipline. Not just the radicalization of the discourse on fornication, and its deployment as part of increasing confessional formation and competition after the 1555 Peace of Augsburg, but also the bureaucratization of proceedings led to the heightened prosecution of fornication from the second half of the sixteenth century.[79] The prosecuting institutions, however, relied on the cooperation of the local population, without which they could gain no information about the offences. After all, fornication – like sorcery – was generally committed in private and only became obvious when a couple was caught in flagrante or when revealed by the pregnancy of an unmarried woman: in this case it became a public "scandal" (*Ärgernis*) in need of prosecution, in which the woman's local reputation – her character, based on observation – played a decisive role. The court records of fornication cases usually only involve women from the urban and rural lower classes, while women of the middle and upper classes generally had the material means to conceal a pregnancy and thus to avoid causing a "scandal."

Since church history, too, is the history of the "victors," it has largely glossed over the fact that the major Protestant churches' understandings of marriage represented only a segment of the broad range of views on matrimony among the Protestant religious movements. In contrast to the monogamous marriage propagated by Lutherans, Zwinglians, and Calvinists, the Anabaptists in Münster, citing the Old Testament and the need to increase the numbers of the "saints," introduced polygamy (*Vielweiberei*), which gave their opponents the opportunity to condemn them as "godless."[80] Landgrave Philip of Hesse (1504–67), who otherwise opposed the Anabaptists, cited the example of the Old Testament patriarchs to justify his bigamous marriage to the Saxon noblewoman Margarethe von der Saale.[81] Among the Anabaptists, those married to a person of another religious persuasion were permitted to separate from their spouses and enter a new marriage.[82] The reformer Caspar von Schwenckfeld (1489–1561), in contrast, preferred the single state in order to devote himself wholly to the service of God, while most of his South German followers chose to marry.[83] In a number of Anabaptist communities, equality was not limited to the common spiritual relationship with Christ; women also had access to clerical office.[84] The belief that the end of the world was imminent played a major role in attitudes towards marriage: thus the radical Pietist Eva Margaretha von Buttlar (1670–1721) rejected marriage; her aim was to restore gender relations as they had existed in the Garden of Eden.[85]

Catholic Reform

The Catholic reform movements culminated in the Tridentine reform. The discussion of priestly marriage and celibacy had played an important role in the consultations of the Council of Trent, without reaching a rapprochement with the Protestants. Rather, the Roman Church retained the principles of clerical celibacy[86] as well as of the sacramental nature and indissolubility of matrimony. Nevertheless, the decree *Tametsi* of 1563 largely followed the Protestant stipulations for a valid marriage – the agreement of the betrothed couple before witnesses and the blessing by a priest before the congregation – in order to do away with "clandestine marriages." Unlike the Protestant churches, however, Catholics did not demand parental consent, defining marriage instead as a process governed exclusively by canon law.[87] Aside from differences of theology and canon law, the institution of matrimony was assigned the same ordering functions in Catholic as in Protestant territories.[88] Both confessions shared the conviction that the social order rested on the hierarchy of the sexes in marriage and that the purity of society was based on the gender relations integrated into matrimony. Thus both faiths were united in their opposition to indecency, profligacy (*Leichtfertigkeit*), and disharmony between spouses. An early example is the duchy of Bavaria, where the dukes clung to the old religion and instituted a strict morals policy even before the Council of Trent.[89] A recent study on the prince-bishopric of Münster documents this for the Counter-Reformation.[90]

Part III: Marriage in the Age of Natural Law and Enlightenment

In the age of the law of reason and the Enlightenment, the institution of marriage retained its central ordering function in society, but in the course of early modern state-building the protagonists of the marriage discourse changed, along with the arguments used to justify maintaining the gender hierarchy in marriage. While in the context of confessionalization marriage policies had been based on the "normative centring"[91] of theological and secular concepts of marriage as well as the coalition between the Christian temporal authorities and the church, the secular interests of the early modern state now gained ascendancy. This process of "secularization" was promoted by jurisprudence, which, together with the law of reason, relegated theology to second place as a central normative authority. But it was not just the "state" that emancipated itself from the authority of theology and the church; it was also civil society, whose leaders included the "upper ranks," the representatives of the rising class of state servants, and the university educated more generally. In the late eighteenth and early nineteenth centuries, the codifications influenced by natural law – particularly Emperor Joseph's Marriage Patent (1783) and the civil code (*Allgemeines Bürgerliches Gesetzbuch*) for the Habsburg lands (1811), as well as the Prussian *Allgemeines Landrecht* of 1794 – document a wide range of effects on marital law. Despite "secularization," however, civil marriage was not introduced in the Holy Roman Empire as it was during the French Revolution. The normative decentring, the separation of law and morals, of law and revelation, sacrament and contract, was still in its inception.

Marriage: Civil Contract as a Contract of Submission

In the late sixteenth century, natural law began to influence thinking about legitimate authority and thus about authority within marriage. Only rational grounds, and no longer reference to unquestioned authorities, now determined the relationship between ruler and ruled, who were conceived of as equals "by nature." This relationship was legitimized in a social contract within which the subjects subordinated themselves to the sovereign. In analogy, the relationship of domination in marriage could no longer be founded on the divine order of creation alone, as formulated in the church marriage vows.[92] If marriage was viewed as a *res politica* (Martin Luther), it was necessary instead to define it as a civil contract between equal partners in which the wife had to submit voluntarily to the rule of her husband in order to legitimize the existing inequality between husband and wife.[93] Despite the challenge to the *imperium maritale* as not founded on "nature," husbandly, paternal, and patriarchal competences continued to exist: disposal over the property that the wife brought into the marriage and its usufruct, claims on her person (deciding the family name and domicile), and labour, whether in the household or in his trade, as well as rights to her body, in order to guarantee the legitimacy of the children who were born into the marriage and thus entitled to inherit. If the wife violated her duty to obey, the husband could discipline her. The wife, in turn, had a right to be kept in a manner befitting her rank and to the representation of her interests in legal matters.[94] Only in cases involving disposal over her children[95] did she exercise rights as a mother. Only if he gravely abused his power in matters of property could a wife take her husband to court.

The tension, typical of the Reformation, between the spiritual equality of men and women and the social form of marriage as a gender hierarchy thus persisted under new conditions. For women, particularly if they were married, there was no provision for legal "emancipation from tutelage," for in civil society the presumed pre-social equality of the sexes could not be transformed into positive law. To this extent, one can agree with Ursula Vogel, who sees the sole benefit of natural law and the Enlightenment in the fact that they at least kept the idea of gender equality present.[96]

Nonetheless, natural law notions of marriage broke a number of intellectual taboos: thus Hugo Grotius (1583–1645) called monogamy into question because natural law did not exclude polygamy,[97] and for Christian Thomasius (1655–1728), polyandry was also conceivable.[98] In "Amazon marriage" the woman ruled over the man if the couple agreed to this.[99] That spouses could live and work together as legal equals remained inconceivable, however. It was not until the French Revolution that Olympe de Gouges developed such a model of marriage. More radically still, the German late-Enlightenment thinker Theodor von Hippel called for public higher education to be opened to the female sex, paving the way for their access to public office.[100]

Welfare and "Domestic Happiness"

The objectives of early modern rule were increasingly influenced by the subjective logic of political action and focused on the intramundane "blessedness" (*Glückseligkeit*) and welfare of subjects. It made no difference here whether the state in question was Protestant or Catholic.

The temporal authorities, which had already assumed the task of preserving the moral order in the fifteenth century, continued with this politics in the age of Reformation and Counter-Reformation. We shall see how in France especially, where the decree *Tametsi* of 1563 was not enacted, the king ("state") – in keeping with regalist theory – claimed jurisdiction in matters of marriage (Lefebvre-Teillard 262–71).[101]

The institution of matrimony was assigned new ordering tasks in the context of cameralism, particularly the preservation of the peace and state demographic policy (*Peuplierung*). When it came to attaining its objectives, the early modern state was woefully understaffed, so that apart from the personnel of the churches, it had to rely on its subjects in the guise of the married couple, as well as the local political community. In addition, policing legislation bolstered the authority of husband and wife as Christian parents[102] by assigning public authority to punish their children and servants to the paterfamilias and materfamilias. In this way, all unmarried persons were to be subject to the control of the pater- and materfamilias, along with all married persons of inferior legal status who lived in the house.

The prerequisite for the authority of the heads of household (*Hauseltern*), however, was that they lived in a "lawful marriage" as regulated in the church ordinances. Territorial rulers were thus disturbed by the impossibility, even in the eighteenth century, of enforcing the church wedding ceremony universally as the official beginning of marriage and thus of legitimate sexual intercourse. Instead, in rural society the betrothal was still regarded as the beginning of marriage, so that intercourse before the church wedding was considered not illegal.[103] Such circumstances were lamented in Lutheran Württemberg and the Reformed landgravate of Hesse-Kassel, but also in the Reformed Basel countryside.[104] A countermeasure adopted in Hesse-Kassel, for example, was to make the betrothal a public affair: before the church proclamation, all subjects who wished to marry had to appear with their parents or guardians and put their material circumstances on record to the local authorities, after which they were to marry as soon as possible. This was intended to prevent "premature intercourse" (*verfrühter Beischlaf*), which became public when a child was born too soon, for example only eight months after the wedding.

Apart from this bureaucratic hurdle to marriage, the aforementioned social and economic barriers also still had to be overcome. First and foremost, young people had to get their parents to consent to their choice of partner and the date of the marriage, whereby economic reasons were often central. Similarly, many villages and towns made consent to marriage dependent on property or sufficient income, which diminished the chances of legitimate marriage for a growing number of individuals in precarious social circumstances.[105] Church consistories in Württemberg refused permission to marry when the couple could not produce the demanded property.[106] Guilds in the imperial city of Augsburg scrutinized all artisans from outside who wished to marry to determine whether their economic circumstances allowed them to do so.[107] The early modern states enacted temporary (delaying) restrictions on marriage. In the duchy of Bavaria and later in the Electorate, the age of marriage for servants was raised to cope with the labour shortage in the countryside;[108] in the landgravate of Hesse-Kassel (and other midsize German states) non-commissioned officers, cavalrymen, and musketeers who wished to marry had to obtain the consent of their regimental commanding officer and from 1710 also to pay a marriage tax of eight *reichstaler* to benefit the military hospital. From 1727 all lackeys, coachmen, and equerries in the service of the landgrave needed permission to marry, and from 1751 all chancery clerks and copyists as well. Finally, from 1800 on, all marriages of the landgrave's civil servants depended on his consent.[109] Generally the concern was to forbid "beggars' weddings" to spare the poor box and only to allow couples to marry who were guaranteed to pay taxes.

It was thus not made easy for young people to enter into a "lawful marriage." For that reason it is not surprising that the various restrictions on marriage encouraged couples to live together unlawfully and increased the numbers of illegitimate children. While in the sixteenth century the offence of fornication was created to promote and protect the institution of matrimony, the new restrictions on marriage worked to increase cases of fornication, above all in the lower social strata.

Fornication, referred to as *Unzucht*, *Liederlichkeit*, or *Leichtfertigkeit*, was an offence in both secular and canon law and subject to secular penalties and ecclesiastical penances[110] if it became a scandal – that is, public. Cases were heard first by the secular lower courts, which passed sentence where appropriate, before a church penance was determined, although this was by no means common everywhere.[111] The German territorial states and city-republics imposed a great variety of legal sanctions: in Catholic Bavaria, for example, the most severe punishment was imprisonment, a monetary fine, and public penance, while in the Protestant margravate of Baden, offenders faced the public confiscation of their property and banishment, public flogging, and a church penance.[112] These draconian punishments were actually imposed but by the seventeenth century frequently reduced, since it was left up to officials to set the punishment "at will" (*willkürlich*), that is, as they saw fit.[113] When a shaming penalty was imposed on female fornicators this was not merely humiliating but could also have far-reaching consequences. If, for example, the executioner, his assistant, or a beadle performed the public flogging, a shaming punishment meted out exclusively to women, it rendered the women dishonourable[114] and could mean their exclusion from society. Aside from the loss of home and livelihood, they also had a much harder time finding a husband. In Bavaria, where offenders were not obliged to submit to punishment in their home city or village, many took this opportunity to avoid the mockery and malice of those who knew them.[115]

By the early seventeenth century, a connection had been constructed between punishments for fornication, public penances, and infanticide, such that only unmarried pregnant women were treated as potential infanticides, although married women were certainly among the accused and arrested.[116] This connection is not substantiated by the testimony of women tried for infanticide; nonetheless, it provided an important argument for the Enlightenment debate on infanticide in the second half of the eighteenth century.[117] As a form of kin murder deemed particularly despicable, infanticide was punishable by drowning. In order to prevent it, unwed women were supposed to report to their pastor as soon as they realized they were pregnant.[118] By the first half of the eighteenth century, however, in many places public penance was replaced by private penance (*Privatzensur*) to preserve women's honour and aid in the reintegration of fornicators. For that reason, fornicating couples who were prepared to marry received a reduction in their monetary fines, and their children born out of wedlock were legitimized. The bride, however, was not allowed to marry wearing her hair down and a bridal crown,[119] and in some towns also not publicly in church. This documents the authorities' anxiousness to see as many persons of marriageable age as possible in the married estate as a site of orderly gender relations – if necessary against their will.[120]

The mitigation of punitive practice on the ground contrasted with the legal situation, which in many German territories remained unreformed until the end of the eighteenth century, so the assumption that the Enlightenment, which after all came "from above," was the source of this mitigation proves untenable.[121] Isabel Hull's reflections on the subject appear more plausible. She points out that fornication trials took place before the lower courts, whose officials were orientated towards local conflict regulation and sought to pacify local society. Thus when hearing cases of fornication, they relied largely on the shaping of opinion in local society, that is, on the reputation of the persons involved and their economic and social standing in the community.[122] In this way the lower courts increasingly departed from legislation, thereby creating a space for responses to enlightened ideas. Thus the view that fornication – at least when it was a first offence – was rooted not in sin but in "human frailty" doubtless promoted the mitigation of penalties.[123] Moreover, in the meantime begging and vagabondage had come to be regarded as far more harmful to society than fornication. When prosecuting women charged with infanticide, officers of the court applied a stricter yardstick to investigating the circumstances of the case and also began to take into account the precise details of the offence,[124] leading to a drop in the number of women executed for infanticide.[125]

In an age characterized by a general bellicosity in relations between states, marital peace was regarded as central to the inner peace of society, whereby the old Christian ideal of "peaceful marriage" was laden with new demands on spouses. Using the example of seventeenth-century Bavarian suits for separation, Rainer Beck has impressively illustrated the potential for conflict in marriage in all its economic, social, and emotional dimensions.[126] The virulence of marital discord is also evident in cases of Protestant couples who sued for divorce.[127] From this perspective, it becomes understandable how marriages between members of different confessions could imperil marital peace and with it the public order because of the couple's separate religious practices and conflicts over the religious education of their children.[128] It is part of the logic of this concept of marriage to resolve marital conflicts, wherever possible, not through separation – whether through separate households or divorce with the right of the innocent party to remarry – but instead by keeping the couple together through forgiveness and reconciliation. In this way, "domestic happiness" in a "peaceful marriage" was closely intertwined with the "general happiness" of society.

Yet another important objective for which the early modern state relied on the "domestic happiness" of its subjects was population policy, or *Peuplierung*. The general welfare could only be achieved with economic and demographic growth, as Veit Ludwig von Seckendorff, the most influential political thinker of his day in the German-speaking world, noted in his 1678 *Teutscher Fürsten-Stat* (*The German Princely State*), where he stated "that the ruler's greatest good fortune lies in the number of his subjects and that they represent the true wealth of the country."[129] The number of subjects was not all that counted but also their heightened productivity. To achieve this aim, many German states pursued a dual strategy: first, the recruitment of qualified skilled workers (preferably with their families) from abroad, for example, the Huguenots in Brandenburg-Prussia;[130] and second, the general promotion of manufacturing. Thus poverty and begging were to be combatted not just with marriage restrictions but also by creating new opportunities for labour. At the same time, Prussia also pioneered the introduction of new policies towards unwed mothers, illegitimate children, and divorce. As early as 1746, Prussia banned church penances for single mothers. In 1765, after the end of the Seven Years' War, the state also abolished the secular penalties for fornication (*Hurenstrafen*), not least in order to prevent infanticide.[131] What is more, Cocceji's 1749 *Project des Corporis Juris Fridericiani* already provided for divorce where one party felt an insurmountable aversion towards the other, as long as both parties agreed, since the very purpose and meaning of marriage could no longer be fulfilled in such cases. This provision was based on the idea that discord-filled marriages produced too few children, so it was better to permit divorce to prevent the children from being damaged by the bad example of their parents and to allow the wife another chance to marry with the prospect of bearing more children.[132] Thus it was only consistent if, in addition to reproducing, parents were required by law to take good care of their children and raise them to be useful citizens for the community.

How "family" replaced marriage as a social model of order, now legitimized by natural law, becomes evident here. In the 1749 *Project des Corporis Juris Fridericiani, status familiae* already follows *status libertatis* and *status civitatis*: "The family is a domestic society established by Nature herself."[133] It includes the *paterfamilias* and *materfamilias*, "who with her will follows the *paterfamilias* into his home, and thereby is constituted a member of her husband's family," as well as their common children. The broader understanding of family in the sense of "all relations" is not the subject of *jus naturae privatum*. The Prussian *Allgemeines Landrecht* also retains this definition.[134] Despite the utilitarian thrust of the new legal provisions outlined here, at the same time they quite obviously also redefined relations between spouses as well as paternal and maternal roles. Spouses should be united in "friendship." Moreover, according to medical policy, it became the first duty of mothers to breastfeed their children for two years.[135] Among the upper classes, where wet nurses predominated, the propaganda in favour of mothers nursing their own children in Jean Jacques Rousseau's *Emile* (1762) proved more effective than legal provisions in enforcing this maternal duty.[136] In the pedagogical century, education and child-rearing assumed enormous importance, not only in the expansion of the public school system but also and particularly in education at home.[137]

While these developments were part of a learned tradition going back centuries, they took a new turn with the broad reception of Rousseau. "Domestic happiness" now encompassed the married couple united in "rational love" who tended lovingly to their children, as the Berlin painter Daniel Chodowiecki effectively portrayed in his illustration for Theodor von Hippel's book on marriage (Figure 3).[138] "Rational love" meant founding marriage on inclination and "friendship" without losing sight of economic and social conditions. What this precarious balance might mean for young women of marriageable age is evident, for example, in the correspondences of the daughters of Göttingen professors, who ultimately chose husbands who could guarantee them a way of life in keeping with their station.[139] The merchant's daughter Margarethe Milow also had to give up her first love, a commercial clerk employed by her parents, and marry a man whose age and life experience would have made him a better match for her mother.[140] Contrary to popular opinion, it was not until the twentieth century that "romantic love" had a chance as the basis for marriage.[141] It is equally clear that this concept of marriage and family applied to the living conditions of the "middle class," in which wives and mothers had sufficient time to devote to their children, while this was not the case in the lower strata. Whereas married couples of the lower classes were brought together mainly by household economy and labour, upper-class spouses found shared interests in child-rearing and living in a manner befitting their social status.

"The Message of Virtue"

The call for gender equality based on natural law, while remaining only an idea when it came to legal equality between spouses, was not wholly without consequences for shaping conditions within marriage. In the early Enlightenment debates on gender, leading philosophers supported the position that the inequality of the sexes could not be justified by women's inferior intellectual capacity, which was in fact equal to men's, albeit not adequately developed because of their lack of education. Parents should thus educate their daughters as carefully as their sons. In making this argument, the older humanist (Platonist) notions of equality between men and women were updated. As early as 1500, German humanists tried to distinguish themselves from their

Figure 3. Daniel Chodowiecki, *Domestic happiness*. Illustration of Theodor Gottlieb von Hippel's book *Über die Ehe: Mit Illustrationen von Daniel Chodowiecki*. Berlin, 1774.

Italian counterparts by conducting their marriages as learned partnerships with their wives and also providing their daughters and sons alike with a scholarly education.[142] In his dialogue between a cultivated lady (*Erudita*) and an abbot (*Abbas*) in 1526, Erasmus of Rotterdam championed the view that a learned wife was better able than an unlearned one to create common ground with her (learned) husband, and thus was a guarantee of concord between spouses.[143] When considering this concept we need to keep in mind the social context: it refers to the nascent academic stratum, which clearly developed its notions of marriage based on learned friendship among men, which applied to celibate learned clerics.

The figure of *Erudita* continued to influence the education of daughters of some reformers, followed by the female Pietists of the seventeenth and eighteenth centuries, who were motivated by the desire to study the Scriptures in the original languages. It particularly influenced the late-humanist education of women of the royalty and the (high) nobility, for whom, with the rise of court culture, educated, "civilized" sociability between men and women became an important field of representation and prestige. A learned education was an aristocratic privilege, tied to disposal of free time, which women of the other estates did not have. The early Enlightenment figure of the "learned lady" (*gelehrtes Frauenzimmer*), in contrast, served as a yardstick for a far wider social formation: the *gehobene Stände* (elevated classes), which included in particular high-ranking state officials and academics but also country squires who by 1700 were referred to as an "intermediate rank" (*Mittelstand*) between the high nobility and the urban middle classes.[144] It was, however, less a matter of promoting the same educational subjects for the female and male sexes than of the equal cultivation of the mind, and thus less about classical scholarship based on the ancient languages than about the "fine arts" and "useful sciences" in the service of the "message of virtue."[145] Christian instruction continued to be fundamental for women's future lives as wives and mothers, but this Christianity was not to remain purely external. Instead, women were supposed to internalize and reflect upon it in dialogue with contemporary "worldly knowledge" (*Weltwissen*). Cultivating the lady's mind was necessary in order to train her powers of judgment, which were deemed essential if she was to be her husband's companion, the educator of her children, and a wise housewife. In the upper classes, education attained the status of a dowry in its own right.[146] During marriage, however, such a "learned lady" was to devote only her "leisure hours" to this cultivation,[147] a restriction that applied equally to husbands, whose "main hours" were spent with business and official duties, for erudition as a main occupation was reserved to certain men; it was no privilege of the male sex.

At first, the most important medium for disseminating the message of virtue was the moral weeklies (*Moralische Wochenschriften*), which, following English models (*The Tatler*, 1709–11; *The Spectator*, 1711–12, 1714; *The Guardian*, 1715), discussed questions of everyday, personal, and civic life with moral, edifying intent, and thus with an eye to the common good.[148] In the *Patriot*, the Hamburg poet and patron Barthold Heinrich Brockes (1680–1747) called for the "rational" education of the female sex both to improve household management and for the purposes of "devotions and edification." With this end in mind he compiled German titles (including many translations from the French) for a *Frauenzimmerbibliothek* (library for ladies), which document the reading matter deemed useful and seemly for the cultivation of women's minds.[149] Absent from this library were the much-read novels with their tales of love, miracles, and adventure, the very quintessence of the "irrational." Only from the mid-eighteenth century, in the wake of English models such as Richardson's epistolary novels *Pamela* and *Clarissa*, did the novel achieve the status of a literary genre capable of transmitting the message of virtue.[150] An outstanding example is the epistolary novel *Geschichte des Fräuleins von Sternheim* (1771), with which Sophie von La Roche (1730–1807) established her literary reputation. Other female authors followed in her footsteps, treating not just "seduced innocence" but also the everydayness of marriage; foremost among them was Wilhelmine Karoline von Wobeser, who published the extremely successful and much-emulated novel *Elisa oder das Weib wie es seyn soll* (Elisa, or the woman as she should be) in 1795.[151]

Since the moral weeklies addressed women in particular, women were also the actual or fictitious editors of a number of such magazines. Particularly important among them was *Pomona* (1783–4), edited by Sophie von La Roche, who regarded herself as the "teacher of her own sex," that is, their instructor for the wifely role.[152] While the *Frauenzimmerbibliothek* promoted self-study, articles in the moral weeklies modelled on the "invented families" in *The Guardian* were intended for domestic discussions not only in the circle of kin as one's "closest friends" but also among friends in the sense of the like-minded.[153] This convivial education was at the same time training for sociability between men and women, a civilized meeting of the sexes.[154] The "salon" that the widow Christiana Mariana von Ziegler (1695–1760) held from about 1723 in the lively trade fair and university city of

Leipzig bore essential characteristics of such an education of manners and morals,[155] and it differed from traditional urban sociability such as the "Vertrautes Consortium" in Leipzig, which was founded to celebrate baptisms.[156] In this way the culture of sociability among cultivated women and men – which had its origins in Italy, was further developed in France, and influenced the many German courts in particular – also became established in Ziegler's environment, the upper classes of high officials and the university educated.[157]

The normative demand to educate sons and daughters went beyond the responsibility for Christian education we find in the seventeenth century, for instance in the intensive shared religious practice of parents and children in the form of prayer, singing, and music-making. We should not be too quick to assume that this signalled a new emotional relationship between parents and children, however, for the eloquent language of sensibility (*Empfindsamkeit*) readily conceals the power differential between parents and children and the enormous moral pressure exerted by the former. This is forcefully documented by the 1792 "Agenda for my daughter Sophie, as the best Christmas gift I can offer a child who wishes to please her parents ... If your heart desires to make us happy, if you wish for blessings from heaven, if you wish for people to love and honour you with good reason, then follow my advice."[158] The author was Sophie von La Roche's daughter Maximiliane von Brentano. In the autobiography of Margarethe Milow of Hamburg, too, father and mother appear above all as figures of respect, while she emphasizes positive emotional relationships with her siblings, especially her elder brother.[159] It seems surprising to us today that mothers of the upper classes, such as Katharina Elisabeth Goethe or Margarethe Milow's mother, thought nothing of placing their small children in a dame school for several years instead of raising them at home.[160] In early modern times, mother love was apparently judged by different standards than in modern Germany.

The Codifications

The great codifications of the second half of the eighteenth century only partially reflect the outlined developments in marriage concepts, the privileging of marriage over other relationships between men and women, and the practices of the courts that dealt with marital matters within the political and social dynamics of the seventeenth and eighteenth centuries. It is doubtless no coincidence that in Prussia

Cocceji's 1748 *Project* began with marital and inheritance law. This was the area in greatest need of order, given the significance of marriage for the internal peace of society and the system of property ownership that depended on it. The *Allgemeines Landrecht für die Preußischen Staaten*, the new Prussian legal code conceived in the 1780s but only published in 1794, was conservative when it came to marital law – for example in its insistence on equality of rank between spouses, particularly in the nobility[161] – and also retained the exchange of vows in church as the beginning of civil marriage. In divorce law, however, as in the *Project* of 1749, the *Allgemeines Landrecht* retained the facilitation of divorce.[162] New was the legal codification of parental duties (the mother's duty to breastfeed, the father's to educate his children); the husband's right to discipline his wife is not mentioned any more.[163] Joseph II, in contrast, promulgated the Marriage Patent for the Habsburg lands in 1783, which defined marriage as a civil contract but still made no provision for divorce with the right to remarry because the canon law stipulations on marriage remained in force.[164] Unlike France, where civil marriage was introduced in 1792, neither Prussia nor Austria instituted a separation of church and state in marital law. In Prussia, civil marriage was only implemented in 1874 in the wake of the *Kulturkampf*, the political struggle between the Prussian state and the Catholic Church.

Overall, the codifications inspired by natural law made only modest contributions to restructuring the institution of marriage. They are characterized by the tension between the tendentiously equal status of man and women in personal law (*Personenrecht*) and the unequal status of husband and wife in marital and property law. While in the nineteenth century unmarried women and widows attained legal capacity, wives – along with their common children – were subject to the husband as head of the family, who merely delegated the management of the household to his wife. He could represent his wife in legal matters, continued to manage her assets unless otherwise stated in the marriage contract, could dispose of her property and decided whether paid employment was consistent with her marital duties. Although women gained political rights, it was not until after the Second World War that patriarchal family law was recast according to the postulate of equality: in the German Democratic Republic this already occurred in the constitution of 1949, but in the Federal Republic not until the *Gleichberechtigungsgesetz* (Equal Rights Act) of 1958 and the *Erstes Gesetz zur Reform des Ehe- und Familienrechts* (First Act on the Reform of Marital and Family Law) of 1976.[165]

NOTES

1 Harrington 1995, 11.
2 Ibid., 97–8.
3 See, in this volume, Donahue 33–4.
4 Borgolte 2004b.
5 Tacke 2006.
6 Helmholz 1974, 5; Signori 2011.
7 Müller 1994.
8 See, in this volume, Lombardi 99, 100, 101; Usunáriz 202, 203, 205.
9 Köbler 1984, 138–54.
10 Rogge 1998, 36–9; Köbler 1984, 140. See, in this volume, Usunáriz 206.
11 Deutsch 2005, 74–5.
12 Ibid.
13 Schröter 1984; Weigand 1984, 173. A case of recourse to both courts is described, in this volume, by Lombardi 105–7.
14 Schuster 1995, 75–6; Günther 2000.
15 Zink, *Chronik*.
16 Völker-Rasor 1993; Noodt 2000; Hagemann and Wunder 1995.
17 Beer 2001; Nolte 2000.
18 Jancke 2002; Wunder 2002, 27–32; Wunder 2001.
19 Zink, *Chronik*, 140.
20 Brandis, *Diarium*, 31–3.
21 Zink, *Chronik*, 135.
22 Burghartz 1999, 143–8.
23 Roper 1989, 148–50; Bastl 2000, 25–83; Hufschmidt 2001, 173–82; Spieß 2003; Essegern 2003.
24 Maschke 1980, 21.
25 Deutsch 2005, 39–41, 268–88; Becker 1978.
26 See, in this volume, Lombardi 94–5, 99–101. See also Cristellon 2008, 389.
27 Schnell 2002.
28 Zink, *Chronik*, 138.
29 Ibid., 122.
30 Wunder 1998, 317.
31 Deutsch 2005, 266.
32 Schuster 1995, 301–41.
33 Roper 1987; Schuster 1995, 80–6; Schuster 1992, 147–53.
34 Schreiner 1984, 342ff.; Thum 2006, 27–32.
35 Meckseper 1985, 603ff.
36 Wagner 2007, 31–49.

37 Eyb, *Ob einem manne sey zunehmen ein eelichs weyb.*
38 Christ-von Wedel 1995, 138.
39 Hamm 1996, 73–6.
40 Borgolte 2004a, 28–33; Schmidt 1992, 14–15.
41 Sprengler-Ruppenthal 1982; Sprengler-Ruppenthal 1992.
42 Völker-Rasor 1993, 159–71.
43 Rogge 1998, 34–5.
44 Burghartz 1999, 74.
45 Puppel 2003, 160; Sikora 2007.
46 Wunder 1980, 175–6.
47 Sibeth 1994, 240.
48 Wunder 1980, 173–7; Dürr 1995, 174–6; Kohl 1985, 165.
49 Rublack 1977; Hufschmidt 2004.
50 Freist 2002. This subject is more fully treated by Cristellon, chapter 10.
51 Moeller 1987; Wunder 1992, 65–6; Burghartz 1999, 38–49; Plummer 2012, 11–50.
52 Schorn-Schütte 1991.
53 Burghartz 1999, 62.
54 Wunder 2009, 770–1.
55 Scharffenorth 1982.
56 Schmidt-Voges 2013.
57 Heckel 1973, 158–9.
58 Koch 1991, 76–81.
59 Lanzinger et al. 2010; Langer-Ostrawsky and Lanzinger 2005; Schattkowsky 2003; Ingendahl 2006; Kruse 2007.
60 Kartschoke 1996; Eming and Gaebel 1988; Bachorski 1991.
61 Lenz 1986.
62 Hufschmidt 2000.
63 Vanja 1996.
64 Schwerhoff 1991, 171.
65 Schild 1989. See, in this volume, van der Heijden 157.
66 Enderle 1993, 206; Rogge 1998, 49.
67 Lutz 2006, 68.
68 Dieterich 1970; Safley 1984; Karant-Nunn 1997, 6–42.
69 Sibeth 1994, 155ff., 240ff. See, in this volume, van der Heijden 163.
70 Schild 1989, 341. See, in this volume, Donahue 36, Lombardi 102–3.
71 Schild 1989, 339–41. See, in this volume, van der Heijden 160–1.
72 Lutz 2006, 134.
73 Sibeth 1997.
74 Möhle 1997, 34–9.

75 Lutz 2006, 127–31; Westphal 2008.
76 Frassek 2005.
77 Sibeth 1994, 179–80.
78 Roper 1989, 89–131; Sibeth 1994, 99–125; Hull 1996, 65.
79 The criminalizing of extramarital sexuality is the central theme of chapter 6, which deals with the Protestant Swiss cantons and southern Germany.
80 Schnabel-Schüle 1997, 281.
81 Buchholz 1991, 149–50; Mikat 1988. The case is contextualized by Burghartz, 182–4, and is sketched by Seidel Menchi, 326–31.
82 Schild 1989, 343ff.; Grochowina 1999.
83 Gritschke 2006, 72–4, 187–208.
84 Schild 1989, 344.
85 Hoffmann 1996, 106–20; Gleixner 2003.
86 Labouvie 2000.
87 See, in this volume, Donahue 35–7.
88 Conrad 1999b; Henze 1999.
89 Breit 1991; Beck 1992; Strasser 2004, 46–51.
90 Holzem 2000, 310–72.
91 Hamm 1996, 73–6.
92 Buchholz 1988, 19–25.
93 See, in this volume, Donahue 49.
94 Duncker 2004, part 3.
95 Bartsch 1903, 124, 128, 130, 141.
96 Vogel 1997, 291–2.
97 Buchholz 1988, 25–42.
98 Schwab 1967, 179.
99 Bartsch 1903, 162.
100 Hippel, *Über die bürgerliche Verbesserung der Weiber*, 199–200, 233–4.
101 See also Schwab 1967, 70–103.
102 Schorn-Schütte 1991.
103 Head-König 2003.
104 Sibeth 1994, 224ff.; Schnyder Burghartz 1992, 262–3.
105 Schnyder Burghartz 1992, 256–8.
106 Schnabel-Schüle 1997, 287–9.
107 Werkstetter 2001, for instance 430.
108 Breit 1991.
109 Sibeth 1994, 233–4.
110 Kluge 1977.
111 Ulbricht 1990, 278–83.
112 Hull 1996, 99.

113 Dettlaff 1989, 346; Hull 1996, 124; Gleixner 1994, 59.
114 Dettlaff 1989, 328–9, 342–3, 355.
115 Hull 1996, 124.
116 Zimmermann 1991, 81.
117 Ulbricht 1990, 217; Hull 1996, 111–16; Michalik 2006.
118 Ulbricht 1990, 347–9.
119 Göttsch 1996, 209–11. The same prohibition was enacted in Sweden (see Korpiola 249–50).
120 Dettlaff 1989, 362–3; Sibeth 1994, 242.
121 For instance Watt 1992, 264; see also Ulbricht 1990, 329–54; Schnabel-Schüle 1997, 284–6.
122 Ulbricht 1990, 70–4; Gleixner 1994, 195–201.
123 Hull 1996, 124.
124 Ibid., 115.
125 Zimmermann 1991, 78–80.
126 Roper 1989, 165–205; Beck 1992.
127 Sabean 1990, 124–46; Schnabel-Schüle 1997, 192–4; Lutz 2006, 188–301; Schilling 1994.
128 Freist 2002; Lutz 2006, 289–301. The subject is treated more fully in chapter 10.
129 Seckendorff, *Teutscher Fürsten-Stat*, 163–4: "daß an der Menge der Unterthanen das gröste Glück des Regenten gelegen und daß solche der rechte Schatz des Landes sey."
130 Hintze 1892.
131 Gleixner 1994, 59; Hull 1996, 127.
132 See Stefan Buchholz, "Ehe," in *Handwörterbuch zur deutschen Rechtsgeschichte*, Lieferung [fascicle] 5, 1192–213, esp. 1206–7; Blasius 1987, 27.
133 Cocceji, *Project des Corporis Juris Fridericiani*, 14: "Es ist die Familie eine häusliche Societaet, welche die Natur selbst gestiftet hat."
134 Koselleck 1975, 62.
135 Toppe 1999, 133–41.
136 Ibid., 203–14.
137 Herrmann 2005.
138 Hippel, *Über die Ehe*.
139 Panke-Kochinke 1993, 187, 189–94.
140 Milow, *Ich will aber nicht murren*, 100–2.
141 For a different opinion on this point, see Lombardi 104, Introduction 28, and Seidel Menchi 323, 325, 331.
142 Hess 1988.

143 Fietze 1996, 125–7.
144 Stollberg-Rilinger 2000, 93.
145 Martens 1968.
146 Tolkemitt 1998, 173–4.
147 "Kinder-Zucht" in *Universallexikon*, 15:654–62, particularly 659–62.
148 Martens 1968, 19.
149 Kopitzsch 1982, part 1, 276–7.
150 Martens 1968, 510–18.
151 Meise 1988, 443–4; Spitzer 2002, 69–89.
152 Weckel 1998.
153 Martens 1968, 45ff.
154 Becker-Cantarino 1997.
155 Schneider 2000, 144, 146–9.
156 Helbig 1980.
157 Battafarano 1991.
158 Maier 2004, 168: "Tagesordnung für meine Tochter Sophie als dass beste geschenk zum Cristkindgen dass ich weiß einem Kind zu geben, welches wünscht, seinen Elteren Freude zu machen … wen dein hertz uns wünscht glücklich zu machen, wen du Seegen vom Himmel wünscht wen du mit recht von menschen geliebt, geehrt Seyn wilst, so folge meinem Raht."
159 Milow, *Ich will aber nicht murren*, 20ff., 128.
160 Hering 1932, 415; Milow, *Ich will aber nicht murren*, 460.
161 Koselleck 1975, 105–15.
162 Blasius 1987, 27–33.
163 Döhlemeyer 1997, 640.
164 Schwab 1967, 208–15.
165 Schwab 1997, 805–12.

Chapter 3

Marriage in Italy

DANIELA LOMBARDI

Married or Unmarried?

Our modern rigid dichotomy between married and unmarried is of no help in understanding the fluidity of marital status in the premodern period. During the centuries that preceded the Reformation, a man's or woman's marital status was not easily defined.[1] People commonly spoke of "beginning" and "completing" or "perfecting" a marriage, which confronts us with a crucial question: When precisely did someone attain the status of husband or wife?

It is important first of all to understand that getting married was not a single act but a process, sometimes a long one.[2] It encompassed a series of steps, beginning with property agreements, which involved the families of both bride and groom, proceeding to the marriage promise, or betrothal, and finishing with the gift of the ring and the couple's cohabitation under one roof. Over the course of this process, the actors were able to adapt to their own needs the times and manner of forming the new couple. For the most part, they tended to lengthen the time involved, either to gather the resources necessary for forming a new family, especially the dowry, or to await the marriages of older brothers or sisters, or to persuade family members who were opposed to the union. But either party could break off the process before reaching the end point. The betrothal, in fact, could be dissolved, though in theory only when authorized by an ecclesiastical court and for the serious reasons envisaged in canon law.

In practice, however, it often happened that one member of a couple changed his or her mind and broke off the relationship without seeking the permission of a judge. We sometimes see such an event when the abandoned party turned to a court for recognition of the bond. This happened in the case of Caterina Belli, a woman from the Florentine countryside. Caterina, whose father was dead, claimed to have married a labourer named Sandro di Betto Bolzoni. In support of her story, she presented as witness a peasant from the hills near Florence for whom Sandro worked. This employer knew the facts of the situation well because Sandro had enlisted him to act as mediator between Sandro and Caterina's brother, who in the absence of their deceased father was responsible for his sister's marriage. Having obtained her brother's consent, Sandro came to Caterina's house along with his employer and other friends. Here "Sandro took Caterina's hand and ... kissed it, saying: I take you for my wife [*donna*] and I am your husband [*marito*]." The ceremony concluded with a dinner during which Sandro and Caterina joked together, "as is common between wife and husband." A few days later, Sandro sent a pair of shoes and a garland to Caterina.

The marriage process broke off shortly thereafter. Sometimes this happened because of disputes over property settlements – above all the size of the dowry – or because of familial resistance. In this case we know that Sandro's father opposed the marriage, and Caterina, perhaps with Sandro's consent, turned to the diocesan court in Florence.[3] But not even the trial reached a conclusion. Litigants frequently reached an agreement outside of court before the judge issued a decision. A trial could serve as a way to resolve disagreements, to overcome resistance, and to reach a solution advantageous for both sides. It was in the ecclesiastical judge's interest to act as a mediator because the purpose of a marriage suit was not to punish a wrongdoer but to resolve a conflict about the parties' marital status – and to avoid disorder and confusion by doing so as quickly as possible, more quickly than the normal judicial process. The judge acted according to the canon law principle *favor matrimonii*, according to which a marriage was to be protected in every circumstance. In this case, he would probably have tried to convince Sandro to complete the marriage. Only rarely do traces of such informal resolutions survive. In fortunate cases, the record of a marriage that brought an end to a trial might be found in a parish register. In the countryside, however, marriage registers generally did not begin until the seventeenth century, so we do not know whether or not Caterina and Sandro finally managed to complete their marriage process.

Caterina and Sandro behaved like most couples who decided to wed. The preliminary negotiations had been entrusted not to one of the professional marriage brokers used by the elite[4] but to Sandro's employer – that is, a connection of the future husband – because it was up to the man to initiate marital negotiations. But how did a man choose a bride? We do not know where or how Sandro got to know Caterina. In the countryside, dances and evening gatherings known as *veglie* were the traditional places for courtship. One young woman outside of Florence who met her future husband at a dance said, "while dancing together I fell in love with him and from that point on I always loved him."[5] Women and men of the popular classes might also meet in the workplace – in the fields and workshops – and court at doorways of houses or through the windows that allowed young women to converse with passers-by. A young carver from Vicenza declared that he had courted his beloved for three years "with our eyes, and sometimes talking ... under the portico through a small window."[6] Courting meant visiting, becoming acquainted, and beginning to express affection, if only with glances.

The next step involved the two families and had as the principle actors only the menfolk, often with the help of intermediaries. Although formally excluded, mothers and daughters still actively participated in the choice through informal channels, such as gossip. Upper-class women, for example, would scrutinize potential daughters-in-law from afar during church services, analysing their physical appearance in merciless detail in order to report back to the son, who would make the final decision.[7]

Property matters were discussed at meetings between the men, as was the timetable for the conclusion of the marriage. Dowry contracts (*scritte di dote* or *scritte di parentado*) are very common documents in Italian archives. They were generally drawn up and signed by the parties who arranged the exchange of goods, the bride's father and the future groom, who settled the amount of the dowry and the husband's contribution (*controdote*). Among the elite, the amounts of the transactions required the use of a notary, who put the agreements in writing. The popular classes who could not afford to use a notary drew up private agreements in the presence of witnesses, or else turned to the local priest, who in small rural communities also fulfilled the functions of a notary. It was important to put the economic transactions in writing because the dowry remained the wife's property – her husband only had its use – and was intended to support her in case she were widowed.[8] However, information about dowries is not always found in marriage suits – there is no information in Caterina and Sandro's – if it was not pertinent to proving the case.

After the conclusion of the financial arrangements, the bride and groom met at the bride's house to exchange marriage promises before their families and friends. As we have seen in the opening chapter, the couple's consent expressed in the future tense (*verba de futuro*) constituted the promise, and the consent expressed in the present tense (*verba de presenti*) created the sacramental, indissoluble marriage bond.[9]

Despite the great importance canon law placed on verbal expressions, men and women very rarely used words that had absolutely unequivocal meaning. Take Sandro's words, for example: "I take you for my wife [*donna*] and I am your husband [*marito*]." How should they be interpreted? Do they express consent for the present or for the future? Often the laity was not capable of making such grammatical distinctions. What was important to them was expressing consent that would move the marriage process forward. In this particular case, the witness did not confine himself to recounting the words he heard but lingered on what he saw. Sandro touched and kissed the bride's hand, ate and joked with her, sent her gifts. These were gestures and behaviours that expressed a familiarity characteristic of the relationship of a couple. The witness was anxious to describe them and to add that they were "common between wife and husband." Is this a marital bond? It seemed so to the friends and relatives who visited the new couple. Yet Sandro's family appears not to have been present, and the fact that his father opposed the marriage was an important obstacle to the conclusion of the union. Indeed, Caterina did not go to live with Sandro. It was clear that Sandro and Caterina had not finished getting married. This, however, was clearer from their behaviour than from their words.

Such behaviour had to be public for a couple's union to be recognized as legitimate and to guarantee the legal effects of marriage, that is, the legitimacy of children and transmission of goods. Consent exchanged in secret united a couple before God and their own consciences but not before the world.

In the absence of unequivocal words, the gestures and behaviour that characterized the various steps of the formation of a marriage also had legal value. Judges could use these rituals as proof in the resolution of disputes. Rituals did not replace the exchange of consent, but they were external signs of that consent.[10] They were not necessary for the formation of the marital bond; without such signs, though, it was less easy to recognize a legitimate union.

In the cities of north-central Italy, caution drove some people to marry before notaries, who presided over the ceremonies and put in writing not only the property agreements settled at the time of the *sponsalia*, but also the act of giving the ring to the bride, which preceded cohabitation. In the countryside, as we have seen, priests were often substituted for notaries, as they were frequently the only literate inhabitants of a village. The priest's presence did not confer any religious form on the marriage contract but gave it public sanction. Practices in the Kingdom of Naples were different. Here already in the late Middle Ages there was a public form of celebration that had a marked religious character. Beginning in the twelfth century, the Norman kings were concerned to impose by legislation the solemn celebration of weddings before the church and in the presence of a priest. Fifteenth- and early sixteenth-century notarial records attest to the spread of these ceremonies. It is surprising to find the kings championing religious ceremonies. The explanation probably lies at least in part in the Byzantine caesaro-papal tradition that made the emperor the most zealous protector of the Christian faith.[11]

Although the pre-Tridentine norms required neither a religious ceremony nor a solemn public ritual for a valid marriage, ecclesiastical authorities repeatedly enacted measures calling for the publicizing of weddings. Iconography was probably used by the church to circulate a model of marriage as a solemn religious event. The numerous representations of the marriage of the Virgin taking place in a sacred space, in front of the temple and in the presence of a venerable priest, probably had a specific propagandistic function. The work of Giotto and his assistants is found in Tuscany and Umbria, precisely the regions where this wedding model struggled to establish itself.[12] The absence of a religious ceremony, however, must not lead us to think that marriage was secular. In whatever way it was celebrated, marriage was understood by the laity as a profoundly religious event.[13]

The doctrine of *matrimonium praesumptum* – or presumed marriage – opened an alternative path for marriage formation, one that did not rely on the exchange of present consent. As we have seen, and as we shall see in more detail, if a marriage promise was followed by sexual relations, it transformed consent *de futuro* into consent *de presenti* (Donahue 34, Lefebvre-Teillard 261–2). In other words, such importance was ascribed to the sexual act that it impeded the dissolution of a marriage promise.[14]

The link between promise and sexual relations sanctioned by the doctrine of presumed marriage had important and long-lasting consequences. As the initial moment of the marriage process that culminated in cohabitation, the promise legitimated sexual intimacy between fiancés based on the reasoning that the marriage was already initiated and was only awaiting conclusion. A young woman from the Florentine countryside expressed with great clarity the importance that the laity attributed to the promise: her man, she said, "has always continued to come home to see me, like those men who come to see their brides, and I received him like the girls do their husbands, and so every time that he came I accepted him and received him like my husband and not otherwise, and if he had not promised me I would not have accepted nor received him into my house."[15] A betrothed woman acquired a status that distinguished her from a single woman and that gave her privileges similar to those of a woman who was married.

This conception of the promise explains why premarital sexuality was so well tolerated. The youthful sexual activity that a pregnancy brought to light did not necessarily damage a woman's honour. If the young woman had succumbed to the man's blandishments only after having received a promise of marriage, and if friends and neighbours testified that there had not been other men in her life, her reputation was safe. The relationship in mid-fifteenth-century Florence between Lusanna, the daughter and widow of artisans, and the wealthy merchant Giovanni della Casa, which was broken off by Giovanni after 12 years, did not harm Lusanna's honour, and she in fact later received many proposals of marriage from other men. She had always asserted that she had received a ring from Giovanni and that she had always behaved with him as his legitimate bride, even though the marriage still needed to be concluded with a public ceremony and cohabitation. In court she managed to defend herself energetically and to discredit the man who had deceived her.[16]

Clandestine and Multiple Marriages

According to the consensualist doctrine, a marriage was fully valid even if a couple had exchanged consent in secret. The practice of secret marriage is well attested in the Italian states between the thirteenth and the sixteenth century, despite the fact that a public form of marriage celebration was known to be necessary to protect the marriage from challenge. Such marriages, which the church defined as clandestine, enabled young people to evade their families' control and make autonomous choices. Secret marriages could also easily become instruments of seduction and deceit. It was inevitable that they would arouse the hostility of many people, especially members of the highest social classes who wanted to intervene directly in the matrimonial choices of their children in order to protect their large fortunes.[17]

There was also another reason for this hostility. Clandestine marriages conflicted with the notion then prevalent in the Christian world that the purpose of marriage was to establish a new alliance between two families, to reconcile battling factions, to bring peace wherever there was war. Those who refused to participate in family strategies and who married clandestinely unleashed hatred and resentment rather than creating friendship. The church doctrine of marital impediments was built on this notion, which St Augustine in the fifth century summarized in the expression "marriage is the seedbed of love" (*matrimonium seminarium est caritatis*). The law of *caritas* required Christians to make matrimonial alliances with those who were not already related to them, in order to extend links of affection and friendship as far as possible.[18] A tight web of impediments was therefore constructed around marriage, impediments not limited to blood relatives but extended to kin by marriage and to spiritual kin (those linked by godparenthood).[19]

But what precisely was meant by clandestine marriage? Did the lack of any form of publicity make a marriage "clandestine"? A fixed definition of clandestinity was impossible because ritual was a matter of custom and varied from place to place. There was, however, substantial agreement that the presence of witnesses was the most effective way to make public the formation of a new couple. Works of moral theology circulating in the decades before the Council of Trent considered contracting marriage without witnesses to be a mortal sin. The reason for this, according to the theologian Tommaso De Vio, known as Cajetanus, was that the publicity of the act guaranteed by witnesses assured the social recognition of the couple and avoided the scandals arising from bigamy. And what about marriages contracted before witnesses but without the solemnities suggested by synods and councils, such as celebration in front of the church, priest's blessing, or gift of the ring? Were these also clandestine? On this there was no agreement. In the 1540s, the canonist Diego de Covarrubias observed that opinions conflicted. His own judgment was that such marriages could not be considered clandestine if the community of the faithful was informed about them.[20]

The centrality that the presence of witnesses assumed as compared to other forms of publicity can also be explained by the need, particularly in court, to identify effective forms of proving the marriage. From the late twelfth century, when the Romano-canonical procedural system was established in ecclesiastical tribunals, proof by witnesses was considered the best form of evidence.[21]

For their part, secular powers were interested in a different definition of clandestine marriage: that contracted without paternal consent. If marriage was above all an alliance, it could not be an issue left up to individuals; it had to involve a couple's families from the beginning to the end of their married life. Many urban statutes between the thirteenth and the fifteenth century established severe penalties for those who married without paternal approval.[22] A mother had a say only in the absence of both the father and of a long list of other male blood kin in the paternal line, who exercised that most exquisitely male form of power, *patria potestas*.

It was not clandestine marriage alone that rendered marital status uncertain. Bigamy was also a common phenomenon. Couples came together not only for reasons of affection but also to combine resources and to provide mutual support. Solidarity was a powerful part of unions, above all when resources were scarce. If the conditions that had created the bond changed, it was considered legitimate to move on to a second or even a third marriage. It is interesting that spouses accused of bigamy – or, perhaps better, multiple marriages – sometimes held their earlier marriage to be invalid. That is, they recognized the canonical rules and adapted them to their own needs but considered it unnecessary to go before the ecclesiastical court to obtain an annulment.[23]

Thus, pre-Tridentine canonical norms left the laity ample space to conduct their family lives as they saw fit. The ease with which young people could marry by mutual consent at any time and place, without the need for any solemnities, favoured a vision of marriage that gave couples (and their families) a more direct and influential role than the church perhaps would have liked. Unions were both made and unmade without the involvement of the church, to which, however, jurisdiction over marriage belonged.[24]

The geographical mobility of the premodern population probably made enforcing the principle of marital indissolubility more difficult. Marriage was indeed monogamous but not indissoluble. It was considered licit to remarry after receiving *probabilis certitudo* of a spouse's death, generally the husband's, since mobility was primarily a male phenomenon and affected above all the popular classes. If, however, a husband reappeared, the wife had to return to live with him. One of these presumed widows who had remarried declared to the ecclesiastical court of Naples, "I was astonished to see him."[25] These few words express well her dismay at having to renew an old and probably forgotten bond. More commonly spouses who departed – for work, or to escape creditors, the law, or even marital strife – did not return. Abandoning the marital household was the simplest way to end an unwanted union and to begin a new life somewhere else.[26]

These attitudes did not imply disdain for the sacrament of marriage. An inhabitant of Lucca who had left home after just 10 months of marriage and spent the next 10 years travelling in various Italian states, eventually ending up in Lyon, justified his second marriage before the ecclesiastical court in this way: "Because I was told by two people from Lucca that my wife had taken another husband and had two children, so I said I would take another wife."[27] In his succinct and matter-of-fact manner of recounting these events, bigamy appears a banal fact, certainly not a grave sin. That marriage was first of all an alliance between families did not mean that people did not also expect it to provide emotional benefits. Sentiments and material interests were not necessarily opposed.[28] Individuals' desires and destinies were interwoven with those of their families, especially when individuals' resources depended on the family economy. The individual dimension of the consensualist theory in fact coexisted with the familial and social dimensions of marriage.[29]

In order to understand early modern marital relationships it is necessary finally to remember that mortality rates were high and marriages often did not last long. Death ruptured familial bonds, creating large numbers of widows, widowers, and orphans among both rich and poor, so that second and third marriages were common. It was primarily widowers who formed new families because a man's age was less important than a woman's for reproduction. Popular tales about cruel stepmothers were rooted in the hard reality of such families, in which the rivalry between children of first and second marriages could become serious in times of famine or during property division.

Awareness of the precariousness of life, particularly of life as a couple, must have influenced the way people approached marriage, relieving it of the burden of definitive choice. People entered and left the state of matrimony with ease; they lived together and they separated. The early modern family was not stable.

Marital Certainty

The fathers at the Council of Trent (1545–63) initiated reform that subjected marriage to rules, controls, and registration. Their objective was to eliminate clandestinity but to do so without abolishing the consensualist doctrine that had dictated church marriage policy for centuries. They therefore required the presence of the parish priest and of two or three witnesses for a marriage contract to be valid, but not parental consent. The parish priest, after having announced the forthcoming marriage at Mass on three Sundays, had to question the couple to ascertain their mutual consent and to pronounce these or similar words, "I unite you in marriage" (*Ego coniungo vos in matrimonium*), as determined by local custom.[30] He was also required to record the marriage in the parish register.

This reform decree – known from its opening word as *Tametsi* – introduced a new conception of marriage, transforming "marriage from a social process which the church recognized into an ecclesiastical process which the church controlled."[31] The celebration of this rite was for the first time removed from familial and community management and completely subjected to ecclesiastical authorities. Excluding paternal consent from the requirements for a valid marriage meant accentuating the authority of the church at the expense of that of fathers.

The choice of the parish priest as the guarantor of the legitimacy of marriage was in line with his role as caretaker of souls that the Tridentine decrees more generally emphasized.[32] The laity quickly came to understand that in order to marry they needed to go to the parish priest.

Church doctrine that considered the bride and groom themselves to be the ministers of the sacrament of marriage remained in force, however. This meant that, while the priest did indeed need to be present, he did not need to be consenting. Couples who suddenly appeared in the church or sacristy, taking an unsuspecting priest by surprise and exchanging consent in the presence of two witnesses, contracted marriages that were fully valid. These so-called "surprise marriages" were often referred to as clandestine because they had not been preceded by the customary three readings of the banns and the couple had not obtained the required dispensation from the bishop to omit them. Surprise marriages allowed rebellious children to escape family strategies and to marry people of their own choosing even if their fathers opposed them. Such marriages were considered to be gravely sinful and were strongly opposed by clergy and laity alike. From the ecclesiastical point of view, they made the parish priest look ridiculous and enabled the laity to appropriate a sacrament that Trent had entrusted completely to the priest. From the lay perspective, they were a very serious affront to the authority of the *paterfamilias*.[33]

The Council of Trent's decisions created conflict between the church and families. Children's freedom of choice – regarding the religious life as well as marriage – meant reducing the powers of the *paterfamilias*. Such powers were particularly strong with regard to daughters, who were often committed to marry as adolescents. Those ecclesiastical judges who were more attentive and sensitive to the changes introduced by the Council might undertake to convince young betrothed women to open their hearts and express their wills freely. This practice was not, however, new. In cases when it was feared young women had not freely consented to marriage, canon law required judges to question them in a secure place away from family coercion. In Venice this rule had been applied since the fifteenth century.[34] In Florence such interrogations became common in the years following the Council of Trent. For some of these young women, who moved temporarily to a convent for a period of solitary reflection far from family pressure, the interrogations were a path towards greater self-awareness.[35]

Margherita Guardi, a Florentine girl, found the strength to challenge parental opposition after just one day in a convent. Despite the fact that her father was against it, Margherita had put in writing her promise to marry a knight of the Ordine di Santo Stefano. The conflict had come into court on the initiative of the knight, who was seeking to obtain the fulfilment of this promise. Here are some passages from Margherita's interrogation:

> It was asked who had induced her to make the promise to take the knight as her husband.
>
> She replied, The love that I had for him.
>
> It was asked if she is saying these things out of fear.
>
> She replied, No, my lord. I am saying them out of love.

Margherita's determination convinced the judge to have the marriage celebrated the next day in the very convent where she was staying, providing a dispensation from all three required publications of the banns. Her father could not oppose it.[36]

Judges' commitment to young people's freedom of choice in marriage tended to weaken over the course of the seventeenth century, however. As the Tridentine model of marriage spread and ecclesiastical control over the institution became more secure, churchmen became more amenable to meeting familial needs, and the conflict between churchmen and fathers of families gradually lessened.

Jurisdictional Pluralism

The most obvious effect of the Tridentine decrees of 1563 was the shift in the site of couples' legal conflicts from the marriage to the promise (or betrothal). Before the Council of Trent, the most common type of suit argued before diocesan courts was that regarding the validity of marriages celebrated without publicity – clandestine or presumed marriages. The number of these conflicts began to decline at the end of the sixteenth century because the Tridentine rules had drastically reduced uncertainty about marriage. At the same time, there was a corresponding increase in the number of suits to obtain the fulfilment (or, more rarely, the dissolution) of marriage promises. In the diocese of Florence, where it is possible to reconstruct marriage litigation from the sixteenth to the eighteenth century, this trend is clear.[37]

Men or women who earlier would have claimed the status of husband or wife, by asserting they had contracted a clandestine or presumed marriage, under the new rules could only lay claim to a marriage promise and appeal to its binding nature when faced with a partner who had become recalcitrant. The outcome was uncertain, however, because the unwilling party could only be induced to keep his or her promise by persuasion, not force. There was another route that could be used if a woman had become pregnant, because pregnancy was considered definite proof of defloration. This was a suit for non-violent rape – or seduction – preceded by a promise of marriage, which could be adjudicated before either ecclesiastical or secular court.

In 1576 a young Florentine woman named Caterina delle Macchie took both of these jurisdictional routes. Along with her father, she turned first to the secular and then to the ecclesiastical authorities to denounce her "rape" by one of her neighbours in Florence, Baccio Segni. Both parties belonged to the artisan class: 20-year-old Caterina was the daughter of a tailor, while Baccio, aged 23, worked in the wool sector as a *cimatore* or shearer. Their families lived next door to each other. It was easy to slip from one house to the other by means of the roof, and this proximity facilitated the young couple's encounters. We have, however, two contradictory versions of events and of the emotions that drove them.

The first version is provided by Caterina's father. Appealing directly to the supreme authority – Grand Duke Francesco I de' Medici – the father sought justice for his daughter, who he claimed had suffered "rape." He declared that Baccio, entering Caterina's room at night while she was working and her two younger sisters were sleeping, seized Caterina and bound her mouth with a handkerchief to keep her from calling for help, "so that *by force* the poor girl, simple and frightened, *consented* to the sinful desires of the said Baccio."[38] At this time, the word "rape" (*stuprum*) did not primarily mean carnal violence but rather defloration of a virgin or sexual relations with a widow. The victim's respectability was a requirement for such defloration to be considered a crime, violence being an aggravating circumstance, albeit one that carried the death penalty. In this case Caterina's father made a complaint of rape that claimed violence, but the terms he used – the verb "consent," even though combined with "force" – and the continuance of the sexual relations for several months allow some doubts about this violence. The resulting pregnancy gave rise to the complaint, but behind the pregnancy lay a long-term relationship and a habit of shared intimacy. The principal criminal court of Florence, the Otto di guardia e balìa, to which the Grand Duke had sent the case, absolved Baccio of the accusation of violence but sentenced him to pay the monetary penalties stipulated in the Florentine statutes of 1415 "in the cause for rape," that is, for deflowering Caterina. The substance of the crime, the taking of virginity, was proven by Caterina's pregnancy. Baccio, however, was spared being compelled to choose between marrying or dowering Caterina.

Caterina and her father were not satisfied with this outcome, and 20 days later Caterina herself turned to the ecclesiastical authorities to begin a civil rather than criminal suit in the archiepiscopal court of Florence. She accused Baccio of a broken promise and of deflowering her. In this second version of the events, the story of violence became instead one of love: Baccio "began to court [Caterina] as is usual among young people," promised to marry her, had more encounters with her, and finally, "in finding himself with her as a young man, acted carnally with her." The sexual activity was presented as something natural for a young man in love, not as a sin or crime to be suppressed.

At this time, the mid- to late sixteenth century, the monetary punishment stipulated in the Florentine statutes of 1415 for the crime of rape began to be replaced by the canon law penalty that the offender either marry or dower the woman he had deflowered. Beginning in the mid-sixteenth century, secular criminal courts in other Italian states and in Spain also began to apply this penalty encouraging the woman's marriage, either to her seducer or else to another man. Often there was additional financial or corporal punishment if the seducer chose not to marry her.[39]

In her complaint, Caterina insisted on her own good reputation and that of her family – demonstrating that the seduced woman had led an honest life was essential to enjoying the protection of the law – and spent some time on the subject of the size of dowry she wanted. Evidently she realized that Baccio had no intention of marrying her. That the goal of the dispute was the dowry is shown also by Baccio's defence strategy, which sought to demonstrate the low social status of Caterina's family, which would have entitled her to a dowry much smaller than the one she was claiming. The ecclesiastical court's decision is a clear example of flexible interpretation of the law and of mediation between opposing parties. Baccio was sentenced to marry Caterina because of the promise he had made, but he was permitted the alternative of giving her a dowry larger than he had proposed but a smaller one than she had requested.[40]

Women in Caterina's situation had the choice of bringing a lawsuit in either the ecclesiastical or the secular court, asking in the first for the fulfilment of a marriage promise or in the second to be either married or dowered, because of "rape" following a promise of marriage. Once they had a decision in one court, however, they could not turn to the other because an offence subject to multiple forums could be adjudicated and punished in only one. Unless, that is, it was both a civil and a criminal offence and could therefore be tried as a civil case in one court and a criminal case in another, as was the non-violent rape that Caterina alleged Baccio had committed.[41]

The ability to make this choice was broader or narrower depending on the relationship between church and state in a particular territory. Secular powers tended to expand their own jurisdiction over the sexual behaviour of the laity and over marriage. In Venice from the end of the sixteenth century and in the principal cities of the Grand Duchy of Tuscany – Florence, Siena, and Pisa – from the first decades of the seventeenth, rape with the promise of marriage became the exclusive competence of secular criminal jurisdiction.[42] After this it was no longer possible to turn to the ecclesiastical court, and suits for non-fulfilment of promises that were adjudicated in these diocesan tribunals no longer made reference to sexual intimacy. Premarital sexuality disappeared from their trial records.

Legal options therefore tended to be reduced for women, who had already had to give up relying on the principle of presumed marriage as a way to gain recognition as legitimate wives. The promise remained at the centre of legal disputes to protect women's reputations.

Licit and Illicit

While the Tridentine decrees helped to clarify the difference between betrothal and marriage, they did not succeed in repressing sexual intimacy prior to the wedding celebrated before the parish priest. To eradicate these sexual practices it was first necessary to transform them into sinful acts and imbue them with transgressive meaning. Paradoxically, this moralizing emphasis, common to both Protestants and Catholics, had the effect of eroticizing the language of the body and accentuating its sensuality.[43] The case of dancing is emblematic. Dancing was a form of courtship very common among the popular classes, which took place for the most part outdoors in association with religious festivals and involving the entire community. In the writings of moralists, however, dancing was overburdened with sexual meaning and offered "occasions for sin," in the words of Carlo Borromeo (1538–84), archbishop of Milan. Authorities thus forbade it on Sundays in order to avoid encouraging immoral behaviour and profaning the climate of religious austerity they were trying to impose upon the faithful.[44]

To suppress such behaviour, however, the Catholic Church did not encourage the use of legal tools. The Congregation of the Council – which was responsible for the interpretation of the Tridentine decrees – in fact condemned the actions of some bishops who subjected couples guilty of sexual relations before marriage to stiff penalties and public penances.[45] As we will see later, at the local level it was not uncommon to find instances of intransigence that demonstrate the repressive capability of ecclesiastical tribunals, but these probably remained isolated occurrences because of the opposition of the Roman Curia. Criminal trials heard before some diocesan courts[46] confirm that when ecclesiastical judges proceeded on their own initiative (*ex officio*) against the laity, they did so not so much to repress premarital sexuality as to repress public concubinage, which the Council of Trent had severely condemned.[47]

The instrument that the ecclesiastical hierarchy held to be most appropriate for combatting premarital sexuality was sacramental confession. Cardinal Prospero Lambertini, who became Pope Benedict XIV in 1740, declared that it was necessary to make use of parish priests as confessors in order to reach the consciences of the faithful, and to make them interiorize a new behavioural model based on the "continence" of betrothed couples.[48] Moreover, confession had itself been transformed from an obligation to be fulfilled once a year at Easter into an experience of introspection to be repeated frequently. Thus, in the secrecy of the confessionals introduced by Carlo Borromeo at the end of the sixteenth century, the sexual life of the laity could be subjected to close control.

Confession, however, did not necessarily guarantee protection against legal sanction. In some Italian dioceses (such as Borromeo's Milan), premarital sex was considered a mortal sin and included among the cases reserved to the bishop. A parish priest who learned of a reserved sin in confession had to tell the parishioner to present him or herself before the bishop (or inquisitor for crimes against the faith) in order to receive absolution. The more uncompromising bishops did not hesitate to arrest the sinner and begin legal proceedings. Thus a secret sin, which the parish priest might have learned of during the obligatory Easter confession, could be subjected to a public and humiliating punishment.[49]

A particularly illustrative example of this took place in Livorno. During Easter confession in 1584, a man named Salvestro confessed to his parish priest that he was living with a woman named Caterina even though they had not yet had a church wedding. Salvestro had in fact already asked the priest to preside over their marriage, but the priest had refused because Caterina had only recently moved to Livorno and the banns had not yet been read the required three times in her parish of origin. Evidently Caterina and Salvestro had been unable to spend the time or money this required but had nonetheless begun to live together, assuming it was enough that they had exchanged promises in the presence of two witnesses and confirmed them with the gift of the ring and clasping hands. The priest, probably fearing this was a reserved case, did not absolve Salvestro but sent him to the archbishop of Pisa, the diocese to which Livorno belonged. Both were arrested and interrogated, Salvestro in Pisa and Caterina in Livorno.

Their interrogations reveal the persistence among the laity of the pre-Tridentine conception of marriage formation. The couple was not ignorant of the new rules instituted by the Council of Trent – they asked the priest to celebrate the wedding – but when they were hindered from putting such rules into effect, they felt authorized to begin living together. They considered themselves already husband and wife. As Salvestro said, "I ... thought that the promise was enough." What probably occasioned Salvestro's confession was Caterina's pregnancy.

Salvestro wanted advice from the priest about how to regularize their situation in order to ensure the child's legitimacy.

Prior to Trent, their union would have been judged a *matrimonium praesumptum* (presumed marriage) on the basis of sexual relations following a promise made according to the local custom, and the judge would have simply asked them to solemnize the union publicly. Instead, the court paid no attention to the fact that Caterina and Salvestro had followed the earlier consensualist doctrine. They were found guilty of clandestine marriage, that is, of marrying without observing the Tridentine rules, and for this – rather than for their premarital relations – they were severely punished. Salvestro was sentenced to be flogged in the piazza in Livorno and was then subjected to two years of forced labour. Caterina had to kneel at the church door holding a lighted candle and was then, pregnant, condemned to three years' banishment. Thus, a confession led to the brutal interruption of their life plans: Salvestro and Caterina were separated and no trace remains of their child.[50]

It is impossible to say how far confession succeeded in transforming previously tolerated behaviour into sins of the flesh. What is certain is that, beginning in the seventeenth century, the language of sexuality used in court changed. Faced with extramarital pregnancies, many men recognized that they had done "wrong" (*il male*) and were ready to make amends by marrying the women whom they had made pregnant. "If I have done wrong, I am also ready to do penance," declared a bricklayer accused by the criminal court of Bologna of having seduced and impregnated a young girl in the 1670s. A century later, Florentines investigated for similar crimes used similar phrases, aware that they could erase the sin through marriage.[51]

Sexual relations following a marriage promise became "wrong"; the erogenous zones became "the shameful parts." But the sense of premarital sex as sin was severely weakened and nearly disappeared when it was argued that marriage would erase any guilt. This idea was so well established that, according to an early eighteenth-century bishop of Cesena, someone who had committed this sin did not even have to confess.[52] Confessors themselves were not always rigorous in condemning premarital sex. In the diocese of Florence in the eighteenth century, some priest-confessors absolved cohabiting couples on the basis of their promise to celebrate the wedding as soon as possible. Precisely to combat such widespread laxity, Girolamo Dal Portico, a member of the Congregazione della Madre di Dio, wrote a long work whose title translates as *Love between persons of different sexes examined according to the principles of moral theology for the edification of new confessors* (Lucca, 1751), in which he denounced too easy absolution in confession and urged confessors to be more uncompromising towards sins of the flesh.

Scandalous Unmarried Women

It was unmarried women without credible marriage prospects – because their lovers were already married or not their social equals or for other reasons – who bore the brunt of the greater rigour secular and ecclesiastical authorities brought to the treatment of sex outside of marriage. Without hope of marriage, unwed pregnant women were easily assimilated into the ranks of women of dubious morals and considered responsible for, rather than victims of, seduction.

In many European countries new legislation was issued aimed at controlling out-of-wedlock pregnancy and preventing abortion and infanticide. In the German Empire, in the Netherlands, in the Swiss cantons, in the Kingdom of France, childbirth became the new frontier in public intervention: protecting and caring not just for the bodies but above all for the souls of the newborn and unborn became the purpose of specific legal measures. It was in particular state authorities who staked out this territory, and the model to follow became the 1556 edict of the French king, Henry II.[53]

In the Catholic world, from the fifteenth century onwards, specialized institutions enabled mothers to abandon their newborn infants, erasing any trace of their sin. Canon law and the culture of the time legitimated abandonment particularly for parents who were too poor to ensure their children's survival, but also for unwed mothers who had to protect their honour. In both cases it enabled parents to avoid difficulties and gave their children a chance at life. In some cities institutions were founded to allow unwed mothers to keep even their pregnancies hidden and thus protect their reputations by giving birth in secret and having the illegitimate children immediately transferred to a nearby orphanage.[54]

After Trent, institutions to aid poor unmarried women multiplied in response to various needs: preserving the (sexual) honour of very young women, restoring the honour of those living a sinful life, and providing dowries to enable the poorest women to marry. Seclusion of fallen women had a punitive and expiatory aspect, but it was aimed at rehabilitating them either for marriage or for entrance into a convent. The assistance offered reinforced customary female roles, encouraging "honest" women to pursue these roles with greater determination and giving "dishonest" ones an opportunity to expiate their sins and return to the right path, which meant above all habituating themselves to obedience.

Repression was particularly severe towards women from the popular classes who had relationships with men of the elite, though it was also directed at such groups as men and women accused of adultery, widows with daughters suspected of licentiousness, and female singers, who were considered a menace to public order. Ecclesiastical authorities used the secular arm to punish them: banishment (albeit temporary) was the most frequent sanction and was intended to remove the scandal far from the community of the faithful. The collaboration between secular and ecclesiastical authorities allowed the punishment of behaviour defined as "scandalous," without the accused parties being able to defend themselves or doing so only with great difficulty.[55]

Separation and Reconciliation

The Council of Trent confirmed the indissolubility of marriage and introduced no innovations in this aspect of marital law. Under canon law separation was possible – *separatio* (or *divortium*) *quoad mensam et thorum*, that is, from bed and board – but remarriage was not permitted. An annulment, in contrast, which could be granted for one of a number of reasons, including defective consent, impotence, bigamy, or insufficient age, declared that the bond had never existed in the first place and therefore opened the way for a future marriage. Separations and annulments appear, however, to have been uncommon. In Livorno between 1766 and 1800, the rate of separations sought was only 2.5 per cent of marriages contracted.[56] But in trial documents from the sixteenth to the eighteenth century, traces of long-standing de facto separations, preceding formal ones granted by the court, suggest that in practice it was possible to separate without recourse to the ecclesiastical authorities.

Separations were not necessarily permanent. Canon law considered separation a temporary measure aimed at the couple's reconciliation,[57] and indeed wives and husbands sometimes used the legal system and their time apart to make adjustments to their life as a couple, to re-establish their relationship on more favourable terms, or to correct behaviour that had become intolerable – in other words, ultimately to continue to live together, though obviously only in cases when conflict was not severe.

It was primarily wives who turned to the courts. Husbands had access to other means, both formal and informal, to readjust the terms of their marriage. They were, moreover, granted a certain leeway in extramarital relationships and could emigrate more easily than their wives to escape an unhappy marriage. One benefit of a legal separation was that the court might in certain circumstances order a husband to restore a wife's dowry to her, although in practice this might prove impossible because the dowry had been absorbed into the family economy.

A husband's violence was the most frequent reason women requested separations. Court records make clear how common such violence was, and the medical documents they contain certifying injuries sustained by wives represent only the tip of the iceberg. Husbands justified the use of violence as their legally sanctioned right and duty to correct their wives.[58] How far such correction could go was the subject of constant debate, however, and wives might turn to the court not so much to obtain a separation as to improve their marital lives. Ecclesiastical judges asked violent husbands to promise to treat their wives well, in the most serious cases binding them with the payment of a guarantee. Another way that wives could put pressure on husbands who were belligerent, drunken, or failed to support their families was to abandon them. In these cases it was the husbands who brought suit to compel their wives to return home and fulfil their marital obligations. For men of the middle and lower classes, it must be remembered, wives' labour, though underpaid, was essential to sustaining a family.[59]

These marital disputes document a less passive female behaviour than is suggested by the treatises and by the literature of advice. In suits demanding that wives fulfil their marital obligations, women insisted on the legitimacy of their rebellions and sought to negotiate more advantageous conditions with their husbands. In 1579 in Venice, for example, Zuana Bagolin was accused of adultery by her husband, a wine merchant. Zuana did not deny her relationship with another merchant but attempted to justify it. Her husband, she claimed, expected to live off her, even forcing her into prostitution; she was therefore obliged to find an honourable man to support her.[60] Wives promised deference and submission if their husbands behaved correctly. When a husband did not, it was considered legitimate for his wife to leave their house and even to make a new alliance. But she would be ready to return if her husband committed himself to changing.

In these situations, the court, which sat in the bishop's palace in the heart of the city, served as a public and solemn space in which the parties could express their personal points of view, declare their reasons, and claim their rights. Husbands and wives had no reticence about revealing the reasons for their disputes. It was probably behaviour already known to all, since the houses in which they lived did not allow privacy. The house was not a private space, and a couple's disputes involved the entire community. Relatives, friends, and neighbours were constantly involved in the life of a couple they knew, and they considered it their duty to intervene to make peace or resolve conflict. For the purposes of the legal proceedings, moreover, it was essential that marital conflicts be in the public domain, because without the testimony of friends and neighbours it would have been impossible to demonstrate to the judges that there were sufficient grounds for a separation.

Enlightenment and Reform

The eighteenth century saw a marked increase in condemnation of youthful promiscuity. Accompanying this was mounting criticism of the binding nature of marriage promises, as well as criticism of rape laws that encouraged the marriage of seducer and seduced. Elite families were preoccupied, even obsessed, with the prospect that the concept of the binding promise allowed their children to evade familial strategies and to transform their passions into marriages.

This debate took place in a period when intergenerational disputes, both legal and informal, seem to have been increasing, while in cities new social spaces – such as theatres and cafés – allowed young people of both sexes and different social classes to meet; at the same time, the practice was spreading among noblewomen of being accompanied in public by a cicisbeo or *cavalier servente*.[61] Not only in novels and plays but also in practice we find evidence of greater freedom of action and more initiative on the part of younger sons, impatient with inheritance practices that denied them marriage, as well as of elite women, who were eager to conquer new areas of social life. Desire for liberty and the pursuit of happiness are themes that spread in the climate of Enlightenment and that also had repercussions on the daily lives of less elevated classes. The popularity of the theatre in cities both large and small probably influenced the language of emotion, which became more explicit and intimate, more focused on probing individuals' hearts and expressing feelings of love. Love was frequently spoken and written of in the eighteenth century. Indeed, in his work *Love between persons of different sexes*, Girolamo Dal Portico called this "the century of love."

The ruling classes worried above all about the many occasions for young people of differing social classes to mix and the consequent risk of the dreaded misalliance. Singers and dancers were considered particularly dangerous because it was feared that they would bring into real life the characters they played on the stage. But the fear of unequal marriages was not restricted to the elite. Powerful pressures from below required secular and ecclesiastical institutions to confront social hierarchy issues. Fathers formally denounced, often vehemently, their rebellious children to secular magistrates, princes' secretaries, and ecclesiastical courts, and they used legal proceedings, police intervention, or informal arrangements to suppress misbehaviour.

Such generational conflicts allow us glimpses of the obstinate resistance, determination, and audacity of some young people who did not want to acquiesce to their families' desires. The pursuit of happiness – individual and earthly – erupted onto the scene, complicating relationships between fathers and children. The principle of authority was called into question. In Venice in 1739, for example, the 23-year-old patrician Pietro Emo married the non-noble Cornelia Gera. They made use of a surprise wedding, presenting themselves without warning with two witnesses before a parish priest unknown to either of them. In response to his father's formal legal complaint, Pietro, desiring to make public the romance impeded by his family, posted throughout the city a statement declaring his love and his resolve to remain with her: "I, Pietro Emo, in love with the lady Cornelia, ... protest to the whole world and swear to blessed God ... that I would sooner send my spirit from my body than I would abandon the lady Cornelia." Three marriages contracted by surprise in the same year led the Council of Ten – the city's supreme magistracy – to issue a law assuming for itself direct responsibility for ensuring that the marriages of the Venetian nobility were celebrated according to the Tridentine rules.[62]

At the same time, changes in social practices reflected a growing sense that marriage promises were not necessarily binding. This is how one Florentine man wrote to his betrothed in 1774:

> I will tell you that you should speak *freely* about whether you want me or another man and explain yourself fully. If you want me I won't withdraw, because it is a thing that is good and right and a matter of duty, and you also know this. But if you desire another ... take him, because I can't forbid you, you are *free*.[63]

Further confirmation of this trend is found in the fact that some couples felt the need for protection in case of a possible change of heart by one party and so provided in the betrothal agreement that if the betrothal should end, the party responsible for the break would pay a penalty. In this way the possible dissolution of a betrothal became a private matter that was resolved directly by a couple without resorting to the ecclesiastical court. But even those who went to court often reached an agreement regarding the end of the betrothal prior to the conclusion of the trial. Many female litigants who sought the fulfilment of a marriage promise actually preferred to withdraw their suits in exchange for financial compensation. In fact, many suits were brought at the moment that the man was about to marry another woman, thus evidently not so much for the purpose of making him marry the plaintiff as to stop this new marriage. A sum of money – we seldom learn the amount – was enough to make the woman withdraw her suit and leave the man free to marry whomever he wanted.[64] Women thus exploited the binding nature of the marriage promise, which according to canon law had to be fulfilled, for the purposes of exacting financial compensation. It was effectively a legal form of blackmail. Betrothal was no longer necessarily a route to marriage.

It was secular authorities who translated these tendencies towards weakening the binding power of betrothal into legal measures. Their goal was not, however, to support greater freedom of choice but to give more power to fathers in a period of strong opposition to the principle of authority. Secular interference in a matter under ecclesiastical jurisdiction was justified by the fact that betrothal was a simple contract with no sacramental aspect. During the 1770s and 1780s, the rulers of the Duchy of Modena, the Kingdom of Naples, Habsburg Lombardy, and Habsburg-Lorraine Tuscany claimed the right to impose as conditions for validity definite proof (in the form of written documents or witness testimony) of the exchange of promises, along with paternal consent for minors. Only those possessing such proof could expect court decisions requiring the fulfilment of a marriage promise. Thus the paternal consent that the Council of Trent had refused to make a condition for a valid marriage made a reappearance in connection with betrothal and prepared the way for more radical intervention, aimed at removing the marital bond itself from ecclesiastical jurisdiction on the grounds that it too was a contract. Abolition of the binding character of betrothal was adopted in Habsburg territories in 1783 (and the following year in Lombardy) by the emperor Joseph II and in Tuscany in 1790 by his brother Peter Leopold.[65] There remained the possibility of going before a secular court to claim monetary compensation.

In this way the concept of the promise as the beginning of the marriage process disappeared from the law. Men lost their rights to their fiancées' bodies and women lost the protection provided by the binding promise. The status of a betrothed woman became perilously near the status – so fragile and insecure – of an unmarried woman.

The issue became more complicated, however, if deflowering followed a marriage promise. As we have seen, the crime of "rape" preceded by a promise of marriage was punished with the obligation to marry or dower the woman. During the seventeenth and eighteenth centuries, this law was harshly criticized for the severity of its penalties by jurists and governing officials, but only the Kingdom of Naples abolished the crime unless it was accompanied by violence. Here seduced women lost the centuries-old legal protection of their honour that had been provided by the definition of defloration as a crime.[66] In other states, such as the Grand Duchy of Tuscany, judicial practice became more cautious and tended to avoid any form of coercion of the deflowerer, in many cases allowing the parties themselves to come to an agreement. In the criminal court of Florence between 1777 and 1790, more than half of the trials were broken off by an agreement reached by the parties before the judge passed sentence. Of these agreements, 64 per cent envisaged the marriage of the litigants; the others were monetary accords. Almost all of the plaintiffs were pregnant or had recently given birth – when faced with pregnancy, many men continued to accept responsibility and kept their word. Therefore, while a "weak" concept of betrothal was becoming widespread, the situation was somewhat different when the woman became pregnant.[67]

An increase in premarital disputes before both secular and ecclesiastical courts in the last decades of the eighteenth century suggests that getting married had become more difficult. Further confirmation of this is the fact that the marriage age began to increase. Economic and political factors – for instance, the famines of the 1760s and the economic policies liberalizing grain selling of some reforming rulers, such as Peter Leopold in Tuscany – tended to hinder unions. In the Italian states no laws hindered the marriages of the poorest who were unable to maintain a family – in contrast to the situation in the Roman Empire of the German Nation (Wunder 78–9) or in Switzerland (Burghartz 190) – but it is quite possible that some parish priests prevailed upon couples to put off their weddings. In such a context, a rape complaint could be used to accelerate a wedding and to overcome obstacles;[68] and a suit for breach of promise enabled a woman to obtain money that would increase her dowry and allow her to find another husband.

The greater ease with which the middle and lower classes could change their minds and dissolve betrothals probably tended to delay marriage. Particularly in the absence of pregnancy, a commitment to marry could be interpreted in a freer manner, allowing for the possibility of going back on one's decision and choosing another partner via agreements and negotiations not necessarily subject to institutional control. It was therefore possible to give more space to individual feelings and desires in the choice of spouse, to speak explicitly of love and happiness as important elements in building a relationship as a couple, as well as of hatred as a good reason for requesting a separation. However, this did not preclude familial consent – imposed by the new laws regarding the marriage promise – which in most cases was needed to start a family. Paternal consent and the emotional dimension of marital choice were not necessarily in contradiction.

The new century – the century of Romanticism – opened with the reaffirmation of the authority of fathers over children and of husbands over wives that the French Revolution had drastically weakened. The Napoleonic Code of 1804, which was imitated by many nineteenth-century European legal codes, envisaged the restoration of paternal authority in order to ensure social and political order following the years of revolutionary upheaval. Patriarchal hierarchies, expressions of emotion, and egalitarian demands were destined to coexist for a long time to come.

NOTES

1 Sarti 2006. On the Italian historical literature on marriage, see Fazio 2009.
2 See Gottlieb 1980.
3 Archivio Arcivescovile di Firenze (henceforth, AAF), *Cause civili matrimoniali*, 17, no. 5 (1561–2).
4 Fabbri 1991; Molho 1994. On marriage rituals, fundamental is Klapisch-Zuber 1979. On the marriage rituals of the Jewish community in Italy, which were very similar to Christian rituals, see Weinstein 2004.
5 AAF, *Cause criminali matrimoniali*, no. 2 (1535).
6 Quoted in Rasi 1941, 259n3 (1568). See also Seidel Menchi 2001.
7 Martines 1974.
8 Delille 1985; Chojnacki 2000, 95–111; Bellavitis 2001; Chabot 2011.

9 See, in this volume, Donahue 34.
10 Bizzarri 1937.
11 Marongiu 1963.
12 Klapisch-Zuber 1979.
13 Zarri 2000, 311–15; Cristellon 2010, 192–3.
14 Lefebvre-Teillard 1996, 132–4. See also Brundage 1987.
15 AAF, *Cause criminali matrimoniali*, no. 2 (1536).
16 Brucker 1986. Lusanna won the first suit but lost on appeal.
17 See, in this volume, Donahue 36, Korpiola 241, and Lefebvre-Teillard 261, 263.
18 Bossy 1985.
19 Alfani 2009. See also, in this volume, Donahue 34–5.
20 De Vio, *Summula*, § "Matrimonium," 274–5; Covarrubias, *De sponsalibus et matrimoniis*, pars II, cap. VI, n. 12, 158.
21 Helmholz 1974; Donahue 1981.
22 Dean 1998; Lombardi 2001, 47–51.
23 See Helmholz 1974, 59.
24 On the uncertainty of marital status under medieval canon law, see Cristellon 2008, 389.
25 Scaramella 2004, 448. From the 1580s onwards, bigamy came under the jurisdiction of the Inquisition. See, in this volume, Usunáriz 217.
26 Siebenhüner 2006.
27 AAF, *Cause criminali matrimoniali*, no. 3 (22 October 1556).
28 Medick and Sabean 1984.
29 Smith 1986.
30 See, in this volume, Donahue 36, 37–8. A dispensation from the publication of the banns could be obtained if there were well-founded fears that someone would try to oppose the marriage with false impediments.
31 Bossy 1985, 25. The literature on Tridentine marriage is vast. I will cite only Jedin 1973–1981 and Zarri 2000.
32 Allegra 1981.
33 A surprise marriage is described in chapter 11 (Seidel Menchi 321–3).
34 Cristellon 2003.
35 Lombardi 2001, 49–59.
36 AAF, *Cause civili matrimoniali*, 22, no. 10 (1574). For the role played by the Spanish Church in favour of young people who rebelled against family strategies, see Casey 2007, 134–8.
37 Lombardi 2001, 167–77.
38 The petition and ruling are conserved in the case file in the diocesan tribunal of Florence where Caterina filed her complaint for broken promise

and defloration. See AAF, *Cause civili matrimoniali*, 24, no. 6 (1576). For Venice, see Ruggiero 1985 and Hacke 2004. For Rome, see Pelaja 1994.

39 Some of the most important legal experts of the day attest to this: Gómez, *Ad leges Tauri commentarium*, "Lex 80," 476 nos. 7, 8; Claro, *Liber quintus*, § "Stuprum," f. 43v. In the Florentine state the penalty of either marrying or dowering a seduced woman was imposed at least from 1559. See Brackett 1992, 115.

40 AAF, *Cause civili matrimoniali*, 24, no. 6 (1576).

41 Rinaldi, *Observationes*, vol. 2, cap. XXIII, 385 nos. 243–7.

42 Hacke 2004; Di Simplicio 1994, 281–2; Lombardi 2001, 340–57; Luperini 2001. In the diocese of Trani in the Kingdom of Naples, suits for rape with a promise of marriage were also moving to the secular criminal court. See Papagna 2006, 479. In contrast these suits continued to be tried before the ecclesiastical court in the diocese of Turin, but diminished notably between the seventeenth and eighteenth centuries. See Cavallo and Cerutti 1990.

43 See Roper 1994, 155–6. For these similarities between Catholics and Protestants, see Lombardi 2008 and Lombardi 2016.

44 De Boer 2001.

45 Lambertini, *Raccolta di alcune notificazioni*, vol. 3, Notificazione V (6 November 1735), 62–8.

46 Criminal trials remain understudied. However, it cannot be said that in Catholic countries ecclesiastical discipline was lacking in a strict sense, as Pieter Spierenburg claims in Spierenburg 2004, 11. The ecclesiastical forum exercised criminal jurisdiction over the laity as well as over the clergy in the case of crimes committed against the church, the faith, and the sacraments.

47 On concubinage, see Esposito 2004, Ferrante 2004, Eisenach 2004b, Luperini 2004a, Romeo 2008, and, in this volume, Seidel Menchi 337–8. On elite concubinage, see Eisenach 2004a and Cowan 2007.

48 Lambertini, *Raccolta di alcune notificazioni*, vol. 3, Notificazione V (6 November 1735), 67. On Lambertini, see Rosa 1969, 49–85.

49 Brambilla 2000, 499–513; Brambilla 2006, 161–8.

50 Luperini 2001. This penalty was later commuted to a fine for Salvestro. Caterina, following six months of exile, was permitted to return to her natal family. See also Brambilla 2006, 164–5.

51 Casanova 2007, 155; Arrivo 2006, 185–8.

52 Fontana, *La santità e la pietà*, part II, ch. IV, 29.

53 Prosperi 2005 and, in this volume, Wunder 79–80, van der Heijden 170–2, Burghartz 189–92, and Lefebvre-Teillard 279–80.

54 *Enfance abandonnée et société en Europe* 1991; Henderson and Wall 2004; Hunecke 1987; Panter-Brick and Smith 2000; Reggiani 2014.

55 Ferrante 2000; Lombardi 1988; Cohen 1992; Groppi 1994; Cavallo 1995.

56 La Rocca 2009.

57 Di Renzo Villata 1989.

58 The same argument was used in the states of the German Empire: see, in this volume, Wunder 73.

59 La Rocca 2009; Luperini 2004b; Ferraro 2001; Seidel Menchi and Quaglioni 2000. On marital violence, see also Cavina 2011.

60 Ferraro 2001, 109ff.

61 Cozzi 1976; Bizzocchi 2008; Plebani 2012.

62 Plebani 2012. See also Cozzi 1976, 206–7.

63 AAF, *Cause civili matrimoniali*, 82, no. 1 (1774), my emphasis.

64 Women used a legal action – in the diocese of Florence called *diffamatio* or *causa jactatoria*, elsewhere "impediment" or *nihil transeat* – which allowed them to impede the wedding that another person was about to celebrate on the grounds of an earlier promise. See, in this volume, Helmholz 146. In the late Middle Ages among the elite of Florence the practice was to make a person who broke a marriage promise pay a large monetary penalty in order to discourage the breaking of such promises; in contrast, in the late eighteenth century a monetary penalty, which was modest, was a way of escaping the commitment. See Cavallar and Kirshner 2004. *Jactitatio* and *diffamatio* (defamation) are one and the same offence. See, in this volume, Helmholz 133, 146.

65 Jemolo 1914; Tosi 1990.

66 Alessi 1989, 1990, and 2006.

67 Arrivo 2006.

68 The ages of such couples were in fact lower than those of other couples in the same area (ibid., 172–3).

Chapter 4

The Legal Regulation of Marriage in England: From the Fifteenth Century to the 1640s

RICHARD H. HELMHOLZ

Introduction

This chapter describes and illustrates the primary changes and continuities in English marriage law between 1400 and the 1640s, when the English ecclesiastical courts were temporarily closed as a consequence of the English Civil War. It also attempts to assess what the law as put into practice meant to the men and women whose lives came into contact with the courts in matrimonial causes. The principal sources upon which any careful assessment of the legal regulation of marriage in England must be made are the documents compiled by the scribes and lawyers whose careers were spent in the courts of the church. They are the sources upon which this chapter is based.[1]

This focus in years and sources, limited though it may seem, is defensible and perhaps even necessary. There are two reasons. First, it fell to the courts of the church to enforce the law of marriage and divorce throughout this period. With few exceptions the royal courts in England made no effort to gain control of this aspect of human life.[2] Second, the legal records and related literature involving marriage from before 1640 have been sufficiently explored, whereas no one has yet investigated the ecclesiastical sources from the period after the Restoration of the monarchy in 1660 in any detail or depth. What preliminary reconnaissance has been done for the later period suggests that the trends established prior to the 1640s continued and even intensified over time. But as yet we do not really know.[3]

If one were forced to choose between change and continuity in describing the overall history of this subject, continuity would necessarily be the choice. The English Church did not adopt the great changes in matrimonial litigation instituted by the Council of Trent's famous decree *Tametsi*. In most aspects of their jurisdiction, the ecclesiastical courts in England continued along medieval paths, and matrimonial law was no exception. As the records make clear, however, overall continuity did not preclude significant change. Altered societal attitudes, enactment of new statutes and canons, and penetration of new ideas among the lawyers who administered the system led inevitably to changes in legal practice.

The historiography of the subject requires a brief preliminary mention. From the time that scientific study of law and society began in the nineteenth century, the church's jurisdiction over marriage has not been neglected. It has claimed the attention of many historians interested in English law. Books were written about the subject,[4] and the greatest of England's legal historians, F.W. Maitland (d. 1906), devoted almost 100 pages of his most famous work to the law of the family.[5] Most of his attention was concentrated upon the law of the church. As he himself said, for all its vaunted insularity, the law of England on this subject was the canon law.[6] England knew no matrimonial law of its own.

At the same time, none of the historians who took an early interest in the subject, including Maitland, seized the chance of examining the records of actual litigation in the church's courts. Their conclusions were based on the formal canon law, supplemented by evidence taken from contemporary literature, commentaries by moralists and social critics, and the fruits of logical deduction. Maitland did not look at court records. He described this as a gap to be filled and as a source of uncertainty. The records, he once lamented, "must have existed." He added the qualification, "I do not know where to look for them."[7] Unfortunately, he never found them.

They do exist. They are being investigated. For England, the situation as it existed in Maitland's day began to change in the middle years of the twentieth century. Studies of ecclesiastical courts that incorporated evidence from consistory court records began to appear in the 1950s,[8] and in the 1970s historians who concerned themselves with the institution of marriage had begun to look closely at actual practice as it is shown in the medieval registers of the church's tribunals.[9] Since then, what began as a small stream has become a flood. An ever-larger body of scholarship devoted to various aspects of the law of marriage and divorce has been written, and much of it has been based on the records of the ecclesiastical courts in England.[10] The research that has gone into these books has shed new light on the history of marriage and the family. This has been a happy development, one that as yet shows no signs of coming to a close. We know much more about all aspects of marriage and divorce than we did 50 years ago. And what we have learned has raised important new questions extending outside the field of legal history.

Along with this expansion has come a second and more recent development, the emergence of a comparative dimension to the subject. Prior to recent years, full comparison was discouraged by the undeniable fact that the same canon law applied throughout the Latin Church. The assumption, a reasonable one, was that it was uniform in its results. Most Continental lawyers also took it for granted that the proper study of legal history did not include the investigation of court records. The law was to be studied, as the jurists of the *ius commune* might themselves have put it, *legibus non exemplis*.[11] To students of the law, evidence of what happened in practice, particularly what had happened in individual cases, was therefore regarded as something of a stepchild.[12]

This attitude has today begun to change, and in Italy for example, works on the history of marriage based on litigation documents have begun to appear. Much of this has occurred thanks to the abilities and hard work of Dr Silvana Seidel Menchi and her several collaborators. They have produced a series of works that illuminate the institution of marriage,[13] and they are not alone. Collaborative volumes, including contributions on Italian marriage by English-speaking authors, have also been published.[14] There are signs that the interest is spreading beyond the geographical confines of England and Italy.[15] Doubts about the possibilities of doing useful work on the history of marriage with material from the archives have thus proved unfounded. This development has opened up the possibility of a true comparative history of the subject. That is the worthwhile project in which this book is meant to share.

This chapter consists of two parts. The first deals with three preliminary questions about this subject. The answers taken from the English records should be compared with the answers about other regions given in other chapters of this volume. The second part deals with the history of English matrimonial law and litigation during the fifteenth century, comparing them with what occurred during the next two centuries. Both formal changes and variations in social attitudes seem significant in tracing what happened. Its purpose is to illustrate and discuss the most important elements of continuity and change that occurred in English court practice as they touched the regulation of marriage during these centuries.

Part I

Three aspects of jurisdiction over English law and marriage are addressed in this part. The first section describes the relevant sources: the records of litigation about marriage and divorce, including some of the literature of practice about marriage that was compiled by contemporary lawyers. The second takes up the relationship between church and state in regulating marriage during the period. The third covers jurisdiction over marital transgressions – matters like adultery, incest, and illegitimacy.

The Sources

The nature and transmission of the sources from which the history of the practice of marriage law can be reconstructed remained much the same in the sixteenth and seventeenth centuries as they had been during the fifteenth. The principal records were the registers and cause papers from the ecclesiastical courts. The biggest change was that there were more of them – more that were compiled and more that have survived. At least up to the present time, it appears that England has the most complete as well as the oldest run of such records of any of the European lands.[16]

Several things about these records should be mentioned as of special importance to the historian of marriage. The most numerous sources of knowledge are the court registers, the books of *acta* from the courts of English bishops and archdeacons. The act books recorded the procedural steps taken by each court in the litigation that came before it. By the early sixteenth century they had become highly formulaic and therefore largely uninformative about the details of each cause brought before the courts. They are not useless on this account. They tell us the names and the habitat of litigants. They also tell us something about the speed of litigation and the various kinds of causes being heard, but they are not informative about the substance of most matrimonial causes.

For fuller information, the second source is more useful – the so-called cause papers. Many diocesan courts retained the documents (the *libelli*, the *positiones*, the *articuli*, the *interrogatoria*, and the *sententiae diffinitivae*) that had been used in pleading and deciding contested causes. We also have the depositions, the *attestationes*, that record the testimony of witnesses and have proved so useful in describing the habits and assumptions of the people.[17] They tell us – at least they seem to tell us – what participants in a marriage actually said to each other. We learn something about confessions of love and about financial negotiations. We must remind ourselves that they were documents prepared for litigation; they distort reality because of their purpose.[18] Still, they provide the most reliable information we have about the ways in which men and women entered marriages. When used cautiously, they open a window on what ordinary people thought.

From a legal perspective, there is an additional point to be made about the records. They demonstrate the existence of many parallels between the nature of the English examples and similar records across Europe. There was a common system of procedure, proof, and record keeping. The *ordo iuris* of the *ius commune* did allow local variation, to be sure, but its principal features were part of the common legal heritage of European countries, including England. We see the results of that common heritage at first hand in the cause papers.

The principal change in the sources that occurred over the course of the sixteenth century was a large increase in the volume of relevant records. The number of act books preserved from the late medieval period is not insignificant – something like 50. But during the reign of Elizabeth in the second half of the sixteenth century, there occurred a positive explosion in the numbers of these procedural records. By 1600, they were preserved as a matter of course in almost all the English dioceses, of which there were then 23, divided between the two provinces of Canterbury and York. The history of these sources is therefore one of continuity and progress in both retention and transmission to us. They exist in virtually unbroken sequence up to the time the English ecclesiastical courts were stripped of their jurisdiction over marriage and divorce in the nineteenth century. The same is true of the cause papers. Whereas only two dioceses have any considerable number of these records for the medieval period, by 1600 most of them do. It is not possible for a historian to do more than sample the records from the later period; but from the medieval period it is possible to read them all.

The greater numbers of records is matched by the compilation of new types of records. Probably because of the initiative of the diocesan registrars, in many dioceses registers of persons under sentence of excommunication were drawn up. Books containing caveats (*cautiones*), or warnings to court personnel not to proceed in particular causes without notifying an interested party, were also put together. New formularies were compiled.[19] It is difficult to know the extent to which such changes aided litigants in matrimonial causes. A more bureaucratic mentality, and nothing more, may have been at work. Even so, these new records might have been useful to the laity, as in a dispute over marriage where a caveat might be entered to prevent enforcement of a marriage contract without hearing what a third party had to say.

The second change in the sources that occurred during the sixteenth century was another addition – the appearance of reports of causes heard in the courts. Most of them are contained in notebooks compiled by the English civilians. These were not official records. Neither were they the *consilia* or the *decisiones* familiar from Continental legal traditions. Instead, they were notes of varying degrees of detail that were made by ecclesiastical lawyers (or perhaps judges) about the causes that had come before the courts where they served. The notes gave something of the facts, the authorities relied upon, the arguments made, and (usually) also the outcome. In their nature, they were not elaborate. Indeed they were more akin to many of the contemporary case reports from the English royal courts than they were to full-blown and scholarly *decisiones*.[20] But they are invaluable to the historian who takes an interest in the law as it was put into effect.

A particular reason for drawing attention to these reports in the context of matrimonial litigation is that these new reports often recorded the motivations of the judges in reaching their decisions – something that is absent from the court records and is highly useful on that account to the modern historian.[21] For example, when Mary Frost sought a divorce *a mensa et thoro* ("from bed and board," a judicial separation) from her husband William, alleging that he had committed adultery, the civilian's notebook records some of the evidence – one witness said "he found [Katherine Audley with] the said [William] in his bed and in his shirt and the door locked fast upon them."[22] The witness did not actually see them committing adultery, but he had seen enough. He "believed they had committed adultery or would have committed adultery." Applying the law of presumptions, and perhaps also because this evidence was corroborated by one other witness, the judge granted the petition for divorce. If we had only the bare act book entry of the cause, we should know only that a divorce had been granted for adultery and that it was being made available to wives as well as husbands. Both facts are worth knowing. But the detail would be missing. So would the importance in practice of the law of presumptions. These notebooks thus reveal important details about the nature of matrimonial practice in the courts and even something about the history of marriage itself.

England has always lacked a strong notarial tradition. This is well known.[23] Although many of the proctors who served in the ecclesiastical courts were in fact notaries public, they rarely drew up matrimonial contracts, as many Continental notaries long did. From the perspective of the available sources, therefore, we lack this important source of information about the terms of entry into marriage. A few such contracts do survive for England – found among the ancient charters preserved in the British Library and in a few other repositories – but examination of their contents suggests they were drawn up only for unusual situations, as where a child was too young to contract himself or where the upper classes were involved and significant amounts of property were at stake.[24] As far as I can tell, written matrimonial contracts prepared by notaries were never introduced as evidence to prove a matrimonial contract. They played an insignificant part in actual litigation. It seems ironic that a procedural system built around the production of written documents should have depended so heavily on oral testimony. But so it was.

Church and State

The second preliminary subject is an outline of relations between church and state in regulating marriage and divorce. For England, this topic does not require extensive discussion. Over the course of the centuries, there was little competition between the temporal and spiritual courts in this area. The disagreement that occurred – and there was some – was about what the law of marriage should be.[25] With few exceptions, however, this disagreement did not take the form of conflict between the courts of church and state. It was reflected instead in social practice and in resistance to legal regulation of any kind. But before the middle of the nineteenth century, the formal matrimonial law of England was the law of the church. From time to time, the royal courts did assert a power to regulate some aspects of the law of marriage, particularly when the canon law seemed to interfere with legitimate secular goals, such as preserving royal jurisdiction over succession and titles to land. Until relatively modern times, however, jurisdiction over most disputes about marriage and about the definition of marriage itself was left to the church. It was not until 1857 that the Matrimonial Causes Act brought this regime to a close by transferring jurisdiction to the temporal forum.[26]

It may be, as has been contended by Professor Eric Josef Carlson, that the longevity and apparent success of ecclesiastical jurisdiction over marriage is best explained by a widespread acceptance among the populace of its legitimacy and effectiveness. The English people, he concluded, "did not complain, because the church's marriage law worked for them."[27] This view may concede more power to public opinion than is likely under the circumstances. Formally at least, the retention of the English Church's medieval jurisdiction was secured by a combination of other factors – the enactment of a parliamentary statute in the 1530s, the repeated failure of attempts at reform, and the weight of lawyerly inertia.[28]

However, in a broader sense, there must be something to be said in favour of Carlson's view. The canon law itself left room for local custom, even in questions involving the formation of marriage, and this would have softened resistance to it among the people who created the custom. It could be relevant in marriage causes when the necessity of avoiding scandal among the people arose,[29] and it was one means of determining whether specific actions of a couple had amounted to their consent to a marriage. Under customary assumptions, for instance, the exchange of gifts between a man and woman was incompatible with anything but an intent to marry, and evidence about such exchanges appears in the formal records as a means of proving a marriage.[30] Similarly, "handfasting" in contracting marriage was customarily done with the right hand; where the woman had first used her left hand, it was argued in one London cause, she could not have done so "fully intending to promise [marriage]" (*integro animo spondendi*).[31] Hence she had given no real consent. Under the canon law, custom could not change the definition of marriage, but it could help interpret human behaviour for judges required to discern whether one had been contracted.

Moreover, as it was put into practice, the canon law in England left more room for active participation by the laity than the formal law allowed. Although the canon law formally prohibited compromise of matrimonial litigation,[32] in practice it occurred throughout this period. In the medieval court records, Frederik Pedersen uncovered many examples of meetings being held between representatives of the community and the families of young men and women being convoked to settle disputes about marriage.[33] The meetings were held "in the shadow of the law." That is, they were intended to explore the issues involved and seek a solution. In most cases, the process was not undertaken to flout the law. It was done outside the law, probably to avoid the courts if possible. Going to an ecclesiastical court was a last resort, something to be done when initial efforts at settlement had failed. Moreover, it is evident in the records themselves that sometimes other secular officials intervened to sort out matrimonial tangles. When in 1595, for example, Edmund Lowes was cited before an ecclesiastical court in Canterbury for unlawfully living apart from his wife, he answered that he had left her company only after being authorized to do so by an agreement made before the mayor of Maidstone.[34] He cannot have been a canonist, but no doubt he had the respect of the couple and their families. Evidence like this suggests that the law of the church was not always applied strictly in practice. If so, the English people may have found the church's jurisdiction more compatible with their own interests and assumptions than appears on the pages of the Gregorian Decretals. This remained true throughout this period.

This continuity of practice being recognized, one significant change occurred during the sixteenth century that led to occasional conflict. This was the enactment by parliamentary legislation of rules to be enforced in the ecclesiastical courts. The English Parliament asserted, and in fact exercised, the power to change the canon law applied in them. Within the law of marriage and divorce, in 1540 Parliament enacted a statute prohibiting dissolution of existing marriages on grounds of pre-contract, a step that would have restricted enforcement of clandestine marriage contracts, but the statute was repealed eight years later.[35] Legislation enacted under King Edward VI abolished laws and canons that prohibited the marriage of priests.[36] And several statutes amended the medieval law that defined the prohibited degrees of consanguinity and affinity, their object being to curtail the scope of those degrees and end the trafficking in papal dispensations that were a part of the prior law's prohibitions.[37] It will be useful to say something more about the fate of the kinship impediments to marriage later, and it should be said immediately that the existence of secular legislation by no means precluded all new ecclesiastical legislation. Convocation, the official legislative body of the English Church, itself enacted statutes regulating marriage and divorce.[38] The difference was that, after the Reformation, they had to share that law-making power with Parliament, and in cases of conflict, the latter normally prevailed. More significant than this potential for clashes was the fact that most parliamentary legislation left the jurisdiction of the ecclesiastical courts intact,[39] that is until the fundamental legislation of the 1850s. What happened before then allowed the ecclesiastical courts to keep to their old paths, and they did so. Their jurisdiction seems to have been subject to a diminishing demand over time, although we still do not know much in detail about what happened after 1660.

Marital and Sexual Transgressions

The third subject is: who took responsibility for punishment of marital transgressions? This category, a long list, included adultery, fornication, cruelty between spouses, illegitimacy and the care of illegitimate children, incest, sodomy, bigamy, infanticide, abortion, failures to solemnize marriages, and miscellaneous violations of positive canonical rules – as for example, marrying during Lent or Advent. The second part of this chapter will discuss in a little more detail the growth of *ex officio* offences during the late sixteenth century, but here it is worth reiterating that the punishment of most of these "transgressions" remained in the hands of the church and its courts throughout the period. Indeed, these transgressions furnished a large part of the *ex officio* matters that came before the courts, as had been true during the Middle Ages. They brought the people into the most immediate contact with the law of the church, and the scoffing epithet attached to the ecclesiastical tribunals by their enemies – "the bawdy courts"[40] – itself reflects the prevalence of what we would today call "morals offences" in the courts of the church.

The most routine offence to come before the courts was simple fornication. In England it was not left to the internal forum, where its commission had become publicly known. Public suspicion led persons suspected of this offence to be cited to appear at a session of a disciplinary tribunal, although such a citation was usually the product of a formal presentment made by the churchwardens of each parish. There the accused persons were made either to confess or to deny having committed fornication. If they chose the latter course, they were normally assigned compurgation. This meant that they were required to take a formal oath that they were innocent of the crime and to find a number of compurgators willing to swear to their belief in the oath they had just taken. If they chose the former (or if they failed in the compurgatory oath), they were required to perform public penance, usually by appearing before the parochial congregation on Sunday dressed in penitential garb and by then making some sort of open confession of sin. For many it would have been a humiliating experience, and the possibility of "compounding," by making a charitable money payment, was left open. Even with this option, compurgation or public penance was the normal course in practice. Seeing one's neighbour doing public penance in church on Sunday would have been a frequent part of life in earlier centuries.[41]

From a lawyer's perspective, this system's weaknesses were all too obvious. It threw the burden of proof on the guilty party, requiring him or her to prove a negative; it encouraged perjury, and it was an unreliable way of arriving at the truth. On the positive side, compurgation was sanctioned by the Decretals,[42] it relieved the judges of the burden of determining guilt or innocence for a crime that is difficult to prove,[43] and it was simple to administer. At least so it appears on the routine pages of many act books. It continued to be used, though it was increasingly confined to sexual offences, until at least the 1640s.[44]

Despite their ordinary simplicity, some of these *ex officio* proceedings turned out to be quite complicated. For instance, in 1598 a man named Arthur Knight was prosecuted for adultery with Dorothy King.[45] When he appeared before the court in the diocese of London, he told a strange story. Indeed it now sounds quite unbelievable. He said that about 14 years before the date of his citation, he had been married to a woman named Denise. Hearing "by credible report" that Denise had died, he contracted a marriage with Anne and lived with her as her husband. But then he learned (he said) that Anne had herself previously married another man, so he left her and subsequently took Dorothy as his wife. It was this woman with whom he was alleged to have committed adultery, and this occurred only because three or four years after his marriage with Dorothy, it turned out that Denise, the first wife, was actually alive. It was a tangle. There is much about this case about which we must remain ignorant. How was it, for example, that Arthur had been able to escape the church's net for so long, and what was it that caused him at last to be cited to appear to answer for his tangled matrimonial history? We do not know. We do not even know how the case was ultimately resolved. However, the story (if true) does well illustrate the continuation of medieval habits of "self-divorce" and perhaps even the effects of a chance enmity (of Arthur's) in the administration of the church's law.

It is not hard to see why the royal courts were content to leave proceedings like these to the church. "More trouble than they are worth" would have been a sensible reaction among the common lawyers.[46] There were, it is true, occasional exceptions to this rule – areas of the law where the temporal courts did intervene in matrimonial affairs, as they had done throughout the Middle Ages. One was illegitimacy of birth. Because illegitimacy could affect inheritance and land – by any standard a secular matter – the common law courts limited the church's jurisdiction over it, though not completely, it should be said. The ecclesiastical courts still had jurisdiction to punish a man for fathering and a woman for giving birth to an illegitimate child. However, their competence was effectively limited by the royal courts' determination not to allow the church to wield its scythe in a secular field, that is to say, in cases where inheritance of land was at issue.

This medieval precedent, well established by 1500, was enlarged in a few other areas of marital and moral transgressions during the sixteenth century. Sodomy became a temporal crime in 1553; prior to that it had been prosecuted only as an ecclesiastical offence.[47] Enforcement of a father's duty to support his illegitimate children was made a duty of the justices of the peace in 1576.[48] Bigamy was made a felony, and hence a temporal crime, by a statute enacted in 1603.[49] Most such statutes contained "savings clauses" for ecclesiastical jurisdiction. Only the course of time and the preferences of the participants moved most of them to the temporal courts, where money could more readily change hands. Overall, however, it is remarkable how slow the movement towards secularization was. Prostitution and incest, for example, remained under the church's jurisdictional umbrella up to the time the ecclesiastical courts ceased to sit during the 1640s. And the staple features of ecclesiastical jurisdiction in England – fornication, adultery, and sexual defamation – were also left under the church's control until then. It was a significant matter too. These offences filled the pages of the act books in the years before then.[50] They brought many ordinary men and women before the courts of the church in what must have been an unpleasant and costly experience.

The sixteenth century was a time of heightened perception of the dangers of social disorder. Greater efforts to control behaviour were the result.[51] They occurred on many levels and in many different kinds of courts. The church's tribunals played their part. In a sense, the punishment of marital transgressions was regarded as belonging within ecclesiastical jurisdiction as a matter of right by the English people, and they would have expected implementation of a policy based on religious standards. The medieval precedents were not overturned by the Reformation in England; they remained "on the books" unless specifically changed by act of Parliament, and where there was statutory change in this area of the law, it usually provided for a sharing of jurisdiction with secular tribunals, not abolition of the church's jurisdictional rights.

The church's jurisdiction over marriage was formally abolished only during the nineteenth century, along with most aspects of the traditional rights of its courts. At some earlier point, however, the ecclesiastical cognizance of most sexual offences had already become obsolete, or at least largely theoretical. As yet we do not know exactly how or even exactly when the loss occurred. We know only that a change in social attitudes, not passage of a parliamentary statute or creation of a new and more restrictive legal regime, was the engine that drove it,[52] and we know also that the change had not occurred by 1640.

Part II

Part II of this chapter deals with changes in English matrimonial law and practice in the century before 1640. It attempts to assess what they meant to the people involved. The topic has its difficulties and even its dangers. By concentrating upon what was new, one can lose sight of the dominant feature of the history of the law of marriage in England: how much remained the same and for so long. Most things did.

In some ways, this result seems unexpected, even unlikely. During the sixteenth century, the English Church broke the ties that bound it to the papacy. The breach would seem to have thrown the future of the canon law of marriage into doubt. It did for a time, but in the end no dramatic change happened. Instead, retention of the past turned out to be the order of the day. Jurisdiction over marriage and divorce was retained by the church. Except at the outer margins, the secular courts did not take over the causes that had once belonged to the church. The substantive law on the subject was also left largely unchanged. Most famously, whereas the Council of Trent changed the definition of a valid marriage by requiring the presence of the parish priest as a condition for a marriage's validity, the medieval law was retained in England. Couples who had exchanged words of present consent could (and did) consider themselves to be lawful man and wife "before God." They continued to have the right to enforce the marriage, if they could prove it.[53] Moreover, although many of the Protestant churches on the Continent moved towards permitting remarriage of the innocent party after divorce *a mensa et thoro*, the prohibition against it was retained in England.

These refusals to change had results that appear in the surviving court records. One was that the cause brought to enforce a contract of marriage – usually a clandestine marriage entered into by *verba de presenti* – remained the most frequent kind of *causa matrimonialis* that came before the courts throughout the sixteenth and early seventeenth centuries. Most of the same problems also arose. For example, one London marriage was contracted under the stated condition "if God so wills." Was it binding upon the parties? To find out, they went to law. On the one hand, it was said that every human action depends on God's will in some sense, so that no real conditional element would have been added by these words. They should therefore be disregarded and the marriage should stand. On the other hand, it was contended that the requirement of freedom in entering marriage meant that the addition of any condition, at least any honest condition, should render this contract inoperative. The person who used the words cannot have meant to contract an absolutely binding marriage, and since intent was what mattered, he was not bound. It was a problem, and it made a contentious cause in court. How could one know whether God in fact willed that the marriage should go ahead? The ensuing debate was recorded in a manuscript report now in the London Metropolitan Archives.[54] The lawyers in it cited the opinions of the Spaniards Didacus Covarruvias (d. 1577) and Tomás Sánchez (d. 1610), as well as older authorities. We do not know the outcome. We know only that this example raised a characteristic problem in English litigation. Causes based upon marriages contracted *verbis dubiis*, as one civilian aptly described them, continued to vex the courts, confuse the people, and enrich the ecclesiastical lawyers throughout the post-Reformation years.[55]

This all meant that litigation brought to secure a full divorce – that is, a declaration of nullity *a vinculo* – remained, if not a rarity, at least a smaller part of English court practice until after 1753 than many historians have thought. There was some greater uncertainty about the impediments to marriage, a subject discussed later, and it did lead to litigation. But it did not oust the dominance of the ordinary *causa matrimonialis*.

The same can be said of judicial separation. More suits seem to have been brought. However, there were built-in limits. The latter might have grown dramatically in numbers had they become a path to remarriage. However, as just noted, after a divorce *a mensa et thoro*, even innocent parties were not permitted to remarry in England. The judges enforced this prohibition. They issued specific mandates prohibiting remarriage, sometimes even requiring that the parties enter into a penal bond not to do so.[56] Reconciliation of a couple after adultery also continued to stand in the way of divorce between them.[57] Somewhat surprisingly, so did mutual adultery. If one spouse committed adultery, the other one could secure a divorce *a mensa et thoro*, but if both did, neither could.[58] These had been the medieval rules, and they remained in place. They discouraged litigation.

Despite these elements of continuity, some significant changes in matrimonial law and practice did occur. Three are particularly noteworthy: changes in levels of litigation, changes in the prohibited degrees of affinity and consanguinity, and changes in the numbers and kinds of offences against public morality that were prosecuted. Each of the three reveals something important about the history of matrimonial law.

Extent of Matrimonial Litigation

Stability in substantive law did not preclude change in levels of litigation. This often happens. For reasons quite unrelated to legal rule, more (or fewer) people may feel compelled (or entitled) to go to law at different periods. One of the most salient features of marriage litigation during the Middle Ages was a gradual decline in the numbers of marriage causes brought before the courts. Whether this was a Europe-wide phenomenon we do not yet know, but it certainly was true throughout England. Both in percentage of total causes and in absolute numbers, matrimonial litigation occupied a smaller part of court practice in 1500 than it had in 1300. Why did this shrinkage occur? No substantive developments in the law took place during the period, and most of the causes were brought to establish the existence of a marriage, not to dissolve one. I have thought – though it is impossible to prove – that the decline reflected a gradual and increasing acceptance among the laity of the church's rules about marriage. In other words, social change left its mark on the records. There were fewer disputes because there was more compliance with the church's requirements that the banns be read and that solemnization of a marriage occur *in facie ecclesie*. Their absence had led to uncertainty and litigation to establish the fact of marriage. Not everyone has accepted this explanation, however. So far it has proved impossible to come up with a better one, but it may be that an argument based on a general acquiescence in the church's rules is mistaken. Nevertheless, the decline in numbers by the end of the medieval period is beyond doubt.

What happened during the sixteenth century? Although more work with the records is necessary before we can be sure, it is my impression that at least a slight increase in the amount of matrimonial litigation occurred during the first third of the sixteenth century, that is an increase over what there had been during the middle of the fifteenth.[59] Thereafter, however, the number of causes declined and that decline carried forward into the seventeenth century. Martin Ingram, who carried out extensive research on the records of the diocese of Salisbury, concluded that "in the period 1570–1640 the flow of marriage contract cases was ... reduced from a fairly low incidence to the merest trickle."[60] The same decline seems to have occurred generally elsewhere in England. Suits brought to enforce marriages entered into by *verba de presenti* remained the norm, but there were fewer of them.

Perhaps acceptance of the church's law on the subject among the populace again had something to do with this outcome. Clandestine marriages became disreputable. Possibly the punishment of clergy who presided over clandestine marriage ceremonies also played a role. However, there is another possible explanation: in day-to-day practice, these suits became harder to win. The evidence from the records demonstrates a growing unwillingness on the part of English ecclesiastical lawyers to enforce doubtful matrimonial contracts, and in this climate of opinion it may be that the decline in number of causes followed from this change of mind. Men and women did not sue to enforce matrimonial contracts when they knew they were unlikely to prevail in litigation.[61] They would naturally have been advised by professional lawyers – the civilian lawyers who served in the courts. These men could have told potential litigants what their chances of prevailing were. In doing so, these civilians might themselves have been informed by three developments in court practice.

The first was to treat as excommunicated the bystanders (and potential witnesses) who had attended clandestine marriages. A common objection made against the practice of the ecclesiastical courts was that they wielded the sword of excommunication unadvisedly and for trivial causes.[62] Of the justice of this complaint, there is scarcely a better example than this practice. It meant a person could be excommunicated for helping a friend. The policy was not implemented uniformly, and so far as one can tell it was not applied to those who had been present at matrimonial negotiations, but a seventeenth-century civilian's notebook now in the Suffolk Record Office in Bury St Edmunds states it as the then current law,[63] and there are many prosecutions for having been present at a clandestine marriage to be found in the act books.[64]

This was a change from the medieval practice in England, when disciplinary action was normally taken only against the couple and (if there were one) the cleric who had joined them together in marriage. The witnesses to the union were not troubled. The indirect but inevitable result of the change was to make it harder to prove marriages. Potential witnesses would naturally have been deterred from helping to prove them, because of the fear of their own excommunication and in part because under the canon law, the testimony of an excommunicated person could not be admitted as legitimate proof.[65] Without proof, there was no way to enforce a contract of marriage. It is true that the canon law made it possible to absolve such persons temporarily (*ad cautelam*) and thus to allow judges to treat their testimony as valid proof.[66] However, this temporary absolution was never a matter of right. The medieval canonists were only enthusiastic about using it as a way of proving the guilt of those they classed as heretics. And at least as it appears in a case recorded in a proctor's notebook now found in the Worcester Record Office, the English courts were unwilling to exercise their discretion in favour of making an exception to the rule excluding the testimony of excommunicates in marriage causes.[67]

The second reason for an increasing difficulty in proving informal marriages was the exclusion of extrajudicial confessions made by the parties from the category of lawful proof. At least such informal confessions seem to have been given less scope than they appear to have been accorded in medieval practice. This is an interesting question (at least for a lawyer), and it ought to figure in assessments of matrimonial litigation. One recognizes at once how often it must have happened that one of the parties to a clandestine marriage contract would have said something afterwards indicating that he (or she) had entered into a marriage contract. People talk. They cannot always help it. Could such a statement be introduced as evidence to prove the existence of the marriage, when the party who made the statement during an unguarded moment later denied its truth? This question was not squarely raised in the English common law, where juries were left to give such weight to evidence like this as they thought proper. In the civilian's world, where there had to be proof by two lawful witnesses or the equivalent, the question raised was whether extrajudicial statements could prevent the party from later denying the substance of the confession. Or, alternatively, could such a statement at least take the place of one witness so as to constitute full proof? If the confession was not conclusive or even probative, it would be harder to enforce a clandestine marriage contract, and fewer people would have sought to do so.

Here the evidence – most of it from the notebooks of proctors and advocates – suggests that at least where either of the parties had entered into a different marriage (which they often did), the extrajudicial confession did not count as conclusive evidence.[68] An example or two will illustrate this. One is a cause from the diocese of Durham in about

1609, where a letter from a man to a woman was signed, "Your loving dnabsuh."[69] The word "dnabsuh" spelled backward is "husband," and the question in the case was whether its use counted as proof of a marriage between them. One might have thought so. What else could it have meant? However, the English ecclesiastical lawyers did not. In the words of the manuscript, "[T]he counsayle of the *doctores* of the Arches [was] that the mariage was not proved." In another cause from about the same time, this one from the diocese of London, a woman being sued for failure to solemnize a marriage was faced with strong evidence that she had previously admitted to having contracted it. She could not deny the confession, but she was allowed to explain that she had never meant to enter into a true marriage. The young man had been sick unto death at the time of her words, and she had said them only to comfort him.[70] She had not believed he would actually recover. But he did, and he sued her to enforce the contract, citing her subsequent confession of having made the initial contract as evidence against her. The manuscript report is not full enough to reveal how this second cause came out, but the fact that the woman made this full argument about what she had meant shows that her prior confession was not treated as conclusive evidence against her. There was support of a sort among the commentators for taking a relatively hard line against according conclusive validity to such confessions,[71] and during the late sixteenth century, the English courts seem to have followed that line.[72]

A third means adopted that discouraged bringing suit upon clandestine marriages lay in stricter application of the general law of evidence. The judges more fully exploited the canonical rule that marriage causes required proof of the clearest kind. Such evidence was not easily uncovered. As an opinion in an early seventeenth-century proctor's notebook now in the Cathedral Library at Canterbury put it, "because marriage causes are arduous and serious," proof in them must be "clearer than the mid-day sun."[73] The judges in the English spiritual courts seem to have acted on this principle – and increasingly so in the sixteenth century – although one assumes that there must have been some variation in practice. It is undeniable that there were cases in which negative sentences were given in suits brought to enforce marriage contracts that otherwise appear to have been sufficiently proved. The sentences are quite hard – indeed impossible – to justify except on the basis of a failure of exacting standards of proof. To a modern student, it is remarkable how often matrimonial litigation descended to minute objections that proof was inconclusive. One finds repeated objections that the testimony of a particular witness was "singular," meaning that it did not agree with the evidence given by another. The lawyer for a defendant in a marriage cause pointed out that one witness testified that his client had said, "I like you … ," whereas the other witness remembered the words as "I thee like …."[74] The difference meant, he argued, that their depositions did not meet the law's basic requirement of valid proof, two reliable witnesses whose testimony agreed. And so it was apparently held.

From a modern perspective, this kind of lawyerly nitpicking seems quite artificial. In practice it nonetheless possessed a certain attractiveness. It meant that fewer men and women were obliged to fulfil a marriage contract that one or both of them had either come to regret or been uncertain about in the first place. For example, in a 1604 cause from the diocese of Ely, during the hearing before the judge both the man and woman admitted to having said, "I am contented to take you as my husband [wife]." Despite this admission, the judge held that this made no marriage.[75] Perhaps it seemed to him that surrounding circumstances were such that the sincerity of their intention to marry was not wholly clear. The words themselves suggested hesitation. And he may also have looked beyond the words. It would have been sensible to do so. A commonplace of the *ius commune* held that in cases of doubt "it was better to elect the more cautious course."[76] For many English judges in the sixteenth century, that course seems to have been not to enforce a marriage contract unless its proof was clear and convincing.

Such an approach was by no means unauthorized under the traditional canon law. The question was always whether the parties had formed the intent to marry and then mutually and openly expressed that intent. The surrounding circumstances and the character of the parties could count in deciding the first part of that question.[77] One may be sympathetic with the English judges in their desire not to force young people into marriage unless they had clearly intended to enter into a lifelong union. The *favor matrimonii* of the canon law was not meant to serve as a means of making it easy to prove the existence of clandestine marriage contracts. There is no denying that one of the by-products of this policy was to create dilemmas of conscience for the parties involved, and from this perspective the Council of Trent was doing something helpful in enacting the simpler rule: no parish priest, no valid marriage. Whether it was also doing right is a different question. Not everyone took an "instrumentalist" view of the subject. One sees the results in the English evidence.

The Prohibited Degrees of Consanguinity and Affinity

The second change in the English Church's marriage law grew out of the reduction in the prohibited degrees of consanguinity and affinity – the medieval rules prohibited marriages between kin too closely related by blood and marriage, unless the man and woman secured a papal dispensation. The old law forbade marriages up to the fourth degree and added a few other prohibitions for good measure. Maitland described all of them as the creation of "the idle ingenuities of men who are amusing themselves by inventing a game."[78] Perhaps that was a little harsh. The canonists did not pass their time by playing board games. A milder form of his view was nonetheless shared by many of the Protestant reformers in England. They desired to simplify the law and to end the trafficking in dispensations to which the old system had led. A Henrician statute, repealed under Mary but revived under Elizabeth, therefore enacted that all voluntary marriages were lawful unless they were forbidden by the Law of God or the book of Leviticus.[79] It was a bold and in some ways a quite admirable step. It promised an end to dispensations and the necessity of paying for them. Some scholars think otherwise, but it requires some explaining to show that there is nothing wrong with declaring a marriage to be contrary to the tenets of the Christian religion and then upholding it as a valid and indissoluble union if the parties are willing (and able) to pay money for it. Under the new regime, that system was to disappear.

To some extent, this laudable aim was achieved. A few dispensations permitting marriages within the prohibited degrees seem to have been issued by the individual bishops or by the Faculty Office, but there were not many.[80] Perhaps it was thought that the authority to issue them at all had disappeared along with papal jurisdiction. However, there was also a "downside" to this. The law of unintended consequences applied here, since the result of the change was to render English ecclesiastical law quite uncertain about what marriages between kin were unlawful. The "trees of consanguinity and affinity" (*arbores consanguinitatis*) familiar in the medieval law had been cast out, but what would take their place? No one knew for sure. The "Law of God" on this subject lacked a defined meaning, and the book of Leviticus was incomplete at best. It became difficult to know who could marry when only the more distant ties of kinship existed between a man and woman. The absence of a system of dispensation only exacerbated the difficulty. The same dilemma arose, it seems, in Scots law.[81]

Some remedial measures were taken in England, most notably a table of prohibited degrees issued by Archbishop Parker in 1564.[82] That table made some things clear, but it left others uncertain. An example of the latter is that it left standing the old rule, one which certainly should have been discarded, that consanguinity arose simply from an act of sexual intercourse, not from marriage. This was an evident source of trouble. An example of the former is that by its own terms it also envisioned that some marriages might be unlawful even though they were not covered by the table. Whether the impediment of crime – applied in some cases where a couple had lived in adultery before marrying – still applied in practice was treated as an open question in one contemporary notebook.[83] In such cases, the couple in question were instructed to "consult men learned in the law; to understand what is lawful, what honest and expedient." This was sometimes done, but what standards the men learned in the law were to use in answering the queries was nowhere made explicit. One supposes they might even have consulted an *arbor consanguinitatis* if they wished.

Many hard cases arose. They have left their traces in the act books and other professional literature of the English civilians, and this literature must reflect widespread uncertainty among the laity whose marriages were affected by the law. One example comes from a manuscript that once was part of a collection in the Berkshire Record Office.[84] The question was whether it was lawful for a man to marry the aunt of his deceased wife. Under the medieval law, they would have been related in the second and third degree of affinity. It had clearly been unlawful under the old law for them to marry without a dispensation. On the other hand, the relationship was not listed in the book of Leviticus or even in Archbishop Parker's table. But as just noted, that factor alone was not determinative. Was such a marriage contrary to God's law? It was not easy to know, and it is no wonder that contemporaries were themselves perplexed. The families may have had other reasons for favouring or opposing the match, but validity depended on the law. Ultimately, two eminent civilians, Sir Julius Caesar and Dr John Hammond, were consulted about the matter. It turned out that they both concluded that the marriage was lawful. How they reached this opinion, the notebook does not provide so much as a hint. Nor does other civilian literature from the time help very much; unhappily the judicious Swinburne did not deal with this question in his famous work *Of Spousals*.[85] Only the movement towards diminishing the scope of the prohibited degrees, a direction also taken by the Council of Trent,[86] is at all certain from a lawyer's point of view. From the perspective of the couple involved in the Trumbull notebook's case, the opinion of counsel found in it may have been the cause for relief, perhaps even for joy. They could be married and, one hopes, live happily together. On the other hand, an opinion of counsel, at least counsel like Sir Julius Caesar, did not come cheap. The couple, or their parents, would have had to pay for it. My own guess – and it is no more than a guess – is that it would have been less expensive to get a papal dispensation.

The result of this development was not limited to the creation of new uncertainty in determining who could lawfully marry that surfaced in instance litigation (*ad instantiam* causes). It also resulted in *ex officio* prosecutions for incest, brought in the ecclesiastical courts and even in the Court of High Commission, when there was doubt about the permissibility of an existing union. For example, Richard Markes was presented for incest before an ecclesiastical tribunal at Hereford for having married his deceased uncle's wife.[87] At York in 1600, William Colson was prosecuted for incest because the second wife of his first wife's father was also the grandmother of the person he had married after his first wife's death.[88] A defendant in a cause heard at Durham in 1592 was tried (and convicted) for incest because (in his own words), "[A]bout six yeres agoe he married Isabella the daughter of Georgia Barre the lait wife of Matthew Erington, deceased, which Matthew was brother on the mother's [side] to this examinate's mother."[89] None of these relationships was found in Archbishop Parker's Table of Prohibited Degrees, but that in itself was not a sufficient defence to a prosecution for incest. Such cases must count as an unintended cost of eliminating the system of papal dispensations without substituting a clear alternative. In modern times, most of us would think that marriages not specifically forbidden should necessarily have been lawful, but that was not the view of the judges of England's ecclesiastical courts.

One thing more needs to be mentioned about this subject. The new regime did not fully end the need for dispensations. Marriages begun without calling of the banns and marriages conducted during the prohibited seasons of Lent and Advent required licenses from the Office of Faculties, and of course these licenses had to be purchased. Without them, men and women who married would be subject to prosecution in the spiritual forum. The records show this happening with some frequency.[90] No doubt a 1640 petition from Kent was exaggerating when it claimed that "almost halfe the yere" had become a forbidden season for marriage.[91] No doubt the drafters were also exaggerating when they claimed the English bishops had "made and contrived illegal canons and constitutions [to] prohibite and grant marriages, neither of them by the rule of Law or Conscience."[92] And no doubt there is some justice in King James I's description of the petitioners who sought to end this regime as men "whose heat tendeth rather to combustion than reformation."[93] However, the drafters of these petitions were not wholly wrong in substance. Money was changing hands for permission to marry. There was something more than religious idealism or simple anti-clericalism standing behind the decision taken in 1653 to replace the law of the church with a regime of purely civil marriages.[94] But this scarcely mattered after 1660. The old regime had returned. The demand for dispensations continued.

Ex officio Offences

In a few areas of the law, the common law courts expanded their competence at the expense of the ecclesiastical courts. This led to a shrinkage of the church's disciplinary jurisdiction. The development should itself be contrasted, however, with a concurrent expansion of ecclesiastical jurisdiction to cover regulation of marriage and sexual offences in new ways. In numerical terms, it seem to have more than made up for the shrinkage. Several examples of expansion in this area of the law occurred during the second half of the sixteenth century and afterwards. The extent of such developments has not always been appreciated by historians, who have concentrated on contemporary attacks against the church and its bishops.[95] Certainly such attacks did occur, but not all were successful, and through them all, enlargements in the scope of ecclesiastical jurisdiction also took place.

First, the sixteenth- and seventeenth-century courts prosecuted married couples – just as they did in the Netherlands (van der Heijden 172) and in the Swiss cantons (Burghartz 187–8) – for having had sexual relations before marriage. The medieval courts normally had not. Many such prosecutions are found in the surviving act books of the sixteenth century.[96] There is an interesting account of this new offence in a circa 1600 civilian's notebook, now at the Borthwick Institute in York. Two proctors pointed out that there was little textual support for it in the ecclesiastical law; in fact the *glossa ordinaria* to the Gregorian Decretals stated, "Matrimony purges all that has gone before."[97] The objection was met by saying that it was the common practice, not to be easily dislodged, in the English courts for such prosecutions to be undertaken.

Moreover, it was said that in doing this the English courts were actually following the common law, which since the council of Merton in 1234 had accorded less force to subsequent marriage than did the *ius commune*. In other words, if there were any illegality involved, the English common law was the culprit. A more overtly spiritual defence of the practice, however, is contained in a manuscript now in Worcester, where the author described prenuptial intercourse as a "secrete poyson which lurkes within marriage" and leads to the encouragement of adultery.[98] Opinions differed. Practice was later returned to its medieval pattern, but only by a statute enacted in 1787.[99]

Second, the offence of "soliciting the chastity" of a maiden began to figure for the first time in the pages of the church's *ex officio* act books during the second half of the sixteenth century. That the development was spurred in any sense by Pope Pius IV's decree of 1561 against clerical solicitation of women, one cannot confidently assert, though I regard it as possible.[100] The language used in the act book prosecutions was designedly archaic – "Thou, Roger Bowyer, at the instigation of the devil, didst attempt to violate the chastity and didst by divers and sundry ways and means attempt to have carnal knowledge of the body of the said Anna."[101] A modern reader cannot avoid being reminded of the modern offence of sexual harassment in reading some of the act book entries. Again, there is unlikely to be any causal link between the two. All the same, the coincidence is thought-provoking, because the substance of the legal wrong was not greatly different.

Third, the offence of harbouring sexual offenders was expanded to encompass the harbouring of pregnant women about to give birth to an illegitimate child. In other words, it was expanded to make unlawful the *result* of illicit sexual relations, not just the sexual relations themselves, and to encompass those who aided the offending couple.[102] Similarly to what we shall find in France, householders were required to see to it that women about to give birth to an illegitimate child were turned out and punished.[103] The post-Reformation act books from all over England contain prosecutions for failures on the part of householders in this circumstance, whereas the surviving medieval act books by and large do not. Some of the stories are quite sad – women about to give birth being turned out into the night. No doubt this development was connected with the sixteenth-century mania about illegitimate children and also has something to do with the parish's responsibilities for them under the Elizabethan Poor Law. However, it was not limited to those concerns, since there were prosecutions begun in which the child was dead at the time of the prosecution or in which the mother and child had fled to a place far away.

Fourth, there was an expansion in making available a remedy for jactitation of marriage. This was an expansion only, because there are very occasional causes related to it in the medieval act books[104] and because it was already in place in at least some courts on the Continent.[105] It is not altogether easy to know why there are so many more brought in England during the early modern period. They were a source of discord and legal uncertainty. The word "jactitation" meant "boasting" falsely of the existence of a valid marriage, typically by a person who claimed to be married to the person bringing the suit. If successful, the defendant was ordered to keep "perpetual silence" and never to repeat the prior boast.[106] The theory was that the boasting was a legal wrong because it damaged the reputation and hindered the marriage prospects of the plaintiff.[107] It raised a controversial question among the advocates early in the seventeenth century: Could a person sued in jactitation bring a separate action to enforce the marriage contract, or were they limited to pleading it in response to the *causa jactitationis*?[108] There was potential overlap, no doubt, but the two remedies seem both to have continued alongside each other in court practice. The wider question of the subsequent history of this remedy remains to be investigated.

Conclusion

Most of the conclusions of this chapter rest on evidence culled from the pre-1640 act books, cause papers, and legal notebooks compiled by ecclesiastical lawyers in England, evaluating the law in terms of change and continuity and speculating about its effects on the English people. This approach differs from that which has been characteristic among many historians, usually those not principally concerned with the canon law or the internal workings of ecclesiastical jurisdiction. They have looked instead at the history of the ecclesiastical courts in terms of their power to compel the obedience of the laity, tracing a gradual but irreversible decline. No doubt there is some merit to that concentration.[109] But it is hard to know the extent to which ordinary men and women had "respect" or only "contempt" for the spiritual tribunals in their hearts. At least the pages of the court records do not tell us. Why should they?

What the records do allow us to do with greater confidence is to reach some conclusions about the nature of matrimonial law and its practice in late medieval and early modern England. They permit us to see elements of both change and continuity over the same period. And both now and in the future they will make it possible to draw some comparisons between the state of things in England and that which obtained on the Continent. When we do, we shall know more about the history of marriage and we shall have a fuller understanding of the inner workings of the canon law. It is in the hope of contributing something to the comparative history of both subjects that this chapter was written.

NOTES

1 The following abbreviations are used in the citation of records found in the archives:

BIHR: Borthwick Institute of Historical Research, York
BL: British Library, London
Bodl.: Bodleian Library, Oxford
CCA: Canterbury Cathedral Archives
CUL: Cambridge University Library
DUL: Durham University Library
HFRO: Herefordshire Record Office, Hereford
LMA: London Metropolitan Archives
RO: Record Office
SKRO: Suffolk Record Office, Bury St Edmunds Branch
WORO: Worcestershire Record Office, The Hive, Worcester

2 The major exception was the Puritan regime of the Interregnum; it instituted civil marriage in 1653, but this change was swept aside in 1660.
3 See Outhwaite 2006, 47–56; Spurr 1991, 209–19.
4 E.g., Lacey 1912.
5 Pollock and Maitland 1898, 2:364–447.
6 Maitland 1898, 39–40.
7 Letter to A.L. Smith (1905), in Maitland, *Letters*, no. 328.
8 Woodcock 1952; Ritchie 1956.
9 See Sheehan 1971; Helmholz 1974.
10 Among book-length works on marriage, see Carlson 1994; Cressy 1997, 233–376; Donahue 2007; Goldberg 1992, 203–66; Hanawalt 1986; Houlbrooke 1979, 55–88; Ingram 1987; McCarthy 2004; McSheffrey 2006; O'Hara 2000; Pedersen 2000; Sheehan 1996; Stone 1990. For the broader history of the subject, the following important works have appeared: Brooke 1989; Brundage 1987; d'Avray 2005; Witte 1997.

11 Cod. 7.45.13.
12 Weigand 1993, 307: "ein Stiefkind der historischen Forschung."
13 See, e.g., Seidel Menchi and Quaglioni 2001. See also Lombardi 2001.
14 See Dean and Lowe 1998; Reynolds and Witte 2007.
15 See, e.g., Arellano and Usunáriz 2005; Hansen 2000; Watt 1992; Poudret 1992.
16 See *Records of the Medieval Ecclesiastical Courts*.
17 Elton 1969, 105: "They take one to the realities."
18 See Stone 1993, 4–7; *Records of the Medieval Ecclesiastical Courts*, 10.
19 See, e.g., Hull 1958, 112–19; *Diocese of Chichester: A Catalogue of the Records*, 16–45.
20 A preliminary look at later reports suggests that the parallel with the common law grew closer; see, e.g., "Ecclesiastical and Admiralty Cases" (ca. 1670–1700), Columbia Law School, New York, MS. M 315; "Proceedings in Ecclesiastical Courts, 1765–69," Spencer Research Library, University of Kansas, Lawrence, KS, MS. E 181.
21 See generally Bryson and Dauchy 2006.
22 Frost c. Frost (1600), Civilian's notebook, Bodl., Tanner MS. 427, f. 14v.
23 See Cheney 1972; Brooks, Helmholz, and Stein 1991.
24 Some evidence on this point is set out in Helmholz 2007.
25 See Stone 1992, 31.
26 20 & 21 Vict. c. 85.
27 Carlson 1994, 141.
28 25 Hen. VIII, c. 19 §7, SR, iii, 460–1; the statute was several times re-enacted; see Helmholz 1990, 36.
29 See X 4.14.3.
30 Gilbert c. Greene (London ca. 1600), Civilian's Casebook, LMA, MS. 011448, f. 2v: "Donariis igitur, consensu partium, carnali copula assensuque parentis etc. precedentibus iustissime contrahatur matrimonium." See also Gottlieb 1993, 79–83.
31 Lee c. Diggins (London ca. 1600), Civilian's Casebook, LMA, MS. 011448, f. 36v.
32 *Gl. ord.* ad X 1.36.11, s.v. "Sacramentum."
33 Pedersen 2000, 105–18.
34 Ex officio c. Lowes (Canterbury 1595), CCA, Act book X.8.15, f. 52v: "[F]atetur that by consent ex utraque parte before the mayor of Maydstone he and his wife doe lyve aparte."
35 32 Hen. VIII, c. 38, SR, iii, 792 (1540), repealed by 2 & 3 Edw. VI, c. 23, SR, iv, 68–9 (1548).
36 2 & 3 Edw. VI, c. 21, SR, iv, 66–7 (1548).

37 25 Hen. VIII, c. 22, 4 (1533–4), SR, iii, 466–7; 28 Hen. VIII, c. 7, 7 (1536), SR, iii, 658; 32 Hen. VIII, c. 38 (1540), SR, iii, 792–3.
38 See the Canons of 1604, c. 62 (on marriage by banns or license), in *Anglican Canons*, 352–3. Another example is the legislation permitting the clergy to marry, which was passed both by Parliament and Convocation; see Parish 2000, 180–1.
39 The greatest exception was Lord Hardwicke's Marriage Act, 26 Geo. II, c. 33 (1753), and it operated only by indirection to curb the jurisdiction of the courts. See Parker 1990 and, in this volume, Donahue 37.
40 See, e.g., Brinkworth 1972.
41 Walsham 2006, 69–73.
42 X 5.34.1.
43 See Whitman 2008.
44 It was abolished by statute. See 16 Car. I, c. 11 (1640), SR, v, 112–13, confirmed by 13 Car. II, c. 12 § 4 (1661), SR, v, 315–16.
45 Ex officio c. Knight, Civilian's notebook, Bodl., Tanner MS. 427, f. 10.
46 See, e.g., Graves v. Blanchet (1704), 2 Salk. 696, 91 Eng. Rep. 589.
47 25 Hen. VIII, c. 6, SR, iii, 441–2.
48 18 Eliz. I, c. 3 § 1, SR, iv, 610.
49 1 Jac. I, c. 11, SR, iv, 1028.
50 See, e.g., Addy 1989, 113–58.
51 See McIntosh 1998.
52 See Makower 1895, § 61; Rodes 1991, 23–32.
53 See, e.g., Rame c. Mende (Archdeaconry of Essex 1577), in *Precedents and Proceedings in Criminal Causes*, no. 515.
54 Anon. (ca. 1620), Civilian's Casebook, LMA, MS. 011448, f. 189.
55 Gilbert c. Greene (ca. 1600), ibid., f. 1.
56 See Helmholz 2004, 267, 555.
57 Thorsby c. Thorsby (London ca. 1600), Civilian's Casebook, LMA, MS. 011448, f. 2v: "Dr Crompton sayd that reconciliatio impedit causam et intentionem divortii."
58 Anon. (ca. 1600), Civilian's Casebook, LMA, MS. 011448, f. 69.
59 See also Wunderli 1981, 118–21.
60 Ingram 1987, 192.
61 For Italy, see Lombardi 105 and Seidel Menchi 339.
62 E.g., The Hampton Court Conference (1604), recorded in Cressy and Ferrell 1996, 125.
63 SKRO, MS. E 14/11/7, no. 20: "All those that are present at a clandestine mariage are ipso facto excommunicated as well as those that were maried."

64 E.g., Ex officio c. William Danbye (Gloucester 1600), Gloucester RO, Act book GDR 86, 156: "for being presente at Mr. Birchhis marriadge being solemnized without bannes askinge or a lawful dispensaion from the ordinary."

65 Hostiensis, *Summa aurea*, Lib. II, tit. *de testibus*, no. 2(m): "[N]on admittitur aliquis, nisi sit fidelis conversationis [citing X 2.20.23], inde est quod excommunicatus testificari non potest."

66 X 2.20.38.

67 Barniston c. Barniston (ca. 1600), Civilian's Notebook "Collectanea B," WORO, MS. 794.093, BA 2470, p. 3.

68 Civilian's Casebook, LMA, MS. 011448, f. 38: "Donaria, cohabitatio, prolis susceptio, nominatio probant matrimonium sed non ad dirimendum sequens matrimonium solemnizatum." There is a full consideration of difficulties that stemmed from clandestine marriages in "Matthew Tabor's book, 1627–29," Somerset RO, D/D/O, fols. 45–50v.

69 Clement Colmore's Book, DUL, DDR/XVIII/3, fols. 231–31v.

70 Web c. Bridges, Civilian's notebook, Bodl., Tanner MS. 427, f. 34.

71 See Mascardus, *Conclusiones probationum*, Lib. II, concl. 1029.

72 Killingworthe c. Harries (London ca. 1600), Civilian's Casebook, LMA, MS. 011448: opinion that a confession of a contract was not sufficient proof of marriage where the contract itself was not sufficiently proved.

73 Taken from Precedent book, CCA, Z.3.27, fols. 70–4, taken from a suit to establish a marriage: Toby Andrews c. Agnes Bylle, with William Prynne intervening *pro interesse suo*. See Valsecchi 1999.

74 Green c. Pashal (London ca. 1600), Civilian's notebook, Bodl., Tanner MS. 427, f. 202v.

75 Ex officio c. Robert Williamson and Margaret Pickeringe, CUL, Act book EDR D/2/23, fols. 22v–23.

76 Gilbert c. Greene (London ca. 1605), Civilian's Casebook, LMA, MS. 011448, f. 1.

77 Other examples: Smart c. Rowe (1602), Civilian's notebook, Bodl., Tanner MS. 427, f. 212 (marriage contract, although proved, held not to bind because made *iocose*); Curson c. Jaxson (1601), ibid., fols. 188v–189 (marriage contract, although admitted, attacked as invalid because one of the parties was of "very weake and simple witte not understanding what a contract meanithe"); Zinzan c. Skelley (ca. 1627), Bodl., Tanner MS. 176, f. 168 (marriage contract attacked as having been made while drunk).

78 Pollock and Maitland 1898, 2:389.

79 32 Hen. VIII c. 38 (1540), SR, iii, 792; 1 Eliz. I, c. 1 § 3 (1559), SR, iv, 351.

80 See Hooper 1910.

81 Sellar 1992, 123–4. Indeed it seems to have been encountered in Calvin's Geneva; see Witte 1998, 24–5, 42. The subject of prohibited degrees of consanguinity and affinity is treated elsewhere (Donahue 34–5 and van der Heijden 161).

82 Cardwell, *Annals of the Reformed Church of England*, 1:316–20.

83 Note in Civilian's Casebook, LMA, MS. 011448, f. 41: "Quaere whether the statute ... [is] understood onlie touching the degree of mariadge."

84 It was Trumbull MS. (1588–1617), D/ED O 48, p. 155. It has now gone either to the Cambridge University Library or the British Library.

85 Swinburne, *Treatise of Spousals*. See Derrett and Martin 1973.

86 Esmein 1891, 2:261–6.

87 HFRO, HD/5 (Visitation book 1584), s.d. 5 May. No result survives. John Coal was similarly presented in 1632 in the diocese of Gloucester for marrying the widow of his uncle: Gloucestershire RO, Gloucester, Act book GDR 179, f. 125v. He was excommunicated after failing to appear.

88 Ex officio c. William Colson and Isabella Moore al. Colson, BIHR, CP.H.5. They were divorced after this had been proved.

89 Ex officio c. Ogle, DUL, DDR IV/3, f. 27. The defendant in the case produced a letter in his favour, but the record concludes the judge's statement, "that he could shew him no favour in that matter for that it was against the lawes of god and man."

90 E.g., Ex officio c. Longe and Knowles (Archdeaconry of Buckingham 1600), Buckinghamshire RO, Aylesbury, D/A.C.25, f. 166: "for being maried upon Shrove Monday last without licence beinge tyme prohibited."

91 "Kent Petition against Episcopacy," No. 20, in *Proceedings in Connection with the Parliaments called in 1640*, 35. An earlier example from 1580 is noted in Strype 1822, Art. 13.

92 "Kent Petition," *Proceedings in Connection with the Parliaments called in 1640*, 30.

93 *Royal Proclamations of King James I*, No. 30, 62.

94 The point is well made in Durston 1996, 215–16.

95 See, e.g., Hill 1956.

96 E.g., Ex officio c. John Gortlie (Archdeaconry of Berkshire 1599), Berkshire RO, Reading, Act book D/A 2/c 42, f. 56v: the defendant admitted that he and his wife "beinge man and wiffe betwene themselves he had carnal knowledge of her body aboute half a year before he was openly married unto her in the church." He was assigned public penance upon this confession.

97 BIHR, Prec. Bk. 11, f. 31, and see *gl. ord.* ad X 4.17.6 s.v. "legitimi": "[M]atrimonium omnia praecedentia purgat."

98 Civilian's Notebook "Collectanea B" (seventeenth century), WORO, MS. 794.093, BA 2470, p. 179.

99 27 Geo. III, c. 44 § 2.

100 See Haliczer 1996, 42–5; Prosperi 1996, 508–42; Romeo 1998, 163–97; and Romeo 2008, 190–5.

101 Precedent book (ca. 1600), CUL, MS. EDR F/5/43, f. 67.

102 For medieval practice, see Poos 2001, s.v. "harboring, fostering, enabling illicit sexual activity." For the Kingdom of France, see Lefebvre-Teillard 278.

103 Evidence on this subject is set out in Helmholz 1998, 258.

104 Ex officio c. Shotleche (London 1512), Act book, LMA, MS. 09064/11, f. 40, "quod iactitavit se commississe adulterium cum Joanna Johnson."

105 Donahue 2007, 308.

106 See Ingram 1987, 59–60. For the same offence in Italy see Lombardi 116 and 121n64.

107 Conset, *Practice of the Ecclesiastical Courts*, pt. 6, no. 3, 257–8.

108 See "Proctor's Summary of Procedural Law," Wiltshire RO, Trowbridge, D 5/24/18, fols. 34–34v.

109 See, e.g., Manning 1969, 212–17; Price 1942.

SECTION II

Licit and Illicit

Chapter 5

Marriage Formation: Law and Custom in the Low Countries 1500–1700

MANON VAN DER HEIJDEN

Introduction

In the late Middle Ages the canon law dictates on marriage formation were pronounced and enforced in church courts in Western Christendom.[1] The belief that marriage was sacramental by nature had resulted in increasing ecclesiastical control over marriage from the twelfth century onward. Protestant reformers, however, insisted that marriage was a worldly matter, subject to the state, not the church. This led reformers in the Netherlands to make legal changes concerning marriage. First, as a consequence of marriage's loss of sacramental status, some marriage rules were loosened while others were strengthened. But most importantly, in Protestant areas, provincial and city councils took over the task of making marriage laws, while urban courts took responsibility for enforcing the moral code. Although lacking legal competence and focused on different issues, church councils of the Reformed Church – consistories – exercised control over the moral behaviour of their Protestant followers as well. This chapter will examine the ways traditional church marriage doctrines were altered in Protestant laws and in matrimonial litigation before secular courts and Protestant consistories in the Netherlands in the sixteenth and seventeenth centuries. It will focus on changing ideas about the marriage contract: the creation of marriage, the interpretations of valid marriages, and the issue of parental consent.[2]

The Role of Secular Courts in Pre-Reformation Holland

As we have seen in the opening chapter, the Catholic Church expanded its control and its jurisdiction over marriage during the course of the

Middle Ages.[3] In the Netherlands, too, marriage was in this period regulated by the church.[4] Secular courts, however, kept or gained control over a few matters, and in a few instances secular law even replaced canon law. In particular, secular authorities in the whole of Western Christendom tended to discourage clandestine marriages by inflicting civil penalties on individuals for contracting them.[5] In the Low Countries, secular law sometimes inflicted penalties in case of marriage-related offences as well. Issues related to disturbing civil order – such as prostitution, adultery, or marital disputes – were handled by secular civil or criminal courts. Dutch magistrates usually dealt with all matrimonial cases that involved disturbing the peace.[6] Some town councils, for instance, made rules prohibiting disturbances during marriage ceremonies. These were aimed at such traditional customs as neighbours and other town inhabitants stopping the bride and groom on the church steps and refusing to let the couple proceed until the couple fully satisfied them with food and drink.[7] Police officers arrested couples especially for public disorder resulting from marital rows or other violence between spouses. Such disturbances could involve neighbours as well, who often complained because they wanted to keep the peace in their neighbourhood or otherwise protect its good name and reputation.[8]

Like ecclesiastical authorities, secular authorities attempted to expand their control over marriage. Although most town councils fully subscribed to church morality and regulations of the church regarding the formation of marriage, they did so with a different accent. While the church focused on enforcing proclamation of the banns and solemnization in church, the secular authorities stressed parental consent and protection of familial interests in controlling who inherited property. City magistrates sometimes disregarded the canonical rule that public solemnization was not necessary for a valid marriage because this rule would interfere with parental interests. The differences in the secular approach were evident in town ordinances and civil court judgments. At a higher level, moreover, Charles V, king of Spain and sovereign over the Netherlands, also supported the customs pertaining to parental consent. In an edict of 1540 he stipulated that females under 20 and males under 25 could enter into marriage only with the full consent of their parents. Orphans were required to ask permission of either their closest living kin or the magistrates of their place of residence.[9] Following canon law, secular law did not declare such marriages invalid, but civil law could inflict various penalties pertaining to property. Individuals who married when under age without parental permission were excluded from their dowries and other material profit deriving from the marriage. In some towns similar arrangements to protect family property interests had already been made by town magistrates in the fourteenth century; many towns followed as soon as Charles V's edict was publicly announced. Obviously, such stipulations were relevant for the upper classes only, however.[10]

Institutional Changes in the Age of Reformation

The Reformation offered both secular and ecclesiastical authorities the opportunity to reconsider various areas of canon law, foremost among them the law of marriage and divorce. Luther and other reformers – including John Calvin, whose thought guided the Dutch Protestant Reformation – questioned whether marriage should be regarded as a sacrament. Calvin rejected the Catholic conviction that celibacy was superior to matrimony, insisting that a married life with sexual activity was in no way less valuable than a celibate life. He asserted that marriage was a sacred institution created by God, but – like all reformers – he did not accept the Catholic belief that marriage was a sacrament.[11] Accordingly, reformers proclaimed marriage to be a public and secular matter which should be treated as such, and not a church matter. These thoughts had major consequences for all Western countries converting to the (Protestant) Reformed religion, because they implied that marriage was subject to the state rather than the church. The northern parts of the Low Countries underwent this institutional and moral transformation as well (see Figure 4).

In 1566 the Governor-General of the Netherlands, Margaret of Parma, granted freedom of religion, which allowed Protestant clergymen to take over Catholic churches. Although nearly half of the Dutch population remained Catholic, after 1572 the Reformed Church became the dominant religion, certainly in the province of Holland. While marriage was transformed in various significant aspects by the new Protestant ideas, clerical control of marriage was reduced to ecclesiastical reprimands, which applied to Protestant believers only.[12]

In the short term, the most radical change did not concern the moral code but rather the institutional framework of marriage control. Since Protestant reformers believed that marriage was sacred but not sacramental, marriage was considered a worldly matter that should be supervised by the secular authorities. Secular governments should thus take responsibility for all matrimonial issues, or at least establish and enforce

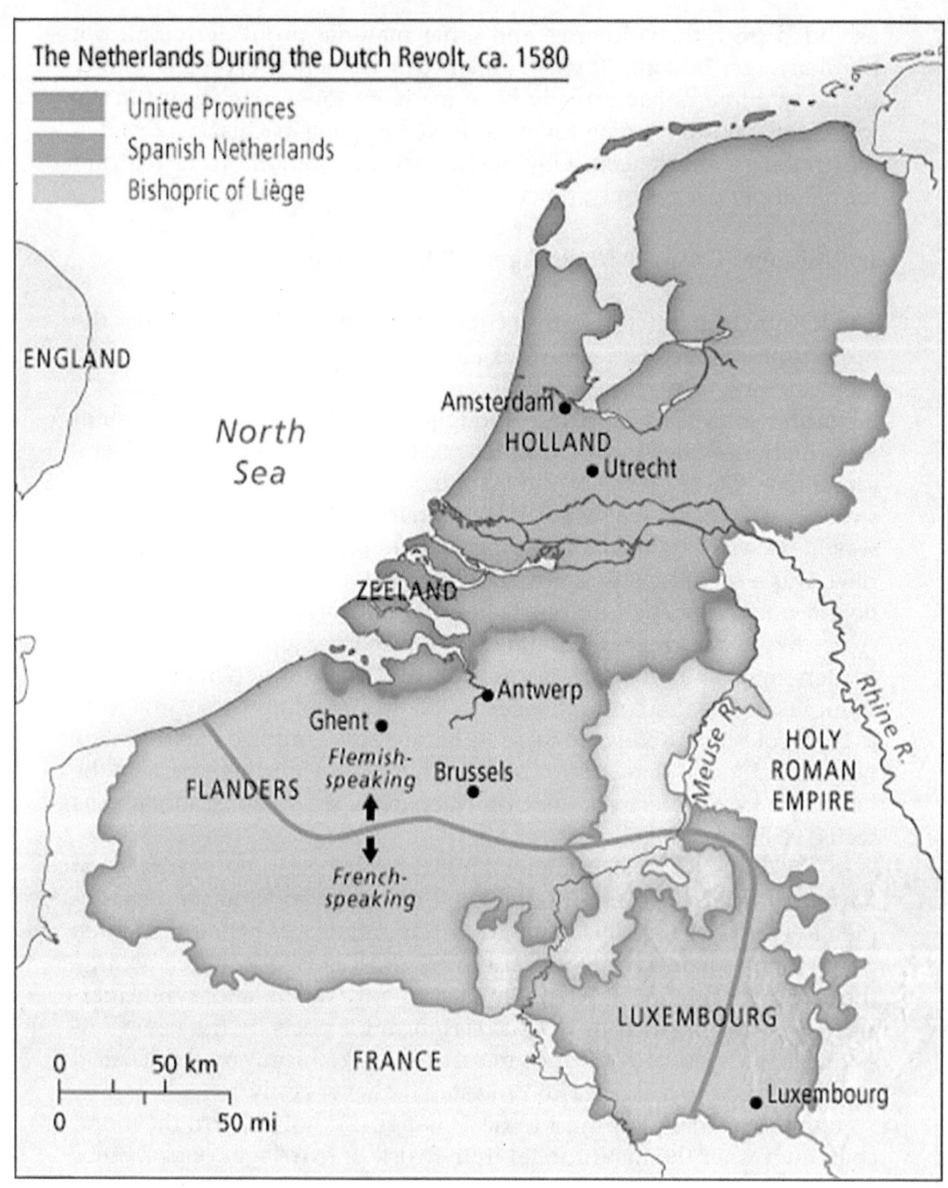

Figure 4. The Dutch Republic, ca. 1580.

marriage laws. Indeed, reorganization of marriage law and legislation began the moment Holland and Zeeland revolted against their Catholic monarch, Philip II, in 1572 (Dutch Revolt, 1568–1648). The new Dutch Republic remained at war with its former monarch until it became officially independent in 1648, meanwhile losing Flanders and parts of Brabant to Spain between 1568 and 1648. Roughly speaking, the southern parts of the Low Countries remained Catholic, while the northern parts converted to Protestantism.[13] In the northern Netherlands, important basic laws were initiated by the province of Holland, now that region's most powerful government. However, most regulations were drafted by town magistrates, who usually dealt with matrimonial matters in their criminal or civil courts. Only exceptional marriage cases, mostly related to contract disputes among the urban elites, were brought to higher courts. Unlike towns in Switzerland (such as Basel, Berne, and Zurich), Dutch towns did not create new tribunals to deal with matrimonial litigation.[14] Secular governments simply incorporated marriage regulations and enforcement into the existing legal system: violators of marriage laws thus came before secular criminal courts.

Although Protestants declared marriage a secular matter, it continued to be a divine institution, and matrimonial matters remained the concern of the church and clergymen. Protestant reformers did not have the competence – which their Catholic predecessors had had – to make laws or to enforce regulations, but they could control their own church members through ecclesiastical discipline, and they did. While secular authorities took over matrimonial jurisdiction, reformers instituted their own Protestant consistories in almost every town in Holland. Composed of clergymen and Protestant magistrates, these consistories kept an eye on their church members' behaviour, especially moral conduct pertaining to marriage and sexuality. Those who treated the Protestant moral code with contempt could expect a visit from the church at home; individuals who failed to improve their behaviour were excluded from the Lord's Supper until they mended their ways.[15]

Moral Change

In the short run, the influence of the Protestant Reformation was visible particularly in the novel reallocation of responsibilities pertaining to marriage that we have just seen. In the long run, however, Protestant thought regarding the formation and dissolution of marriage resulted in much more significant changes. First, Protestant reformers put different emphases on the purpose of marriage. They indeed affirmed the considerable religious value of marriage, recognizing the same principal purposes of matrimony as those described by Catholic theologians. But whereas canon law defined reproduction as the most important goal of marriage, Protestant reformers put more emphasis on marital love. Calvin and Luther did not think procreation was of lesser importance than love, but they considered it the work of God himself. The ultimate purpose of marriage was the loving union between man and wife, because love and companionship was the bond that kept men and women together. These beliefs were strongly expressed in the teachings of the Reformed Church.[16]

A second important change concerned parental consent. In the first and third chapters of this book we have seen how at the Council of Trent the Catholic Church declared marriages without public solemnization and witnesses to be invalid – partly to support parents' interests pertaining to property – but it did not change the rules on parental permission. Therefore, under canon law, children who were of age could still enter into marriage without their parents' permission (or against their will).[17] In contrast, because the Reformed Church understood parental authority as an extension of divine authority, sons under the age of 25 and daughters under 20 were supposed to obtain the full consent of their parents before marrying. According to Reformed rules only marriage vows made with parental consent were valid, and consequently marriages without parental permission or proclamation of the banns were invalid.[18]

The third and perhaps most significant change instituted by reformers concerned the dissolution of marriage. According to canon law – unless one of the spouses died – a marriage was essentially indissoluble. Because the Roman Catholic Church had had a jurisdictional and legal monopoly over marital affairs in the late Middle Ages, it had had the power to outlaw divorce entirely. The church had only allowed the so-called *divortium quoad mensam et thorum*, or separation from bed and board. However, this separation did not end the conjugal union; it permitted spouses only to split up their households; that is, it suspended spouses' obligation to live together.[19] After the Reformation the *divortium quoad mensam et thorum* remained in existence, but reformers also allowed divorce *quoad vinculum*, that is full divorce, the ultimate consequence of the non-sacramental status of marriage. Even so, divorce had strict limitations and was allowed only in case of malicious abandonment or proven adultery. Only the innocent spouse was allowed to request such a divorce in civil court. The main argument behind permitting divorce was that the *divortium quoad mensam et thorum* was clearly unfair to the innocent party.[20]

Although several crucial changes took place after the Reformation, most rules concerning marriage in fact remained the same. Reformers adopted the existing canonical rules unless they were inconsistent with the Holy Bible or Roman law. Marriage promises could only be broken by mutual consent or for valid reasons put forward by one of the parties. The reformers continued to sometimes allow a breach of promise, but illegal breaches were handled with less leniency and did have consequences for the party who had breached his or her promise without valid reasons. One could be forced to marry when untrue or invalid reasons were given. Marriage prohibitions up to the fourth degree of kinship, which had been instituted by the Catholic Church, remained in effect. Both Luther and Calvin discussed the reduction of the forbidden degrees, arguing that the Catholic Church had profited from these regulations by selling dispensations from them. Calvin saw no biblical ground for prohibiting marriages between first cousins but accepted the prohibition against such marriages as being deeply rooted in custom. However, he clearly reduced the ban on marriages between relatives from the fourth to the second degree of consanguinity.[21]

Marriage Formation and the Law

A few years after the start of the Dutch Revolt and Holland's conversion to the Reformed religion, Holland created a whole new set of laws to implement Reformed ideals regarding marriage. The Political Act of 1580 addressed most of the important Protestant marriage-related issues: the transfer of jurisdiction from church to state, the formation of marriage, and parental permission, as well as older issues that had to be reconsidered because they were now handled by secular courts, such as adultery and the forbidden degrees of consanguinity.[22] The focus here is on the issues of marriage formation and consent.

We will start with the new rules regarding marriage formation. Lawmakers were very aware that they were living in an age of transformation. The new rules requiring public proclamation rendered invalid marriages made by mutual consent that had been valid for centuries under canon law (until the Council of Trent decrees in 1563) and were still well-established custom and widely practised in the Netherlands in the 1570s. The secular authorities therefore made an exception for those who had entered into marriage before 1580, when the new Protestant laws came into effect. Individuals who had married without public proclamation and solemnization in the church, and lived together as man and wife before the announcement of the Political Ordinance, were considered officially married. Criminal courts strictly followed this rule.

The following case was heard by the Criminal Court in Delft, Criminal sentence book no. 46, 10 February 1588.

Joris Centen and Maritgen Jaspers exchanged marriage vows followed by sexual intercourse in 1577. Thereafter the couple lived as man and wife and the marriage produced several children who all died. However, in 1588 Joris and Maritgen mutually freed each other from their marriage promises, and both entered new sexual relationships, assuming that they could now lead separate lives because they had put an end to their own marriage. Although their action was not approved by the church or the law, they clearly believed that such a mutual annulment was valid. The criminal court of Delft, however, thought otherwise. Although they had exchanged clandestine marriage vows, their marriage was identified as being legal and valid, because they had exchanged those vows before the act of 1580. According to the act of 1580 a clandestine marriage that was realized before 1580 was identified as being legal and valid, and therefore indissoluble. The court of Delft clearly followed the reasoning of the act of 1580. The statement of the court was as follows:

> "They have lived with each other as man and wife within a shared household and shared their bed for 11 years continuously confirming their marriage promises, and having had several children who died, they are therefore according to the political ordinance of this country identified as married people."

Sentence:

The court sentenced both spouses to 50 years' banishment for committing adultery (the punishment prescribed by the Political Act of 1580).

However, individuals who wished to be married after the 1580 announcement had to report themselves to the magistrate or church of their hometown. The names of the couple would be published (publication of the banns) three times on successive Sundays in order to give parents, relatives, and any others who might be involved the chance to bring forward impediments. Members of the Reformed religion usually married in church, while Catholics and adherents of other religions married in city hall.

The law of 1580 also made parental permission necessary for all minors entering into marriage. It was still possible for young adults to marry without the approval of their parents, but they had to use a special procedure that involved the secular court and the Protestant consistory. This procedure was intended to give parents a final opportunity to be involved in their children's marriage choices. In order to try to reconcile the parties, parents who refused their children's choice were asked to explain their reasons before either magistrates or clergymen. Children whose parents persisted in their opposition would go to court to get permission to marry from the magistrates. Lawyers questioned this roundabout procedure, arguing that it gave parents opportunities to abuse their power and obstruct their adult children's marriages, especially because they could go to higher courts for an appeal, whereas their children could not.[23] Historians have debated whether parents actually took advantage of these options, some insisting that it happened frequently, others concluding that dissatisfied parents rarely went to higher courts to obstruct a child's marriage. The latter opinion was shared by the eighteenth-century Dutch lawyer Eduard van Zurk, who found that parents rarely took legal actions to impede their adult children's marriages, and when they did, the children usually won the case.[24]

Marriage Contracts and the Criminal Court

How were the new rules on marriage formation implemented in criminal court? The Political Act of 1580 had made all sexual intercourse outside wedlock punishable by law. Couples who shared a bed as husband and wife after exchanging clandestine marriage vows violated the marriage laws. The new rules were clear, but long-standing traditions hindered the effective implementation of such rules for decades. Individuals accused by the public prosecutor of fornication after having exchanged marriage promises all stated bluntly that they had done nothing wrong because they were engaged to be married. They might sometimes have exaggerated their ignorance about the marriage rules to plead their case, but well into the seventeenth century girls openly admitted that they had had sexual intercourse only after receiving a promise of marriage, often proving it with a written statement, a marriage coin that would confirm the commitment, or a ring that symbolized their marriage promise. The following case is one of many examples.

Heard by the Criminal Court of Rotterdam, Sentence book no. 246, 14 May 1626.

Janneke Claes from the city of Delft exchanged words of marriage with Roeloff van Bremen, a sailor from the harbour of Rotterdam, stating that he "… had promised to marry and honour her and that he bought her a ring to confirm his faithfulness, that she thereafter also slept with him for two nights, after which he took off and never returned."

Decision: The criminal court acquitted her of the charge of fornication.

Janneke certainly should have known better: the Political Act was more than 40 years old and it must have been common knowledge that any form of premarital sex was forbidden by law. Fornicators could receive banishments up to 25 years and at least risked imprisonment on bread and water. However, criminal courts showed a certain flexibility, sometimes deviating from the letter of the law. As long as there were no impediments to the marriage (earlier promises, blood ties, etc.), the magistrates were generally mild in their sentences, often simply reprimanding the couples for their loose behaviour and pointing out to them that their marriage promises were binding.[25] In implementing the rules secular courts thus carefully combined marriage laws and long-standing traditions. The magistrates' ambiguous stance could cause confusion about the status of marriage promises among young individuals. Indeed, the courts had to deal with many cases in which two lovers told different stories about their alleged engagement. Young men in particular were confronted with a dilemma after a promise of marriage: claiming that they had slept with the young women with serious intentions and only after exchanging promises meant that marriage was practically inevitable, but claiming that there had been no such promises made them guilty of fornication. The following case clearly shows this dilemma:

Criminal Court of Rotterdam, Confession book no. 60, 25 March 1681.

Isaacq de Klerck was accused of fornication because he had had sexual intercourse with Petronella Pieters without being married.

> He confessed that he "had committed himself with marriage words to Petronella Pieters." In the same statement however he said that "he had said that he would marry her, but that he wasn't engaged to her."
>
> The court clearly found his statements ambiguous, and they therefore sentenced him to twenty-four hours' imprisonment.

The flexible attitudes of the Dutch courts were not exceptional in western Europe. Evidence from Switzerland, England, Scotland, and Germany demonstrates that courts everywhere in Protestant areas tended to follow pre-Reformation traditions, considering marriage contracts binding from the moment of consent, not from the formalization of marriage in church.[26] For Neuchâtel, Jeffrey Watt observed that Protestant judges began showing greater flexibility in the seventeenth century, but such conclusions could not be drawn from our Dutch material.[27] Also, comparing the stance of Catholic courts with that of Protestant judges might put the image of growing flexibility in Protestant areas in a different perspective. Thomas Safley, for example, demonstrated that the secular authorities in Protestant areas of southwest Germany were much more stringent in prosecuting infringements of marriage laws than were their Catholic counterparts.[28]

According to the letter of the law, only marriage vows made publicly in church or city hall were valid, but in practice the courts again tended to follow pre-Reformation norms. Judges and plaintiffs often did not distinguish between clandestine marriage promises and public marriage promises; both were accepted by the judges in court. Furthermore, premarital sexual intercourse was allowed as long as couples were engaged to be married. To avoid further breaching of the marriage laws, judges saw to it that such clandestine marriage promises were ultimately solemnized in church or at city hall. The dichotomy between law and practice gave rise to problems concerning the validity of marriage contracts. What proof would young people, and especially young women, need that they had actually received a promise from their alleged fiancés? In such cases, magistrates were convinced only when the woman in question had an impeccable reputation or when she could support her claims with written statements and material evidence. The public support of neighbours or other witnesses might help to convince the judges as well.[29] The courts dealt with a whole spectrum of plaintiffs from a variety of socio-economic levels, each with different intentions and motivations. Obviously, young people whose families were well off and who enjoyed a spotless reputation were usually treated kindly by the magistrates. At the other end of the spectrum, young men and women who had openly slept with each other without the intention of eventually marrying were treated as criminals who had violated the marriage laws.[30]

Marriage Promises Handled by Protestant Consistories

Criminal courts were clearly lenient in their treatment of marriage formation cases. Public prosecutors were reluctant to arrest individuals for breaching marriage promises without the consent of the church or the courts, but they did take action when people openly engaged in sexual relations. How did attitudes in Protestant consistories compare? Before analysing the church's attitudes towards marriage formation, we'll have to keep in mind that the consistories could only discipline their own church members using ecclesiastical sanctions, such as exclusion from the Lord's Supper and excommunication. Furthermore, whereas the criminal courts were intended to try violators of the criminal law, the consistories' purpose was to reconcile church members with the church. Clergymen enforced ecclesiastical discipline on church members to bring their marital behaviour in line with the Protestant moral code. While secular prosecutors primarily brought marriage formation cases to court when unmarried couples had openly engaged in sexual activity, clergymen were much stricter in following the letter of the law.[31]

It appears that most problems pertaining to the validity of marriage contracts involved only the alleged fiancés themselves. Nearly 70 per cent of all premarital cases handled by consistories in Holland in the sixteenth and seventeenth centuries (1572–1700) were in some way related to the breaching of a marriage promise (the breaking of an engagement). Sometimes the lack of parental consent was an issue that had to be dealt with as well, but such cases made up only 11 per cent of the affairs related to premarital issues treated by the consistories. The rules on parental consent in the Political Act of 1580 were clear: minors needed their parents' consent when entering into marriage. Despite that, both parents and children had difficulty accepting the new rules; well into the seventeenth century consistories had to point out to minors that parental permission was required and to parents that their adult children were free to marry without their consent if there were no legal impediments. In 1660 the consistory of Rotterdam still felt it necessary to again announce publicly – explicitly referring to the Political

Act of 1580 – that "from now on no [minor] person may announce the banns before showing their parents' approval."[32]

Most problems involving parental consent came to the authorities' attention when parents submitted complaints to the consistory, protesting that their children had announced their marriages without informing their families. The clergymen followed the letter of the law: all such engagements were illegal and invalid even if the marriage promises were followed by sexual intercourse. However, consistories were sometimes unsure about the competence of the church in matters related to marriage promises, and they put the question to the National Synod of the Reformed Church. In 1581 the National Synod instructed the clergy to advise couples to bring their cases to civil court because the church lacked jurisdiction over such matters.[33] Church records show that pre-Reformation marriage formation customs were still in use even decades after the promulgation of the Political Act.

The following case is recorded in the Consistory Notes of Rotterdam no. 4, 24 June 1654.

After announcing their upcoming marriage for the first time in church on June 7, minors Jannetje Jans and Abraham Willemsen were stopped by his mother, who complained to the consistory that she had not given them her permission. The consistory arranged for a discussion between Abraham's mother and stepfather and the couple, after which the consistory decided that:

1. The proclamation of the banns would cease.
2. The young man was reprimanded with exclusion from the Lord's Supper because he got engaged without his mother's consent.
3. If Jannetje was pregnant, she should go to city hall to the civil court in order to get alimony for her child from Abraham.

The consistories would support a young woman in getting a statement of honour (a written statement confirming that a young woman had acted faithfully and morally) with which she could save her reputation or which might help her obtain child support in a civil court for her illegitimate child, but they would not insist on a marriage as long as parental consent was lacking. Furthermore, as the previous case shows, children were excluded from the Lord's Supper when they had not followed the rules regarding parental consent.

In line with the Protestant emphasis on the value of parental authority, clergymen also punished adult children who withheld information of their intended marriage from their parents. The clergy regularly expressed concern about young people's disregarding of their parents' wishes and insisted that parents be treated with respect. The consistories' primary goal was to bring children and parents together in harmony, and they went to great lengths to reconcile the parties after such disagreements.[34]

More complicated problems arose when one member of a couple breached a clandestine marriage promise, especially because secular courts still accepted pre-Reformation norms. Until the end of the sixteenth century, the confusion was limited to certain cases. A woman who had exchanged clandestine marriage promises lost her rights the moment her lover had marriage banns proclaimed with a new bride in church or at city hall. Public marriage promises with witnesses were thus always favoured over clandestine marriage promises. Until the end of the sixteenth century consistories strictly observed the regulations of the Political Act of 1580. Clergymen insisted that only public promises were identified as an official engagement and clandestine marriage promises were not binding. Those who had exchanged marriage vows the traditional way (by mutual consent and without public proclamation or solemnization in the church) before the Political Act of 1580 were considered lawfully married.

The following case is recorded in the Consistory Notes of Delft no. 2, 24 February 1592.

When Aeltje Elias was caught living with her alleged husband after only having exchanged clandestine marriage vows, the consistory stated:

> "… that secret [clandestine] vows between two persons do not make a marriage, but public announcement, confirmations, and consecration to consummate the marriage do."

Clearly, the clergymen were of the opinion that Aeltje and her husband did not have a valid marriage, because they had exchanged marriage vows by mutual consent and without public proclamation and solemnization in the church. However, as such cases were considered a secular matter, the clergymen sent the case to the Commissionaires of Marriage Affairs, who were the secular officials for civil marriage matters.

In 1598, a couple asked the consistory if they should publicly affirm their marriage because they had been living as man and wife for 25 years and had had many children. The clergymen told them that this was not necessary because they had lived in a decent household as man and wife and their marriage was thus recognized.[35] However, during the first decades after the Act of 1580, in the vast majority of cases consistories defined the validity of disputed marriage contracts according to the letter of the law: a marriage contract was valid only after public proclamation of the banns. Difficult or ambiguous cases were sent to the secular magistrates, who over time became responsible for all matrimonial legal matters.[36]

However, things changed in the seventeenth century, when consistories began to realize that even after 20 years of Protestant law the divergence between Protestant rules and pre-Reformation customs had not been resolved. It appears that they were confronted with canon law marriage traditions on a daily basis in their parishes, because consistory notes begin to show Protestant clergymen using traditional canon law terminology – such as *copula carnalis* and *verba de presenti*. Their interpretation of such vocabulary, however, was based on a combination of canon law traditions and Protestant notions. In 1652, for example, the consistory of Rotterdam claimed that a couple who had exchanged marriage vows in the presence of witnesses and with permission of their family and friends was to be held as man and wife "before God." Instead of following the stipulation of the Political Act of 1580 that marriage vows should be exchanged publicly in city hall or in church, the consistory apparently sometimes allowed marriage vows made outside the church. To legitimate this conclusion, the consistory went on to describe the love and companionship of spouses based on the mutual consent of both parties and the approval of their close family and friends as "the fundaments and the fundamental purposes of a lawful marriage." This formulation seems to mix Protestant and Catholic beliefs. Reformers, like Luther, emphasized love and companionship as the basis of a marriage, but the reference to mutual consent and to "marriage before God" clearly come from the canon law tradition.[37]

The re-introduction of canon law terminology in the writings of Protestant clerics was the result of the vocabulary used by church members who were being disciplined or seeking the consistory's advice. Young men and young women alike did not hesitate to ask the church to support them in their marriage contract disputes, openly admitting that their promises had been followed by *copula carnalis* (which they believed made the promises binding). Clergymen clearly faced a dilemma: officially they were supposed to follow the law, but they were also aware that a strict adherence to the law could bring shame to young women who had lost their virginity while simply following widespread and age-old tradition. Watt has suggested that Protestants in Neuchâtel tended to follow canon law and deem marriage contracts binding from the moment of consent.[38] In contrast, although they showed understanding for the beliefs of individuals who persisted in marrying in private without the required public formalities, Dutch clerics were not inclined to recognize canon law traditions: in the sixteenth century they reprimanded couples for clandestine marriages and sent them to the secular marriage commissionaires. In the course of the early modern period, however, the Dutch clergy became slightly more flexible in their attitude. Consistories in the seventeenth century still did not accept canon law traditions, but the church reacted much less strongly when faced with such situations. They tried to convince couples to sanctify their marriages in church, reprimanded individuals who refused to keep their promises made privately, and helped to restore the honour of girls who were abandoned by their alleged fiancés.[39]

Shifting Boundaries in the Seventeenth Century

Following the Reformation, both secular courts and Protestant consistories in the northern parts of the Low Countries had attempted to deal with the divergence between Reformation laws and pre-Reformation practices. From the second half of the seventeenth century on, however, attitudes towards illicit sexuality and bastardy began to harden, and courts and consistories began to pay more attention to children born outside of wedlock. This shift was partly the result of demographic transitions. During the sixteenth and the seventeenth century, population growth occurred in many parts of western Europe, including England, Germany, and the Low Countries. As the population began to grow, illicit sexuality increased poverty and illegitimacy. The prominence given to illicit sexuality by the courts and consistories from the second half of the seventeenth century was no doubt related to these demographic factors.[40]

In deciding cases of illicit sexual activity, secular judges began to focus on the illegitimate children who were born as a result. In early modern times, sentences were often symbolic of the crime committed. Women found guilty of infanticide or attempted infanticide were displayed on a platform with a doll in their arms after being flogged. Such punishments showed spectators the gravity of the crime and were not imposed on girls who had merely produced children outside of wedlock. Towards the end of the seventeenth century, however, unmarried women who had given birth were sometimes also put on display with a doll in their arms. The judges distinguished between women who had given birth to bastards – especially those who received no financial support from the child's father – and women who had merely committed fornication. When compared to those convicted of fornication, unwed mothers were given more severe sentences that were imposed in a more public way: they received larger fines or longer banishments and were publicly whipped or escorted out of town while being beaten with sticks.[41]

Secular authorities' changing opinions towards bastardy are evident in their regulations as well. The Marriage Act of 1656 required midwives to obtain the names of fathers while their clients were in labour. An unmarried woman who refused to identify the father of her child was to be denied any further delivery assistance. It is uncertain how faithfully midwives followed the new regulations, but unmarried women who revealed the father's name gained certain advantages. A midwife might provide a written statement declaring before a notary that a woman had specified the father's name according to the law. With such a statement the woman could bring a lawsuit against the father to get child support or at least to partly restore her honour and minimize her loss of reputation. Such lawsuits – called paternity actions – were quite common in certain Protestant areas, such as Holland in the late seventeenth and eighteenth centuries.[42]

The urban magistrates' new rules for midwives were intended to reduce the financial burden created by the growing number of illegitimate and abandoned infants. Beginning in the late Middle Ages, churches and secular authorities had established institutions for orphans and widows, the sick, and the elderly to provide support in the form of food or occasionally money. Unmarried women received poor relief for their children as well. These efforts to identify fathers and encourage subsequent paternity actions were intended to reduce the burden on urban institutions. The moral policies of the secular authorities that began at the end of the seventeenth century were primarily based on such economic considerations, but the Protestant emphasis on individual responsibility stimulated the process as well. As both Protestants and Catholics increasingly insisted that premarital sexuality was in no way permissible, they began to stigmatize illegitimate children as the products of sin and a threat to the social order.[43] Protestants, however, tended to emphasize the individual, who was held responsible for his or her own actions,[44] while Catholics generally focused more on restoring the honour of the mothers and caring for the illegitimate and abandoned children.

Although Protestants and Catholics followed different paths in handling bastardy, their approaches had many similarities. In the Low Countries, both churches started campaigns in the sixteenth and seventeenth centuries which initially aimed at strengthening Catholic and Protestant belief in society, but which ultimately came to focus on the control of their church members' sexual and marital conduct. In the seventeenth century, the Catholic Counter-Reformation and Protestant Pietism (which was called "Further Reformation" in Holland) reinforced the values of family life and the importance of legal marriage.[45] In both Catholic and Protestant regions, moralists viewed unwed motherhood with such revulsion that women often faced the dilemma of either suffering the irretrievable loss of their reputation or of protecting their honour at the cost of abandoning their illegitimate child: the line followed by the clergy in the Netherlands is closely paralleled by the discipline set up in the Holy Roman Empire, in Switzerland, and in France.[46] Whereas the secular authorities focused on the financial burden of illegitimacy, the Protestant Church instead focused on premarital sexuality in general. During the last decades of the seventeenth century, consistories strengthened discipline against sexual relationships between fiancés. Even those who married properly in church or at city hall were disciplined if clergymen discovered that they had had sexual relations before the wedding.[47]

Conclusion

The Dutch reformation of marriage underwent three phases in the sixteenth and seventeenth centuries. During the first phase, between 1572 and 1600, secular authorities and the Protestant Church in the north introduced a novel allocation of marriage tasks and established new regulations on marriage formation and parental consent. During this first phase, criminal courts tended to accept pre-Reformation marriage customs as long as couples ultimately married in church or at city hall. The Protestant consistories during this phase more strictly followed the law, focusing on the consolidation of the new Protestant rules on marriage.

As they were constantly confronted with the canon law traditions that persisted among their church members, the consistories' discipline became more hesitant in the first half of the seventeenth century. The Protestant Church still followed the letter of the (Protestant) law, but the clergy showed more consideration for people who continued to follow traditional marriage customs. During the last phase of the reformation of marriage, both secular and religious authorities strengthened their discipline of family life and premarital sexuality. This shift was caused by demographic forces that resulted in increasing numbers of illegitimate children, but it was also stimulated by the aspirations of the Protestant and Catholic churches alike to further strengthen their churches through strict moral discipline. Protestants, Catholics, and secular governments each focused on different aspects of marital life, but in all cases their efforts belonged to the same process of marriage discipline.

NOTES

1 The following archival records will be cited in this chapter:

Criminal Court of Delft, Criminal sentence books
Criminal Court of Rotterdam, Sentence books
Criminal Court of Rotterdam, Confession books
Rotterdam Archive of the Reformed Church, Consistory Notes (Kerkenraadsacta) Rotterdam

2 The material presented in this chapter is for the most part based on my PhD research on secular and ecclesiastical marriage control in Holland in the sixteenth and seventeenth centuries: van der Heijden 1998.
3 See Donahue 33–5.
4 Van der Heijden 1998, 30–5.
5 See, e.g., Lombardi 2001, 42–59.
6 Van der Heijden 1998, 34–5.
7 Van der Heijden 1999.
8 Van der Heijden 2000.
9 Van der Heijden 1998, 46–8.
10 Van der Heijden 1998, 34–7.
11 Esmein 1929–35, 2:144–5; Watt 2001.
12 Van der Heijden 1998, 36–40.
13 For the Dutch Revolt and its political and religious implications see Israël 1995.
14 Burghartz 1999; Watt 1992; Philips 1988; Roper 1989.

15 Van der Heijden 1996.
16 Ozment 1983, 50–72; Roper 1989, 165–205.
17 See Donahue 34, 36, and Lombardi 102–3.
18 Brink 1977, 126–41; Grotius, *Inleiding tot de Hollandsche rechts-geleertheyd*, 16; Ankum 1978.
19 See Lombardi 112–14.
20 Bonfield 2001, 108–12.
21 Watt 2001, 129.
22 The Political Act of 1580 made adultery punishable by secular law, but it did not yet include stipulations on divorce. In practice Holland did allow divorce. The Marriage Act of 1656 did include rules for divorce, declaring that adultery and abandonment would be the only reasons to get a divorce. The act was pronounced in the jurisdiction of the Generality (areas reconquered from Spain, such as Brabant), but it was referred to in the towns of Holland as well: van der Heijden 1998.
23 Ankum 1978, 224–5; Haks 1982, 117.
24 Zurk, *Codex Batavus*.
25 Van der Heijden 1998, 98–102.
26 Outhwaite 1995, 21–2; Smout 1982; Harrington 1995, 248–59; Ingram 1987, 197; Philips 1988, 31; Watt 1992, 91–2. For a different view of the line adopted by the Protestant courts in Switzerland and southern Germany regarding fornication, see Burghartz 187–9.
27 Watt 2001, 138.
28 Safley 1984, 185–95. For Spain, see Usunáriz 207–16; for Italy, see Conclusion 337–8.
29 Van der Heijden 1998, 96–133. See, in this volume, Wunder 74 and Lombardi 107.
30 Van der Heijden 2004.
31 Ibid.
32 Rotterdam Archive of the Reformed Church, Consistory Notes (Kerkenraadsacta) Rotterdam 5, 1 December 1660: "… men sal voortaen niemant ondertrouwen ten sij alvorens ouders consent daertoe betoont wierde. Gelijck sulcx emde brengt de politijcke ordonnantie."
33 *Acta van de Nederlandsche synoden*, 447–8 (Middelburg 1581, article 18).
34 Van der Heijden 1998, 177–201.
35 Delft Archive of the Reformed Church, Consistory Notes (Kerkenraadsacta) Delft 3, 17 August 1598.
36 Van der Heijden 1998, 178–89.

37 Ibid., 40; Rotterdam Archive of the Reformed Church, Consistory Notes (Kerkenraadsacta) Rotterdam 4, 24 January 1652. The clergymen referred to several texts from the Bible: Deut. 20:7, 22, 23; Gen. 29:21; Mal. 2:14; Matt. 1.
38 Watt 1992, 65–70.
39 Van der Heijden 1998, 186–9.
40 Watt 2001, 147–50; Viazzo 2001; Mitterauer 1983; Shorter 1971.
41 Van der Heijden 1998, 121–8.
42 Watt 2001, 149. In Basel alimony was settled in the *Ehegericht*. The Basel marriage law of 1533 stipulated that fathers should take responsibility for their children, or at least assume financial care of them, even if they were not married to the mother: Burghartz 1999, 269–77. See, in this volume, Burghartz 192 and Lefebvre-Teillard 271–8.
43 See Burghartz 189–94.
44 For the new humanist and Protestant approach to poor relief see Matheeussen and Fantazzi 2002.
45 Foster and Kaplan 2005; Storme 1992.
46 See, in this volume, Wunder 80–1 and Burghartz 189–93.
47 See Burghartz 188.

Chapter 6

Competing Logics of Public Order: Matrimony and the Fight against Illicit Sexuality in Germany and Switzerland from the Sixteenth to the Eighteenth Century

SUSANNA BURGHARTZ

Introduction

The reform discussions of the fifteenth century and the debates of the Reformation era criticized the perceived general state of moral disorder and called for a reorganization of social relations with the aim of drawing an unambiguous line between decent and indecent behaviour. As we have seen, the programmatic demands of the reform-minded included rejecting compulsive celibacy and introducing marriage for priests, as well as the moral improvement of Christian life through a revaluation of marriage as the ideal way of life.[1]

Over many centuries, the Christian West had developed two different ordering principles for sexuality and marriage, which I distinguish in this chapter as sexual order and social order. A dualistic separation between body and mind or spirit, along with ancient notions of pollution through sexuality (above all in the religious context) and moral demands for abstinence, led to concepts of purity that juxtaposed celibacy as an ideal way of life with marriage. In the twelfth and thirteenth centuries, this development attained a new degree of legal codification,[2] in which the social organization of sexuality – sexual order – was based on the high value placed on sexual abstinence and on an opposition between chastity and (illegitimate) sexuality.

The generative aspects of sexuality, however, had consequences for the social order, that is, for the organization of society in households, the transfer of goods between generations and families, and property questions. Marriage and inheritance law created regulatory mechanisms for these matters that were intended to create and guarantee social order through the fundamental social categories of household and family.

Although the objectives of these two organizational efforts could converge in certain areas – for example in the avoidance of ambiguous kin relationships and thus ultimately also claims to property – social disorder and sexual disorder were by no means the same thing. This became especially evident in the Reformation-era discussions of clandestine marriages, known in German as *Winkelehen*, literally corner or angle marriages.[3] Although Alexander III's rules on the formation of marriage were intended to prevent illicit relationships, they gave rise – as we have seen – to a centuries-long controversy, since the principle of consensual marriage and the conjugal praxis deriving from it conflicted with family strategies.

The Reformation's fundamental rejection of compulsory celibacy together with the revaluation of marriage as the ideal way of life led to a thorough reorientation of the coordinate system of sexual order. The Reformation's theology of marriage and anthropology of gender no longer relied on celibacy as the societal guarantor of purity; now, the purity of marital sexuality was to guarantee sexual order. As a consequence of this fundamental reorientation, in subsequent decades – at least in Protestantism – the relationship between social order and sexual order had to be redefined. Marriage lay at the heart of this process of redefinition.[4] The discussion revolved around the purity and pollution of the social and communal body as well as the social order of households, intergenerational transfers of goods, and the maintenance and solidification of social groups and mechanisms of distinction. In what follows, I should like to trace the dynamics of the interrelationship between these two ordering principles.

Marriage Law in the Confessionalization Process

Throughout the sixteenth century and well beyond, wedlock, marriage, and illicit sexuality were important topics on the sociopolitical agenda. While the success of the Reformation manifested itself particularly in enacting new marriage ordinances and establishing Reformed marriage courts and consistories in the 1520s and 1530s, the process of confessionalization from the mid-sixteenth century led to a series of new marriage decrees and laws on illicit sexuality in both Protestant cities and territories such as Württemberg or the Palatinate and in Catholic Bavaria.[5]

The matrimonial regime introduced by the Council of Trent replaced the old rules that had generated legal uncertainty and social disorder with new ones which, at least in theory, made it possible to determine without a shadow of a doubt who was married and who was not.[6] This marked increase in formalization and codification shifted the balance between the future spouses, their families, the church(es), and the secular authorities with regard to control over marriage. In Protestant territories, parents (particularly fathers)[7] gained influence, as did secular and/or ecclesiastical authorities, while the future spouses' right to self-determination and the influence of extended families and peer groups waned.[8] In Italy and probably in Spain, on the contrary, the enactment of the decree *Tametsi* encouraged the autonomous marital choices of children, at least in the initial period.[9]

In the long run, the requirement that marriages be contracted publicly and the related increase in legal and ritual formalization led to a clear separation between the assumption of sexual relations and the beginning of legally recognized matrimony.[10] In this way, the new concept of premarital sexuality was born and gradually became a problematic area, not merely at the formal, juridical level but also in the conduct of individuals' lives and in the perception of individuals.

When it came to the concept of matrimony and the distinction between legitimate (and thus pure) and illegitimate (i.e., impure) sexuality, the reform discussions of the fifteenth century and their continuation and radicalization in Protestantism proved a stunning success, at least at the legal and normative levels. With the enactment of the various Protestant – Lutheran, Zwinglian, and Calvinist – marriage ordinances in the first decades of the sixteenth century, and the Catholic reaction at the Council of Trent, the interests of parents, community, and authorities in controlling marriage and the marriage order asserted themselves in the legislation of the political area considered in this chapter.[11] This by no means meant that the battle to establish proper Christian practice in the temporal world had been won, however. Instead, it soon became clear that ever-new threats were being conceived and discovered, which had to be combatted. And they also took on concrete form in the growing debate on illicit sexuality, where they assumed frightening proportions. The decades that followed, up to the mid-seventeenth century, would be marked by this struggle.

Post-Reformation Regulatory Discourses

In the second half of the sixteenth century, the focus of the conflict about matrimony shifted. It was no longer primarily a matter of claiming that the wedded state was divinely ordained for all and therefore requiring priests to marry. Now official regulatory efforts and the educational, theological, and literary discourses sought to anchor the newly recognized ideal of wedlock in Christian practice and imagination, while purging it of all forms of illicit sexuality. Distinct literary forms emerged: *Hausväterliteratur* (household literature) spelled out in sermons and pedagogical writings the ideal of the divinely instituted estate of matrimony, its tasks and forms, as well as addressing questions of courtship, matchmaking, and weddings.[12] The *Teufelsbücher* (devils' books), in contrast, which experienced a boom after 1550, painted a gloomy picture of the unfortunate, sinful, and indecent state of affairs within matrimony and between the sexes.[13] In practice, as we shall see, the reformed legal ordinances, with their new strategies of disassociation and exclusion, and the jurisdiction of the newly installed marriage courts created a whole series of new problems and social frictions. Moreover, subsequent decades and centuries also revealed that regulations and delimitations, once established, had to be addressed, updated, and reformulated repeatedly to retain their power of distinction, as will be seen later.

While in his struggle against actual or imagined abuses Martin Luther polemicized against the prohibition on priests marrying and confronted the problem of clandestine marriage, in 1525 Ulrich Zwingli pursued the legal consequences of the new Protestant theology of marriage by promulgating a new municipal ordinance and setting up a new municipal matrimonial court in Zurich, staffed by both members of the town council and pastors. In the period that followed, various Swiss and South German cities experienced a veritable wave of legislation and foundings of local marriage courts.[14] This set in motion a development that in subsequent decades in Protestant towns and territories would lead to the enactment of ordinance after ordinance, which became over time ever more elaborately detailed. While the initial focus was on establishing rules for marriage and divorce, from the 1560s on, in order to promote the "moralization of life," the surveillance of sexuality, which was explicitly conceived of as a struggle against fornication (*Unzucht*), was increasingly pursued through marital legislation as well as legislation directly aimed at *Unzucht*.

One example is Württemberg, which enacted its first marriage ordinance in 1534. The ordinance retained the necessity of parental consent for the validity of marriage and spoke of clandestine marriages as the source of "grievous perjury, horrible blaspheming against the most holy name of God, perpetual confusion and irredeemable burdens on the conscience ... and other marked and very great damage, harm and danger."[15] The language of sin and contamination is striking here. The text speaks of "bestial, insolent and impudent persons," who pay no heed to the forbidden degrees of consanguinity and cause "offence and all manner of damage." Thus quite early on, the legislation adopted a tone that would increasingly mark the discussion on matrimony in the centuries that followed. The tone of the legislation aimed not merely to create order but also to name, define, and imaginatively illustrate illicit sexuality and its ruinous consequences, making it easier to recognize, avoid, and eliminate it.

The public dialogue on fornication and divine wrath attained a new intensity in Württemberg in 1586 with the "Edict concerning the punishment of carnal offences." This legislation no longer focused on the question of the legal conditions for valid marriages. Instead, it was mainly concerned to define which forms of sexuality were illegitimate in order to distinguish permissible from impermissible sexual relations, a distinction that – as the introductory passage put it – was to facilitate "the possibility of abolishing such disgrace and vice, and to avert the threat of grievous divine punishment" by "sharpening the insignificant and lenient punishments hitherto applied."[16]

Württemberg was by no means alone in this legislative struggle. In Geneva, efforts at stricter moral surveillance were already evident before the actual onset of the Reformation in 1536. As in other Swiss and South German cities, the town council enacted laws against fornication and adultery (1534) and banned prostitution (1536). In practice, however, Geneva only introduced a systematic morals policy after the return of Calvin in 1541, with the establishment of a consistory responsible for the oversight of morals in the city.[17] Beginning in the 1550s, this consistory revealed itself as an instrument to impose "a kind of moral reign of terror in Geneva."[18] Thus in the 1560s, the regulation of marital conflicts and the condemnation of extramarital sexuality were among the central, but by no means the only, duties of the Geneva consistory, while the enforcement of the true faith receded into the background.[19] According to William Monter, by the end of the 1560s the excessive system of moral surveillance had clearly passed its zenith, although it would remain in place for another four centuries. In Geneva, which introduced a reformed morals policy later than other southern German and Swiss cities, the repression quickly attained an intensity whose socially dysfunctional consequences soon revealed themselves, although this did not lead to a complete abandonment of the harsh policing of morality.[20]

Protestant territories such as Württemberg, Hesse, and the Palatinate or Calvinist cities like Geneva were by no means the only ones whose marriage courts shifted their focus in the second half of the sixteenth century from conflict resolution to a repressive targeting of illicit sexuality. Catholic territories such as Bavaria or the prince-bishopric of Speyer also increasingly took this route.[21] Even before the conclusion of the Council of Trent, in its 1553 legal code (*Bairische Lanndtsordnung*), Bavaria stipulated the disinheritance of children who married without parental agreement, as well as the punishment and criminalization of premarital sexual relations. This was intended to bolster patriarchal control over marriage and at the same time to restrict sexual relations among the lower classes.[22] The newly introduced offence of *Leichtfertigkeit* (profligacy) encompassed morally suspect as well as economically undesirable unions. The establishment of a separate wedding office (*Hochzeitsamt*) in Munich in the late sixteenth century combined the moral concern to clearly demarcate impure and illicit sexual relations with an economic interest in forbidding marriages that lacked a sufficient material foundation. This shifted attention back to an issue that had always been central to the social assessment of marriages – their material basis – since in these societies matrimony was the central vehicle for the transfer of goods from one generation to the next and thus, through the dowry, it became a central element in the social system of inheritance. The interest of fathers, as heads of households in urban and rural communities, in ensuring that the households founded by newlyweds had a sufficient material foundation was accordingly great.

With reformist calls to establish matrimony as a universally binding way of life and a new site of sexual purity, which was being propagated as late as Heinrich Bullinger's 1540 treatise on wedlock,[23] the sexual order of society so important to the early reformers was temporarily privileged over the social order. The new Protestant theology of marriage and anthropology of gender had elevated matrimony to the status of a parameter regulative for all and sought to establish sexual order at the marriage courts by conducting cases in such a way as to promote marriages. During this phase, those who went to court to enforce promises of marriage had significant chances of success. In the long term, however, in a society marked by increasing social differentiation and scarce resources, this inclusive attitude, whose essential aim was to recognize marriages, ran up against a judicial practice whose primary interest was social order and which sought to restrict the right to marry.

In the courts, such an exclusionary administration of the law nearly always led to convictions for fornication. Accordingly, the authorities sought to resolve the potential contradictions between the two ordering objectives by adopting an increasingly repressive morals policy, especially towards the lower classes. This policy shift from a more inclusive, pro-marital judicial practice in the first half of the century to a repressive one, increasingly orientated towards the discourse on fornication, had the paradoxical effect, however, of continually recreating the very evil it was supposed to combat, because the courts no longer affirmed contested marriages but instead condemned the relationships in question as illicit.[24]

The Discussion on Polygamy and Morganatic Marriage: Mésalliances among the Nobility

The contradictory ordering objectives resulted in criminalization of sexual behaviour that had long been largely socially accepted within the framework of traditional courtship. While this criminalization affected mainly, if not exclusively, members of the lower orders, at the opposite end of the social scale clear shifts were also occurring in how people viewed hitherto accepted ways of life and behaviours. Marriages between individuals of unequal rank were affected.[25] The reformist pressure, with its new standards of sexual morality for the laity, expressed itself in the discussion of polygamy, which particularly touched the German high nobility.[26]

An especially prominent example was the hotly debated double marriage of the landgrave of Hesse, Philip, who alongside his first marriage to Christine of Saxony also contracted in 1540 an additional and morganatic marriage – that is, a legally inferior or secondary marriage – with Margarethe von der Saale as his secondary wife.[27] Legal developments between the thirteenth century and the late sixteenth century had resulted in the "outlining of full marriage as the only valid and normative legal institution for the binding creation of legitimate couple relationships."[28] While this meant a success in the fight against concubinage and clandestine marriages, and the victory of the principle of monogamy over polygamous tendencies of various types, it also led to new problems, particularly for relationships between noblemen and women of lower rank. Now, among the high nobility, circumventing the restrictions that arose from familial and caste strategies of spousal selection could be judged morally damnable.

Clearly, the intense discussions of matrimony and illicit sexuality during the Reformation period also left their mark on the nobility. In view of the still common practice of "special caste morality,"[29] it is as surprising as it is understandable – against the background of the Reformation-era moral theology debates over celibacy, fornication, and priestly marriage – that Philip, landgrave of Hesse, sought in 1540 to give his relationship with Margarethe von der Saale a form that could count on acceptance under the altered social conditions. Although Luther and Melanchthon had noted that it was not unusual "for princes to keep concubines," this was apparently no longer a viable option under the new circumstances. Since concubines, once deemed acceptable, could now "be viewed as whores," the efforts of Philip, who had been married to Christine of Saxony since 1523, sought a construct that would move beyond "fornication," "for it [i.e., Margarethe von der Saale] is, after all, to be a lawfully wedded concubine."[30] The intense discussion among reformers about polygamy by no means led to easy acceptance of the landgrave's double marriage. Rather, Luther and Melanchthon laid down strict preconditions intended to maintain the secrecy of the prince's relationship, which appeared morally problematic when judged by the yardstick of strict monogamy. That they agreed at all to a legally recognized arrangement illustrates their understanding that marriages of the high nobility had potentially wide-ranging political implications.

Although Landgrave Philip was a partisan of the Reformation who played an important role in its establishment in central Germany and who as a figurehead could have done significant harm to the new movement, in other cases attention focused on dynastic issues of inheritance. Accordingly, a new practice of morganatic marriage emerged at the end of the sixteenth century. Michael Sikora, who has studied the legal development as well as the practice of misalliances in the early modern high nobility, has found numerous examples of such "socially unequal, but fully valid marriages" that opened up a whole range of formalized relationships between concubinage and fully valid and publicly concluded first marriages. He regards the de facto adoption of morganatic marriage from Lombard-Milanese law in the German-speaking region as an attempt to mediate between an increasingly rigid morals policy in matters of matrimony and aristocratic problems and privileges. "Modern church law," notes Sikora, "distinguished only between marital and non-marital unions, while the nobility continued the tradition of differentiating between socially appropriate and inappropriate marriages."[31] Underlying this practice were quite concrete interests, and by no means merely the problem of an absence of attraction – the subject of complaints by both Landgrave Philip and Duke Bernhard of Saxony-Jena – as a result of politically motivated marriages. Reasons for a morganatic marriage could thus be to protect the claims to inheritance or succession of the children from a first marriage in case the monarch was widowed or the regulation of the succession between brothers – for example the elder brother's renunciation of the title in order to avoid a compulsory dynastic marriage – or the interest in the political opportunities offered by establishing a mistress as an "épouse légitime," as in the case of Augustus the Strong and his alliance with Constantia von Cosel.[32]

The development of the legal instrument of morganatic marriage at the end of the sixteenth century and its integration into gradually emerging dynastic law from the mid-seventeenth century by academic jurisprudence plainly illustrate the necessity, in the face of the new doctrine on marriage and fornication, of morally legitimizing the scope of action previously available to noblemen – whom medieval legal practice had offered a spectrum of legally gradated forms of alliance from full marriage to concubinage[33] – by closing the gap between these forms and fully valid marriage.[34] The sharper distinction between matrimony and fornication, which went hand in hand with the clearer formal regulation of marriage, thus affected quite varied social groups in regard to their societal inclusion and exclusion or position: alongside the maidservants and "unwed mothers" for whom the increasingly intense debate on fornication could have grave consequences, which I shall examine later, the socially inferior female partners of men of the high nobility also faced new demands, as well as opportunities.

Display of Social Rank, Social Positioning, and Customary Rituals

Misalliances draw our attention to the symbolic practices of the wedding celebration and the obviously different manners in which they were organized: "the norms of the social hierarchy were superimposed on marriage law."[35] Law and social practice diverged. While church law now only distinguished between marital and non-marital alliances, noble society continued to separate appropriate from inappropriate unions and to express the difference with great precision in the orchestration of wedding festivities. For example, in the case of the morganatic wedding of Archduke Ferdinand of Tyrol to the commoner Philippine Welser, the exact place and time were not even recorded. In marked contrast to this reticence, we have a wealth of documentation about the archduke's appearance dressed as Jupiter at the nuptials of one of his court officials in a carnivalesque procession that formed part of the 10-day wedding festivities.[36]

Other social groups also reveal the tensions and divergences between, on the one hand, the ecclesiastical and legal establishing of a firm definition of valid promises and marriage rituals and, on the other hand, the customary, ritualized forms of courtship and nuptials, whose concrete social practice was associated with informal legal and social signals and expectations. The marriage of Felix Platter and Margarethe Jeckelmann in Basel in 1557, for instance, illustrates how coded and ritualized the various phases of courtship and marriage were for the urban middle classes as well.[37] During this ritualized process, parental (in this case paternal) consent was secured, as was that of the betrothed couple, for both types of consent were legally necessary for a valid marriage. But the various stages from betrothal through nuptials also served to display the social position of the families of origin and of the newlyweds' future household.[38] After a prolonged (and somewhat difficult) period of courtship and preparation, Felix and Margarethe's wedding was celebrated as convention demanded, with 150 guests, a lavish banquet, drinking, and various dances. It was a complete success that demonstrated the material and social rise of the Platter family and their integration into Basel society.[39] In the leading circles of the urban, Protestant middle class, the societal attention paid to wedding festivities did not focus solely on those aspects of the nuptial ceremony relevant to church law – the public announcement and going to church or the benediction of the pastor. It was equally important for such festivities to pay suitable homage to the codes of social networking and positioning.[40]

The regulatory bodies and the social rituals pursued distinct, sometimes divergent objectives and logics. Whereas theologians' primary ambition was overseeing marriage as a Christian way of life and as the sole legitimate site of pure sexuality, popular customary rituals and ritualized ceremonial intended above all to make visible and understood the social relations between the spouses and their social position in the community. Socially coded gestures such as gifts and engagement pledges or ritualized modes of making contact between the sexes, such as visits to private chambers,[41] acted as reliable signs of male-female relationships. Wedding festivities served not just to mark the transition from the single state to membership in the collective of married people, or to celebrate a legally valid marriage and thus to make it known to society at large, but were also intended to highlight claims to social position (e.g., by means of the number of guests who were invited or the sequence of dishes served), as well as the new bond between the two families involved. All of these social and largely ritualized forms may also be interpreted as a conventionalized and recognized set of communicative practices for negotiating relationships in the precarious field of heterosexual contacts and their social meanings.

Sexual Order versus Social Order?

Thus, in the course of the sixteenth, the seventeenth, and the eighteenth century, increasing and visible discrepancies between authorities' aims and social needs gradually emerged in the areas of courtship, marriage, and weddings. Authorities, who were bent on establishing norms and primarily interested in drawing clear lines between pure and impure, moral and immoral, privileged questions of sexual order. In contrast, actual practice, which had deep social roots legitimized by custom, sought above all to stabilize and represent socio-economic conditions, ensure a functioning gender and generational order, and preserve the logic of the culture of honour, thus emphasizing social order.[42] Various supervisory opportunities and bodies emerged to further these objectives. They included the so-called *Knabenschaften* (groups of young unmarried men who organized and oversaw the customary and ritual visits of young men to young women's rooms), bridal processions and bridal wagons (which communicated to the community as a whole the material position of the family of origin but first and foremost of the soon-to-be-founded household), and customs of rebuke such as the charivaris, ritual activities that sometimes opposed undesirable unions with considerable violence.[43] Such practices, with local variations, were found throughout the German-speaking region and beyond. In Schleswig-Holstein they were known as *Nachtfreien*,[44] in Bavaria as *Haberfeldtreiben*,[45] and in Switzerland as *Kiltgang* and *Kammerbesuch*.[46] The young women's *Spinnstuben*, which were common in various regions, also belong in this category.[47]

In a society suffering from increasing social stratification and poverty, the aim of these methods of social control, which were often taken on and enforced by the young unmarried men of the village, was primarily to safeguard the social order by ensuring that courtship and marriage were orientated towards the preservation of economic resources and social status.[48] The community practices that accompanied and supervised the initiation of relationships between the sexes did not merely have socio-economic implications, however. Particularly in regard to the commencement of sexual relations, matchmaking, and responsibility for morally desirable sexual behaviour, these practices led to unequal scopes of action for men and women and thus codified the asymmetry of the gender order as a part of the social order.

"Premature" Coitus, "Untimely" Deliveries, and Threats to the Marital Order

The moral policy promoted by the authorities took on its own momentum. The boundaries between marital and non-marital – that is, between licit and illicit – sexuality, between purity and pollution, were drawn with increasing sharpness in the sixteenth and seventeenth centuries. This was because – as a result of the legal developments following the Reformation and the Council of Trent – formally proper, official marriage in the presence of a pastor or priest had to precede the initiation of sexual relations in order for them to be legally recognized as legitimate. Thus nuptials and sexual intercourse, which still coincided in the canon law concept of presumed marriage (*matrimonium praesumptum*),[49] now diverged temporally and the new offence of premature intercourse between married people could arise without their marital status itself being in question.

The beginnings of this problem, which would become increasingly evident in the seventeenth and eighteenth centuries as a conflict between differing systems of values and social logic, may be traced back to the Reformation period itself. As early as 1534, the first Württemberg marriage ordinance devised and named the offence of "untimely, disorderly, and improper coitus" between betrothed persons before their actual church wedding.[50] This was the first time a law separated betrothal and subsequent intercourse from formal marriage – i.e., celebration including the public announcement and consent expressed before the congregation – in a manner relevant for criminal prosecution, although it still left the punishment open. The second Württemberg marriage ordinance of 1553 set a penalty of eight days' imprisonment in a tower for men and of four days for "female persons" for "clandestine coitus." This punishment applied to couples who had only married after a marriage court had passed judgment on the validity of their promise to marry. Their offence was having had sexual intercourse before the wedding, which was legitimized only retroactively by the court sentence to marry.[51] Later, the definition of this offence was expanded to include uncontested marriages. Thus in Hesse-Kassel as early as 1556, the synod imposed a church penance on premarital coitus (*anticipatio*), and the Hessian Reformation ordinance of 1572 demanded in addition that the bride not wear a wreath at the wedding and that the celebrations take place in private; furthermore, a penalty for fornication was imposed in the case of "premature" delivery (*partus septimestris*).[52]

This normative development, which spread only gradually through the German-speaking area in the decades that followed,[53] clearly privileged the purity of marital sexuality over the preservation of social order. At the same time, however, this had the potential effect of casting a slur on socially uncontroversial, recognized, and unproblematic marriages. Honourable male and female burghers whose weddings did nothing to disrupt the social order were compelled to explain themselves before the courts for their "profligate nature" and do penance.[54] This could expose recognized, legitimate marriages to arraignment in a fornication trial. The new legal assessment of premarital sexual relations, however, was only put into practice – that is, expressed in judicial sentences – towards the mid-seventeenth century, when it took place in several places at the same time. This development represented a new high point in repressive policies towards fornication. In Basel, for example, convictions for so-called premature coitus represented a significant portion – 20 to 30 per cent – of the total number of convictions for fornication during this period.[55]

The introduction of this new offence, however, revealed the limits of the morals policy and its discursive dynamics. Because the new offence could place legally contracted marriages under suspicion of fornication, vehement resistance soon emerged. And although soon after the introduction of the new offence the penalties were regularly reduced and trials assumed a highly stereotypical character, in the long run, Basel burghers, for example, found this criminalization unacceptable when it touched on their own wives. Thus as late as 1708 they argued in petitions that such trials were a danger to the health of mother and child, in order to avoid their wives' personal appearance in court. Here notions of sexual order plainly collided with the needs of the social order. The expansion of the notion of fornication had reached a limit beyond which lay dysfunction.

This became evident above all in the eighteenth century. As Christian Simon and Albert Schnyder have shown, as late as the eighteenth century the authorities failed to impose in the Basel countryside their view that the beginning of marriage coincided with the church wedding and that couples therefore could not engage in sexual relations prior to this. The persistent penalization of the rural practice of engaging in sexual intercourse after the promise to marry and considering it legitimate had no visible effect on sexual behaviour.[56] The example of Hesse-Kassel points to a similarly tense competition between sexual order and social order. While penalties for premature coitus were implemented comparatively early here, this sanctioning was hotly debated from its introduction.[57]

The Criminalization of Lower-Class Sexuality and the Invention of the Unwed Mother

In principle, the morals policy enforced by the authorities in both Catholic Bavaria and Protestant Basel, as well as in other (imperial) cities and territories, continued to intensify. Ulinka Rublack has described the heightened "moralism" in Württemberg, which was expressed from the second half of the sixteenth century in a proliferation of morals decrees and a more severe prosecution of "sexual immorality."[58] Legislation sanctioning "carnal offences," as they were referred to in a general rescript of 1630, reached a high point in the seventeenth century, peaking regionally at different times.[59] While in Württemberg this process was completed by the mid-seventeenth century, in Schwäbisch Hall the first relatively mild penalties were issued in 1643, followed in the final third of the century by a large-scale criminalization campaign. It mainly targeted domestic servants and, as Renate Dürr's studies show, may be read as a shift in the early modern concern for order.

The stereotype of the disorderly, sexually profligate servant was built up into a threat to an increasingly socially stratified early modern society. This stereotype aimed at social marginalization and could serve at the same time as part of a competitive debate about the Christian character of the various territorial powers. In this process criminalization and marginalization took the place of sanctification through admonition and reconciliation. Renate Dürr's research on the imperial city of Schwäbisch Hall reveals with particular clarity the significance and dynamism of this increasingly obsessive early modern struggle for order.[60] In Hall, the penalties for fornication, which could affect women of all social strata, were probably disproportionately imposed on maidservants; in the same way, the discursive attribution of fornication to domestic servants reached a peak in the second half of the seventeenth century.

This occurred in a period marked by especially low rates of illegitimacy.[61] Thus, the societal focus of the fornication controversy on the specific group of domestic servants by no means corresponded to an actual social problem with high rates of illegitimacy, growing poverty, and the attendant potential burden on municipal poor relief. Instead, the development in Hall proved to be a further manifestation of the increasingly repressive discourse of order with its fears and harsh judgments.

The figures for illegitimate births in Hall are similar to Rainer Beck's findings for Upper Bavaria (Unterfinning) between the final third of the seventeenth and the end of the eighteenth century. He ascribes the very low illegitimacy rates to a traditional culture of honour, in which young people's sexual behaviour was marked by "chastity." In this culture, sexuality and economics were closely intertwined, and the code of honour ultimately guaranteed the close connection between pregnancy and weddings.[62] In a study on profligacy offences in Bavaria in the seventeenth and eighteenth centuries, Stefan Breit modifies the link between honour and low illegitimacy rates, stressing that "honour or virginity became a key form of capital" when no other (concrete) capital was present for women of the lower classes.[63] In a long-range overview, however, Breit too concludes that in late seventeenth-century Bavaria, moral and religious concerns were still in the forefront of state penalties for fornication, while by the end of the eighteenth century they had been displaced by social concerns. In the long term, this led to the abolition of penalties for "profligacy" in 1808, but also to the perfecting of restrictive state marital policies.[64] Breit and Beck both emphasize premodern Bavarian rural society's acceptance of premarital sexuality, and Beck regards his finding of the combination of a high rate of premarital pregnancy and a low rate of illegitimacy as important evidence of the failure of the repressive efforts of church and state authorities.[65]

Heinrich R. Schmidt reaches similar conclusions for the Berne communes of Vechingen and Stettlen. He sees, beginning in the mid-seventeenth century and above all in the eighteenth century, "the overall situation in the area of premarital sexuality as changing for the worse: the age of consent was raised, penalties for fornication and adultery increased, the campaign against bridal pregnancies was stepped up, prohibitions of marriage among the poor amounting to compulsory celibacy intensified, and infanticide became more frequent."[66] At this time Berne, too, criminalized bridal pregnancies ("untimely deliveries"): they were made punishable in 1686 and prosecuted until about 1770, a remarkably short period when compared to other regions. In the long run, prosecutions for fornication (*Hurerei*) increased in the villages studied by Schmidt, as did the number of paternity suits. Until around 1735 the church court (*Chorgericht*)[67] pursued cases involving sexual relationships between unmarried persons, whether or not the woman became pregnant, but after that period only those contacts in which a pregnancy occurred were actually prosecuted as fornication.[68] At the same time, the ratio of marriages to unwed pregnancies changed fundamentally. Whereas in the seventeenth century there had been ten marriages for every unmarried pregnancy, in the eighteenth century the ratio was two to one. Thus, principally in the eighteenth century there is no evidence of an effective policing of morals that reduced the number of illicit sexual relationships.[69]

While Schmidt rejects the thesis that social discipline was successful in the long term in the area of non-marital sexuality, when it comes to the regulation of marital conflicts, he proposes that a coincidence of interests led to an "alliance" between women and the authorities with the aim of disciplining men.[70] According to Schmidt, the "paterfamilias ideology" aimed programmatically at the "moral reform of its main protagonists, men," and "therefore represented a weapon in women's hands for the domestication of men."[71] This thesis may possess a certain plausibility for the regulation of marital disputes by the church court in the Bernese villages Schmidt has studied, but it cannot be generalized into positing a growing rapprochement between vertical domestication by the authorities and horizontal domestication by wives, given the growing repressiveness of the marriage and morals courts in the sixteenth century and even more so in the seventeenth century. Similarly problematic is Safley's thesis that the Reformation and its efforts at morals policy engendered "a greater sensitivity ... to the needs of petitioner."[72] Beginning in the second half of the sixteenth century, women and men were equally unsuccessful in suits involving marriage or divorce: they found themselves confronted with increasingly repressive sanctions as part of an ever more rigid morals policy.[73]

Watt's studies of Neuchâtel also substantiate this interpretation. The Reformed city of Neuchâtel witnessed a clear and lasting criminalization of pre- and non-marital sexuality.[74] Parallel to the massive rise in fornication trials in the seventeenth century, the number of suits brought by women for breach of marriage promise, which now had scant chance of success, fell drastically.[75] In the seventeenth century, during the consistory's struggle against sexual impurity and on behalf of a pure, Christian life, nearly equal numbers of men and women were punished for fornication, but in the eighteenth century the number of women sentenced rose sharply by 51 per cent, while the number of men convicted during the same period fell by 150 per cent.[76] Watt suggests that there was a direct connection between the court's interest in illegitimate children and the potential burden on poor relief associated with them.

Heinz Schilling has noted a similar intensification of sexual discipline, which largely targeted illicit sexuality and fornication (*Unzucht, Hurerei*) and thus primarily unmarried women and mothers, in the city of Emden as well. There, however, the harsher repression only began in the later seventeenth century, particularly in the 1690s under the Pietist church council.[77] In Emden, the stigmatization of *anticipatio* did not begin until the 1740s, far later than elsewhere.[78]

Thus, two contradictory tendencies manifested themselves earlier or later depending on the region or territory. Beginning in the second half of the sixteenth century, an increasingly repressive morality policy was enforced in the marriage and morals courts. From the late seventeenth century onwards this led to a shift from a paternity to a maternity principle in the matter of responsibility for the support of illegitimate children.[79] Whereas previously fathers had been responsible at least de jure for rearing their illegitimate children (which meant that they also disposed of their labour power), now the principle of the mother's responsibility for children born out of wedlock was normatively enshrined. This development was accompanied by the increasingly decisive exclusion of illegitimate children from any inheritance claims and by the increasingly distinct construction "unwed mother, illegitimate child" – a unit for which the father appeared to bear ever less responsibility.

To a growing degree – and to some extent in step with a critique of domestic servants, which applied mainly to maids – this development held unmarried women responsible for the purity of the social body or, to put it another way, for the maintenance of social order and the prevention of illicit sexuality. In fornication trials, however, society by no means let the men involved get off scot-free. At the same time, the number of fornication trials rose markedly in the course of the eighteenth century in some regions. This quantitative growth cannot be read simply as an expression of increasing repression. Rather, scholars have also ventured the interpretation that the increase in trials reveals a discrepancy between the values of various social groups, since the sexual norms for unmarried persons previously pursued by the church and secular authorities and rooted in Christianity were no longer shared by all.[80] Heinrich R. Schmidt notes the existence of a veritable "flood of violations of Christian norms governing sexuality" in Berne in the period after 1700 and "an increasingly refractory and resistant group of people," who no longer obeyed church norms or communal village principles but rather took up sexual relations without intending to marry. He proceeds from the assumption that this group, lacking communal and agrarian ties, could ignore economic considerations and accordingly found it easier to resist supervision – by ecclesiastical and secular authorities as well as by communal control institutions and peer groups – and as a result engaged in more individualistic behaviour. He believes that this development was directly related to an increasingly cavalier attitude towards the fate of unwanted children and the rapidly rising rate of "children of illicit relationships who died before birth or baptism." Contrasting sharply with medical progress, the mortality rate rose from "less than one-quarter to over two-thirds in the eighteenth century."[81]

Although the growing acceptance of bridal pregnancies and illegitimate children, which Brigitte Schnegg has also found for the Bernese region in the eighteenth and nineteenth centuries, does not apply equally throughout the German-speaking world or to all social groups, it is at least clear that the undiminished condemnation and criminalization of illicit sexuality was called into question in the eighteenth century and that people began to express different and indeed contradictory positions. These in part unconnected and in part openly antagonistic tendencies are revealed in exemplary fashion in the intense debate on infanticide and the associated criminal policy at the end of the century.

The Debate on Infanticide as a New Regulatory Discourse

A gradual modification of absolutist patterns of sexual regulation occurred over the course of the eighteenth century in the German territorial states, and at the centre of these modifications stood the figure of the unwed mother. Infanticide became the point at which society's handling of the regulation of sexuality met the discussion of the legitimacy of capital punishment, and the subject where the debate on the abolition of the death penalty overlapped with that on the general revision of sexual legislation.[82] Women who committed infanticide became the focal point for key questions about the relationship between state laws, social customs, and the individual, as well as for considerations of the social, biological, and psychological causes of sexual behaviour.[83]

The infanticide debate in this form was a specifically German phenomenon, which preoccupied dramatists, novelists, and essayists from the mid-1770s.[84] In July 1780, more than 400 authors from various disciplines responded to the famous essay contest in Mannheim on the best means of preventing infanticide.[85] Ultimately, the debate on infanticide proved to be an intense controversy over a way of life centred on illegitimate birth understood as the product of disorderly sexual behaviour. Thus once again, issues of the boundaries between licit and illicit sexuality, between legitimacy and illegitimacy, and the question of opportunities and the right to marry became the object of fervent societal debate. Infanticide and punishment for fornication were linked here through the topos of the young, innocent, fallen woman who, fearing public disgrace, became the murderess of her own child – the victim of an unscrupulous male seducer, abandoned by the law, which was after all supposed to prevent, not promote, crime. The elements of this discourse – the innocent girl who went wrong because of love, the aristocratic seducer who ruthlessly exploited his social superiority, the wanton whore, the question of natural maternal love – brought together all of the important ingredients that had been assembled and developed over centuries of debate on notions of sexual and social order as applied to wedlock and marriage.

In the course of this, the debate on infanticide and its punishment expanded to encompass new questions. Initially this occurred through integration into a general reform discussion, which sought to replace punitive responses with prevention and prophylaxis, while also considering the sense and legitimacy of the death penalty and seeking to abolish penalties for fornication in favour of educational measures. The question of the emotional quality of the relationship between the infanticide and the seducer also became part of the growing eighteenth-century interest in the emotional quality of marriages, which left traces in trials for breach of promise as well as those for divorce.

Also amply evident were the irresolvable tensions between the need to fulfil the demands of the sexual order as formulated by the Christian authorities and the need to do justice to the requirements of the social order. These tensions manifested themselves in the highly indecisive and indeed contradictory manner in which practical legislative reform proceeded.[86] Isabel Hull has vividly traced the contradictions in the reform debates and policies of the eighteenth century, which ranged from radical abolition of all penalties for fornication to complete rejection of any revision of the law. Thus shortly before the punishment for fornication was lifted in 1800, first in Prussia and then in the other German states,[87] the basic problem that had accompanied the regulation of marriage in the preceding centuries re-emerged clearly: in the face of increasing social stratification and high rates of impoverishment, the desire for the purest possible society, coupled with the call for marriage as a universal way of life, had actually increased the amount of criminalized illicit sexuality and the rates of illegitimacy.[88]

Despite reforms to the penal codes in the nineteenth century, one key boundary, which the reformers had done their best to draw with absolute clarity, was left indistinct. The new zone of premarital sexuality, which had emerged with the institutionally orientated formal demands on marriage in the Reformed and Tridentine marriage ordinances, was never closed. The beginning of sexual relations and formal, official marriage thus remained legally and temporally separate.

NOTES

1 Burghartz 1999, 14–21. See Wunder 68–70 and van der Heijden 159–61.
2 Harrington 1995, 52–8.
3 On the enduring continuity of the discussion, see Harrington 1995. In this volume, see Lombardi 99–101, Lefebvre-Teillard 262, and Seidel Menchi 319–21.
4 Burghartz 1999, ch. 2. As the paradigm of confessionalization has impressively shown for German-speaking Europe in particular, this also applied to Catholic regions. On Bavaria, see Strasser 2004. On the relationship between the state, couples, and families more generally, see Burguière 1987.
5 Harrington 1995, 98–9.
6 See Donahue 36–8, Lombardi 102–3.
7 See, in this volume, the imposition of parental control in the Holy Roman Empire and Holland, 72–3, 160.
8 See, for example, the prohibition of the *Spinnstuben* (spinning rooms), in Benker 1986, Schnyder 1996, Medick 1980; or the observations for Piedmont in Cavallo and Cerutti 1990.
9 See, in this volume, Lombardi 104–5 and Usunáriz 208–9.
10 Burghartz 1999, 80–1 and 175–7 (for Basel); Breit 1991, esp. ch. 2.3.2, pp. 78–83 (for Bavaria).
11 Harrington 1995, 96–100.
12 Ibid., 78–84.
13 Stambaugh 1972–80.

14 Köhler 1932 and 1942. Marriage courts were set up in Berne in 1528, Basel in 1529 (Köhler 1932), Strasbourg and Konstanz in 1531, Ulm in 1533, and Augsburg in 1537 (Köhler 1942).

15 *Sammlung der württembergischen Gesetze*, vol. 4, part 1, 66–9, esp. 67. For a general account, see Rublack 1999.

16 Here the different kinds of illegitimate heterosexual relationships were brought together under one heading, starting with simple fornication – i.e., sexual relations between unmarried persons – and "untimely" (*unzeitlich*) sexual intercourse of couples who in principle wanted to marry, and extending to various forms of adultery and incest (*Blutschande*).

17 The Geneva consistory, an institution referred to in other Reformed cities as a marriage court (Zurich and Basel) or church court (*Chorgericht*, Berne), consisted of the city's pastors and 12 elders of the congregation. Convening under the chairmanship of the mayor, the consistory dealt with questions of faith, morals legislation, marital issues, and fornication cases (Köhler 1932 and 1942 and Kingdon 1972). Whether the consistory was primarily a repressive disciplinary authority or one that mainly played an intermediary role and served to regulate and reconcile conflicts is a matter of dispute in the current scholarly debate. See also Manetsch 2006 and Grosse 2008.

18 Kingdon 1972, 12. On southern Germany, see in particular Schuster 1992 and Schuster 1995.

19 Monter 1976, esp. 473–4. Manetsch 2010, 300, confirms these numbers and states, "Stefan Zweig's indictment that Calvin initiated a moral reign of terror in Geneva seems almost justified," but at the same time he points out the commitment of Geneva's ministers to pastoral care. A more conciliatory reading is offered by Witte and Kingdon 2005, 414. Following George Bernard Shaw, who "once called the period between a couple's engagement and wedding 'the perilous interval,'" they emphasize that the "Genevan authorities regulated this perilous interval in some detail in their statutes and cases," without questioning the very idea of "a perilous interval," which seems to be a slightly anachronistic or at least one-sided argument in favour of the reformed side.

20 Monter 1976, 484.

21 For the prince-bishopric of Speyer, Andreas Blauert in particular has pointed to the phenomenon of "moral reform as crisis management" and cites the adultery cases listed in the privy council minutes (Blauert 1993). Another focus can be found in Harrington 1995, esp. 214, which, while also stressing the marked similarities in Reformed and Catholic development between the Palatinate and the bishopric of Speyer, more strongly

underscores the continuity in marriage policy and above all the limited options available to the authorities.

22 Strasser 2004, 47.

23 Bullinger warned against using the argument of "beggars' weddings" to discourage young people from timely marriage and proposed that sons be married early, before they could become accustomed to a dishonourable way of life, in order to prevent fornication. Burghartz 1999, 67. See Wunder 78–9 and Burghartz 190n66.

24 Burghartz 1999, 122–5.

25 For a more general account, see Sikora 2005. See also Heinig 2006.

26 Mikat 1988.

27 For a detailed account of this case, see Rockwell 1904 and more recently Sikora 2012. For a brief exposition of this bigamy case together with a definition of morganatic marriage, see Seidel Menchi 326–31.

28 Sikora 2005, 16.

29 Ibid.

30 Ibid., 26; Rockwell 1904, 1–5.

31 Sikora 2005, 48.

32 Ibid., 13. For more on Constantia von Cosel and her relationship with August the Strong, see Hoffmann 1984; see also Oßwald-Bargende 2000.

33 On the broad spectrum of marital and extramarital relations between the sexes in the (early) Middle Ages and the legal history terminology associated with it, see Esmyol 2002 and Mazo Karras 2012.

34 Sikora 2005, 15, 25.

35 Ibid., 48.

36 Ibid., 44. On marriages and wedding celebrations among the high nobility, see also Spiess 1993, ch. 2.5, pp. 113–30.

37 Burghartz 1999, 138–43.

38 Platter, *Tagebuch*, 120–1.

39 Ibid., 327. For a psycho-historical interpretation of this passage, see Schröter 1991, esp. 384–8.

40 On autobiographical accounts, see Völker-Rasor 1993.

41 See Schnyder Burghartz 1992, ch. 4.1.2, pp. 264–74, or Lischka 2006, part C, ch. 1, esp. 126ff.

42 Burghartz 2004.

43 For examples of the extensive scholarly literature on charivaris, see Zemon Davis 1975, ch. 4; Thompson 1991, ch. 8; Klapisch-Zuber 1985b; Schindler 1996.

44 In Schleswig-Holstein, the term *Nachtfreien* (literally, night courtship) referred to ritual, controlled evening courtship visits of young men to young women.

45 In Bavaria, *Haberfeldtreiben* was the name given to a nocturnal tribunal of rebuke run by young men, which mainly punished "moral misconduct in gender relations, which was not pursued by the public courts": Ruth Schmidt-Wiegand in *Handwörterbuch zur deutschen Rechtsgeschichte*, cols. 644–5.

46 The term *Kiltgang* refers to forms of regulated courtship by young men mainly in rural areas in which individuals or groups visited young women of marriageable age in their rooms at night; see Paul Hugger, "Kiltgang," in *Historisches Lexikon der Schweiz*, 7:206.

47 On the various forms and the scholarly literature, see Lischka 2006, esp. part C, ch. 1, 121–3.

48 Schnyder Burghartz 1992, 390; Beck 1983.

49 See, in this volume, Introduction 22, Lombardi 98, 110, and Lefebvre-Teillard 261–2.

50 *Sammlung der württembergischen Gesetze*, vol. 4, part 1, 69. An undated regulation for Zurich probably comes from the same period; see Köhler 1932, 104ff., and for the seventeenth century Bänninger 1948, 42-50.

51 *Sammlung der württembergischen Gesetze*, Zweite Ehe-Ordnung (1 January 1553), vol. 4, part 1, 88.

52 Sibeth 1994, 156–7. On the bridal wreath, see Göttsch 1996, 209–11, and, in this volume, Korpiola 249–50.

53 Rublack 1998, ch. 5, and esp. 203–9. Basel introduced such legal condemnation of premature coitus and untimely delivery only in 1637 (Burghartz 1999, 175–7), and Berne not until 1686 (Schmidt 1995, 200).

54 For Basel, see Burghartz 1999, 177.

55 Ibid., 119.

56 Simon 1981, 124ff., and Schnyder Burghartz 1992, 262–4.

57 Sibeth 1994, 145–6, 217–20.

58 Rublack 1999, 10–11, 199–209, and esp. 203–9.

59 Ibid., 257.

60 Dürr 1995, ch. 6.

61 Ibid., 229–30.

62 Beck 1983, 122, 135–8.

63 Breit 1991, 109.

64 Ibid., 290–2. This development away from religious justifications and towards arguments in terms of welfare and the common good is also evident for Baden-Durlach. See Hull 1996, 108.

65 Beck 1983, 131.

66 Schmidt 1995, 202. Thus in Berne, for example, the age of majority for marriage was raised from 19 and 20 years, respectively, in the Reformation ordinance of 1529, to 25 years in the ordinance of 1723: Ibid., 190, 195–7.

67 The church court (*Chorgericht*) – presided over since the mid-sixteenth century by the pastor – consisted of six men elected by the congregation, who met once a fortnight to decide cases of marriage and morals. Schmidt 1995, 45–58.
68 Ibid., 220.
69 Ibid., 236.
70 This argument is already put forward in Safley 1984. On Basel, see 176–9.
71 Schmidt 1998.
72 Safley 1984, 180.
73 This sanctioning practice affected men and women quite differently, at least in the long run. We need only think of the history of "unwed mothers" and the abandonment of the principle of paternity. See Burghartz 1999, ch. 7.4, as well as Schmidt 1995, 236–40.
74 Watt 1992, 107.
75 Ibid., 112.
76 Ibid., 181–3.
77 Schilling 1989, esp. 292–3.
78 Ibid., 299.
79 For Berne, see Schmidt 1995, 198; Sutter 1995, esp. part B. For the discussion of the maternity and paternity principles in Prussia in the nineteenth century with reference to historical arguments, see Bors 1998, esp. 31–7.
80 Edward Shorter already makes this argument in *The Making of the Modern Family* (Shorter 1975).
81 Schmidt 1995, 239.
82 Hull 1996, 107–16.
83 Ibid., 111.
84 Ulbricht 1990, 231–44. Ulbricht (232) explicitly points out that it was not literary authors who unleashed the debate on the issue: Enlightenment thinkers had already discussed the problem of infanticide. Ulbricht and Rebekka Habermas (see Habermas and Hommen 1999) both emphasize the very tenuous connections between the literary treatment of the issue (Goethe's *Faust* is a concrete example) and the judicial trials. Thus Habermas writes of the analogies between the case of Susanna Brandt and the figure of Gretchen: "Brandt and Gretchen have little in common. The focus of these literary interpretations is not maidservants, but middle-class girls; their seducers are not commercial clerks or journeymen, soldiers or day laborers, but utterly decadent, immoral and unscrupulous members of the nobility. Moreover, in her literary incarnation, the child murderess is ultimately wholly innocent in contrast to her aristocratic seducer, a

middle-class girl who loses her honour solely because of the aristocratic haughtiness that forbade marriage with a commoner" (ibid., 39).

85 Ulbricht 1990, 217–328.

86 The contradictory approach is especially evident in Baden: Hull 1996, 108–11, 116–22.

87 Ibid., 127, and Mitterauer 1983.

88 Mitterauer 1983, 23–4. On high rates of illegitimacy in nineteenth-century Europe as a result of the green revolution, see ibid., 111.

Chapter 7

Marriage and Love in Sixteenth- and Seventeenth-Century Spain

JESÚS M. USUNÁRIZ

Church and State: The Regulation of Marriage as an Aspect of Political History

In Spain, marriage law was developed and formalized by the monarchy, particularly in Castile, by the *Siete Partidas* (Seven-Part Code) of Alfonso X of Castile, a thirteenth-century code which influenced Spanish law for centuries.[1] The relevant provisions are clustered in *Partida* IV, which is concerned with "marriage, which joins [man and woman] together," and is located in the middle of the *Siete Partidas*, "as the heart is placed in the middle of the body," to emphasize its importance. This *partida* contains the distinction between marriage and betrothal (*desposajas*). The latter is understood as "a promise which persons [*los omes*] make orally when they desire to marry" (*Siete Partidas*, IV.i.1). The law explains that the marital union can be created *per verba de futuro*, that is, by the exchange of promises accompanied by traditional exchanges of wealth, property, or wedding tokens (*arras*), including the ring that the groom put on the bride's finger, which had a prominent symbolic value (IV.i.2). To bring the union into full effect, however, a celebration before the parish church (*in facie ecclesiae*) had to follow the promise, legitimizing the couple's sexual relations. If in contrast the groom said "I take you" as wife in place of "I will take you," he contracted a marriage *per verba de presenti*, creating with the woman whom he addressed, and who uttered a reciprocal phrase, a marital bond that had full and immediate effect, because, the text explains, "there is no difference or distinction ... between one [marriage] contracted by words relating to the present time, and one that is consummated by the husband having carnal union [*ayuntamiento*] with his wife" (IV.i.4).[2]

Synods held in the dioceses of Spain during the Middle Ages were also concerned with marriage, as were catechisms. The catechism of Gutierre de Toledo (1377), for example, declared that a marriage had to be entered into publicly (*in facie ecclesiae*) and that it was a sacrament as the result of which the man and woman "could join together carnally in [one body]." The marriage was created by words in the present tense that demonstrated "that one party consented to [take] the other [as wife/husband]."[3]

Was parental or familial consent necessary to contract a marriage? Prior to the thirteenth century, secular law required it. Ecclesiastical law of this period punished couples who married without their families' consent, although the lack of this consent was not enough to invalidate the bond. In contrast, the consent of individuals marrying was absolutely necessary.[4] The *Siete Partidas* were a synthesis of secular and ecclesiastical legislation and, faced with the fact that the church did not deny the validity of a marriage contracted without parental or familial consent, in the end equated this kind of marriage with clandestine marriage.

The *Siete Partidas* thus forbid clandestine marriages (*encubiertos*) – that is, marriages that were contracted without witnesses and that therefore could not be proven – as well as marriages contracted without the presence of the bride's parents or other kin and without the traditional exchanges of wealth, property, or tokens (dowry and *contrados*) between the bride and groom. Similarly forbidden were marriages that were not celebrated *in facie ecclesiae* or not preceded by banns (IV.iii.1). Severe punishment was prescribed for those who violated these prohibitions. The marriages that were celebrated without following these requirements were nonetheless declared valid: the man and woman who contracted such a (prohibited) union had to be considered husband and wife and were joined to each other in the forum of the conscience (IV.iii.2). In short, the *Siete Partidas*, following the doctrine expressed by Pope Nicholas I in his letter to the Bulgarians in 866, held that "consent alone, with the desire to marry, constitutes matrimony between a man and a woman" (IV.ii.5).[5]

Thus the Castilian code left the door open to clandestine marriages. Severely prohibited in theory, they were nonetheless valid and legally binding.

The matrimonial legislation introduced by the *Siete Partidas* remained for the most part in force until the eighteenth century. In 1505 the *Leyes de Toro* (Laws of Toro) introduced some innovations, above all regarding property relations between spouses, adultery, and clandestine marriage. Thus modified, the marriage laws of the *Siete Partidas* were included in the *Nueva Recopilación* (New Compilation) promoted by Philip II in 1563 and promulgated in 1567.[6] Further, on 12 July 1564, Philip II announced the forthcoming enforcement in the Kingdom of Spain of all the decrees issued by the Council of Trent (1545–63).[7] Thus the matrimonial legislation enacted in the *Siete Partidas*, together with the modifications introduced by the *Leyes de Toro* and by the *Nueva Recopilación*, and the rules established by the Council of Trent would remain in force in the Spanish monarchy until the ordinances of Charles III of 1776. During these centuries of essential legal continuity, one constant element stands out with particular clarity: the tendency of the Spanish monarchy to delegate matrimonial matters to the church. One of the Laws of Toro, for example, defines clandestine marriage as "that which the church will deem clandestine," while limiting itself to prescribing confiscation of goods and exile for those (including witnesses) who participated in the celebration of such forbidden rites and to recognizing a father's right to disinherit a daughter who contracted such a union.

For its part, the Spanish Church prior to the Council of Trent focused particular attention on two questions relative to the formation of the marital bond: ensuring the publicity of the wedding and identifying possible impediments to the union, particularly those of kinship. Synodal assemblies concentrated their efforts on the first of these two problems in their attempt to halt the serious disorders that, to judge from the repeated prohibitions, were the result of non-publicized unions. Such efforts had already begun in the thirteenth century as a result of the implementation in Spain of the decrees of the Lateran Council of 1215, as well as in accordance with the royal legislation of the *Siete Partidas*, which followed to the letter the Lateran provisions on matrimonial matters. The synod of Segovia of 1325, for example, decreed that clergy needed to be informed that the exchange of consent *per verba de presenti* constituted marriage, because "the law [i.e., the *Siete Partidas*] presumes that this is marriage."[8] Similarly – according to the same synod – if a man standing before the door of the church presented wedding gifts to a priest who then uttered the words, "Lord, bless these tokens [*arras*]," and if the man then placed a ring "on the fourth finger" of a woman, he was united to her in matrimony (as the synod explained, there is a vein in the ring finger that leads directly to the heart, so one puts a ring on that finger to "unite their hearts").[9]

The synod of Salamanca of 1410 was inspired by the same doctrine. In chapter 68, in fact, marriage was defined, in terms similar to those used in the *Siete Partidas* (IV.ii.1), as "the union of man and woman, made between legitimate persons [*personas legitimas*]" – that is, able to contract marriage – defined as "indissoluble" ("that cannot be undone") and that had to join "the hearts."[10] Chapters 66 and 67, however, go beyond this definition, providing more detailed information on how to create the marital bond. The means to create a marriage was a "promise that the man and woman exchange to contract marriage in the future" or "in the present." This obligation could be expressed either as "a simple and naked promise" (*simple y desnuda promisión*) – the man saying "I will take you as wife" and the woman saying "I will take you as husband" – or by "giving each other their faith," that is, confirming the pledge with an oath, or by performing the ritual of giving the ring accompanied by the binding words. As these alternatives show, precisely which act or series of steps of the marriage process created the irreversible bond was neither clear nor unambiguous.[11]

The tenor of the synodal decrees discussed here takes for granted the publicity of the union and presupposes the parents' approval; at the same time, however, these decrees leave the bride and groom ample freedom for actions that escaped any regulation. These implicit features – the publicity of the union, parental consent, and ecclesiastical jurisdiction – were difficult to reconcile with a form of marriage that the young couple could legitimately contract with the simple exchange of words *de presenti* and confirm with subsequent sexual relations. This fully valid form of marriage relegated fathers and even the priest to secondary roles. The contradiction between these two forms of marriage became a more serious issue as clandestine marriages became less rare.

The problem of clandestine marriage was not new. The synods of Segovia in 1216 (chapters III, 3, and 21), of León in 1267 and 1303 (chapters 36 and 38, respectively), of Avila in 1384 (chapter 4), and of Santiago in 1289 and 1328 had earlier expressed opposition to clandestine marriage, insisting above all on the absolute necessity of the banns (*amonestaciones*) being read prior to a wedding in order to halt a practice that the church opposed just as much as families did.[12] But it was primarily in the fifteenth and sixteenth centuries that the Spanish Church intensified its efforts to establish – with ever greater precision – the boundaries of the bride's and groom's freedom and to contain a phenomenon that was clearly widespread across the peninsula. The Spanish clergy's sensitivity on the subject is explained by the social tensions and damage to the moral order that clandestine marriages caused. As the first two chapters of the synod of Zamora in 1479 declared,

> What great damages and evils follow and can follow clandestine and secret marriages is demonstrated by experience, both because of the enmity that is created between the kin of the bride and groom, as a consequence of the doubts to which these marriages give rise, given the impossibility of proving them – which [proof] would be possible if they were celebrated publicly – and because [in publicly celebrated unions] the matrimonial impediments between the bride and groom could be known and the betrothal and marriage contracts [*desponsorios* and *matrimonios*] could be proven clearly and fully.[13]

On the one hand, this passage provides a glimpse of a society harmed by conflicts between clans that were set against each other by a marriage opposed by one of the two families involved, who perceived it as an abuse and a trick. On the other hand, it shows us an ecclesiastical community exposed to the dangers of incestuous unions and the disorder of bigamy. All this had direct consequences for the validity of marital contracts and repercussions for the family economy.

The synods of Salamanca in 1451 (chapters 9–10) and 1497 (constitution 42),[14] of Coria in 1457–58 (chapter 11), of Segovia in 1472, and of León in 1440–59 and 1485–1500 (various chapters), the aforementioned synod of Zamora in 1479 (chapters 1–2), and the synods of Plasencia in 1499 (chapter 21) and of Tuy in 1482 (chapter 33) issued regulations aiming to curb this disorder. Similar decrees were issued by most of the synods held in Spain prior to 1563. In these regulations, the figure of the priest had a leading role.

The laity, who until late in the sixteenth century played an active – and often the central – role in the celebrations of betrothals and marriages, were progressively marginalized and excluded from all the nuptial rites. Severe penalties were prescribed for transgression. The acts of the synod of Salamanca in 1451, for example, say, "It has become known that some lay persons, men and women, are present and celebrate marriages *de presenti* and *de futuro*, and unite the hands [of the bride and groom] without the intervention of the priest or competent curate, and they pronounce the words used for making the contract of holy matrimony." The synod prohibited this type of lay-directed wedding celebration and punished with a fine of 200 *maravedíes* any layperson "who has celebrated or participated in such clandestine and secret marriages contracted without banns (*moniciones*)" and without the participation of a priest or curate. The practice of laymen officiating at weddings, however, proved tenacious, for the clerics meeting in the synod of Segovia in 1529 felt the need to establish that all marriages celebrated without the presence of a clergyman had to be contracted a second time within a month before a priest on pain of a fine of 10 gold florins (chapter 514). The persistence with which Spanish synodal assemblies returned to these subjects demonstrates the importance they attributed to the problem.[15] In terms that were peremptory but by no means resolved the matter, the synod of Cuenca in 1531 declared that "no layman should dare celebrate such a marriage," under pain of excommunication *ipso iure* and a fine of one gold mark.[16]

The Spanish clergy's preoccupation with the formation of marriage as it appears at these synodal assemblies was an expression of the disquiet that assailed the higher social strata of the laity. We find evidence of this uneasiness in a particularly authoritative source, petitions (*peticiones*) presented to the *Cortes*. The *Cortes*, political assemblies with consultative power that periodically brought together representatives of the three Spanish estates – the nobility, the clergy, and the bourgeoisie – were convened by the king, who presided over them; but the delegates had the right to present petitions, which the king could accept or reject. In the petitions of the Castilian *Cortes* of the sixteenth and seventeenth centuries, the painful subject of undisciplined marriage often appears. A petition presented at the *Cortes* of Madrid in 1551, for example, condemned as an "act of great ugliness" the marriage of a son under the age of 25 who contracted the union against the will of his father (petition 105).[17] A petition of the *Cortes* of Valladolid in 1537 asked that the penalty of disinheritance, which applied to daughters who married clandestinely, be extended to include those who were older than 25, that is, who were legally of age (petition 4).[18] In a petition of the *Cortes* of Toledo of 1538, it was proposed that disinheritance apply not only to daughters but also to underage sons who contracted marriages their relatives opposed (petition 91). Similar petitions are found in the acts of the *Cortes* of Valladolid in 1555 (petition 72) and in 1558 (petition 74) and of Toledo in 1559 (petition 75).[19]

Do the arguments made in these documents give us a taste of the fears that children's freedom of marital choice inspired in fathers of the noble and bourgeois classes? In my opinion, the tenor of these petitions does support this conclusion. Consider this sampling of examples. From the *Cortes* of Toledo in 1538: many young men "of few years," the assembly complains, without the permission of their parents marry "persons of low condition and bad reputation" (petition 75). From the *Cortes* of Valladolid in 1542: while daughters are subject to the authority of their parents (*recogidas en poder de sus padres*), sons have "greater freedom to destroy their fathers' memories," that is, to threaten the family honour (petition 11). From the *Cortes* of Valladolid in 1548: the marriages that the sons of "great knights and eminent persons" contract with persons of much lower status "usually produce great scandals and conflicts," and some of these unions are judged to be the results of persuasion or deception (petition 127). From the *Cortes* of Toledo in 1559: it is right "that children are in some way obligated to marry according to the wishes of their parents, especially children of the elite, because it is to be believed that their parents will make a suitable choice" for them (petition 75).[20]

Over the course of the sixteenth and seventeenth centuries, the Castilian *Cortes* succeeded in strengthening the *Leys de Toro* of 1505, which had already severely repressed clandestine marriages, with the aim of guaranteeing fathers complete control over the marriages of their sons and daughters. As the next section will demonstrate, however, this objective was never completely achieved.

Love and Marriage: Spanish Sources for a History of Emotions

Studies of marriage formation in Spain tend to agree that during the early modern period marriage was under the control of fathers (or family heads), a finding consistent with the legal developments discussed in the previous section. "It was the interests of the family that presided over the establishment of conjugal bonds."[21] In spite of the provisions of the Council of Trent (which left children at least theoretically capable of choosing their own spouses), "the economics of sentiment were subordinated" to the dominant practice of family interventionism.[22] The decisive factors in the choice of a spouse were "social status and economic considerations."[23] Given that matrimonial alliance was the way to preserve and transmit family wealth and property, heads of families allowed that goal to direct their negotiations, in which the parties primarily interested did not participate.[24] There is no lack of historians who declare flatly that in the Christian West love and marriage were incompatible.[25]

Cause papers from the ecclesiastical courts, on the other hand, tell a different story. From these documents, in which the Spanish archives are particularly rich, emerge characters and episodes that suggest this widely held opinion should be revised. The following suit is just one from a series of extremely varied cases.

San Sebastian (Navarre), 1602. One late afternoon in September, a public street became the setting for a promise of marriage. The woman and man involved were Águeda de Arbizu, the 18-year-old daughter of a local notable, and Juan Salmón de Camargo, an *alférez* (i.e., a junior military officer). The presence of spectators was no accident. "You are witnesses," Juan told passers-by, "that this lady and I give each other our faith and word to be husband and wife." In confirmation of this promise, the two joined hands. Later, when the case came to court, the witnesses recalled an extended two-year courtship that culminated in the public promise. The couple met at the house of a soldier who lived in front of Águeda, the captain Miranda, and as time went on Juan began to accompany her back to the door of her house. Frequent conversations "from one window to another" soon followed, along with meetings in which "words of great love" were exchanged, as were gifts, above all from Águeda (a decorated black velvet sleeve, a pouch, some fruit). In the surviving letters from Águeda to Juan, the "great love" uniting the couple finds passionate expression:

> "My husband, so great is the love that I bear you and the affection I have for everything of yours that your absence has meant that love pierces me body and soul ... I don't think to be of any use in the world except to you, my husband. You alone will be *mi bien* [my good] and my hope. You can believe in me and rest assured, my love, that I would never give you up for another, even if he were the Crown Prince of Spain."
>
> "Goodbye, my love; goodbye, my soul; goodbye, my vital core; goodbye, mine own heart; goodbye, my hope; goodbye, my love and gift of my body and soul; farewell, comfort of this world. I would like to go now, but I cannot manage it. What a comfort it is for me to say: as you are mine, I am yours, unto death!"[26]

The intimacy created by such shared rapture was not loath to show itself in public, as when the couple were seen seated together on a chest wrapped in a tender embrace. In greater privacy, their "great affection" expressed itself in sexual intimacy, something that was evidently not unusual, for the woman confessed to one of her maids that she had shared her bed with the *alférez* for 23 or 24 nights. Still, the young soldier perceived their bond to be fragile. When his imminent departure threatened them with a separation – Juan was going to court to receive the command of a company – he felt impelled to confirm their mutual commitment, even at the cost of introducing a note of violence into their relationship. One night, taking advantage of her father's absence, the young officer surreptitiously entered his lover's house, surprising her in a secluded room in the company of a servant. Taking her by the hand, he vehemently expressed his need to have her close and asked her to confirm immediately her commitment to be his wife and no one else's. The young woman, perhaps frightened, was reluctant to accede to this request and was only convinced to do so – she later said – because she believed herself to be completely at the young man's mercy.

The relationship was in fact fragile, because the woman's father was not aware of it. Águeda confided to her spiritual father: "Having confessed, her confessor told her that [the betrothal and promise to marry] could not be made without her father's permission; but that [once made], it had to be kept, despite her father's opposition." From the context in the document, it is clear that Águeda did not need to hear this information from the priest. Like many of her contemporaries, she was well informed about the rules governing couples' relationships. Indeed, her letters express her great certainty:

> Husband of my heart, as you know well there is only one faith and one God. And since you have given me [your faith], you are bound to keep it, as am I. Even if my father wants to marry me to the richest man in the world, I wouldn't trade: I would let myself be torn to pieces rather than break my promise to you … [And similarly:] And I also tell you, my heart, that if my father let me choose among twenty thousand other husbands, I would not deny you. And when he arranges to marry me off and the banns are read in church to publicize the marriage, I would send you a message [so that you would present yourself in church] in place of that one of the twenty thousand.[27]

Included in this correspondence is an early example of the symbolic language of love: the heart pierced by an arrow, sent by Águeda to her lover.

The young couple's correspondence shows very clearly, moreover, the cause of this anxiety and uncertainty about the future: Águeda's father was not only unaware of their relationship, but he might well refuse his consent. Distinct social and wealth differences divided the aspiring bride and groom, and Águeda's father could hope to "marry

Figure 5. The heart pierced by an arrow, sent by Águeda to her lover.

his daughter elsewhere" – as in fact he told the mediator whom Juan had sent to present his suit – that is, to make a more advantageous marital alliance. Informed that his daughter had bound herself by a promise, he threatened Águeda not only with complete disinheritance but even with death if she did not withdraw from the commitment. The servant whom Águeda sent at this point to her lover to explain that the marriage could not take place was told to emphasize the insurmountable obstacle: her "fear of her father."

> "And although [Juan] had slept with her for more than twenty nights, she let him free. And her father promised her he would fix it by artificially restoring her virginity, as he had done for her servant Mariacho, who had got married in Astigarraga after having been in their house for two years. And she [Águeda] had to live with her father and had to do what he wanted because otherwise her father" – supported by his kin, friends, and clients – "would have killed her."[28]

We know about the case of Juan and Águeda in such detail because Juan turned to the ecclesiastical court to demand that Águeda keep her promise to marry him. But theirs is not an isolated case. It was selected as a representative example from a vast body of similar cases that survives in Spanish archives. The case of Juan and Águeda is typical first of all from a numeric point of view: broken marriage promises account for 57 per cent of the causes of marriage-related litigation in the ecclesiastical court of Pamplona between 1511 and 1700.[29] These statistics tell us that in Spain as in other Catholic countries following the promulgation of the Tridentine decrees on marriage, couples' disputes moved from marriage – which the Tridentine codification had rendered no longer a cause of dispute – to the promise of marriage.[30] But looking beyond the numbers, the case of Águeda and Juan is also representative of love and marriage in early modern Spain for three other reasons:

1. because of the nature of the marriage promise and the use of rituals;
2. because Golden Age Spanish culture appears here as the site where a new language of passion was forged;
3. because of the role that sexuality plays in this case.

These themes will be examined in this order.

The marriage promise rituals enacted by Águeda and Juan are common to many European cultures in certain respects. The exchange of words in particular was an essential requirement for the valid manifestation of consent. According to the Roman Catechism, which took shape in precisely this period, in the absence of words, neither marriage nor betrothal could exist.[31] For Juan and Águeda, however, the ritual words were not enough, and their behaviour is the demonstration of a clear change in the requirements for validity. It was no longer sufficient for a couple only to exchange words of promise; it was now necessary to have witnesses to the exchange. The episode on the public road in San Sebastian demonstrates their conscious search for publicity. The next step was the couple's sense that they needed the even stronger guarantee of a promise in writing, as was also the case in France, particularly following the royal decree of 1639,[32] and in Italy.[33] Written promises by both men and women that come from Spanish archives are both varied and eloquent. This example of a written promise is from San Juan de Luz in the middle of the seventeenth century:

> The thirteenth of May in the year sixteen hundred sixty-two, in the locality of San Joan, I have given my word and faith to marry María de Echeverri, and thus in the presence of honourable women I remain firm in this [promise] forever, Joan de Perusqui.[34]

And here is an example from 40 years earlier, this time written by a woman:

> I, Donna Mariana de Arzalluz y Loidi, declare that the doctor Hernando de Lortia, physician of Tolosa, in sign of being my husband gave me the ring that he wore on his hand. In a sign of the same kind, I gave him the one that I wore on my hand, with some conditions. And in the case [these conditions] cannot [be met], I declare that once he proves his nobility as he must, at the Royal Council of Pamplona, I will be his bride. And this being true, I write the present [document] on 20 April 1622, in Regil.[35]

In addition to this sort of betrothal certificate, there are also documents in which both the man and the woman reciprocally declare their love and promise to marry. Documents of this kind – along with love tokens exchanged in the same circumstance, especially rings, and love letters – were requested and saved as potential legal proofs of the promise, to be exhibited if necessary in court. It was well known that such documents could be important if the promise became contentious or was denied.

But before it was ever a question of its being legal proof, the written promise had a very important social function as well as a fundamental psychological effect. When a public promise was not enough to reassure the woman, and above all the community, of the solidity and durability of the bond, lovers turned to writing. Consider, for example, the behaviour of the sailor Joanes de Ansa, who hailed from San Sebastián (Guipúzcoa) in the Basque Country. At first he gave his promise to marry to Joana de Alzueta in the presence of "many people." It was Joanes himself who sent Joana to "find witnesses before whom to make the marriage promise," and it was he who in front of the five neighbours Joana had collected together took Joana's hand and said, "Gentlemen, you will be witnesses to how I take Joana de Alzueda as my wife and betrothed, swearing that, God save me, I will keep this faith and word that I give her."

Their bond was a well-known fact, the couple had regular sexual relations, and the priest had begun to read the banns for them in the parish church. However, when the sailor told his fiancée that his ship was about to sail for Ireland, his imminent departure frightened her:

> "And so, Joanes, you are leaving without marrying me as you promised! How can you expect God to help you?" And he responded, "Joana, bring

me paper and ink, because I want to leave you a document written and signed by my hand. So if today or tomorrow I die without doing what I promised, that is, marrying you, you will be able to show it."[36]

The signed document that resulted from this discussion became a further step in the marriage process, a more solid and reassuring guarantee:

"I promise and give my faith and word – by the faith that I have in God – to be the husband of Joana de Alzueta and she my wife. And since I give this faith, I sign with my name Joanes de Ansa."[37]

A document of this sort served to guarantee the legitimacy and the solidity of the union not just in the eyes of the fiancée but as well in the eyes of the community, which considered itself responsible for public morality and oversaw the behaviour of its own members. Joanes's commitment had an effect. When he had already had several children with Joana, without however having kept his promise to marry her, a neighbour woman commented thus upon his return from a voyage, in the course of which, by his own account, he had barely escaped a shipwreck: "God allowed you to avoid this fate [the shipwreck] to remind you of your children and the obligation you have toward Joana."[38]

The second notable trait that our representative case of Juan and Águeda displays is the language that Águeda used towards Juan. Her letters are fragments of an amorous dialogue that as far as we know has few parallels in the Europe of this time. That women like Águeda, from outside the highest classes, had such skill with words and writing is a phenomenon that reveals that Golden Age Spain was the site where the vocabulary of passion was rediscovered and circulated even outside of elite circles. Armed with this language – which is to say, with self-awareness – young women formed by the cultural climate of early modern Spain claimed independence and ventured out autonomously onto life's paths. In the town of Villanueva de Salazar in Navarre, Joanes de Garayoa, age 28, and Juana de Moricorena, age 21, exchanged marriage promises without any witnesses on a night in August 1605. It was well known that Juana's parents would not welcome the union, which is why the lovers made their promises privately. But when Joanes brought up the risks attendant on "going against parental wishes," Juana replied resolutely that "even if it isn't the desire of her parents, she intends to marry him, even if he has to take her to the ends of the earth."[39] In other words, Juana was ready to run away with him.

Even more than in these quotations, the language of passion has left a decisive mark in letters. Read how Donna Isabel de Errazquin, a contemporary of Águeda, addressed Francisco López de Dicastillo in the early seventeenth century:

> My loving cousin, sweet enchantment of all my love, my beloved. Although I am sad because you have gone away, my soul, nonetheless I live joyful in hope, my beloved husband, because only four days remain until I will find myself in your arms. Ah, my lord! What happiness! Since my soul worships you, it is not strange that it yearns for this happiness. Ah, Franco of my life, how I am yours! And you, adored lover, are all mine. Tell me this, ecstasy of my tenderness and charming lord of my entire soul that faithfully loves you. My cousin, send me the linings so that I can repair them, whereas the stockings, well, you can bring them to me when you come, and I will put them on in your presence. Will you do that, my husband? I have no doubt of it, since you are already all mine and I all yours until death! I am entirely constant and submissive to your will, your wife who adores you, steadfast lover, your cousin.[40]

The symbol of a heart pierced by one or more arrows – already seen before as one of Águeda's expressive resources – also appears in this letter, accompanied by a verse:

> This sad heart
> Signifies great sadness
> But my heart knows
> How to wear pain as a badge of honour.[41]

The frequent references to clandestine meetings that are scattered throughout these messages leave little doubt about the nature of these shrewdly arranged encounters: "And you know that you promised me that when you came you would come secretly and would remain with me eight days at the house in Triana. Do it, my love, since you can do it very well," one young woman wrote to her lover.[42] And another: "And I beg you to come to San Juan, because it seems that we will not have people here and we will be able to find some time [for us]."[43] And even more explicitly: "I made sure that the back door, which earlier made a noise, doesn't anymore, because I had it cut down a little at the bottom ... , even

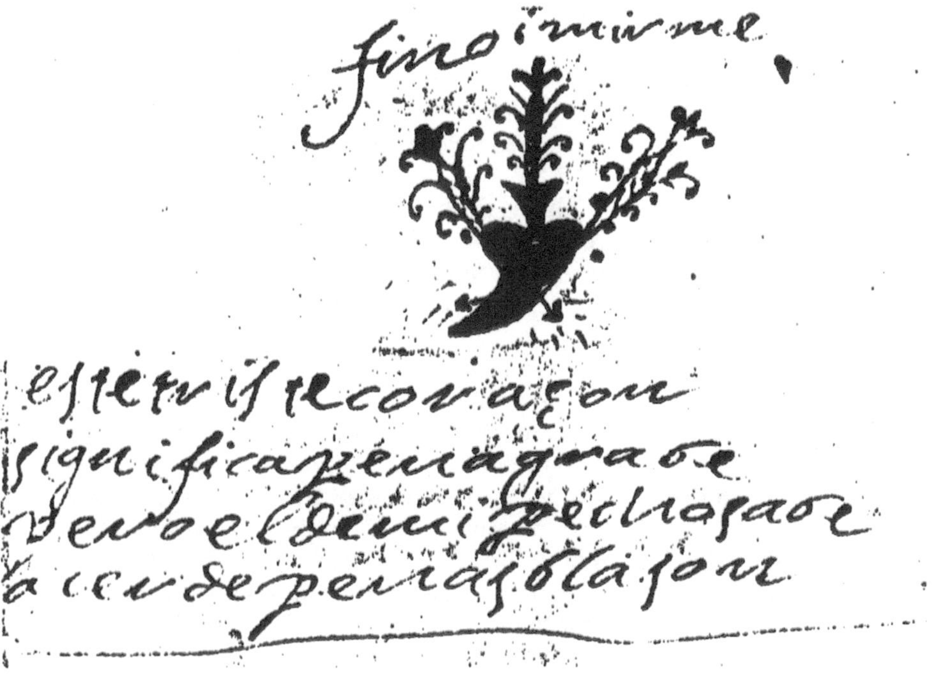

Figure 6. The symbol of a heart pierced by arrows accompanied by a verse.

if you don't need to come in that way, because my father has gone down to sleep in the lower room. So that you can come in by the [front] door safely as my husband, which you will be unto death."[44]

There were times when the emotional fervour caused mothers, who generally identified with the interests of lineage, to side instead with their rebellious daughters. In 1716 in Estella in Navarre, Maria Rosa Donado, in love with a certain Yoldi, learned that her father intended to marry her off instead to a relative and that he had already begun the process of obtaining the necessary dispensation from the impediment of consanguinity. "In times of affliction," she wrote to her lover, "a consoling angel is never lacking, and thus my mother, seeing me so tormented and afflicted, has acted as a mediator to alleviate my many woes."[45] More than just a mediator, her mother seems to have served Maria Rosa as a ready ally:

> My mother (who is well aware of my diverse inclination), compassionately … , has put herself very strongly against my father, telling him that

> he should not settle me in a manner so contrary to my desires nor to do me violence, because there is still time to marry me off. This has restored my soul to my body. So, to gain time, a letter has been written telling them [the family of the fiancé] that the prospective marriage was not well defined and that they should therefore consider it further.[46]

The evidence reviewed here clearly shows that this universe of emotions did not remain confined to the realm of words. These Spanish documents demonstrate that a promise of marriage signalled the beginning of a couple's sexual relations not only for the lower classes but also among the literate and wealthy. To conclude that sexual activity was legitimated by a marriage promise – as happened in Italy[47] – would be reductive. In Spain it was a question not of acceptance into the social context but of an internal conviction of the lovers themselves that they were in the right. The initiation of sexual relations was understood as a requirement that accompanied the promise and that was necessary to formalize the relationship between the betrothed in the eyes of the community. The community did not just absolve a betrothed woman who was involved in a regular sexual relationship with her fiancé; it became the depository for the memory of her rights and, if necessary, proponent of her cause.

It is probable that the magistrates were not unaware of the community's opinion. In most of the cases considered here, the ecclesiastical judges pronounced in favour of the celebration of matrimony. When one of the parties presented love letters as proof, the sentence of the diocesan court obliged the couple to marry in 65 per cent of the cases, and to do so within a very short period of time (10 days in the case of Águeda de Arbizu and Juan Salmón de Camargo, the same in the case of Joanes de Ansa and Joana de Alzueta).

Marital Transgressions and Their Control

Both ecclesiastical and civil authorities devoted a great deal of effort to the control and repression of behaviours that threatened to violate marriage as a sacrament. Because marriage "was perceived as the only social space capable, because of its sacramental effects, of providing the [spiritual] help the faithful needed to support the burdens that derived from the marital union and from the obligation to raise and educate children,"[48] both the church and the state were equally interested in protecting it. The misbehaviours and disorders of married couples' lives were *crimina mixti fori*, or crimes of mixed forum, falling under the jurisdiction of both ecclesiastical and secular authorities.[49] Included among these transgressions were adultery,[50] cohabitation,[51] defloration (*estupro*),[52] incest,[53] and pandering or abetting sexual transgressions,[54] all crimes that could be prosecuted by either ecclesiastical or secular courts. Considered particularly serious was bigamy, that is, the crime of a person who took a second wife or husband while the first was still living. In Spain, as in Italy, bigamy fell under the jurisdiction of the Inquisition, because it was considered a deviation from the Catholic doctrine of the sacraments.[55]

From the very rich documentation in the Archivo General de Navarra, now being explored and analysed, there emerge fragments of a lively community life, in which low-profile matrimonial transgressions – almost always within the competence of the secular courts – are part of the day-to-day experience of the inhabitants and generally do not provoke strongly hostile reactions. The transgressors themselves seem to be well integrated into the social body and do not behave like guilty sinners. In Burguete, for instance, a husband, Hernando de Roncesvalles, denounces to the royal tribunal the adultery of Arnaute Aldasoro with Catalina de Ilzaurralde, Hernando's wife and the mother of his two daughters, declaring that he has surprised the two lovers in intimate circumstances: this discovery, instead of inducing the adulterers to repent – the exasperated husband declares – has induced them to flee and has hardened their hearts to their sin (1544).[56] That sexual sins were treated with a certain indulgence is suggested also by the way the community of Navarre reacted to *amancebamiento* (concubinage, i.e., cohabitation). Juan de Sola, an inhabitant of Orbanos – although well known to be married – is living in public concubinage with Juana de Garayoa, of Larrasaoaña, without the supposed "public scandal" mentioned in the denunciation imposing on them the slightest discretion: it is the *fiscal del reino* (i.e., the public prosecutor) who initiates proceedings against him, but he does so using a terminology that betrays the insubstantial nature of his charges (1598).[57] The practice of the matrimony of mere consent, without any ecclesiastical solemnization, is also part of day-to-day experience for these communities. Ecclesiastical anathemas and the prohibitions raised against "clandestine marriages" by the *Siete Partidas* – we met them in the first part of this chapter – are not sufficient to dissuade, for example, Juan Ibáñez and Pascuala de Olazagutía from their nuptial plans: meeting in a wood, on a Sunday, the two of them enact their own marriage in the presence of the four witnesses they have brought with them, scrupulously observing the traditional ritual, which requires the touching of hands, and choosing particularly solemn phrasing as *verba de presenti* – "I give you my faith, o Pascuala, as husbands and wives do, and I take you as my wife" and "I too, Johane, give you my faith as husbands and wives do, and I take you as my husband, Johane" (1548).[58]

Among the sexual sins that proliferated in the Spanish air we need finally to consider ordinary fornication, which on the Iberian Peninsula was not only an act or a series of acts but was also an opinion or complex of opinions. The view that venal sexual relations between an unmarried man and an unmarried woman are not sinful was so deeply rooted that the Spanish courts had very little success in combatting it. Officially, this belief was regarded as heretical blasphemy in as much as it violated the sacrament of marriage. So we find the peasant Miguel Merino – to cite just one among dozens of similar examples – convicted for having maintained that "having congress and carnal copulation with a public woman is not a sin" (ca. 1586).[59]

We will conclude this brief survey with a case argued in Pamplona in 1577, which unlike the earlier ones illustrates how communities were able to exercise careful control over matrimonial transgressions – and activate a disciplinary procedure – when such behaviour was judged harmful to society.[60]

In that year, before the royal tribunal of Navarre appeared a young vegetable grower named Sancho de Valcarlos, an inhabitant of the *rione* of Santa Maria Magdalena on the outskirts of Pamplona. He had been called to testify at the trial of María San Juan, called "la Basca," who was accused of facilitating (or abetting) illicit sexual activities. Valcarlos had known this woman for several years because she had lived in a rented house in the same neighbourhood. It was rumoured that "while living there the said accused had many friendships and conversations [i.e., relations] with many men and women and girls who came to the river" – to wash bedclothes and clothing – "who were accustomed to go in and out of her house many times." It was even said that "day and night she hid a girl in the company of a man." Because of this, the inhabitants of the district had decided to "take note of who entered and left her house at night," putting the house and its occupants under surveillance. One of those carrying out this surveillance showed himself to be particularly diligent: one day "he saw a man enter the house of the said María la Basca one hour after nightfall, and since he did not come out," the watcher informed the district leaders. These men went from house to house summoning the district inhabitants, who then as a group entered the suspect house and searched the rooms one by one. In an upstairs room "they found a beautiful woman in a bed" – but she was alone. Everything fed the suspicion that while María had delayed answering the door to the searchers, the man who had been seen entering the house under cover of darkness had jumped out a window and fled through the gardens that lined the Arga river alongside the house, or that "he was hidden in some corner of the house itself." The search was thus unsuccessful, but the suspicion of evil conduct and the woman's bad reputation were enough to provoke a denunciation by her neighbours – mostly peasants and vegetable farmers – against "la Basca." A few days later "by order of the district," the district leaders expelled her as an "abettor" or facilitator of sexual crime (*encubridora*).

A little while later, "la Basca" reappeared in the neighbourhood of San Cernin, inside the city walls. Here again she lived in a rented house, with an annual rent of six ducats. The two-room dwelling had two entry doors, each opening onto a different street, which allowed her visitors to go in and out with the utmost discretion. One of the two rooms contained a fine feather mattress, which all the witnesses in the case recalled with impressive precision. The entire neighbourhood, in fact, either knew or suspected the activities that took place in these rooms. María, one of the witnesses tells us, possessed neither house nor goods but "always goes about with various people and has more acquaintances, both men and women, than any other woman in the neighbourhood, and always draws numerous people to her lodgings, as many men as women and girls, under the pretext of having meals; thus the rumour is that she provides a cover for people [i.e., their illicit encounters], and doesn't live in any other way [i.e., she has no other income] and of such [i.e., of abetting] she was accused."

A scandal discovered within her walls – one that ended without tragedy thanks to the intervention of "certain respectable persons" after a betrayed husband had surprised his wife in María's house – resulted in the public prosecutor's opening an investigation into the woman's occupation. Various witnesses testified about those they had seen go in and out of her house: "a beautiful woman, who they say lives with her patron in that city"; a girl from Baztan (in Navarre) "with a beautiful face, who was said [to live] with a leading man of that city, and the said accused woman [la Basca] used to make her come to her house and from there [the girl] went to the house of her male friend and then she came back to the house of the accused"; a man "whose name will not be said for decency's sake," who had been seen in one of the rooms with a girl, "while eating some fresh fish," and so on. Moreover, another witness declared, "they generally entered by one door and left by the other, which is confusing, and when they entered her house she [María] went to fetch wine, and left them in her room, and she lived by that, and not a girl passed on the street who wasn't her friend, and she lodged some of them in her room, and she lived by this."

Some witnesses added – and this was a great scandal to the neighbourhood – that María San Juan had tried to lead her own daughter into concubinage. According to Inés de Roja, the wife of a gunner, two years earlier, in 1575, one of her acquaintances had asked her to host in her house a friend's protégée, whose marriage he was trying to arrange. Until the marriage took place, the friend asked Inés to give hospitality to the girl and "to teach her to sew and other refined skills." Inés's husband, once consulted, accepted the proposal but on the condition that no man should enter his house while the girl was lodged there. The girl, Joana, was no other than María la Basca's daughter. Joana told her hosts that her mother had by trickery taken her from the house where she had been entrusted to the care of one of the most influential men in the city and had then tried to arrange for her to become a concubine. The girl had resisted: "she said she was still a maiden and that she begged not to be thrown into perdition." She managed to free herself, for the moment.

Not surprisingly, the public prosecutor, highly alarmed, concluded that "with little fear of our Lord God and of our royal justice," the accused "had exercised the profession of procuress and of public abettor for every sort of person, and with largesse and payments and other illicit means had persuaded and convinced many married and unmarried women" to put themselves in the power of "some influential persons of this city." María la Basca was condemned to banishment from the city and its territory for the period of one year.

Conclusion

The phenomenon of marriage has been treated in this chapter from two opposed and complementary points of view. In the first part, marriage was viewed from the more established and traditional historiographical perspective, while in the later parts it was examined from a more current perspective that is attuned to potential future historiographical developments. These two perspectives have two corresponding types of sources. The normative, institutional, and impersonal sources of the first section of the chapter contrast with the more individual sources in the later sections, which document, often meticulously, the concrete experiences of couples, reconstructed both by means of the testimony of the parties themselves and by the voices of the people around them.

The normative sources – secular law and ecclesiastical regulation – in the first part of the chapter focus on marriage as the object of a dialectic between ecclesiastical and secular powers. This aspect of the political and institutional history of Spain can be fruitfully compared to other political-cultural areas of Europe (particularly France, Italy, and England). The distinctive trait of Spanish history in this regard is the continuity of the collaboration between the monarchy and the Catholic Church, in which the former submitted without protest to the directives of the latter, reproducing them in its own legislation.

The documents that form the basis of the later sections are, on the other hand, the matrimonial cause papers that furnish the connection between all the chapters in this book. In these documents, which have only recently become the object of Spanish sociological and historical attention, the concrete case comes to the forefront of the discussion. The placement of the concrete case at the centre of scholarly discourse has recently received a great deal of attention as a methodological issue, especially in France.[61] From this point of view, the Spanish records are particularly distinctive. The files produced by the chancelleries and scribes of the Spanish courts – when misunderstandings, tensions, or conflicts arising between the couple bring before ecclesiastical or secular judges the man and woman, their families, friends, neighbours – are rich mines of information for the history of emotions, which is today one of the most fascinating lines of scholarly investigation.[62]

NOTES

1 The following abbreviations are used in the citation of records held in archives:

ADP: Archivo Diocesano de Pamplona
AGN: Archivo General de Navarra

2 This article of the *Siete Partidas* obviously refers to *matrimonium praesumptum*. See, in this volume, Lombardi 98–9, 109–10, and Lefebvre-Teillard 261–2.

3 Aznar Gil 1989, 53–5.

4 See Donahue 34.

5 On this, see Rodríguez Arango 1955, 737, and, in this volume, Lombardi 99–100.
6 *Nueva Recopilación*, book V, title 1, law I, f. 2.
7 Tineo 1996.
8 *Synodicon Hispanum*, 6:45.
9 Ibid., 6:321.
10 Ibid., 4:274ff.
11 Charageat 2011, 37–43; see Donahue 34 and Lombardi 97.
12 *Synodicon Hispanum*, 1.
13 Ibid., 4:437–9.
14 Ibid., 4.
15 See also the synods of Palencia in 1500 (ch. 106) [*Synodicon Hispanum*, 7], of Badajoz in 1501 (ch. XIV-1) [*Synodicon Hispanum*, 5], of Burgos in 1503–11 (ch. 309 and 407) [*Synodicon Hispanum*, 7], of León in 1526 (book XXX, ch. 1–3) [*Synodicon Hispanum*, 3], of Tuy in 1528 (book IV, I) [*Synodicon Hispanum*, 1], of Mondoñedo in 1534 (ch. 18) [*Synodicon Hispanum*, 1], of Plasencia in 1534 (ch. 22) [*Synodicon Hispanum*, 5], of Palencia in 1545 (book IV, title II) [*Synodicon Hispanum*, 7], of Oviedo in 1553 (book IV, I, ch. 1) [*Synodicon Hispanum*, 3], of Astorga in 1553 (book IV-11, ch. 1, 2, 3) [*Synodicon Hispanum*, 7].
16 Nalle 1992.
17 *Cortes*, 5:545.
18 *Cortes*, 5:664, 773.
19 *Cortes*, 4–5.
20 Ibid.
21 Morant 1991, 577.
22 Rodríguez Sánchez 1990, 377–80.
23 Rothe 1978, 139, 141.
24 See Isabel Testón on the family in Extremadura: Testón 1985, 53.
25 Rougemont 1962.
26 "Esposo mío, es tanto el amor que tengo y afición para tus cosas pues tu auçençia a causado, que se me entra amor en mi cuerpo y en el alma. Pues ya sabías que en mi pecho cuán poco dexastes. No pienso servir en este mundo sino a ti, esposo mío. Tú sólo eres mi bien y mi esperansa. Que podrás creer y estar satisfecho de mí, amor mío, que jamás te trocaré a otro, aunque fuese el infante de España, como no lo será … Adiós, mi bien; adiós, mi alma; adiós, mis entrañas; adiós, corazón mío; adiós, mi esperanza; adiós, bien mío y el regalo de mi alma y de mi cuerpo; adiós, descanso de este mundo. Quisiese partir, pero no puedo. Que me alivio en decir: '¡qué bien tú mío, yo tuyo, hasta la muerte!'" ADP, Sojo, c. 114, no. 6, unpaginated.

27 "Bien sabes, esposo de mi alma, que no hay más de una fe y un Dios. Y pues me la diste, estás obligado de guardármela, como yo lo hago. Que aunque me quisiese mi padre casar con el más rico del mundo no te trocaría; antes me dexarías de hacer pedazos que negarte la fe que te he prometido"; "Y más te digo, corazón mío, que si mi padre me diese a escoger veinte mil maridos, no te negaría. Y cuando procurase el casarme y que se hiciesen las proclamas en la iglesia para conocer, te enviaría un propio a los veinte." ADP, Sojo, c. 114, no. 6, unpaginated.
28 ADP, Sojo, c. 114, no. 6, f. 6r, 55v–56v, 60v.
29 Campo Guinea 1998, 60.
30 See, in this volume, Lombardi 105–8 and Lefebvre-Teillard 271–2.
31 *Catecismo Romano*, 1:357–8 (English translation, 227–8).
32 Flandrin 1984, 79.
33 See Lombardi 116.
34 ADP, Oteiza, c. 1071, no. 27, f. 11r.
35 ADP, Ollo, c. 658, no. 1, f. 46r.
36 ADP, Ibáñez, c. 426, no. 2, f. 47r.
37 Ibid., f. 11r.
38 Ibid., f. 49v.
39 ADP, Secretario Marichalar, c. 459, no. 21, f. 10r–10v.
40 "Amoroso primo mío, dulce hechizo de todo mi amor, mi bien. Aunque ayer quedé triste porque te fuiste, alma mía, pero con la esperanza vivo gustosa, amado esposo mío, que me faltan cuatro días para verme en tus brazos. ¡Ay dueño mío! ¡Qué dicha! Si el alma te adora no es mucho que anhele esta dicha. ¡Ay Francho de mi vida y que tuya soy! Y tú, querido amante, eres todo mío. Dímelo, embeleso de mi cariño y atractivo dueño de toda el alma que fiel te ama. Primo mío, envíame las fundas para que las tenga compuestas, que las medias, el día que vengas, me las traerás y en tu presencia me las pondré. ¿Querrás, marido mío? No lo dudo; ¡si eres ya todo mío y yo toda tuya hasta morir! Mi bien firme y rendida a tu voluntad, tu mujer, que te adora, firme amante, tu prima." ADP, Ollo, c. 884, no. 14, f. 69r (the original at fols. 62r–66v).
41 ADP, Ollo, c. 884, no. 14, f. 69r.
42 ADP, Sojo, c. 114, no. 6, unpaginated.
43 ADP, Ollo, c. 1488, no. 19, f. 86r–86v.
44 ADP, Sojo, c. 114, no. 6, unpaginated.
45 ADP, Ollo, c. 1488, no. 19, f. 88r–v.
46 Ibid., f. 88r–v; fols. 90r–91r.
47 See Lombardi 110–11.
48 Bel Bravo 2000, 161.

49 Candau Chacón 2004, 406. See Lombardi 105–7.

50 Charageat 2011, 171–92.

51 Barahona 2003, 94–118; Charageat 2011, 171–92.

52 Barahona 2003, 18–19, 41–93, 158–9.

53 Here incest means a marriage within the prohibited degrees of kinship that was contracted without first having obtained a dispensation from the Apostolic Penitentiary. See Schmugge 2008, 58–61; Salonen and Schmugge 2009, 22–3, and Donahue 35.

54 See, this volume, Usunáriz 218–20.

55 Siebenhüner 2006. For bigamy in Spain, see Tanco 2002.

56 AGN, Procesos, no. 066206.

57 AGN, Procesos, no. 283813.

58 Lizarraga Artola 1991, 349.

59 Chavarría Múgica 2001. "Heretical" opinions of similar content are documented in southern Italy, Romeo 2008, 201–3.

60 AGN, Procesos, no. 4521.

61 Passeron and Revel 2005.

62 Usunáriz 2004; Usunáriz 2005; Usunáriz 2012; Usunáriz and García Bourrellier 2012; Usunáriz 2014.

Chapter 8

Marriage in Sweden 1400–1700: Formalism, Collectivism, and Control

MIA KORPIOLA

Introduction

On 26 April 1598, vicar Hans of Södermalm appeared at the Consistory of Stockholm together with a Scottish Flax-weaver named Sander and Sander's daughter.[1] They explained that Johan Persson, an apprentice of Nils the Flax-weaver, had lawfully trothplighted Sander's daughter and that they had had intercourse. In fact, Sander's daughter – whose name is never mentioned in the source – had already given birth to Johan's baby. The court decided that Johan Persson was to be heard the following Wednesday. When he appeared, obeying the summons, he was asked three questions: First, if he had indeed trothplighted the maid. Second, if he had given her gifts. Third, if the trothplight had taken place lawfully, in the presence of "good and major witnesses." Johan Persson answered affirmatively to all points. The engagement had taken place in the presence of the girl's parents and Johan's master Nils the Flax-weaver. Two other witnesses, Henrik Viborg and his wife, also seem to have attended. In addition, Johan had given his fiancée a ring as a pledge. Sander and his wife affirmed that they had been present at the trothplight and consented to it. The Scot also submitted to the tribunal Johan's letter to him in which the youth referred to the girl as "his heart's dear betrothed." After such unambiguous and uncontested evidence, the Consistory of Stockholm declared them to be married by virtue of "God's word and the Church Ordinance [of 1571]." Their vicar, Hans of Södermalm, then solemnized the marriage.[2]

As Johan Persson did not dispute any of the alleged facts, he seems only to have needed the smallest nudge to have his union with his fiancée, the mother of his child, solemnized by the church. Indeed, this was probably Sander's intention in taking the matter to court. Johan Persson's meek and honest admission of all the allegations made by his father-in-law is unusual, but otherwise the case displays the basic features of early modern Swedish marriage disputes with the clarity of a model example. In most cases, intercourse had taken place either before or after the engagement. Parental consent, the presence of witnesses, and engagement gifts were necessary formalities for a valid engagement, while intercourse transformed the union into indissoluble matrimony. The ecclesiastical courts investigated the circumstances of the trothplighting to determine if intercourse had been accompanied by an exchange of consent and sufficient formalities had been performed for the relationship to be considered a marriage.

The starting point for this chapter is that Swedish marriage was a process composed of several acts with legal meaning, and the status of the future spouses changed gradually during the course of this process. The various acts – betrothal, wedding, transfer of the bride to the groom's house, bedding, and sleeping together – constituted the marriage process recorded in the medieval secular laws. Each stage was properly accompanied by festivities and attended by witnesses. Only after all these stages had been completed was a couple considered married.[3] The laws prescribe how and when property consequences and the transfer of the woman's legal guardianship came into effect, which happened in a piecemeal fashion.

In contrast to this, the church's canonical doctrine of marriage was based on a conception of marriage as created at one clearly defined moment.[4] Over the course of the Middle Ages, the growing influence of this notion blurred the collectivism and formalism of the Swedish system. The ecclesiastical conception of the sacrament of marriage had tendencies towards individualism, as represented by the acceptance of informal and unwitnessed exchanges of present-tense consent as sufficient to create a binding marriage. Although the church doctrine upheld informal marriages, it also introduced in Sweden ecclesiastical solemnization preceded by the reading of the banns. The publicizing of the banns and ecclesiastical solemnization came to be included in the medieval laws as the detailed description of the stages of the marriage process faded away. At the same time, solemnization became an integral part of the Swedish marriage process because it was a way to ensure the publicity and control that secular society also desired. The influence of canon law also contributed to the birth of the institution of trothplight as a more informal equivalent of betrothal, but the canonical distinction between *verba de futuro* (which amounted to engagement) and *verba de presenti* (which created a marriage) was never truly accepted in Sweden. Consequently, the Swedish Lutheran Church dropped the distinction after the Reformation, when the tense of the words of consent lost relevance because all vows made prior to the wedding or solemnization were perceived as engagements.

The Lutheran Church opposed the informality of marriage vows and engagement that the Catholic marriage doctrine had permitted. Instead, as in the previous case, it required that couples observe certain formalities. If these were disregarded, even a consummated exchange of consent could be dissolved at the request of one of the parties. Otherwise, the church accepted that a formal engagement (betrothal or trothplight) accompanied by intercourse constituted a marriage. However, engagements could be – and were – regularly broken by the ecclesiastical courts, that is, the bishop acting together with his cathedral chapter. While divorce in the modern sense, meaning dissolution of a valid marital bond so that at least the innocent party might licitly remarry, had been forbidden by the Catholic Church, the Reformation (re)introduced divorce in Sweden. Divorces were generally granted for adultery and malicious abandonment, but occasionally also for other reasons, until the late seventeenth century, when the ecclesiastical courts became more rigorous. By this time, however, the kings had begun to grant divorces on other grounds, using their power to grant privileges and pardons.

Over the course of the seventeenth century, ecclesiastical surveillance of the marriage process increased as the more rigid Lutheran orthodoxy set in. The Lutheran Church also opposed various popular marriage customs, alleging that they caused scandal and disorder or that they were associated with beggary.[5] Reports of sexual crimes multiplied, mainly because systems of control became more effective. The Swedish marriage process became less clearly defined and shorter under the combined influences of ecclesiastical pressure and German and learned (Roman) law. While the introduction of the Law Code of 1734 meant the demise of many medieval legal norms, it could not entirely obliterate the perception of marriage as a process.

Matrimonial Jurisdiction and Legislation in Later Medieval and Early Modern Sweden

Late medieval Sweden, which comprised much of present-day Sweden and Finland, had been effectively Christianized only in the twelfth and thirteenth centuries. From this period on Catholic notions of matrimony and canonical marriage norms influenced local law and practice. The first sporadic sources that deal with matrimony in Sweden date from the late twelfth century. More material, such as papal letters and synodal statutes, survives from the latter half of the thirteenth century. The oldest secular sources, the provincial laws (ca. 1280–1350) and royal statutes date roughly from the same period. The laws of King Magnus Eriksson (reigned 1319–64) for the towns and the countryside (Magnus Eriksson's Town Law and Magnus Eriksson's Law of the Realm) became the most influential laws in medieval Sweden. In 1442, a revised version of the Law of the Realm was promulgated, but it only began to supplant the older law in the second half of the sixteenth century. The Town Law was applied in all Swedish towns, the largest of which was the capital, Stockholm, with 5,000–7,500 inhabitants. These two laws were abrogated only when the national 1734 Law Code came into force.

Sixteenth-century Sweden was a poor, peripheral, agricultural country. In 1527 it became the first realm outside the German-speaking lands to embrace the Protestant faith. The Swedish Lutheran Church was under the supremacy of the king. It retained its own separate jurisdiction, but bishops lost much of the economic and political power and independence they had had prior to the Reformation. The king became the highest ecclesiastical judge in the country, granting the first divorces in the 1530s. When he and his bishops disagreed, as in 1552 when the clergy protested against King Gustav I Vasa's (reigned 1523–60) marriage to his deceased wife's niece, the king did as he pleased.[6]

Marriage (excluding property matters) and sex-related issues had formed a large part of the practice of the medieval ecclesiastical courts of Sweden. The records of several Swedish ecclesiastical courts have been preserved from the 1590s on, whereas none exists from the Middle Ages. A bishop's register and some scattered documents are all that remain of the medieval and early Reformation period. The influence of medieval canon law in Reformation and early modern Sweden has not been thoroughly researched. Clearly, however, in matrimonial matters it remained considerable. The new Reformation legislation mainly regulated forms of engagement, solemnization, and grounds for divorce, but as this hardly covered all aspects of marriage, the old canon law remained in the background, seldom directly referred to but applied as custom especially in connection with matrimonial impediments.[7]

Both secular and ecclesiastical law continued to control marriage-related matters. Marriage formation was regulated by both legal systems.

The secular courts adjudicated matters relating to the marriage process, matrimonial property issues, engagement gifts, inheritances, and child support. Secular courts completely took over the punishment of sexual offenders after the Reformation, although such offenders also had to undergo ecclesiastical censure imposed by the chapters and consistories. These church bodies mainly evaluated the validity of engagements and marriages, imposed ecclesiastical censure on offenders, acted as marriage counsellors, and dissolved engagements and marriages. Royal supremacy over the church and sexual crime excepted, the jurisdictional division was not much altered from the Middle Ages.

The 1571 Church Ordinance and the 1686 Church Law were the main sources of ecclesiastical law and, supplemented by secular legislation and diocesan statutes, the most important sources of rules regulating marriage. Before and between these two laws, there were some attempts at legal reform, but these came to nothing. The 1686 Church Law was a monument of rigid Lutheran orthodoxy that adjusted the balance between ecclesiastical and secular jurisdiction slightly to the advantage of the worldly authorities.[8] The tradition of issuing synodal statutes on the diocesan and provincial level also continued. The secular Code of 1734 was the result of nearly half a century of drafting. No Enlightenment codification, it was instead conservatively based on the legal practice (norms and precedents) and the value system of the late seventeenth century.

The Swedish secular legal system was in the hands of laymen without university training. In the countryside, the courts were staffed by mostly noble judges with peasant juries as co-judges, and in towns by burghers. These laymen applied Magnus Eriksson's or King Christopher's laws supplemented with the provincial laws and statutory legislation. When the 1442 law was printed in 1608, giving Sweden its first printed law book, it finally replaced Magnus Eriksson's Law of the Realm. The formal reception of the Bible, or the "Law of God," as a legal source took place in this same year. Court sentences began increasingly to be justified by Bible citations, an indication of the increasingly strict Lutheran orthodoxy which was soon visible in all fields of life, including marriage and sexuality.[9]

In its seventeenth-century heyday, Sweden expanded into a European great power that required a large hierarchical bureaucracy to take care of administration, taxation, and conscription. Local communities were supervised on an unprecedented scale. Centralization had a price, however, and at the parish level, medieval local freedom, independence, and discretion were largely sacrificed for the benefit of state formation.

The Swedish Marriage Process and Rituals

As discussed, the medieval ecclesiastical notion of marriage focused on a decisive moment in marriage formation, namely the couple's exchange of present-tense consent. In contrast, the Swedish secular late thirteenth- and early fourteenth-century provincial laws describe marriage as a process with several stages upon the completion of which the couple was finally considered married.[10] The couple was transformed gradually into husband and wife, and the accompanying spousal duties and rights took effect along the way.[11] The provincial laws describe this process in more detail than did later medieval laws. As there were no legal consequences relating to the man's presentation of his suit, it was not described in the laws. However, from scattered mentions and sixteenth-century evidence, we know that the suit was often presented by an intermediary, the *böneman* (literally "praying-man"), who could act as an extra witness and a guarantor of the prospective groom's respectability and the honesty of his suit.[12]

The betrothal (*fästning*), the actual agreement to the marriage made between the groom and the woman's marriage guardian (her closest male relative), was a formal occasion. Originally, the bride's presence had been considered unnecessary, but by the mid-fourteenth century, it had become a precondition for a valid betrothal. In addition to the three principals, the law required that several witnesses be present. The parties negotiated the size of the dowry or dowries and especially the morning gift. Afterwards, there was a party with ale drinking. Following the betrothal, both spouses were under an obligation of fidelity towards each other.[13] Although the betrothal could be broken by the bishop at the request of just one of the parties,[14] it had created a duty to conclude the marriage with a wedding. If the bride's marriage guardian kept stalling and postponing the wedding without a legitimate reason, the groom could take the matter to the local secular court, where he could be authorized to take his bride by force in what would be considered a valid and lawful marriage. Such cases must have been extremely rare, but this was a way out of an impasse. Moreover, children born to a betrothed couple were considered legitimate.[15]

In the late Middle Ages, a new institution, trothplight (*trolofning*), can be found alongside the betrothal. While in everyday parlance the words trothplight and betrothal could be used more or less interchangeably, the two institutions were of different origin and ideology. The trothplight was probably influenced by the ecclesiastical marriage doctrine, as it focused more on the mutual exchange of consent creating the personal bond between the bride and groom and on their reciprocal rituals and gifts. It was not regulated by or mentioned in the medieval Swedish laws. Both parties of the trothplight were considered active and relatively equal participants, whereas the betrothal was originally an act between the groom and the woman's marriage guardian. The betrothal focused on the relationship between the two men, the active parties, even though the bride was involved as the passive object of the contract. The betrothal gifts mentioned in the laws were given by the groom to the marriage guardian and possibly also to the bride's other relatives.[16]

The 1571 Church Ordinance confirmed that a trothplight made with due gifts and witnesses and followed by intercourse constituted a valid marriage.[17] According to the 1686 Church Law, trothplights necessitated the presence of parents and guardians as well as of two witnesses, one from each side. Handclasping was necessary; gifts were not.[18] Because the medieval laws remained applicable until the 1734 Code came into force, the betrothal continued to exist in theory, although by that time trothplighting had come to replace it in practice. According to some studies, engagements seem to have become more difficult to prove in the latter half of the seventeenth century.[19]

The wedding (*brudlop*) was the execution of the agreement made at the engagement. It consisted of several parts: the marriage guardian's handing over of the bride to the groom, the transfer of the bride to the groom's house, her arrival there, and the wedding feast. In the evening, the couple was publicly put to bed together, while guests also witnessed the presentation of the morning gift on the morning following the couple's wedding night. However, it must be observed that over the course of and following the Middle Ages, the role of ecclesiastical solemnities tended to be emphasized at the expense of the other stages. Ecclesiastical solemnization, preceded by the triple publication of the banns, was already mentioned in the thirteenth-century provincial laws (ca. 1280–1350). It was strongly advocated by the church as a means of controlling the impediments to marriage and thus avoiding bigamy and incest. By the mid-fourteenth century, the ecclesiastical ceremony performed by the priest at the church door was mentioned in the law as a normal part of the marriage process.[20] Yet, at this stage, solemnization was only an integral part of the marriage process of the nobility. Sixteenth-century ecclesiastical court records indicate that among poorer people, many engaged couples both in towns and in the countryside were still postponing church marriage. They were, however, pressured by ecclesiastical authorities to marry under the supervision of their parish priests. Those who did not could be subject to fines or other penalties.[21]

During the seventeenth century, ecclesiastical supervision of the marriage process became more effective. Synodal statutes regularly began to insist that not only weddings but even betrothals be performed and supervised by priests. Secret promises were no longer considered binding. The reading of the banns was still urged, but it was now recommended that this take place earlier, before the betrothal. Priests were instructed not to perform any engagements unless the wedding date had been confirmed. Couples were also forbidden to live under the same roof prior to the wedding.[22] Bishops ordered parish priests to keep records of all couples who married and also of all children baptized and their parentage. In this way, through improved documentation, the investigation of impediments was gradually made more reliable and effective. During this period, attention was also increasingly turned to ensuring the knowledge of the articles of faith and catechism. Any person wishing to be trothplighted or married by a cleric had to demonstrate his or her knowledge of the faith and ability to read.[23] In fact, the old, the demented, the mentally retarded, or those suffering from other disabilities could be denied marriage altogether. However, as long as solemnization was not an absolute requirement for marriage, these people could still contract informally.

Property and the Marriage Process

Property and marriage had always been intricately interconnected as matrimony also united two families and family wealth and property. Eventual children would seal the union of the kin groups and their possessions. The Swedish inheritance system was based on partible inheritance, but in the countryside, a son's portion was double that of his sister, while in town their shares were equal. Daughters had an equal right to all kinds of property, not only cash or moveables. Moreover, a daughter was not excluded from parental inheritance through her dowry, though all inheritance advances (such as the dowry) were taken into consideration in the final division of the estate. Inherited land enjoyed a special status as it was to remain in the kin line, so it could not be freely alienated by sale or barter or through a will. If alienated without the consent of the next of kin, who as the closest relatives had a preferential purchase right, the kin had the right to redeem the sale or get back the land. Thus, the Swedish inheritance system sought to balance a variety of principles: the reciprocity of inheritance rights, the special status of inherited land, and the rule that the property passed down to the next of kin regardless of gender.

Property exchanges came into the picture when the marriage process was initiated. The courtship could involve small tokens of affection, but these were not regulated by the law. Similarly, one may assume that when the suit was presented, the parties initiated preliminary discussions about the dowry (or dowries) and morning gift. However, any such talks hardly ever left traces in written sources. Where the medieval provincial laws do mention property issues is in connection with the betrothal. According to some laws, the groom was supposed to give the bride's family "friend gifts" (*vingäf*), irreversible when given, while the gift given to her marriage guardian only became irreversible at the bedding. Other laws refer to the betrothal gift (*fästnaþäfä*) from the groom to the bride's marriage guardian.[24] However, the mid-fourteenth-century royal laws no longer mention friend gifts, probably indicating that the importance of their role was decreasing with the growing influence of the ecclesiastical notion of marriage as a mutual sacrament between the spouses. Gifts and pledges were increasingly mutual exchanges between fiancés. Yet we cannot know to what extent the friend gift was being replaced by mutual gifts at this time, as neither left any traces in the sources. We have more information, however, from the fifteenth century and even more from the sixteenth, in which periods there is no mention of any other gifts apart from those that the fiancés gave each other. At the end of the seventeenth century the legal and financial role of trothplighting gifts probably diminished, again possibly as a consequence of the emphasis on solemnization, but they certainly were still given as tokens of love and pledges of intention.[25]

After the bedding, the husband became his wife's legal guardian and had extensive powers to manage her property during the marriage, although his rights to alienate her inherited lands were very limited, and he generally needed her permission to do so. The marriage also created property rights to the joint estate. Apart from some personal property, two-thirds of all chattels and acquired lands were to go to the husband (or his heirs), while the remaining third went to the wife or her heirs. Inherited land was excluded from this joint estate. In towns, both spouses shared the joint estate equally.[26]

According to Swedish law, both sons and daughters could receive a dowry (*ormynd*, *hemfylghþ*). However, as it was not customary in Sweden to make detailed marriage contracts, we have very little knowledge of the property included in the dowry. Probably it usually consisted of moveable goods. Dowries were important, but they reverted back when the parental inheritance was ultimately divided between the heirs. Instead of marriage contracts as in many other parts of Europe, from the medieval and early modern period we have hundreds, if not thousands, of morning gift letters. As mentioned before, the morning gift was given by the groom to his new wife on the morning after the wedding. In noble families the size of the morning gift and the lands given – or the equivalent of their annual yield – were specified in the letter. If the wife was widowed, she would receive the morning gift, which would contribute to her upkeep in widowhood and that she could dispose of as she wished. If their children ultimately inherited the property from her, it was to be considered maternal inheritance. In the later medieval laws, the permitted maximum size of the morning gift varied according to the donor's status. In practice, however, because the morning gift had developed into an important status symbol, the maximum amounts were generally disregarded.[27] Inflation and currency fluctuation make it difficult to calculate the price of morning gifts, but, for example, around 1440, the noble Eskil Isaksson gave his wife Cecilia Haraldsdotter a morning gift property worth approximately 95 marks, while he was only allowed to give 10 or 20 marks, depending on whether he was an ordinary nobleman or a higher-ranking squire. Knights, who – in a country like Sweden lacking hereditary noble titles – were a very aristocratic group, were allowed to give property worth 40 marks.[28]

By the sixteenth century, as family correspondence makes clear, the morning gift had become an important factor in marriage negotiations. Responsible fathers and guardians of noble girls bargained over large morning gifts as a provision for widowhood and a way to honour the bride by publicly acknowledging her status in society.[29] But precisely because of the expectations related to the morning gift in noble circles, allegations were made that the grand morning gifts impoverished the nobility. These complaints became part of more general efforts among the nobility to restrict the access of noble women to land, especially inherited land, and thereby also to favour the patrilinear family and estate. Indeed, the late sixteenth-century Swedish nobility tried to compel monarchs to limit morning gifts to cash or life interests, and female dowries and inheritance to cash or chattels, and to restrict the female right to redeem noble lands. The different and conflicting interests of widows and widowers as well as sons and daughters limited the success of these efforts, however, until the noble privileges of 1644. Nor was the nobility unanimous on the matter. While some families wished to preserve the pooled property in the male line, it was to the advantage of others to ensure the possibility of upward mobility and social advancement by matrimony.[30]

Legitimacy, Children, and Controlling the Marriage Process

Whereas Swedish perceptions of legitimacy and illegitimacy, linked together with the right to inherit, had earlier been more fluid, by the early fourteenth century these conformed largely to those of the church. Children were divided into three categories: legitimate children (*aþalkunu barn*, literally "true wife's child"), natural children (*frillobarn*, literally "concubine's child"), and adulterine children (*horbarn*). The inheritance rights of natural children were restricted to a small sum, while adulterines had no inheritance rights.[31] In Sweden, children born to their parents after betrothal or trothplight were considered legitimate and able to inherit even if their parents never completed the marriage process with a wedding or solemnization. Legal cases show that the existence of engagement and cohabitation was sufficient for children to be considered legitimate even if the groom died before the intended solemnization.[32] One such tragic event was addressed in 1586. A man named Silvester had lived with his "trothplighted wife" for four years and they had had two daughters together. The wedding had been arranged, but only a few days before the event Silvester was killed. The archbishop deemed the couple lawfully married and the daughters legitimate, and the secular court resolved the inheritance dispute accordingly.[33]

As in canon law, in Swedish law the difference between natural and adulterine children was the parents' capacity validly to contract matrimony with each other. The existence of an impediment precluding marriage between the parents resulted in an adulterine child. This impediment was usually a pre-contract (at least one parent was already married) but could also be consanguinity, affinity, or ecclesiastical status (at least one parent was a monk, a nun, or a priest).[34] Swedish law had adopted the canon law institution of legitimization by subsequent marriage (*legitimatio per subsequens matrimonium*), according to which two single people who had conceived a natural child could by subsequently marrying each other legitimize it. It would then inherit as a legitimate child because "when he [the father] bettered the woman, then he also bettered the child."[35] An example of this is King Karl Knutsson, who, just prior to his own death in 1470, legitimized his small son by marrying his concubine.[36]

There is no evidence that Swedish kings legitimized illegitimate children by decree, so legitimization by marriage was the only route available. This could be done even if one or both parents had been married to other people in the interim before eventually marrying each other.[37] It should be noted, moreover, that ecclesiastical solemnization – or even a wedding – was not a precondition for legitimization: betrothal alone sufficed.[38] In this sense the institution of legitimization by subsequent matrimony fitted well into the Swedish marriage process.

In the Reformation period, new efforts emerged to control couples who were in the midst of the marriage process. One means to do this was through the birth of their children. The Lutheran Church wanted to bring the marriage process more effectively under its supervision and to emphasize the distinction between respectable matrons and women of loose morals. The ecclesiastical rites of baptism and churching (purification of the mother after the birth of a child) were easily turned to these purposes, and ecclesiastical sources from the 1570s on demonstrate an increasing tendency to punish women whose relationships with the fathers of their infants were found to be non-marital. When a baby was to be christened, the priest was instructed to inquire of the godparents who the child's parents were. If it transpired that the parents were not married to each other, the officiating cleric was to denounce them to the authorities. Moreover, baptisms of illegitimate children were not to take place at the same time as those of legitimate babies.[39] Negligent or corrupt priests were to be punished with suspension.[40]

For the Lutheran Church, churching – basically a ritual of thanksgiving – became a showcase for demonstrating the difference between morality and immorality. This subject appeared fairly regularly in synodal statutes from the 1570s onward.[41] If an unmarried woman wished to avoid penance and to be churched as an honest wife, she had to prove that she and her baby's father were in midst of the marriage process. Evidence of a trothplight or betrothal sufficed. In the absence of the infant's father, the mother had to establish his promise of marriage by means of witnesses, letters, or display of the engagement gifts. The chapter could then impose the condition that the couple solemnize their marriage once the father returned.[42] The mothers of illegitimate children were to be churched differently from those of legitimate offspring: with less ceremony, with different formulas and prayers, after a longer waiting period, on different days of the weeks or times of the day, in a different part of the church building, and so on. The practices varied from diocese to diocese, but the common goal was to demonstrate that a line divided virtuous matrons from wanton women. The Church Law of 1686 allowed brides who were pregnant at their solemnizations to be churched like other honest wives, but also required payment of a fine for prenuptial fornication. If the childbirth preceded solemnization, however, the betrothed mother had to be churched by using special prayers in the church manuals.[43] Naturally, unmarried or unbetrothed mothers could expect even more branding treatment emphasizing their sin.

Dissolving Marriages: Reformation Changes

As mentioned earlier, one of the most fundamental changes made by the Reformation was the (re)introduction of full divorce in the modern sense, that is, *a vinculo* with remarriage, which had been forbidden by the Catholic Church in Sweden since the twelfth century.[44] By personally granting the first divorces, King Gustav I Vasa – from 1527 the new supreme head of the church – came to authorize the Swedish post-Reformation divorce practice even before the establishment of new legislation regulating divorce. After the Reformation, the bishops were given the power to grant divorces, but the king remained the highest judge in both the secular and ecclesiastical judiciary, which meant that he could permit divorces or marriages otherwise forbidden by clerics. This policy became especially pronounced in the late seventeenth century as a result of royal autocracy.

In 1537 King Gustav Vasa authorized divorce for female adultery but also for illness.[45] In the early days of the Swedish Reformation, the Bible was the main normative basis for divorce, notwithstanding the divorces granted by the king. Accordingly, a statute in 1541 allowed divorce only for adultery and similar sexual offences.[46] Later, malicious desertion was included, as in many other Lutheran regions. In addition to adultery and malicious desertion, the 1571 Church Ordinance cited impotence, but in practice this was actually considered cause for annulment, not divorce, in accordance with medieval canon law. Divorce on the grounds of illness such as leprosy was explicitly forbidden.[47]

However, the divorce policy became somewhat more flexible in practice than it was in theory. The practice of four Swedish ecclesiastical courts demonstrates that, of the divorce suits brought between 1593 and 1610, nearly half involved adultery, while malicious desertion pure and simple was behind almost a third.[48] During his visitation in 1596, Archbishop Abraham Angermannus granted at least one divorce on the basis of a mutual wish to divorce as well as an illness that made the wife incapable of performing the conjugal debt.[49] In such cases usually only a separation from bed and board was granted, not a divorce with the right to remarry. In this period, divorce causes were initiated more or less equally by men and women, although it appears that later in the seventeenth century women may have started divorce proceedings more frequently. However, around 1600, cases initiated by women had a better success rate. Men and women cited adultery as grounds for divorce more or less equally, while women were the initiators in a clear majority of the cases citing malicious desertion. Here the situation may also have changed during the seventeenth century, as some studies indicate that wives initiated almost 9 out of 10 cases of divorce on the grounds of adultery and about 65 per cent of desertion cases.[50]

The Swedish Church Ordinance of 1571 mentions no waiting period following spousal desertion during which the deserted spouse was to inquire diligently of relatives, employers, and acquaintances into the whereabouts and fate of the absconder. In practice, though, it appears that a minimum waiting period of three years between the disappearance of the spouse and bringing a divorce suit was necessary for success. Some deserters had been gone for up to 14 years before the innocent spouse took the matter to court. While the chapter records from the 1590s show that occasionally even the guilty spouse was allowed to remarry after a lapse of several years, it was extremely rare that marriage with the co-adulterer was authorized. As the church did not want to reward sin and crime, such marriages were usually – but not always – forbidden.[51] However, in some cases of lengthy desertion, the innocent spouse had become engaged or married to another person while the first marriage bond was still intact. Instead of trying these spouses as bigamists in the secular court and executing them, the bishops and the chapters adopted a more pragmatic approach. The ecclesiastical court accepted the second union as valid – though premature – and ordered the couple to solemnize the union. Thus, the divorce was obliquely granted by authorizing the second nuptials. In a case not involving bigamy, for example, Bengt Persson had had sex with a married woman whose husband had run away nine years earlier, fleeing a larceny charge, and of whom she had not had tidings since. During the archiepiscopal visitation of 1596, Bengt and the woman were allowed to be married in church immediately, but they had to pay a fine for their illicit and unauthorized intercourse.[52]

Many aspects of how divorce was practised in Sweden testify to a certain pragmatism. Although the law only allowed divorce on two grounds, adultery and malicious desertion, on occasion divorces were also granted for other reasons, such as permanent and serious discord or illness. At the Diet of Norrköping in 1604 the clergy may have accepted divorce on the grounds of implacable hatred between the spouses.[53] In the mid-seventeenth century, despite the fact that it had been expressly forbidden by the 1571 Church Ordinance, the chapter of Turku (Åbo) on many occasions granted divorce on the grounds of leprosy when the wife had been interned in a hospital for seven to nine years and the husband lacked "the gift of continence."[54] In the 1660s, several divorce cases claiming discord and refusal to pay the conjugal debt were submitted to the king, who referred them back to the clerical estate, authorizing the chapter freely to resolve the cases in accordance with their consciences.[55]

Towards the end of the seventeenth century, in the more conservative atmosphere of the Lutheran control state, the chapters seem to have become increasingly reluctant to grant divorces on grounds not mentioned in the 1571 Church Ordinance. Nonetheless, the chapter of Växjö, for one, did grant some divorces on the basis of abuse and violence.[56] Subsequently, it appears that the conservative Church Law of 1686, which upheld that divorce could only be granted for malicious desertion and adultery,[57] induced the ecclesiastical courts to follow the letter of the law and to stop dissolving marriages on grounds other than the two specifically authorized. Thus the earlier, more liberal practice seems to have given way to a more rigid regime, and the number of divorces decreased.[58] The practices of the late seventeenth- and eighteenth-century Swedish consistories, however, require more research.

While ecclesiastical courts were becoming more rigid in granting divorces, it appears that a parallel secular system of granting divorces was growing up thanks to the increasing juridical power of the monarch. The growth of the monarch's power curtailed the independence of both the ecclesiastical and secular justice systems. In the 1610s and 1620s, for example, secular courts of first instance were required to adhere to the letter of the law when adjudicating, while discretionary powers were henceforth reserved to the royal Courts of Appeal and, ultimately, to the monarch. Moreover, despite the fact that an appeal system had been established, the custom of presenting inquiries to and asking for guidance directly from the king persisted. Divorce petitions were also presented directly to the monarch. By the 1690s, an even larger spectrum of causes was referred first to the king, who then empowered the chapter by submitting the cases for it to hear and decide. Consequently, a practice of divorce by royal dispensation based on precedents and test cases began to take shape in the 1700s.[59] The reliance on precedents and previous practice meant that the routine of granting divorces more freely by dispensation continued to develop even when King Karl XII (reigned 1697–1718) personally felt bound to follow the letter of the Bible.[60] Thus, the seventeenth- and eighteenth-century "juridification" of the practice[61] also helped to legitimize and standardize divorce by dispensation in the eyes of individual monarchs.

In short, Swedish divorce law was always more liberal in practice than it was in theory. Although the marital bond could be broken, it was not done lightly. But generally no moral discourse or condemnation accompanied the divorce sentences either.[62] Priests were expected to attempt reconciliation, and out-and-out pressure could be put on spouses to forgive and forget the other's transgressions. But looked at pragmatically, divorce could also mean a fresh start for gravely dysfunctional households, in which the discord of the couple might be threatening communal peace or one spouse's desertion meant that the other struggled with maintaining the farm alone. In such cases, divorce was in the interests of both the parties and the community. It also went hand in hand with the pastoral concerns of the church.

Lutheran Orthodoxy, the State, and the Defence of Marriage

If one were to sum up in three words the goals of the Swedish Lutheran Church for marriage in the seventeenth century, they would be propriety, sobriety, and control. These values were also largely shared by the state authorities, whose war efforts demanded a well-ordered system of administration and control. The church set out to put its marriage objectives into practice in the second half of the sixteenth and in the seventeenth century. The enforcement of these values, however, meant different things for the various stages of the marriage process.

One of the aspects of propriety related to the parity of the couple. The church opposed any grave disproportion between the future spouses whether of age, condition, or status. If there was a considerable age gap between the future spouses, and particularly if the bride was much older than the groom, the church was reluctant to authorize the union. Such women were usually widows who could provide younger men with access to land and a farm. The clergy was probably concerned that older wives would soon be unable to perform the marital duties because of illness and that the younger husbands would as a consequence succumb to the lure of housemaids or loose women. Clerics also voiced doubts if the bride was suspected of grave immorality. In some cases of disparity, the couple was given time to consider the matter and their commitment to each other, but in other cases solemnization was denied outright.[63]

Another aspect that featured even more prominently in the late sixteenth and the seventeenth century was disparity of birth. Marriages between nobles and commoners were among the recurring complaints of the nobility. Finally in 1622 the noble estate persuaded the king to penalize misalliances with the forfeiture of land to the next of kin.[64] The earlier penalty had only been the loss of the tax exemption of their land. For example, the noblewoman Elin Tönnesdotter of the Tott family had fornicated with a student in her youth and later married another commoner. Elin's siblings disputed her right to inherit as well as her ability to hold noble, tax-exempt land. The matter had already been resolved by the king in 1616, who confirmed Elin's inheritance rights because her father had pardoned her sexual crime and recognized her rights, but without the noble tax exemption. However, fortified by the later 1622 privileges of the nobility, Elin's siblings again denied her property rights, which she only managed to have reconfirmed after a long legal battle that stretched from 1627 to 1629.[65]

Disparity of faith naturally became a more prominent obstacle to marriage after the Reformation. There remained a small Catholic minority after the Reformation but, as in England, for political reasons Catholicism and treason were associated in the eyes of the government. Unions with suspected crypto-Catholics, religious nonconformists, or members of other reformist creeds were forbidden. For example, if a Calvinist foreigner wished to marry a Swedish Lutheran, the Calvinist had to convert.[66]

Control of the clergy was of paramount concern to church authorities, as laxity of men of cloth permitted immorality, disorder, and impropriety to thrive among the laity. The marriage customs of the clergy were monitored by the chapters, as the parish priest was expected not only to supervise his parishioners but to set an example by his own behaviour. Clerics were forbidden to marry former concubines of noblemen, for example. Moreover, priests had to conform to the ideals of chastity. Premarital sexual adventures threatened a man's chances of obtaining clerical office, and offending clerics were temporarily suspended or perpetually defrocked. An example of this is the disciplining of the priest Matthias Jonae Helsing for sexual intercourse with a distant relative of his. When the incest was investigated in 1597, Matthias was jailed for several weeks. He was suspended from office, excommunicated, and told not to reside in Hälsingland, the scene of the crime, for a period of time. Instead, he was to stay with his brother-in-law, also a cleric. Later, after a suspension of one and a half years and after payment of a special bond for good behaviour, he was reinstated.[67] The secular power supplemented the network of control. For example, the statute of 1665 threatened clerics who presided over the clandestine marriages of noblemen or noblewomen with jail terms and perpetual banishment.[68]

The propriety and sobriety of wedding celebrations were also controlled by sumptuary laws. In Sweden, such rules had existed since the Middle Ages, but they seem not to have been strictly enforced at that time. In the class-conscious seventeenth century, however, sumptuary laws gained renewed impetus as a way to keep each estate in its proper place and to restrict the excessive spending at weddings. Such statutes could also seek to minimize the disorder associated with wedding feasts that lasted for many days. Authorities frowned upon the often elaborately sumptuous wedding processions that were intended to display the wealth of the participants, as well as upon the noise and drinking at the many festivities. The number of dishes served, the number of guests attending, the gifts given, the cloth used for weddings clothes – all inspired minute regulation.[69] Similar complaints of disorder at baptisms and churchings were also voiced. Women were accused of being drunk at the ceremonies and of arriving late to church on Sunday morning, in which cases the rite was to be denied and a fine paid.[70] While the effect of these regulations is difficult to measure, their mere existence does demonstrate the desire to restrain and monitor various aspects of marriage formation and festivities. Because the effectiveness of the system relied on the efforts of local clerics, who were expected to exercise vigilant control over their parishioners, to denounce them to the authorities, and to act as good role models, the actual level of control varied from parish to parish depending on the clerics' zeal.

The Role of the Reception of Roman Law

As discussed, the canon law regulated many aspects of marriage, and in medieval Sweden, Roman law played only a marginal role in marriage matters. However, beginning in the later Middle Ages and particularly in the seventeenth century, foreign, especially Roman, law made inroads into Swedish matrimonial law via Germany.

This seventeenth-century influence of Roman law manifested itself in various ways but above all in the field of matrimonial property law. This influence had three major effects. First, jurists influenced by Roman law put pressure on curtailing the Swedish marriage process – which happened to be in line with the aims of the church. Second, they critiqued the Swedish matrimonial property transactions and their links to bedding and spending the wedding night together. Third, they bolstered a stricter interpretation of the medieval Swedish law regarding the disinheritance of wayward children, which strengthened patriarchal trends in Swedish society.[71]

Swedish commentaries on domestic law also started to appear, written by some of the few legal experts who had studied Roman and German law in Continental universities. Their ambivalent attitudes towards the Swedish marriage process as well as the morning gift may have influenced the legal practice of the important Svea Court of Appeal, established in Stockholm in 1614. Johan Skytte (1577–1645), a judge of the Court of Appeal and a high royal official who was the author of one of the first commentaries on Swedish law, was puzzled by the conflicts between Swedish law and principles of Roman and canon law. He observed, for example, that in Sweden the matrimonial bond was not perfected until consummation.[72] This was so despite the Roman and canon law rule that "consent, not intercourse, effected marriage" (*consensus efficit matrimonium et non concubitus*). Nor did Skytte understand why in Sweden community of property was only created by the bedding, not by the actual creation of the marriage bond by consent.[73]

Morning gifts proved to be another area of discrepancy between Roman and Swedish law. As classical Roman jurists had forbidden gifts between spouses, under Roman law the couple could only make prenuptial agreements. The Swedish morning gift in particular, which was given on the second wedding day after the couple had married, was in obvious conflict with the notion that married couples were not to give valuable gifts to one another. An illustration of the uncertainty caused by a growing awareness of the disparity between Roman law and Swedish law was an early seventeenth-century Swedish law proposal. It would have placed the morning gift between the trothplight and solemnization, making the morning gift more or less like a prenuptial marriage settlement (*pactum antenuptiale*). This proposal would also have transferred the husband's assumption of guardianship of his wife to after the solemnization instead of after the bedding.[74] Thus, as the number of learned lawyers in Sweden increased, the Roman law notion of forbidding property transactions between spouses, and the canon law focus on the moment of the exchange of marital consent, began to undermine the traditional Swedish marriage process.

Other factors also contributed to curtailing the Swedish marriage process. Because of the German influences, a new institution, the prenuptial marriage settlement, started to appear even in court practice. Especially in the seventeenth century, Swedish courts had to interpret the contracts of German couples who had settled in Sweden. These contracts included such matters as stipulations on spousal rights to the joint estate but also agreements concerning property after death.[75] The custom of making marriage settlements then also started to spread in Sweden, reducing the traditional importance of the morning gift.

In addition, influenced by northern German towns, medieval Swedish Town Law had already stipulated that morning gifts were to be given, despite their name, on the first wedding day, before the bedding and wedding night, though after the bride had been consigned to the groom and possibly after solemnization had taken place.[76] In northern Germany during the sixteenth century, the bedding also became simply a formality that was performed during the wedding feast and after which the new couple rejoined their celebrating guests.[77] In seventeenth-century Sweden, this practice of giving the morning gift on the first wedding day spread from Stockholm to some areas in the surrounding countryside governed by the 1442 law instead of the Town Law. Even the Svea Court of Appeal accepted this custom, in stark contrast to the law that unambiguously stated that the morning gift was to be given the morning following the wedding night.[78] Some couples performed the bedding on the wedding day before the wedding meal, but this aberration from "the good old custom" the church disliked.[79] The trend towards compacting the marriage process led to strange results. In 1693, for instance, the synod of Uppsala was shocked when the question was posed whether the bedding ought to take place in church or elsewhere. The thought of the bedding taking place in a church was quite outrageous. The bishop and chapter allowed the priest to accompany the couple home, but the parish cottage or parish clerk's cottage were considered possible locations for this.[80] Shortening the Swedish marriage process was in the interests of the church, as this meant the strengthening of the position of the ecclesiastical solemnization, but without preposterous times and places for the bedding.

Even though the earlier seventeenth-century law proposals did not become reality and prune the lengthy Swedish marriage process, attitudes among the laity and lawyers were in a state of change. However, the law remained unaltered until the 1734 Code came into effect. The growing influence and reception of learned law combined with the professionalization of Swedish lawyers made it increasingly difficult to sustain the traditional Swedish marriage process. As in the Middle Ages, university-trained lawyers wanted to define the precise moment when an indissoluble marriage was created. The law commission established in 1686 to draft a new law code, the future 1734 Code, spent much time deliberating upon this issue. The commission observed that the current practice was that solemnization alone sufficed to create a marriage. Consequently, the commission decided that in the future law, all marital property rights and legal guardianship had to be dependent on the ecclesiastical ceremony.[81]

In the early modern period, Roman legal influences also helped strengthen parental authority. During the Middle Ages and the Reformation period, Swedish parents could punish their daughters with disinheritance for either fornication or marrying without their consent. This disinheritance penalty did not extend to sons, while other filial misbehaviour or ingratitude that fell short of causing or attempting the parent's death did not even merit forfeiture of inheritance.[82] However, various late sixteenth- and early seventeenth-century Swedish legal sources demonstrate that Roman legal norms concerning disinheritance (*Novellae* 115.3) were both known and influencing attitudes in Sweden.[83] Under Emperor Justinian, Roman law had listed many filial offences that were considered acceptable reasons for the disinheritance of children in the sixth century. This list found its way to an abortive law proposal from the early 1600s that would have adopted it in its entirety.[84] In 1608, Johan Skytte observed the differing treatment of sons and daughters in cases of unauthorized marriage, namely, that the law was silent on disinheriting sons, though it allowed disinheritance of disobedient daughters. But in the 1620s things began to change. In a 1621 commentary, Hans Olofsson argued that despite the existing law, it would be just and fair for sons to be disinherited in cases where parental wishes was defied and the bride's family was dishonourable.[85] In 1630, Benedictus Crusius (d. 1633) went further to opine that, as the law did not expressly forbid disinheriting sons for contracting marriage without parental consent, the silence ought to be interpreted to mean that sons, like daughters, could be disinherited for showing such disrespect.[86] Thus, the interpretation of the medieval law had totally changed within some decades because of growing patriarchalism bolstered on Roman law.

The royal statute of 1665 against the illicit and secret marriages of the nobility targeted those sons and daughters who contracted marriage without the consent of their parents and guardians. Offenders were threatened with temporary or permanent forfeiture of property and with exile.[87] Indeed, jurists writing in the 1670s rejected the view that sons enjoyed complete freedom of marriage. Their view is also visible in the 1686 Church Law and the discussions of the commission drafting the Law Code of 1734.[88]

The Marriage Process and Sexual Crime

In Sweden, as in many other countries, a courtship could go one of two ways: either down the aisle or down the drain. Just as the marriage itself developed through the various informal and formal stages of the marriage process, so too did the couple's intimate relationship. Unchaperoned courtship could lead to fondling, foreplay, and ultimately sexual intercourse. Especially in the upper echelons of Swedish society, girls were supposed to enter the marriage bed with their virginity intact, but even in those circles fornication occasionally took place.[89]

Swedish medieval law distinguished between three kinds of sexual relations between unmarried and unrelated people: simple fornication, violation of a virgin, and prenuptial fornication. Simple fornication (*lönskaläge*, Old Swedish *läghär*) was the oldest of the three, already mentioned in the provincial laws, which considered fornication largely a secular offence for which the man, the culprit, paid a fine to the injured party or parties, usually the woman's relatives or marriage guardian. The woman was not punished. The amount of the fine could vary depending on whether the woman was a virgin or a widow and how many times she had previously committed fornication. The fine for fornication with a virgin was the highest, with each subsequent instance of the woman's fornication reducing the amount.[90] However, several medieval laws placed restrictions on accusing a man of fornication. Such a charge was only permitted if the woman became pregnant, the man confessed to the sexual relations, or the couple had been caught in the act.[91]

The church perceived fornication as a crime that came under the spiritual oversight of priests and for which penance had to be performed. According to late medieval Swedish penance lists, simple fornication merited a three-year penance with regular fasting.[92] However, originally fornication seems not have come under formal ecclesiastical jurisdiction in Sweden but belonged only to the internal forum. Perhaps because of this, late medieval Swedish ecclesiastical councils saw fit to repeat the statutes of church councils denouncing as heretical those denying that fornication was a capital sin.[93] By 1412, however, when a Swedish ecclesiastical provincial statute imposed a three-mark fine on fornicators, it had become a crime falling under church courts.[94]

Prosecutions for simple fornication hardly ever appear in pre-Reformation secular court records. In one rare case from 1503 from the town of Arboga, Olof Bengtsson was fined three marks for fornication committed on the night of a feast day. His partner was not mentioned.[95] In contrast to the rarity of fornication proceedings, however, violations of virgins appear in medieval secular court records with some frequency. The crime of violating a virgin first appeared in the mid-fourteenth-century town laws, from which it was incorporated into the 1442 law that applied to the rest of the country.[96] The punishment for violating a virgin was a 40-mark fine, which was perceived as compensation to the woman's marriage guardian for despoilment of the woman's virginity. The payment was distributed in equal shares in accordance with Swedish custom: one-third each to the injured party, the king, and the hundred.[97] The fine was reduced by half if the man was prepared to remedy the situation by marrying the "damaged" woman.[98] If the seducer was already married, the transgression was considered adultery and the woman was also punished. In the early seventeenth century, compensating seduced virgins with a dowry gained additional support after the acceptance of the Bible, especially the Law of Moses, as a direct source of law. The woman did not have to claim a marriage promise for the offence to be taken to court and the fine to be levied. Nor does it seem that a pregnancy was necessary for a case to come to court. But the woman had to be a virgin – or at least not previously involved in a sexual crime and not have given birth to a child. In a case from 1597, the court tried to determine the time when each individual lover had fornicated with Kirstin Pedersdotter in order to establish which of them had taken her maidenhead. Per Olsson, who had lain with her eight days before Christmas 1595, was fined 40 marks for violation of a virgin, while Jöns Hemmingsson paid only 3 marks for fornication that had taken place three weeks before Michaelmas 1596.[99]

Following the Reformation, the church's right to pass sentence on sexual crimes (incest, adultery, and fornication) was abrogated, and the secular courts became the places where these crimes were tried. Nonetheless, the church retained its right to prescribe penance to sexual offenders in addition to secular punishment. In the latter half of the seventeenth century, the proportion of sexual crimes compared to other crimes tried in secular courts increased considerably. This was partly due to rising intolerance both among the clergy and in the larger society for lesser extramarital sexual crimes, particularly male adultery and fornication. But also important was the growth of state power. In the earlier period, parties had preferred to settle disputes outside of court (e.g., with financial compensation or child support), with the result that many never made it to court at all. But over the course of the sixteenth and seventeenth centuries, the local royal and ecclesiastical administrations increasingly denounced sexual offenders and demanded that they be punished according to the law.

In the seventeenth century, the legal distinction between violation of a virgin and simple fornication began to break down. This can be seen at the level of penalties. In some regions, a distinction was made between the violation of a maiden, in which the seduced maiden received compensation, and fornication, where both parties were deemed equally guilty. In other regions, this difference was abolished in the 1650s, and all men had to pay a 40-mark fine regardless of the woman's sexual history. The woman was not everywhere fined for her first offence, that is, if she had been a virgin, although she did have to perform penance. However, this regional variation came to an end in 1694, when King Charles XI (reigned 1660–97) unified the legal system. Thereafter, all women convicted of fornication were fined 20 marks as criminals regardless of whether or not they had been virgins.[100] This result neatly illustrates the black-and-white morality of Lutheran orthodoxy: now all extramarital sexual activity was to be punished. Seduced virgins were perceived no longer as innocent and dishonoured victims needing compensation and performing penance, but as willing wantons deserving of shame and punishment.

The third type of fornication, prenuptial fornication, was committed by a betrothed couple who had sex before their wedding. Although according to canon law sexual intercourse between fiancés transformed their union into a marriage (*matrimonium praesumptum*), the church nonetheless considered such sexual relations unacceptable and sinful. In fact, it had become punishable in fifteenth-century Sweden first in ecclesiastical statutes and then in secular law. For a period following

Figure 7. Olaus Magnus Gothus's *Historia de gentibus septentrionalibus* (Liber xiiii, "De nuptis plebeiorum," cap. ix, Romae, 1555). Image courtesy of the National Library of Finland. Photo: Pentti Niemimaa

the Reformation, the penalty was abolished based on the reasoning that the intercourse had transformed the union into matrimony. However, by the end of the sixteenth century fines for prenuptial fornication appear again.[101] The offence usually became known only if the bride was heavily pregnant at the wedding or gave birth to a child less than eight months after marriage.

Prenuptial fornication was related to the so-called crown offence. It was customary in Sweden that virgins went about bareheaded, while wives, widows, and all other women who had lost their maidenhead covered their hair. In medieval Sweden, virgin brides wore their hair down and a crown on their heads when their marriages were solemnized in church (Figure 7).[102] However, in the 1570s and 1580s, it became an offence punishable with a fine for deflowered brides to wear crowns when their marriage was solemnized. Instead, sexually experienced brides were to cover their hair, but they were allowed to wear a wreath.[103] Cases involving prenuptial fornication were discussed in cathedral chapters, while the punishments for these "crown offences" and prenuptial fornication were repeated in numerous synodal statutes in the seventeenth century, and they were included in the 1686 Church Law.[104]

In the seventeenth century, the Swedish Lutheran Church started to oppose rural courtship practices, especially so-called night-courting or bundling, more vigorously than before. In many regions in the countryside, courting couples occasionally slept together in the outbuildings where young unmarried women spent their nights in the summer months and their suitors visited them. Naturally, such nocturnal encounters occasionally resulted in sex and pregnancy. The church considered this custom both suspicious and immoral and attacked it in its synodal statutes. However, in these rural regions night-courting was not seen as licence for vice but as ordinary interaction within the peer groups. It was regarded as socially acceptable even for girls from better-off families, and community elders and parents could not be prevailed on to quash the custom (which is one that we have already encountered in rural Switzerland).[105] Thus, in more peripheral and socially relatively egalitarian regions in Finland, Sweden, and Norway, the custom lived on until the late nineteenth and early twentieth centuries.[106]

For much of the early modern period, the relatively pragmatic Swedish society showed some understanding towards couples who were engaged in traversing the multi-step marriage process, as well as towards illegitimacy, even if the atmosphere became increasingly intolerant as state and church control intensified. In the seventeenth century in particular, however, this pragmatism gave way to the religious zeal of black-and-white Lutheran orthodoxy. Before the close of the century, all extramarital sexual acts were punished in both the secular and the ecclesiastical spheres.

Conclusion

The peaks of Swedish political absolutism and religious orthodoxy coincided at the high point of Swedish state control in the later seventeenth and early eighteenth centuries. After nearly five centuries of labour (initiated by the Catholic Church), the Lutheran Church had finally largely managed to make ecclesiastical solemnization standard behaviour. Rowdy wedding customs were discouraged and illicit sexuality was severely punished both by secular sanctions and by ecclesiastical discipline. Sexual offenders had to sit in the stocks and ask publicly for the forgiveness of the congregation for their crime in humiliating ceremonies during the Sunday service. In serious cases, they had to undergo multiple public whippings with a birch rod at the church door. Unwed mothers were churched using liturgies and customs intended to shame, while the control system based on the local clergy made it nearly impossible for such women to escape penalties. Nonetheless, a continuing fundamental societal pragmatism meant that one out-of-wedlock pregnancy did not usually completely destroy a woman's chances of marriage.

The orthodox Lutheran Church collaborated with the monarchy to create a strong state, contributing to Sweden's rise as a European great power over the course of the war-dominated seventeenth century. Essential to this project was the enforcement of cultural and religious unity, which enforcement relied in turn upon a relatively effective central administration. The cooperation and growing control are clearly visible in the fields of criminal and matrimonial law. The growing severity of secular punishments and ecclesiastical censure both at the normative level and in court practice was already discernible in the late Middle Ages. By the seventeenth century, the Swedish war-state was bent on punishing offenders in order to avert the wrath of God from the larger community. The well-developed administrative and control networks at the parish level ensured that it was difficult for offenders to escape the due penalties.

The long-awaited legal code enacted in 1734 broke well-established tradition by making solemnization of marriage compulsory. Most marital property consequences were now attached to the church ceremony, and bedding became redundant as a legal act. While the morning gift retained its old name, it was to be given prior to the solemnization.[107] Still, the Code of 1734 did not wipe clean the slate of Swedish matrimonial law. The weight of tradition was too great to allow an abrupt break with the past.

According to the Code of 1734, when a betrothed couple had intercourse, a marital bond was created that was to be perfected by solemnization. This was in line with traditional doctrine. However, also according to this new law, if after intercourse either fiancé(e) was reluctant to proceed with the wedding and solemnization, the other could take the matter to the secular court and there be declared the reluctant fiancé(e)'s spouse. The innocent party insisting on solemnization obtained marital rights to the other's property, including financial support, and the children were considered legitimate. However, the couple could not be forced to live together, nor did the husband become the wife's guardian. The union created by the judicial procedure declaring fiancés spouses was called an incomplete marriage (*ofullkomligt äktenskap*). In contrast, if there had been no betrothal in the presence of witnesses and marriage guardians, but only informal promises of marriage, the case was judged somewhat differently. Marriage promises could be annulled at the guardian's request. Moreover, if the couple had intercourse after a private promise of marriage, the woman could also take the matter to court and have the man adjudged her husband and their relationship an incomplete marriage.[108] The new law may have been trying to strike a balance between requiring solemnization and the consent of the guardian on the one hand and penalizing private marriage promises and seducers on the other.

The children of formally betrothed couples were considered legitimate, as were children born under private promise of marriage, with the result that it was still possible to sire legitimate children without ever having been married.[109] The consequences of the Code of 1734 thus remained restricted. The length and complexity of the Swedish marriage process were diminishing, but many of its traditional features were still very much alive in eighteenth-century Sweden, and in more remote regions of Sweden and Finland they persisted until the twentieth century.

NOTES

1 The following abbreviations are used in the citation of records held in archives:

LiDP: Linköpings domkapitels arkiv (Archive of the Chapter of Linköping), A Ia:1 Protokoll 1600–1632

SstA: Stockholms stadsarkiv (Municipal Archive of Stockholm, Sweden)

SDP: Stockholms domkapitels protokoll (Records of the Chapter of Stockholm), A I:1 Protokoll 1595–1600, A I:2 Protokoll 1600–1605

ULA: Upplands landskapsarkiv (Regional Archive of Uppland, Uppsala, Sweden)

Dalarnas dombok: (Kopparbergs län) (Court Records of Dalarna, province of Kopparberg), Domböcker 1544–1559 A Ia:1

UDP: Uppsala domkapitels arkiv (Archive of the Chapter of Uppsala), A I:1, Protokoll 1593–1608

VaLa: Landsarkivet i Vadstena (Regional Archive at Vadstena)

VDA: Västerås domkapitels arkiv (Archive of the Cathedral chapter of Västerås, Västerås, Sweden)

VDP: Domkapitlets protokoll m.bil. huvudserie (Chapter Records with Appendices, Main Series), A I:1: 26.3.1595–1.12.1603, A I:2: 1598–1602

2 SstA, SDP A I:1, 26.4.1598, 3.5.1598, 122, 125.

3 See also in this volume 230–2.

4 See Donahue 34, 36–7.

5 On the prohibition of marriage among the poor see Wunder 78–9.

6 *Svenska riksdagsakter*, 1:2, doc. 227, esp. pp. 615, 617; Korpiola 2006, 163.

7 Söderlind 1969; Korpiola 2011; *Johan Skyttes kommentar*, 25.

8 For instance, 15:1, in *Kircko-Laki Ja Ordningi 1686* (Church Law of 1686), pp. 21–2.

9 Korpiola 2014.

10 For similarities to Italy, see Lombardi 94–8.

11 For a more thorough analysis of the Swedish marriage process, see Korpiola 2009, 19–88.

12 Korpiola 2009, 39–41.

13 For instance, Giftermålsbalken (chapter on marriage) 6, in *Magnus Erikssons landslag*, 41.

14 For instance, Kyrkobalken (chapter on the church) 15:1, Upplandslagen, in *Svenska landskapslagar* 1:25; e.g., 14.4.1526, *Biskop Hans Brasks registratur*, 424, p. 449.

15 For instance, Giftermålsbalken 2:4, 4, in *Magnus Erikssons landslag*, 39–40.

16 Korpiola 2009, 191–7.

17 Om åtskildnat j Echtenskap, *Den svenska kyrkoordningen 1571*, 126–7.

18 15:10–12, in *Kircko-Laki Ja Ordningi 1686*, p. 23.

19 Lennartsson 1999, 160–1; Pylkkänen 1990, 236–40.

20 For instance, Giftermålsbalken 2:3, in *Magnus Erikssons landslag*, 39.

21 Korpiola 2009, 341–7, 356–61.

22 Kyrko-ordning för Vexiö Stift 1619, in *Ecclesiastique Samlingar* 8:598–601.

23 For instance, King Karl XII's letter to the Consistory of Växjö, 2.11.1699, in *Ecclesiastique Samlingar* 8:163–4.

24 For instance, Giftermålsbalken 10:2, 26, Östgötalagen, in *Svenska landskapslagar* 1:105, 111; Ärvdabalken (chapter on inheritance) 1–1:3, Upplandslagen, in *Svenska landskapslagar* 1:63–4.

25 Korpiola 2009, 69–70, 194–6.

26 Erickson 2005, 7–13; Ågren 2009, esp. 28–32.

27 Korpiola 2009, 70–2, 78–85; Carlsson 1965, 209–24; Ylikangas 1988, 89–96; Petersson 1973, 69–87, 100–4.
28 Petersson 1973, 373.
29 Lahtinen 2011.
30 Korpiola 2007; Ylikangas 1967, 185–9.
31 For instance, Ärvdabalken 17–18, in *Magnus Erikssons landslag*, 63; Ärvdabalken 14–15, in *Magnus Erikssons stadslag*, 60–1.
32 For instance, Giftermålsbalken 2:4, in *Magnus Erikssons landslag*, 39.
33 9.3.1586, in *Upplands lagmansdombok*, 178–9.
34 See Ärvdabalken 18, in *Magnus Erikssons landslag*, 63; Ärvdabalken 15, in *Magnus Erikssons stadslag*, 61.
35 For instance, Giftermålsbalken 2:5, in *Magnus Erikssons landslag*, 40; Giftermålsbalken 2:4, in *Magnus Erikssons stadslag*, 38–9.
36 Korpiola 2012.
37 Petri, *Kommentar till Stadslagen*, 322; 14.4.1549, in *Diplomatarium Dalekarlicum*, vol. 3, doc. 890, pp. 217–18; ULA, Dalarnas dombok (Kopparbergs län) Domböcker 1544–1559 A Ia:1, 16.12.1552, Mora Soken, 222v.
38 *Biskop Hans Brasks släktbok*, 92.
39 Lempiäinen 1965, 54, 87–8; Agricola, *Käsikiria Castesta*, 5; 11, Synod of Strängnäs 1585, *Svenska synodalakter 2*, 25; *De Ceremoniis et Ecclesiae constitutionibus*, dioc. of Uppsala 1607–8, *Svenska synodalakter 1*, 18.
40 VDA, VDP A I:1, Synodal statutes of Västerås 1596, 19v; 10.12.1614, in *Stockholms stads (och Norrmalms stads) tänkeböcker*, 53–5; 5.9.1632 and 12.9.1632, in *Utdrag ur Åbo stads dombok 1626–1632*, 150–1.
41 3, Nova Ordinantia, *Kyrko-Ordingen och Förslag dertill före 1686*, 226; 2, Synod of Strängnäs 1585, *Svenska Synodalakter 2*, 24.
42 For instance, SstA, SDP A I:1, 9.4.1600, 163; ULA, UDP, 22.4.1596, 115; SstA, SDP A I:1, 4.6.1600, 29.6.1600, 170, 172; VDA, VDP A I:2, 28.12.1598, 5v; VDA, VDP A I:1, 16.12.1597, 46v.
43 *Kircko-Laki Ja Ordningi 1686*, 5:2, p. 10.
44 *Diplomatarium Suecanum*, vol. 1, doc. 42, pp. 61–2.
45 5.2.1537, *Handlingar till Sverges reformations- och kyrkohistoria*, 2:86; 2.10.1540, Ibid., 2:146–7.
46 Articuli Ordinantiæ of 1541, in "Bidrag till Svenska kyrkans historia i sextonde århundradet," 17.
47 Om åtskildnat j Echtenskap, *Den svenska kyrkoordningen 1571*, 124–6.
48 These cases come from the chapter of the archdiocese of Uppsala (23 cases, ca. 31.3.1593–1596, 1598–1601), its subordinate consistory of Stockholm (24 cases, 1.9.1595–1605), the chapters of the dioceses of Linköping (29 cases, 1.4.1600–1602, summer 1605–9.7.1610) and Västerås (14 cases,

26.3.1595–1.12.1603). The material is culled from the following sources: the ULA; UDP; SstA; SDP A I:1 Protokoll 1595–1600 and A I:2 Protokoll 1600–1605; VaLa; LiDP; VDA; VDP A I:1: 26.3.1595–1.12.1603 and A I:2: 1598–1602.

49 *Ärkebiskop Abrahams räfst*, 87–9.

50 According to Lennartsson 1999, 214, 230, 238, perhaps even up to 75 per cent were started by women.

51 For instance, *Ärkebiskop Abrahams räfst*, 6.

52 For instance, *Ärkebiskop Abrahams räfst*, 125.

53 Pietilä 1903–1904, 151. However, I have not been able to confirm this in the version of *Cleri Comitialis Circulaire* 1604, printed in *Ecclesiastique Samlingar* 5:164–5.

54 For instance, *Consistorii ecclesiastici aboënsis protokoller* I–II, 235, 284, 378, 447, 454.

55 Nylander 1961, 112–15.

56 Lennartsson 1999, 210–11, 216.

57 *Kircko-Laki Ja Ordningi 1686*, 16:6, 9, pp. 26–8.

58 For instance, Lennartsson 1999, 226.

59 Nylander 1961, 116–28, 164–8, 171–2, 187–9.

60 Ibid., 120; Wedberg 1944, 34.

61 On the standardization of mitigating sentences in the Court of Appeal, see Thunander 1993, 106–7, 118–26, 149–55, 171–3, 197–8.

62 See also Lennartsson 1999, 243.

63 For instance, SstA, SDP A I:1, 2.5.1599, 147; SstA, SDP A I:1, 13.6.1599, 150; Söderlind 1967, 76–86.

64 Summary of the 1622 privileges of the nobility, in *Kongl. Stadgar*, 217. The privileges also enacted that the children born of the union between a nobleman and a commoner who had married without royal permission lost their right to his lands and to noble privileges. His lands were instead to go to his closest relatives.

65 Korpiola 2007.

66 For instance, 9.7.1642, 8.11.1643, *Kulturella interiörer*, 106, 121.

67 VDA, VDP A I:1, 26.10.1597, 43; VDA, VDP A I:2, 20.11.1598, 4.

68 Royal resolution on unauthorized solemnizations (10.3.1665), in *Kongl. Stadgar*, 436–7; Ylikangas 1967, 118–20.

69 For instance, Söderlind 1950; 17.12.1644, in *Kongl. Stadgar*, 239–45.

70 For instance, VaLa, LiDP, 5.3.1602, 1.10.1609, 10, 46.

71 See also Korpiola 2005.

72 Here Skytte confused symbolic consummation (*consummatio de iure*) and simply having sexual intercourse (*consummatio de facto*). The latter was required in Swedish law, not the former.

73 *Johan Skyttes kommentar*, Giftermålsbalken, ch. 6, 26.
74 Giftermålsbalken 6, Giftermålsbalken 9, Carl den Niondes lagförslag, *Lagförslag i Carl den Niondes tid*, 123, 125.
75 Ylikangas 1967, 143–5.
76 Giftermålsbalken 6:3, 9:2, in *Magnus Erikssons stadslag*, 41–2.
77 Carlsson 1965, 186–7.
78 Petersson 1973, 188–93; Ylikangas 1967, 199–202.
79 17.12.1631, 33.8.1640, in *Kulturella interiörer*, 29, 97.
80 Synod of Uppsala 1693, *Svenska synodalakter 1*, 183.
81 Ylikangas 1967, 199–202.
82 For instance, Giftermålsbalken 3, in *Magnus Erikssons landslag*, 40; Ärvdabalken 9, in *Magnus Erikssons stadslag*, 60–1.
83 Uppsala universitetsbibliotek (Library of the University of Uppsala), Uppsala, Sweden, legal manuscript B 40, 133–133v is only one of over 20 existing legal manuscripts with the text.
84 Det Rosengrenska lagförslaget, *Lagförslag i Carl den Niondes tid*, Erfda Balken 2, 320–1.
85 Uppsala universitetsbibliotek, legal manuscript B 190a, 19; *Riksrådet Johan Skyttes kommentar*, 34n2; *Johan Skyttes kommentar*, 25.
86 *Vår äldsta kommentar till landslagen*, 27.
87 Royal statute on the unlawful marriages of the nobility (7.3.1665), in *Kongl. Stadgar*, 426–9.
88 Ylikangas 1967, 57; 15:6, in *Kircko-Laki Ja Ordningi 1686*, p. 22; Lagkommissionens förslag till Giftermålsbalk 1689, *Förarbetena till Sveriges rikes lag 1686–1736*, 16.
89 Korpiola 2011, 2007.
90 For instance, Ärvdabalken 22:2, Upplandslagen, in *Svenska landskapslagar* 1:74; Ärvdabalken 16, Östgötalagen, in *Svenska landskapslagar* 1:131.
91 Ärvdabalken 22:2, Upplandslagen, in *Svenska landskapslagar* 1:74; Ärvdabalken 16, Östgötalagen, in *Svenska landskapslagar* 1:131; Ärvdabalken 15, in *Magnus Erikssons landslag*, 63.
92 Kk 15:1, Östgötalagen, in *Svenska landskapslagar* 1:13; *Beiträge zur Geschichte des Buss- und Beichtwesens*, vi, ix, xix.
93 For instance, statutes of the provincial council of Uppsala 1368, *Diplomatarium Suecanum*, vol. 9, doc. 7777, p. 454; "Provinsialkonsiliet i Söderköping år 1436," 277. See also Brundage 1987, 381, 459, 517.
94 17, provincial statutes of Arboga from 1412, *Synodalstatuter och andra kyrkorättsliga aktstycken*, 30.
95 5.4.1503, *Arboga stads tänkebok*, 135.

96 For instance, Giftermålsbalken 2:3, in *Magnus Erikssons stadslag*, 38; Giftermålsbalken 3:1, in *Kuningas Kristoferin maanlaki 1442*, 44.
97 The hundred was a territorial administrative unit.
98 Giftermålsbalken 3:1, in *Kuningas Kristoferin maanlaki 1442*, 44.
99 4.10.1597 Oppunda, *Sörmländska härads domböcker*, 89–90. See also 1.7.1458, *Arboga stads tänkebok*, 88.
100 Aalto 1996, 116–19; Lennartsson 1999, 317–18; Thomson 1966, 166–7; King Charles XI to the Svea Court of Appeal 2.1.1694, in *Kongl. Stadgar*, 1357.
101 *Svenskt Diplomatarium*, vol. 2, doc. 1616, 5, p. 542; decision of the provincial synod in Arboga from 1412, issued for the diocese of Linköping, 23, *Synodalstatuter och andra kyrkohistoriska aktstycken*, 31; Giftermålsbalken 2:3, in *Kuningas Kristoferin maanlaki 1442*, 44; Ordinance of Västerås, *Svenska riksdagsakter*, I:1, p. 92; Thomson 1966, 37–41.
102 Korpiola 2009, 380–3.
103 Thomson 1966, 35–7; Synod of Strängnäs 1583, *Svenska synodalakter 2*, 5; Synod of Strängnäs 1584, *Svenska synodalakter 2*, 13; Circular of the diocese of Växjö 1584(?), *Undersökningar och aktstycken*, 53.
104 See, for example, the Synod of Uppsala 1611, 3, *Svenska synodalakter 1*, 25; Kyrko-ordning för Vexiö Stift 1619, *Ecclesiastique Samlingar* 8:601–2; *Consistorii ecclesiastici aboënsis protokoller* I–II, 159, 161; Söderlind 1950, 28–43.
105 See Burghartz 186, 189, 198n56.
106 Söderlind 1950, 3–5; Gaunt 1996, 23–34.
107 Giftermålsbalken 3:8, 9:1, 10:1, *Sveriges Rikes Lag*, 5, 10–11.
108 Giftermålsbalken 3:9, 10:7, *Sveriges Rikes Lag*, 5, 12; Missgiernings Balk 54:1, *Sveriges Rikes Lag*, 168; Hemmer 1954, 49.
109 Giftermålsbalken 5:1, Ärvdabalken 8:1–2, *Sveriges Rikes Lag*, 7, 27.

SECTION III

Uniformity and Singularity

Chapter 9

Marriage in France from the Sixteenth to the Eighteenth Century: Political and Juridical Aspects*

ANNE LEFEBVRE-TEILLARD

Introduction

The history of marriage in France from the sixteenth to the eighteenth century was profoundly shaped by political interests. Increasingly influenced by currents in political thought that considered marriage the "foundation of the families that make up republics," the monarchy attempted to take juridical control of the process of making marriages, an area that had been the exclusive province of the church until the mid-sixteenth century. The way the monarchy set about this task of taking into its own hands that foundational act, the "source and origin of civil society," was by reinforcing the authority of parents over their children's marriages without challenging the competence of the church and its courts. That the task was a long one is illustrated by the royal Declaration of 1639, which retraces the principal stages of the state's increasing control over the institution of matrimony, while also revealing the duplicity inherent in this process. Although by the latter half of the seventeenth century the bishops were cooperating with the monarchy, many difficulties still lay in the way. People did not easily accept the innovation that parental consent to the marriage of children, even of a relatively advanced age, was obligatory, particularly as the Catholic Church had rejected this requirement at the Council of Trent.

The monarchy not only attempted to control marriage but also claimed jurisdiction over carnal relations outside of marriage, particularly regarding acts that obligatorily led to marriage under canon law, as was the case when carnal relations were preceded by an exchange of promises between the man and the woman. As we know, if there was no diriment impediment to marriage, carnal relations transformed a promise to marry into a *matrimonium praesumptum*, because engaging in sexual relations was taken to indicate that a promised couple had given "present consent," which canon law held created a marriage. But when the Council of Trent, followed by royal legislation, decreed that public and solemn celebration of marriage was necessary for its validity, this change barred the route to presumed marriages.[1] The related idea that a "seducer" was expected to marry his "victim" nonetheless remained stubbornly anchored in people's minds, and many "seduced" women, particularly if they were pregnant, continued to refer to it as they pursued the avenues of action against their "seducers" available to them in canon law. As the royal courts took over hearing such suits, their jurisdiction gradually became exclusive, and as such legal actions came to be influenced by various cultural and social factors, they evolved in a direction less and less favourable to the woman.

Part I: The Growing Predominance of the State

An examination of the growth of state control over the formation of the matrimonial bond from the sixteenth to the eighteenth century contributes to our understanding of the process of secularization of marriage that culminated under the Revolution.

The royal Declaration of 26 November 1639, registered with the Parlement of Paris on 19 December of that year, serves as the basis for this discussion.[2] This highly important document concerning marriage was published at a key moment in the evolution of royal legislation that had begun in the mid-sixteenth century, during which the juridical control of marriage passed from the church to the state. Behind the Declaration lay the famous affair of the marriage of Gaston d'Orléans, the brother of King Louis XIII and heir presumptive to the throne. In 1632, Gaston d'Orléans, a man in perpetual conflict with Richelieu, had more or less secretly – at night and before a monk delegated by the bishop of Toul and a few witnesses – married Marguerite, the sister of Charles IV, Duke of Lorraine and a dangerous enemy of the king and the cardinal. Obviously, he did so without the consent of his brother the king, who suspected the marriage had taken place but had no confirmation of it until 1633. This affair inspired lively reactions regarding the king's rights in matrimonial questions that were still very much current in 1639.[3]

The very long preamble to the royal Declaration permits analysis of the motives behind the French monarchy's intervention in this domain and also shows why that intervention began as early as the sixteenth century. The text, as we shall see, contains a certain ambiguity, because in theory the king could not concern himself with the validity of the sacrament of marriage, which remained governed by canon law. In practice, however, the monarchy found a variety of means to extend royal control over the formation of the matrimonial bond.

How the king proceeded is clear from the main dispositions of the Declaration. For the most part, they recall earlier decrees of 1556 and 1579, which were here renewed and given strengthened penalties – penalties disproportionate to the stated aim of the measure, to require parents' consent to their children's marriage. The king did not yet dare "go all the way" and nullify marriage without parental consent. His courts, however, would over time see to that task. Furthermore, an examination of the final articles of the Declaration, concerning suits brought before the ecclesiastical courts – the *officialités* – for enforcement of promises to marry, which were still particularly numerous in the sixteenth century, will lead to consideration of the various means that the monarchy used not just to restrict the jurisdiction of the ecclesiastical courts but also to constrain them to apply royal dispositions on marital matters.

The Royal Declaration of 1639: The Preamble

"As marriages are the seed-beds of states, the source and the origin of civil society, and the foundation of the families that make up republics ...." This phrase, of clearly Ciceronian inspiration, opens the preamble to the 1639 royal Declaration and presents the essential reason for the monarchy's move to take control of the institution of marriage: the importance of the legitimate family as the foundation of the state. This notion, taken from the Roman world and diffused in France during the sixteenth century, in particular by Jean Bodin,[4] was an essential and durable one in political thought. "The good order of families creates the good order of the state," declares the treatise on marriage written several decades later on the order of Colbert for the instruction of his son, Monsieur de Seignelay.

The monarchy moved to regain control of marriage, the founding act of the state, by reinforcing parental authority, because "the natural reverence of children toward their parents" was similar to "the tie of legitimate obedience of subjects toward their sovereign." This was by no means an easy task, despite the support that Gallican jurists gave the king,[5] for the

Catholic Church opposed it – the church that had reasserted its exclusive competence in marriage-related questions during the Council of Trent and which the king did not want to defy openly.[6] The preamble to the royal Declaration insists on the convergence of the interests of French monarchs, who were eager to "make laws to promote public order, exterior decency, honesty and dignity," and the interests of the church, which had transformed marriage into a public and solemn act at the Council of Trent. According to the Declaration, the royal legislation simply took control of "ceremonies that have been prescribed as essential by the holy councils and by them declared to be not only necessary as a precept but also for the sacrament." This was a justification for royal legislation regarding marriage that went back to "the kings, our predecessors," in particular an initiative of Henry II in 1556, which the preamble felt it necessary to justify at some length, and the *Ordonnance* of Blois in 1579.

Henry II's Edict of 1556

In reality, as both the date and the tenor of Henry II's 1556 legislation regarding "clandestine marriages" show, the monarchy took advantage of the weakness of a church under attack from the Protestant Reformation to intervene in a domain that had until then been reserved to the church. This legislation was certainly strongly affected by an affair that touched the king directly. François de Montmorency, the son of the famous constable, revealed his "clandestine" marriage to Jeanne de Piennes on the eve of the day on which his father was to marry him to Diane, the legitimized daughter of Henry II.[7]

The censure that had long fallen on marriages contracted without proper publicity,[8] coupled with Erasmus's and Luther's criticism of such "clandestine" marriages, their challenges to the sacramental nature of marriage, and Luther's insistence, citing the Bible, on the need for parental consent for marriage were all arguments that aroused echoes in France, then torn between Protestants and Catholics.[9] Given this theological atmosphere, it is hardly surprising that Henry II's edict prohibiting clandestine marriages was based on the Decalogue, but this may have been only a pretext to mask pressure from the aristocracy that was increasingly eager – like the constable de Montmorency – to retain control over its alliances. As the preamble to the 1639 Declaration recalls,

> Although this enactment was founded on the first commandment of the second table containing the honour and the reverence that is due to

> parents, it was not strong enough to halt the course of the evil and the disorder that has troubled the repose of so many families and dimmed their honour by unequal and often shameful and infamous alliances.

In order to permit parents to punish "their children who might contract clandestine marriages without their consent," Henry II's legislation had turned to the time-honoured punishment of disinheritance, which did not touch the marriage bond but only its civil effects and was by tradition within the competence of civil law.[10] As the 1639 preamble recalls,

> But aside from the punishments indicated by the councils, some of our said predecessors have permitted fathers and mothers to disinherit their children who contracted clandestine marriages without their consent and to revoke each and every gift and advantage that they may have made to them.

Henry II deemed parental consent necessary up to the age of 30 for male children and 25 for females.[11]

This was a first and timid measure taken by a monarchy that still hoped the Council of Trent, which had not yet concluded (it closed seven years later, in December 1563), would subject the validity of marriages to parental consent. That hope proved vain. At the urgent request of the king of France, Charles IX, the Council Fathers examined the question during the summer of 1563, but they refused once and for all to make parental consent a condition of the validity of a marriage.[12] This was one of the reasons – although not the only one – for France's refusal to accept the decrees of the Council of Trent.

The Ordonnance of Blois of 1579

A second and extremely important stage in the development of royal control of marriage is reflected in the *Ordonnance* of Blois of May 1579. This sweeping reform measure contained several articles concerning marriage. The preamble to the 1639 Declaration summarizes article 40 of the *Ordonnance* of Blois, saying that the problem of clandestine marriages

> has since given rise to other *ordonnances* that advocate the proclamation of banns, the presence of [the couple's] own parish priest and of witnesses to the nuptial blessing, with sanctions against the parish priests, vicars, and others who celebrate the marriages of children of well-to-do families [*enfans de famille*] if they cannot demonstrate the consent of fathers and

> mothers, guardians and caretakers, on pain of being punished as guilty of the crime of abduction, as authors and accomplices to illegitimate marriages of the sort.[13]

In article 40, the *Ordonnance* of Blois took from the canons of the Council of Trent what was important to the king: the need for banns, for celebration of the marriage in the presence of the "parish priest, vicar, or other," and for four witnesses (rather than the two or three required by Trent). Above all, however, it reinforced parents' control over the marriage of their children by assimilating the lack of parental consent to "abduction." In article 42, in fact, the *Ordonnance* considered to be abduction – *rapt* – the marriage of all minors under age 25 concluded without parental consent.[14] The parish priest who married such "children" without ascertaining the consent of the father, mother, or guardian, even risked being punished as an "accomplice in the crime of abduction" (article 40). And abduction, which fell under the exclusive jurisdiction of the royal courts, was punishable by death. With this terrible penalty the king hoped to achieve respect for his edicts against "clandestine marriage" (i.e., marriage without parental consent), which he did not dare to declare invalid. Was this punishment too harsh to be effective? This would seem to be the case, given that the preamble to the 1639 Declaration states,

> In spite of whatever order has been brought until now to reestablish public virtue [*honnêté*] and such important acts of law, the license of the century [and] the depravation of mores have always prevailed over our so holy and so salutary *ordonnances*, the very vigour and observation of which has often been relaxed by the consideration of fathers and mothers who remit their own offense, even though they cannot remit the offense to our public laws.

In any event, the penalty was soon put into effect when another type of abduction, "abduction by seduction" (*rapt de séduction*), was assimilated to this abduction by violence (*rapt de violence*). This appeal to the notion of "abduction," a fundamental innovation in the 1579 *Ordonnance*, and the presumption that accompanied it are a key to the juridical evolution that followed.

The Rapt de Séduction

Assimilating "abduction by seduction" to abduction per se – that is, forcibly carrying someone off – first of all allowed the removal of a large number of matrimonial cases from the ecclesiastical courts, because the crime of abduction fell under the exclusive jurisdiction of the royal courts, where it had to be heard before any civil suit could be brought.[15] But equally importantly, the assimilation of these two types of abduction also eventually permitted the declaration that a marriage contracted without parental consent was invalid. In its twenty-fourth session the Council of Trent had decreed there could be no marriage between an abductor and the abducted girl or woman so long as the latter remained under the power of her abductor.[16] Any marriage concluded under such conditions was null. Here the council meant abduction by violence.[17]

The idea that abduction could be carried out by "seduction" as well as by force was already common among certain French jurists by the latter half of the sixteenth century.[18] The same idea is manifestly present in article 42 of the *Ordonnance* of Blois,[19] observation of which the king's 1639 Declaration demands (in article 2), along with all of the items contained in that *ordonnance* and in the edict of 1556. The 1639 royal Declaration even strengthens the sanctions:

> The content of the edict of the year 1556 and of articles 41, 42, 43, and 44 of the *Ordonnance* of Blois are to be observed; and adding to these, we command that the penalty for abduction still remain, notwithstanding the consents that may have occurred after the fact on the part of fathers, mothers, guardians, and caretakers, in express derogation of the customs that permit children to marry after the age of twenty without the consent of the parents. And we have declared and do declare that the widows, sons, and daughters under twenty-five years of age who may have contracted marriage against the tenor of the said dispositions be deprived of and have forfeited [their rights] by this act alone, together with the children who will be born [of the union] and their heirs, as unworthy and unable forever to [inherit] the estates of their fathers, mothers, and grandparents and all other direct and collateral [kin], as is also true of the rights and advantages that may be acquired by them through contracts of marriage and by testament in the customs and laws of our kingdom, even [concerning] the right of legitimate succession; and [we declare] the dispositions that will be made to the prejudice of this our *ordonnance*, either in favour of the married persons or by them to the profit of the children born of these marriages, null and of no effect and value. It is our will that things thus given, bequeathed, or transported, under whatsoever pretext, remain in this case irrevocably acquired to our treasury, our being able to dispose of them only in favour of hospitals or other pious works.

It was one thing to stiffen penalties, increase formalities,[20] and threaten

> very express prohibitions to all priests, both secular and regular, to celebrate any marriage except between their true and ordinary parishioners, without the written permission of the parish priests of the parties or the diocesan bishop, despite immemorial customs and privileges that might be alleged to the contrary. (article 1)

It was quite another to declare a marriage null and void. The solution was to emphasize the notion of marriage as a contract, until then considered indissociable from the sacrament of marriage, and to treat it separately.

The Notion of Marriage as a Contract

This was precisely what the Parlement of Paris did when its *arrêt* of 5 September 1634 declared the marriage of Gaston d'Orléans "not validly contracted" because *rapt de séduction* was involved. The notion of contract as applied to marriage was an old one; it appeared in civil law theory towards the end of the eleventh century, and thereafter was used by the canonists and, with a bit more reserve, by theologians, who applied it to a close analysis of the consent of spouses.[21] This appeal to the juridical notion of contract, even if it was considered at the time indissociable from the sacrament of marriage, nonetheless rendered that sacrament more fragile, as it opened the door to an eventual separation. In their discussions of marriage reform, the fathers of the Council of Trent had made intensive use of the distinction between contract and sacrament – in effect giving excessive importance to the contract – and thus opened the way for the French monarchy later to invalidate clandestine marriage. Those discussions were soon turned against the church.[22] Gallican jurists profited from the situation, cleverly pursuing the distinction while also demanding that the king have competence over establishing the form of the contract. When Pope Urban VIII protested against the 1634 decree,[23] Richelieu responded,

> There is this difference between the ecclesiastical tribunal and the courts of Parlement: that the first, in dissolving a marriage, declares it null, which involves the sacrament, while the courts say only "not validly contracted," which concerns the contract alone.[24]

This clever response did not deceive anyone regarding the monarchy's intention to use indirect means to separate the contract and the sacrament.

It is in relation to that aim that the terms "validly contracted" or "not validly contracted," used by both the *Ordonnance* of 1579 and the king's Declaration of 1639, take on their full meaning. Not only does the Declaration render "not validly contracted" marriages concluded without parental consent, but it does so "in conformity with the holy canonical decrees and constitutions," since abduction was presumed in such cases. In practical terms, this juridical subtlety was aimed at asserting the invalidity of marriages so contracted, but without directly countering canonical precepts.[25] When a marriage contract was declared invalid, this inevitably nullified the associated sacrament, according to the opinion defended by the Gallican jurists and backed by some eminent theologians, in particular regarding the marriage of Gaston d'Orléans.[26] Some theorists went so far as to assert that the king could create diriment impediments on his own authority,[27] which the king took care not to do, given that by using his parlements as an intermediary he had effective and more supple control over the formation of the matrimonial bond.[28]

The "Appel Comme d'Abus"

The parlements did in fact have one quite effective way to oblige ecclesiastical judges to respect royal decrees based on an edict of 1606: the *appel comme d'abus*.[29] The *appel comme d'abus* was invented in the latter half of the fifteenth century and further developed in the reign of Francis I.[30] It permitted, on appeal by the accused or the king's prosecutor assigned to the ecclesiastical tribunal, to invalidate as illegal all the acts (citations, sentences, etc.) of the ecclesiastical judges that, in a general manner, interfered with the king's rights and, in this particular instance, failed to respect the royal *ordonnances* and their interpretation in jurisprudence. Penalty was seizure of temporal revenues. The *appel comme d'abus* permitted the annulment of clandestine marriages and, to the extent possible, limited the jurisdiction of the ecclesiastical courts.

Marriage promises, to which canon law accorded a great importance, offer a good example of this process. In the first half of the sixteenth century, cases concerning promises or betrothals (*fiançailles*) still represented a large part of the activity of the church courts.[31] Not only did the royal jurisdiction prevent the *officialités* – the ecclesiastical courts – from taking cognizance of suits to gain recognition of marriage promises when an accusation of abduction was entered at the same time, but in the name of the "freedom of marriages" they were gradually forbidden to hear any such cases.[32] In connection with a suit brought by one Anne Miloy in 1636, Talon, the king's advocate-general, expressed the official thesis:

> It being said that there is no act among human beings in which liberty and openness is as fully and absolutely necessary as in a marriage, to the solemnity of which no one can be constrained, even though there be written promises, even made before notaries, ... it follows that the jurisdiction of the *officiaux* [the ecclesiastical judges] ... is superfluous and useless.[33]

In spite of this, the king found it necessary in the 1639 Declaration to prohibit "all judges, even those of the church, to receive evidence from witnesses of promises of marriage in any other form than written and attested to in the presence of four close relatives of each of the two parties, even if they are of low condition." The king's subjects were clearly reluctant to abandon time-honoured traditions.

In the interest of avoiding "unhappy surprises" to families haunted by the fear of misalliances, the king went so far as to declare "incapable of all successions, along with their posterity," children born of a secret marriage (article 5) and children legitimated by their parents' marriage *in extremis* (article 6).

The Royal Legislation and the Reaction of the Clergy

Not only did the king dictate laws on marriage, but those laws obtained the support of French bishops during the seventeenth century. Most of the bishops, who were named by the pope but presented by the king,[34] came from aristocratic backgrounds, which means that they were close enough to the monarchy to share its concerns – perhaps too close – although they were also well able to defend the interests of the church. In the second half of the seventeenth century, synodal statutes and rituals began to reflect the royal demands by requiring parish priests to make careful inquiries about parental consent at the stage of the marriage promise. The ritual of Bourges, for example, redacted in 1666, prescribed that parents or "other persons asked to do so" must present the couple to the priest. Several years later, the ritual of Reims stated that the priest must interrogate the couple in the following terms: "Is it with the participation and consent of your parents that you claim to contract this alliance together? Yes, Monsieur. Are they here present? Yes or No, Monsieur."[35] Parish priests were not to publish the banns of minors "under the age of twenty-five unless they had ascertained the consent of their father, mother, guardian, or caretaker." This requirement, formulated in the ritual of Sens in 1694 among others, became widespread in the eighteenth century.[36] Certain rituals, as in Bourges, went so far as to prescribe that parish priests obtain parental consent in writing if they thought that the parents might disavow their oral consent.[37]

The king had definitively taken control of the formation of the matrimonial bond.

Part II: Marriage and Carnal Relations Outside of Marriage

"Unless he prefers to marry her": *Si mieux n'aime l'épouser* was how a number of plaintiffs in the eighteenth century concluded their petition when they brought suit in secular courts against their "seducers." For many of these women, forcing their seducer to marry them was their last hope. One of these was Marie-Thérèse Douchet, who brought suit against Jean Baptiste Dubus on 28 July 1768 demanding that he "be declared the father of the child, [and] in consequence [be] condemned to dower her, repay her childbirth expenses, [and] pay her each month the sum of three florins for the nourishment, nurturing, and education of the child ... unless he prefers to marry her."[38] All or nearly all these women claim to have yielded to the men's demands following promises of marriage. But by the eighteenth century the time had long passed in which such a promise followed by sexual intercourse (*copula carnalis*) was sufficient to create a marriage, as had been the case when the church was uniquely competent to set matrimonial legislation.[39] The only marriages that were now valid, according to the conditions fixed by royal legislation, were those celebrated publicly (*in facie ecclesiae*).[40] Girls or women who had been seduced thus had no recourse other than a suit for one or more of the three forms of support mentioned in Marie-Thérèse Douchet's suit: a dowry, payment of childbirth expenses, and recognition of paternity. These three complaints had originated at a time when the ecclesiastical courts believed they had exclusive competence in matrimonial matters and held the right to condemn all carnal relations outside of marriage. For the church, such relations had constituted an offence that involved civil reparations over and above the penal sanction that the two guilty parties would eventually have to face.

Although ecclesiastical competence was quite real in the early sixteenth century, as we have seen, the church courts lost that power to royal jurisdiction by the early seventeenth century. Notably, however, the royal courts simply took over the legal actions that the *officialités* – the ecclesiastical courts – had created, modifying them little by little. I shall attempt to note the principal events and situations that contributed to this shift over the course of the seventeenth and eighteenth centuries.

It is important to make one preliminary observation. While in this domain some rules and regulations were fixed by canon law, other aspects were left to the initiative of the judge and to jurisprudence. Case studies reveal significant diversity in the ways courts resolved the dual problem of reparations to the woman and responsibilities towards the child, even though the basic principle and the resulting legal actions were the same. The influence of the environment in which the ecclesiastical judge – and later the secular judge – operated plays an important role here. Mores and customs varied from one region to another and according to whether the population of the region was rural or urban, and the regulations guiding the authorities who provided assistance to the poor and had charge of abandoned children affected such cases differently. Such variations existed not only across space but also over time. This treatment will thus necessarily be general.

The Church Courts and Penalties for Carnal Relations Outside Marriage in the Sixteenth Century

During the first half of the sixteenth century, the ecclesiastical courts' competence over the domain of carnal relations outside of marriage was broad but not exclusive. The secular jurisdictions not only denied the *officialités* the right to set penal sanctions for adultery,[41] but in practical terms they represented a competing competence, especially regarding the *provision*, or payment of the mother's expenses for and after childbirth. Nonetheless, especially as long as promises of marriage followed by carnal relations sufficed to create a valid marriage, female plaintiffs generally preferred to bring their suits before church judges. The issue of competing competencies was settled by deferring to the earlier decision and does not seem to have given rise to major jurisdictional conflicts at the time.[42]

The jurisprudence of the *officialités* will serve as a guide for this first part of my discussion,[43] keeping in mind that informal settlements or compromises were and remained numerous, although such arrangements did not prevent eventual recourse to a judge.[44] By and large we know only of those cases that were brought before the ecclesiastical courts. Still, these are highly instructive.

For the church, any carnal relation outside of marriage was a transgression. It was a simple misdemeanour when it occurred between two persons capable of marriage to one another; it was a crime when it involved a person who was already married (adultery) or who was a blood relation within the prohibited degrees of kinship (incest).[45] Like all sins, it carried an obligation to make reparation, an obligation that weighed on the man regarding both the woman and the child born or to be born.

When marriage was juridically possible, it constituted the best form of reparation: it effaced the offence and retroactively gave the child legitimate status.[46] But this was not always possible or desired by the man. Hence the church chose to support the woman so that she would not undergo the consequences of this transgression alone. The church offered her three quite separate possible actions: the suit for a dowry (*actio dotis*), the suit for expenses (*actio provisionis*), and the suit for acknowledgment of paternity (*actio captionis vel susceptionis partus*). In practice these were often combined, and in the early sixteenth century they were frequently attached to a suit to recognize a promise of marriage (*matrimonium per verba de futuro*) followed by sexual intercourse (*carnali copula subsecuta*).[47] There was no need for official ceremonies sealing the marriage promise, or even for a sworn statement: a simple object accepted in the name of marriage (*nomine matrimonii*) sufficed,[48] provided the promise preceded the carnal relations. In such a situation, the female plaintiff might decide that the marriage needed to be "solemnized." Other demands were only secondary. Here, for example, is how a woman named Marion la Brune worded her petition:

> Regarding Marion la Brune, plaintiff suing for marriage or nuptials, dowry, deflowering, provision of expenses, and acknowledgement of paternity, against Jean Harangier, defendant, the citation being founded. The plaintiff … demands solemnization of the marriage and, in case of insufficient proofs, the award of a dowry, for the which dowry she demands the sum of fifty *livres tournois*; the usual provision, to wit: during the six weeks before childbirth, eight *sous parisis* per week, and during the period immediately following childbirth, sixteen *sous parisis* per week for four weeks; and acknowledgement of paternity when the child arrives in the port of Salvation; and payment of expenses.[49]

Had Marion la Brune been taken advantage of under promise of marriage, or had she perhaps hoped, by giving in to Jean Harangier's advances, to force him into marriage? Marion's statement shows how difficult it was for a female plaintiff to prove her claims, as well as how hard it was for the ecclesiastical judge to discern the truth.[50] It often happened that a man who was sued to acknowledge a marriage would deny the promises of marriage but admit to the carnal relations and be happy to get off relatively easily. This did not always happen, however. The seduced woman could then turn to the three legal actions described earlier to lodge a complaint against her seducer, whether a cleric or layman, unmarried or married.

The plaintiff could choose between two procedural avenues. She could accuse her seducer directly, according to the normal procedures; or she could take the avenue of inquisitorial procedures and invest a *promoteur* with responsibility for the case, permitting him to act *ad denuntiationem* and direct the inquiry. In either case she would be required to swear an oath, in principle limiting the risk of calumnious accusation or denunciation.[51] In certain situations, the *promoteur* had the power to act *ex officio*.[52]

Finally, the plaintiff could initiate one or more of the three actions just discussed.[53] The first of these, the suit for a dowry (*actio dotis*), however, was reserved to a quite specific category of plaintiff. Based on a passage from Exodus (22:15–16), the suit for a dowry was applicable only to a young woman who had been deflowered[54] and was aimed at offering reparation for the harm done to her by the loss of her virginity through the provision of a dowry. In principle, the dowry was calculated according to the financial means and the social status of the parties (*secundum facultates et qualitates partium*), but in practice the ecclesiastical judge often tended to conform to local custom, which dictated compensation of 10 *sous tournois* in Montivilliers (Normandy), to pick one example. The defendant could avoid paying the dowry if he offered to marry the young woman, on the condition that the marriage was possible and she consented to it. The *official* of Troyes formulated this alternative of "marry or dower" (*duc vel dota*) in the following terms: "The said François has been sentenced to marry the said Louise or dower her, giving her and paying her thirty-five *sous* by way of dowry."[55]

In principle, the *actio dotis* (suit for a dowry) required dual proof: that of carnal relations and the more delicate proof of a previous state of virginity. If the man admitted to carnal relations but denied defloration, he would often be found liable, for there was a presumption of a young woman's virginity, which derived from the Exodus text and which would be set aside only if the defendant successfully showed that he had not been the first (*probare antecessorem*) or, even better, could plead the exception of a woman of bad repute (*filia diffamata*).[56]

The two other legal actions were aimed at coming to the aid of a girl or woman who discovered she was pregnant. She customarily sued for support before the birth of the child, but she might also act afterward, for example, if her seducer had promised to contribute to the child's upkeep but had failed to keep his word. There was no specified time limit.

The suit for expenses (*actio provisionis*) was intended to assure payment of the mother's expenses for several weeks before and after childbirth and the costs of childbirth. In Paris the sum to be paid was fixed at 8 *sous parisis* per week before the birth and 12 after it. More than the mother, it was the life of the child that the law sought to protect by this measure, so that when the child arrived "in the port of Salvation" (*ad portum salutis*) it could be baptized.[57] In order to obtain provision for herself and the child, the plaintiff did not have to prove that the defendant was the father of her child but only the plausible existence of carnal relations.[58] If the man admitted relations but denied paternity of the child the woman was carrying, he could still be sentenced to pay the expenses. If at a later time it turned out that he was not the father, the sum collected by the *official* would be restored to him.[59] In practice, when the suit for expenses (*actio provisionis*) was joined to the suit for acknowledgment of paternity (*actio captionis vel susceptionis partus*), the plaintiff would attempt to bring evidence to prove carnal relations at the presumed moment of conception, in order to obtain payment of the expenses but also make the defendant take responsibility for the child.

The suit for acknowledgment of paternity was aimed at getting the defendant to accept material responsibility for the child, whose rights were essentially limited to nourishment.[60] No child was excluded from that right, whether simply illegitimate or the fruit of adultery or incest. The goal of this suit was not directly to force the defendant to declare his paternity but rather to sentence him to pay for the upkeep of the newborn.[61] If paternity was proven, the child would have the right to bear the father's name.[62]

But how could it be proven that the defendant was indeed the child's biological father? The canonists drew from the Decretals a presumption in favour of a concubine that weighed more heavily on the man and shifted the burden of proof to him.[63] In practice, in cases of "concubinage" the woman usually brought a suit for recognition of "consummated marriage," a move that forced the man to admit paternity even if he denied promises of marriage. This presumption, based on cohabitation, could be extended to a female servant because she lived in her master's house.[64] More often than not, this presumption pushed a master to confess to carnal relations, the most frequent evidence for paternity, if he had no valid argument to the contrary. Social pressure on the father to acknowledge the child was still strong in the early sixteenth century and was reflected in customs, fairly broadly respected in certain regions, like bringing the child to the dwelling of the supposed father a few days after its birth.[65] Social pressure and the weight of his conscience could easily lead a man to admit to carnal relations, but if he had doubts about his paternity, either because his relations with the plaintiff did not correspond with the presumed time of conception or because the plaintiff had a bad reputation or was considered "promiscuous" (*filia diffamata* or *plurium concubentium*), he could use these as arguments. If he failed to be sufficiently convincing, he would be found liable.

Aside from the man's admission, recourse to witnesses was a possible but much less frequent course, given that at most the evidence was observation of certain familiarities or indications (such as seeing the defendant alone with the woman) that might imply intimate relations. When this was the case, the proof had to be completed by a supplementary oath (*serment supplétoire*) on the part of the plaintiff.[66] In principle a sworn statement, even when given by a young woman who had been deflowered and was pregnant, was insufficient to prove paternity; but it provided strong pressure, given that popular practice in some regions attached great importance to it, especially when it was delivered "in the throes of childbirth" (*in partus doloribus*).[67]

In its efforts to substitute its own control over the institution of marriage for that of the church, the monarchy intensified pressure to remain sole judge in these matters when suit was brought against a layman.[68] Between the end of the sixteenth century and the end of the seventeenth century, the church courts were dispossessed of their competence,[69] but this transfer of jurisdiction was gradual and accompanied by a transfer of juridical solutions.

In order to understand the legal developments during the last two centuries of the Ancien Régime, I will first survey their principal motivations, then examine their typical traits, keeping in mind that the situation did not change everywhere at the same pace. This was also true of the three legal actions available to female plaintiffs.

1. Contributing Factors

Many factors contributed to the evolution of this transfer of jurisdiction, and they did not always work in the same direction.

The first of these factors was the transformation of marriage into a solemn and public act effected by the Council of Trent in its penultimate session, 11 November 1563. This was accomplished by the famous decree *Tametsi*. As we have seen, this decision made by the church – though with heated debate – carried considerable weight.[70] Although the Council was not officially "received" in France – in large part because of current conflicts between Catholics and Protestants – its principal dispositions were incorporated into royal legislation as part of its efforts to make the legitimate family the foundation of the state, and hence to control marriage, its founding act.[71]

The second and determinant contributing factor was the development of royal legislation, as we have seen in Part I.

In this way, marriage gradually passed under the control of the state, obliging the church courts, which theoretically still retained competence in marriage matters, to respect royal legislation (edict of 1606). The *appel comme d'abus* proved to be a useful tool in this connection, as it permitted the accused to have decisions of ecclesiastical judges overturned as "abuses" when they overstepped their competence or failed to respect royal legislation and its interpretation in jurisprudence.[72] Not content to place marriage under its control, and well aware of the importance of marriage promises, the monarchy went so far as to require written proof of marital intent, "even among people of low condition" (Declaration of 1639), thus dealing a severe blow to the role that promises played before the church courts.[73] The vice was tightening around illicit carnal relations.

A third factor made it easier for legislators to tighten that vice: the reaction against the laxity of mores following the Protestant Reformation and the Counter-Reformation. In the seventeenth century that reaction led to increased rigour within the magistrature, reflected, especially, in the Jansenism of some members of the Parlement of Paris. That increased rigour worked to the profit of the state, which, arguing from the respect due to "religion" in general and the sacrament of marriage in particular, worked to control the mores of its subjects through royal legislation and the royal courts. The influence of those courts was in turn reinforced as magistrates and lawyers increasingly occupied a prominent place in juridical literature in the late sixteenth century, leading to the diffusion of a progressively more rigorous attitude towards women. In this context the woman, once a "victim," gradually came to be seen as "guilty." No longer dishonoured, she dishonoured herself, and only promises of marriage could still excuse her for having given herself to her seducer. Overcome with shame, many young women attempted to hide their pregnancies and go to the city to give birth anonymously.[74]

Child abandonment, an option that increased in frequency during the sixteenth century and grew even more prevalent in the seventeenth and especially the eighteenth century, was both a contributing factor to these changes and a consequence of them. It was a question that soon preoccupied the local authorities, given that responsibility for abandoned children fell either to lords or to community organizations or cities.[75] Local attempts to reduce child abandonment were made, in some places even before the edict of 1556 regarding declarations of pregnancy.[76] Child abandonment often led to abuses on the part of seigneurial or municipal judges, who attempted to put pressure on the women who declared their pregnancy, or on midwives, to learn who the father was, thus preserving the collectivity's taking responsibility for the child. The various parlements reacted – sometimes fairly late – against such abuses. In 1668 the Parlement of Dijon forbade obliging a woman or a midwife to provide the name of the father (and, for the midwife, the name of the mother).[77] In 1704, the seneschal's court in Lyon passed a ruling requiring persons to inform the authorities if they received girls or women in their homes to give birth; but in 1712, the Parlement of Paris annulled this ruling.[78]

2. *Aspects of the Shift in Jurisdiction*

Change came slowly. Very old traditions are not given up easily, and many unmarried women in the early seventeenth century still believed that promises of marriage, followed by sexual relations, were enough to constitute marriage. These were not just country women. The *Journal des audiences* reports a decision handed down by the *grande chambre* of Parlement of Paris on 2 September 1637 regarding an earlier suit brought in the church court by one Anne de la Gadaigne against Sieur Phelippeaux, councillor to the royal court, with such a claim. Parlement declared illegal the "citation given by the *official* of Paris *in causa matrimonii incoepti* [in the suit of an initiated marriage] and the ensuing ruling that the marriage thus begun had to be formalized."[79]

"Most of the difficulties that cause so many disputes in questions involving marriage," the *avocat général* Bignon stated in 1632,

> come from [the fact that] people confuse the maxims of the old canonic jurisprudence with the new. It is true that, following the old canonic jurisprudence, promises of marriage, followed by the union of the flesh, are transformed into a true and presumed marriage ... However, those presumed marriages are today entirely abrogated, *moribus nostris* [according to our customs]. It has been thought that it was indecent to give the name and the effect of marriage, which is a great sacrament, to an illicit, impure, and dishonest union.[80]

Still, for some time to come promises of marriage followed by *copula carnalis* continued to imply marriage, even if juridically the seduced woman could claim only damages and the accrued interest. The plaintiffs and the judges themselves remained persuaded of this view – whatever they may have said – and the use that was made of the charge of *rapt de séduction* during the seventeenth century bears witness to its persistence.

The overall evolution of the trend I am tracing was also influenced – but to an extent difficult to determine – by the edict of February 1556, a measure intended to combat infanticide, that introduced declarations of pregnancy and of childbirth but failed to make them obligatory.[81] This act was poorly redacted – for example, it fails to state to whom the declaration was to be made – and it was interpreted liberally, except perhaps in the late sixteenth century, by a justice system that wanted to avoid condemning to death a woman judged guilty of abortion or infanticide.[82] The declaration was not only not considered obligatory but it might be made to anyone – the parish priest or a midwife, for example – capable of being called as a witness. Nonetheless, the edict certainly encouraged the local authorities to reinforce their surveillance and to attempt to force unmarried mothers not only to make such a declaration but to denounce their seducer in order to avoid having responsibility for the child fall on the community.[83] Such a declaration was made under oath and often, as at Cambrai, had to be repeated "in the pains of childbirth."[84]

How numerous were such declarations to the "authorities"? It is hard to know for sure. Despite the pressures exerted on the women involved, they often preferred not to make such a declaration, especially because in certain provinces (Languedoc, for example) they were liable to a tax when they did so.[85] At Cambrai only 26 out of 253 suits debated and judged by the church court, or 10 per cent, mentioned the existence of a declaration of pregnancy.[86] The insistence with which the parlements of the late seventeenth and early eighteenth centuries ordered judges to make sure that parish priests read the edict once every three months during their Sunday sermons seems to bear witness to the same reticence.[87]

The overall evolution was also marked by a provisional reinforcement of the penal basis of certain legal actions by their assimilation to seduction or abduction. The *rapt de séduction* served not only to punish the marriage of a minor without the authorization of his or her parents or guardian;[88] it was also used by a seduced woman, or her parents if she was still under age, in particular if she was pregnant.[89] The accusation involved arrest (*prise de corps*) but also the risk of being condemned to death, "unless he prefers to marry her" (*si mieux n'aime l'épouser*). This was not really a choice, or at the least it was subject to certain conditions: consent of the parents for minors, equal social conditions, and proposal by a sovereign court.[90] Pierre Jacques Brillon states that this choice disappeared in the late seventeenth century. "One should not condemn someone who has made a girl pregnant under promise of marriage to marry her or be hanged, but only to damages and interests fitting for the circumstances and the social rank of the parties," he writes in his *Dictionnaire des arrests*, basing his argument on an *arrest* of the Parlement of Paris of 28 April 1691, so confirming a shift that, according to Brillon, was discernible as early as 1660.[91] This procedure, which was the exclusive competence of the royal courts, was in fact excessively severe in its end result. Originally favourable to the seduced girl, it ended up turning against her as the judges showed themselves more and more mistrustful. Moreover, that proceeding led to marriage, whereas in appealing to the notion of "abduction by seduction" the monarchy pursued the opposite aim of preventing "unworthy alliances."[92] Incontestably, these changes affected the internal evolution of the various legal actions that lay tribunals had taken over.

3. *The Evolution of the Legal Actions*

We continue to find the three legal actions that we have been following – the suit for a dowry, the suit for expenses, and the suit for acknowledgment of paternity – up to the end of the eighteenth century. They evolved, however, under the influence of the various factors that I have noted.

As they became increasingly tied to one another, they gave rise to a certain degree of confusion.[93]

The dowry granted for loss of virginity during the early decades of the seventeenth century gradually disappeared unless the young woman had been deflowered under promise of marriage. In the eighteenth century such promises, increasingly invoked by plaintiffs to justify their ceding to the seducer,[94] became the chief argument for the damages and interest granted for them. Moreover, jurists increasingly tended to take the plaintiff's pregnancy as an indispensable proof of deflowering.[95] The suit for a dowry (*actio dotis*) slowly lost its original *raison d'être,* becoming a compensation granted to the pregnant woman that gradually became inseparable from the other two actions.[96] Towards the end of the Ancien Régime, a suit for a dowry was hardly ever admitted except in cases of pregnancy; damages and interest were considered uniquely "a result of her pregnancy,"[97] and were granted only when it could be presumed that the girl had succumbed following promises of marriage, which was impossible when the man in question was married or a priest and had not dissimulated his condition.[98] In making such a move jurists did their utmost to connect carnal relations outside of marriage to a future marriage towards which the seducer was to be urged – provided that social "conditions" were appropriate – even without "bodily seizure" (*prise de corps*). As a consequence, the penal tradition faded to the point that in 1781, at the end of the Ancien Régime, Jean-François Fournel, the author of a *Treatise on Seduction Considered within the Judiciary Order,* failed to comprehend why "the common opinion regards seduction as a crime."[99]

The other two legal actions available to female plaintiffs evolved in a way similar to the action for a dowry described above. But this evolution was also influenced by the authorities' attitude to child abandonment. As we have seen, one of the legal recourses open to a seduced woman was to file a suit for expenses against her seducer (*actio provisionis*). Even if, in principle, proof of carnal relations remained necessary, there was a tendency (due to a sense of urgency and a desire to avoid having responsibility fall on the community) to be content with a simple presumption if the man failed to admit his fault – a presumption in favour of the servant woman who accused her master and in favour of the virgin, a presumption which shifted from the state of virginity to the state of pregnancy. This resulted in granting expenses even when the question of the child's paternity had not been established definitively. It was within this framework that the maxim forged by

Antoine Favre, "One should believe the virgin who says she has been known carnally by someone and impregnated by him" (*creditur virgini dicenti se ab aliquo cognitam et ex eo pregnantem esse*), was applied.[100] Presumptions of this sort would be eliminated during the course of the eighteenth century. Some jurists, reacting to the overly great ease with which certain of their colleagues had admitted such presumptions, tended to demand real proof of carnal commerce, both for granting expenses for the mother and child and for establishing paternity.

Paternity was impossible to prove. This means that it continued to be presumed in the case of avowed cohabitation (through inquiry or testimony). In contrast, the presumption concerning paternity in favour of the female servant, still present in the early seventeenth century, was seldom retained by the end of that century. This meant that the woman had to prove (e.g., by means of specific evidence or testimony concerning certain "familiarities") that her master was indeed the father of the child she was carrying.[101] His admission remained the only genuine proof.[102] If the man admitted to carnal relations at the moment presumed to be that of conception but denied being the father of the child, he would not escape condemnation unless he could successfully plead that the woman was known to be sexually promiscuous (*filia diffamata* or *plurium concubentium*). On this point the law remained constant, as it did on the possibility of escaping a sentence by marrying the child's mother. What gradually changed, however, was the attitude of the men, who were increasingly quick to brand as "unchaste" (*impudique*) the girl who had ceded to them, and who were less and less apt to assume responsibility. Social pressure then focused on the mother. She was forbidden both to have the child brought to the dwelling of the claimed father and to have the child inscribed in the baptistry registers under his name if paternity had not been proven.[103] Increased demand for proof was simply the reflection of a more general attitude that, by the end of the eighteenth century, led increasingly to an essentially voluntary avowal of paternity. Implicitly eliminated by the law of Brumaire, An II, the search for paternity was prohibited by the Code Civil of 1804.

NOTES

* The (more detailed) French version of Part II of this chapter was published in Anne Lefebvre-Teillard, *Autour de l'enfant* (Leiden: Brill, 2008), 31–51.

1 See Donahue 38 and Lombardi 109–10.

2 Text in Isambert, Jourdan, and Decrusy, *Recueil des anciennes lois françaises*, 16:520–4.

3 On the considerable importance of this affair, both on the religious and the political planes, see Blet 1959, 404–45. More particularly concerning the political context, see Hildesheimer 2004, 251–4, 341ff. On the many negotiations with the Holy See about this affair, which ended only after the birth of the Dauphin in 1641, the death of Richelieu in 1642, and the pardon granted by Louis XIII, see Blet 1959, 409–10, 429–45. For a detailed description see, in this volume, Seidel Menchi 319–21.

4 In his *Les six livres de la République*, first published in 1576, Jean Bodin gives a definition of the Republic (in the sense of *res publica*) that emphasizes the family as the basic political cell: "It is the right government of several households and of what is common among them with sovereign power."

5 "Gallican jurists" were the jurists who defended the *Libertés de l'Eglise gallicane*, i.e. supported the sovereign's claims to a high degree of autonomy of the French Church vis-à-vis the Holy See.

6 Council of Trent, sess. 24, *Canones super reformatione matrimonii*, Canon 12: "If anyone says that matrimonial causes do not belong to ecclesiastical judges, let him be anathema," *Canons and Decrees of the Council of Trent*, 182.

7 Henry II's edict on clandestine marriage is dated February 1556 under the old calendar, in which the year began on Easter, and is therefore 1557. According to the investigation conducted in October 1556, the marriage between François and Jeanne was contracted in August 1556 *per verba de presenti*, without witnesses or blessing, but was never consummated. Such a marriage was valid although it was illegal. Pressured by his father, François requested a dispensation for an "unconsummated marriage" from Pope Paul IV, which was refused. This affair ended poorly in a false declaration under oath by François: see Morel 1979.

8 Synodal statutes of the medieval period struggled indefatigably against clandestine marriages, in particular by recalling the measures of publicity prescribed by the Fourth Lateran Council (1215) and prescribing that promised couples solemnize their marriage within a brief period of time (usually 45 to 60 days). To the extent that "clandestine" marriages were valid, however, this effort proved to be of little effect: see Lefebvre-Teillard 1973, 164–71. This was why a strong movement grew up within the church for the reform of marriages, as is stressed in Gabriel Le Bras, "Mariage," in *DTC*, IX, 2, 2123–317, esp. section 3, "La doctrine du mariage chez les théologiens et les canonistes depuis l'an mille," in particular cols. 2232–3 (Le Bras's essay is cited hereafter as Le Bras 1927).

9 On the challenge to the sacramental nature of marriage in Protestant doctrine, and more generally on the marriage of French Protestants before the revocation of the edict of Nantes (1685), see Bels 1968.

10 On the long-standing existence of recourse to the punishment of disinheritance for marriages concluded without parental consent, see Lefebvre-Teillard 1996, no. 114. The church was competent to judge the validity of the matrimonial bond itself, but it was the task of secular law to draw the patrimonial consequences. On this fundamental distinction, which went back to the Middle Ages, see Lefebvre-Teillard 1996, no. 106.

11 Article 5 of the edict states that sons and daughters over these ages still owed it to their parents "to seek out advice and counsel" from them. For the complete text of this edict, see Isambert, Jourdan, and Decrusy, *Recueil des anciennes lois françaises*, vol. 13, no. 363.

12 This was true even though, as the text of the Council of Trent's decree *Tametsi*, Session 24, ch. 1, states, "The holy Church of God has for very just reasons at all times detested and forbidden" unions without parental consent (*Canons and Decrees of the Council of Trent*, "Decree concerning the Reform of Matrimony"). See Gaudemet 1987, 290–5, and in this volume Donahue 36–7.

13 "... which has ... given rise to other *ordonnances*." In spite of this plural, the preamble is aiming in particular here at the *Ordonnance* of Blois, which remained the base for the entire later evolution of the question.

14 "And yet we wish that those who are found to have suborned a son or daughter of less that twenty-five years of age, under the pretext of marriage, or other, without the express desire, knowledge, will, or consent of the fathers, mothers, and tutors, be punished with death without hope of grace or pardon: notwithstanding all consents that the said minors may later allege having given to the said abduction [*rapt*] at the time or before, and similarly extraordinary punishment awaits all those who have participated in the said abduction and who have given advice, comfort, and aid in any manner whatsoever."

15 "When the charge of abduction goes [as far as] corporal punishment," writes Laurent Bouchel (d. 1629) in his *Bibliothèque ou Trésor du droit français*, 3:48, "the case that is before the judge about the bond [of matrimony] ceases, even though in former times the judge did not fail to pursue the matter, therefore what people say, that 'there is no good marriage that rope cannot break' ... But when the complaint touches only the interests, the judge is sure to pursue the case." (On the latter point, see Part II of this chapter, "Marriage and Carnal Relations Outside of Marriage"). In February 1580, the king had been forced to moderate the ardor of his judges in this domain: "We prohibit our judges," states article 25 of the edict, responding to

complaints from the clergy, "in cases involving marriage that are pending before the said ecclesiastics, to raise objections to disregard the decisions of the same, under pretext of abduction, without great and apparent reason, with which we charge their conscience and honour."

16 *Canons and Decrees of the Council of Trent*, canon 6, 452–3.

17 See Esmein 1929–35, 2:283.

18 "For a woman is abducted [*ravie*] not only when she is ravished [*violentée*] and transported from one place to another by force, but also when she is seduced and suborned by ruses, fine statements, promises, and false persuasions": see Coras, *Arrest du Parlement de Tolose*, under "Rapt," cited in Demars-Sion 1988, 722.

19 See this chapter, note 14. Moreover, this is the sense in which jurists soon understood the question: "Hence it is known that the *ordonnance* does not at all speak of abduction by force, violence, and carrying off girls … but that the said *ordonnance* concerns only abduction achieved by persuasion, induction, and subornation." This is the opinion expressed by Brisson, *Code du Roy Henri III*, 207. On this work and its author, a major servant of the royal power, see Olivier Descamps, "Brisson, Barnabé," in *Dictionnaire historique des juristes français*, 137–8.

20 Notably concerning the proclamation of banns, which must be made "by the parish priest of each of the contracting parties, with the consent of the fathers, mothers, guardians, or caretakers, if they [the marrying parties] are children of well-to-do families [*enfans de famille*] or under the power of others" (article 1).

21 On the appearance of the notion of contract in this context, see Gaudemet 1987, 191–3.

22 As Le Bras 1927 rightly stresses in "Mariage," 2261. In fact, the redaction of *Tametsi*, ch. 1 in the Council of Trent's *Canones super reformatione matrimonii*, emphasizes the contractual aspect of marriage. It decrees, "Those who shall attempt to contract marriage otherwise than in the presence of the parish priest or of another priest authorized by the parish priest or by the ordinary and in the presence of two or three witnesses, the holy council renders absolutely incapable of thus contracting marriage and declares such contracts invalid and null, as by the present decree it invalidates and annuls them" (*Canons and Decrees of the Council of Trent*, "Decree Concerning the Reform of Matrimony," ch. 1, 184).

23 The pope was right about the real consequences of the *arrêt* issued by the Parlement: see Blet 1959, 407.

24 Cited in Le Bras 1927, 2263.

25 This aim appears unambiguously in the edict of 1606 concerning ecclesiastical jurisdiction (the text of which is quoted in note 29), which refers to the penalty "stipulated by the councils." Article 169 of the *ordonnance* of 1629 known as the "Code Michau" reiterates: "It is our will, following the holy canonical decrees and constitutions, that such marriages made with those who abducted the said widows, sons, and daughters, be declared null and of no effect and validity, as not validly or legitimately contracted." The Code Michau, the work of the chancellor, Michel de Marillac, was registered without enthusiasm and did not survive the disgrace of the chancellor, which followed soon after. This may be why the king did not cite it by name. Subtle references to it appear in his Declaration, however, in particular in article 3.

26 On the king's request for an opinion addressed to the assembled clergy of France in 1635, see Blet 1959, 412–29; Le Bras 1927, 2263.

27 As did the Gallican canonist Jean Launoy in 1633: see Le Bras 1927, 2263–5.

28 On the jurisprudence of the parlements in this domain, see Duguit 1886 and, for a more extensive survey, Ghestin 1956.

29 Article 12 of the 1606 edict reads, "We desire that cases concerning marriages be of and belong to the cognizance and jurisdiction of the church judges, with the charge that they be held to keep the dispositions, even the *Ordonnance* of Blois in its article 40, and following these, declare marriages not performed and celebrated in church and with the form and solemnity required by the said article null and invalidly contracted, according to the indications of the councils. And in order for the bishops, each in his diocese, and the *curés* in their parishes be advised of this, and avoid violating the said *ordonnance*, it will be renewed and published immediately, so that the said bishops and their judges may from this moment on be able to judge in accordance with these."

30 See Lefebvre-Teillard 1973, 69–70.

31 The ecclesiastical courts encouraged each of the promised spouses to demand the right to oblige the other to contract marriage (absent a legitimate excuse): see Lefebvre-Teillard 1973, 147–63. When an exchange of promises was followed by "union of the flesh," promises sufficed to create a marriage (see, in this volume, 34 and "Part II" of this chapter). Suits involving marriage promises accounted for 60 per cent of the matrimonial cases heard by the archdiocesan tribunal of Paris between 1499 and 1503.

32 On the evolution of jurisprudence regarding such suits, see Lefebvre-Teillard 1978.

33 Reported in Bardet, *Recueil d'arrests du Parlement de Paris*, tome 2, 232.

34 The concordat of 1516 gave the king a right of presentation to the major benefices; the candidate's nomination, if he proved qualified, was the privilege of the pope. This arrangement persisted until the Revolution. At the end of the eighteenth century, it covered 129 bishoprics or archbishoprics, 750 religious houses for men, and almost 1,000 for women: see Barbiche 1999, 245.
35 "Rituel du diocèse de Bourges," 681; "Rituel de la province de Reims," 16.
36 "Rituel de la province de Sens," 256.
37 "Rituel du diocèse de Bourges," 381.
38 This example is taken from Demars-Sion 1991, 218.
39 See Donahue 34 and Lombardi 98–9.
40 On this legislation, see "Part I" of this chapter.
41 In the south of France in particular, but also in the north, if we can judge by the famous "decree against immoral husbands," the text of which was published later in Dupuy, *Libertés de l'Eglise gallicane*, ch. 26, no. 7, p. 866, and 3rd ed. (Paris, 1731–51) II, 148.
42 I am basing this judgment on the registers of the Parlement de Paris, which I have explored on the basis of Jean Le Nain's Table, a manuscript repertory consultable at the Archives Nationales, Paris. When called before the court of the archdiocese of Paris, Jean Marays stated that he had already been sentenced to take responsibility for the child by the secular judge of Villiers-Adam: see Pommeray 1933, 399.
43 Lefebvre-Teillard 1973, 207–14.
44 This is shown by a case brought before the archdiocesan court of Paris in 1518 in which the defendant in a suit for deflowering was ordered to pay a security deposit despite an agreement drawn up before two notaries of the Châtelet: see Lefebvre-Teillard 1973, 212n343.
45 On incest, see Lefebvre-Teillard 1973, 121. Relations with a male or female religious or a priest in major orders were also deemed criminal.
46 Thus declared Pope Alexander III in his famous decretal, *Tanta* (X 4, 17, 6), refusing that possibility to the child born of adultery. On the retroactive effect of legitimation in canon law, see Lefebvre-Teillard 2002, reprinted in Lefebvre-Teillard 2008.
47 Canon *Veniens* (X 4, 1, 15). For the doctrine laid down by Alexander III and the principle of *matrimonium praesumptum* see Donahue 34, Lombardi 98–9. On the elaboration of this doctrine, see Gaudemet 1987, 180–1. In practice this principle was based on a strong interpretation of *verba de futuro*, equating them to *matrimonium initiatum*: see Lefebvre-Teillard 1973, 148–61. The expression *matrimonium consummatum*, used by the ecclesiastical judges, is revealing.

48 Lefebvre-Teillard 1973, 150.

49 Archives Nationales, Z 1° 14, fol. 322r, extract of a sentence handed over by the judge of the archdiocese of Paris on 18 September 1518, the initial portions of which summarize the demands of the plaintiff. For the expression "to come to the port of Salvation," see note 57.

50 Was this a godsent aid to young women seeking a husband and who permitted themselves to be deflowered in the hope of marriage (*in spe matrimonii*)? Or was it a trap? See Lefebvre-Teillard 1973, 174–9. The two might overlap and it was not always easy for the *official* to evaluate the extent of the good faith of either party.

51 Obviously, this oath is not to be confused with the one she might eventually be required to take to prove her accusations (discussed later).

52 This was often the case when a priest stood accused: see Lefebvre-Teillard 1973, 80. Thus on 10 April 1511 Gilbert Guyard, a priest of the diocese of Bourges, spontaneously admitted his paternity of a child: Archives Départementales du Cher, 8 G 292, fol. 22r.

53 Occasionally the *official* reserved to himself the right to pronounce on the three actions separately.

54 The text of *Decretals* based on Exodus reads, "If a man seduces a virgin who is not yet betrothed and sleeps with her, he will dower her and take her as his wife. If, however, the virgin's father does not want to give her to him [in marriage], [the seducer] will pay money equivalent to the dowry that virgins normally receive" (X 5, 16, 1).

55 Archives Départementales de l'Aube, G 4199, fol. 151v (November 1529). The alternative *duc vel dota* was less severe than the obligation in Exodus, where the man was obliged to supply a dowry in all cases.

56 See Lefebvre-Teillard 1973, 209.

57 In order to be baptized, and thus to have access to life eternal, the child had to be born alive; it was recommended to midwives that they baptize the baby during childbirth if there was any danger of its death. The expression *dum venit ad portum salutis* ("until he came to the port of Salvation"), routinely used by the judges to designate birth, clearly reveals this concern.

58 According to circumstances and if he thought the suit well founded, the *official* could accord provision while waiting for proof to be established (Pommeray 1933, 398).

59 See the example given in Pommeray 1933, 575.

60 "Nourishment" was understood in a broad sense to include everything a child needed until he or she could take responsibility for his or her own needs. The juridical condition of the bastard was in reality very different

according to the social condition of the parents: see Lefebvre-Teillard 1996, nos. 214, 229, and 240.

61 On the different forms of responsibility for the child, which began on the day of its birth, see Lefebvre-Teillard 1973, 217–21. The general trend was increasingly toward the father's taking total responsibility for the child.

62 Lefebvre-Teillard 1990, 60–9, esp. 66.

63 Canon *Michaël* (X 1, 17, 13). The *Glossa ordinaria* to the *Decretals* of Pope Gregory IX redacted by Bernard of Parma develops this claim under the term *"constiterit."* Presumption of concubinage originally served to refuse to an illegitimate son of a priest the right to succeed his father in his office. On this presumption, see Demoulin-Auzary 2004, 265–70.

64 The master's putative abuse of his authority could also be argued. A number of criticisms were directed at the practice of extending this presumption to female servants: see Lefebvre-Teillard 1997, reprinted in Lefebvre-Teillard 2008.

65 On this custom, see Lefebvre-Teillard 1973, 216.

66 The *official* might administer the accused a decisory oath (*serment décisoire*), which would be taken as conclusive, but this very rarely happened. For one example, see Lefebvre-Teillard 1973, 216.

67 This oath *in partus doloribus* was used in particular by lay judges to obtain provision for the child: see Demars-Sion 1991, 15 and 136. Many nuances of time and place should be taken into account on this point: see Lefebvre-Teillard 1996, no. 229. On doctrinal discussion of the force of the sworn oath in this context, see Lefebvre-Teillard 1997, reprinted in Lefebvre-Teillard 2008.

68 Fevret, *Traité de l'abus, et du vray sujet des appellations qualifiées de ce nom d'abus*, a work that went through many editions, cites, after Chopin, a decree of the Parlement of Paris of 1560 that recognized the citation of a layman "for the dowry and feeding of the child" (*de dote et alendo partu*) by an ecclesiastical judge as an abuse of jurisdiction: see vol. 1, livre 5, ch. 1, no. 16.

69 Leaving aside such exceptions as Cambrai, which was attached to France at a late date and enjoyed special status: see Demars-Sion 1991, 35.

70 On the difficulties encountered in the adoption of this decree, see Gaudemet 1987, 290–5. Trent's decrees applied only in lands that officially accepted the council's decisions. In principle earlier canon law continued to apply to Catholics elsewhere, which meant that clandestine marriages were valid. Such presumed marriages (*matrimonia praesumpta*) were not eliminated by canon law until 1892.

71 See, in this volume, 263 and Lefebvre-Teillard 1996, nos. 122–7.

72 See 269–70.
73 On the importance of marriage promises and the many suits regarding them before the ecclesiastical courts in the sixteenth century, see Lefebvre-Teillard 1973, 148–54. On the way in which the *officialités* were deprived of their competence in this matter during the course of the seventeenth century, see Lefebvre-Teillard 1978.
74 This flight to the city prompted strong reactions, in particular on the part of certain of the larger urban centres (discussed later).
75 On this increase in child abandonment and the reaction to it of local authorities, see Demars-Sion 1983.
76 In this connection, see Phan 1975, 66n39, where she quotes a 1537 act of the Parlement of Toulouse cited in La Roche-Flavin, *Arrests du Parlement de Tolose*, L. II, vol. 3, "containing instruction to all judges and senechals and lords having jurisdiction, in which any unmarried woman who is pregnant will be put under their surveillance, so as to avoid the inconveniences that daily follow from this." Although this ruling did not set up formal procedures (as the edict of 1556 would do), it nonetheless reveals a similar concern for preventing infanticide.
77 See Demars-Sion 1983, 503.
78 Parlement de Paris, *arrêt* of 15 April 1712, cited in Le Ridant, *Code matrimonial*, 2:637.
79 The *Journal des audiences* gives the *arrêts* of that body from 1622 to 1722: this *arrêt* is published in vol. 1, livre 3, ch. 44. See also the ruling of the Parlement of Dijon mentioned earlier.
80 Bardet, *Recueil d'arrests du Parlement de Paris*, tome 2, livre 1, ch. 21.
81 The text reads, "We state, ordain, will, order, and it pleases us that any woman who will find herself duly charged and judged to have hidden, covered, or disguised both her pregnancy and her childbirth without having declared the one or the other and having taken sufficient witness of the one or the other, even of the life or death of her child when it issued from her womb, and thereafter it is found that the child was deprived of the holy sacrament of baptism and of public and customary burial, such a woman will be held and reputed to have murdered her child. And in reparation [she will be] punished by death and by the extreme penalty, with such rigour that the particular quality of the case will merit, so that it be an example to all and that afterward there be no doubt nor difficulty": Isambert, Jourdan, and Decrusy, *Recueil des anciennes lois françaises*, 13:472–3.

82 In order for the mother to be condemned for infanticide she must have hidden her pregnancy or her childbirth, but also her failure to baptize the child or to provide normal burial had to be proven. Moreover, in order to set off the legal process, a child's body had to have been found: see Carbasse 2000, no. 186. The judges of the lower courts seem to have been less "liberal" than the appeal judges in their interpretation of this edict.

83 This led to legislation against abuses, as has been shown. In the case argued before the Parlement of Dijon in 1668, the *syndic* of the city of Dijon did not hide the fact that this denunciation was aimed at "bringing relief to the hospital, because when the fathers are known, they are obliged to nourish their children."

84 Demars-Sion 1991, 124.

85 In 1747, upon learning of this "usage," Chancelor d'Aguesseau had the intendant of Languedoc address a letter to the officers of the seneschalcies of the province condemning it, in fear of keeping "seduced young women from making a declaration." The content of this letter is given in Fréminville, *Dictionnaire ou traité de la police des villes*, "Grossesse."

86 See Demars-Sion 1991, 121. This result may perhaps have been influenced by the exceptional situation of Cambrai, where the *official* retained jurisdiction.

87 See Phan 1975, 70. Reading this edict had been prescribed by an edict of Henry III in 1586, repeated by Louis XIV in 1708.

88 See this volume 262–8 regarding the *Ordonnance* of Blois on marriages.

89 On the notion of abduction by seduction and the use made of it, see Demars-Sion 1988. The connection between seduction and abduction had been made in the latter half of the sixteenth century by Jean de Coras (d. 1572), the most prominent of the Protestant members of the Parlement of Toulouse, in his *Arrest du Parlement de Tolose*, under "*Rapt.*" On Coras see Jacques Poumarède, "Jean de Coras," in *Dictionnaire historique des juristes français*, 203–4.

90 The seneschal of Angoumois was formally reminded of this principle by the Parlement of Paris in a decree of 2 January 1638, as cited in Bardet, *Recueil d'arrests du Parlement de Paris*, tome 2, livre 7, ch. 1.

91 Brillon, *Dictionnaire des arrêts*, "Grossesse." See also Demars-Sion 1991, 84, which stresses that the provincial parlements would follow the Parlement of Paris in this direction somewhat later.

92 This was why the royal power forcefully denounced this use of procedure in a declaration of 30 November 1730: "Whereas true abduction by seduction must put an obstacle to marriage, the debauchery given the

name of 'abduction' becomes a step to reach that end": see Demars-Sion 1988, 747–50.

93 Lefebvre-Teillard 1976, 251–69, reprinted in Lefebvre-Teillard 2008, 259–273.

94 See Demars-Sion 1991, 85, for Cambrai and its surrounding territory. Phan 1986, 130, reaches similar conclusions. Between 1755 and 1786, three-fourths of seduced women who had recourse to the law claimed promises of marriage. The same tendency existed in Nantes and Lyon, according to studies cited in Demars-Sion 1991, 63.

95 See Durand 1974, 285; Demars-Sion 1991, 25.

96 See Demars-Sion 1991, 213. This shift seems to have occurred more slowly in the south of France than in the north: in only one-third of the cases that came before the Conseil Souverain of Roussillon was the plaintiff pregnant: see Durand 1974, 285.

97 See Demars-Sion 1991, 217.

98 On this "presumption," see Fournel, *Traité de la séduction*.

99 Fournel, *Traité de la séduction*, 5. The terms in which Fournel, a lawyer to the Parlement of Paris, views the question reveal much about the frame of mind of a number of men of law at the end of the Ancien Régime. He states, "If jurisprudence on this matter is filled with contradictions and incertitudes, it is for not having determined in a precise fashion the nature of the action that is proper to a woman who has been abused against the author of her dishonour. The common opinion regards seduction as a crime that gives the abused girl the right to pursue reparation against the guilty party, but this is visibly an error: seduction is neither a public nor a private crime." For Fournel, the only justifiable action is that of a woman who has been abused by promises of marriage; it is such promise, a "convention presumed to have been made with her seducer," that constitutes her title for suit (p. 8). Fournel further states, "By means of the presumption of a promise of this sort there is no more absurdity in the action initiated by the abused girl … She does not complain of an outrage that she had permitted; she complains only of an infidelity, a failure to keep his word, and of failure to execute a contract. Her title does not derive from her pregnancy; pregnancy is but the evidence of the previous agreement made between the parties" (p. 10).

100 On how Antoine Favre (1557–1624) came up with this adage, to which he refused any application against a married man, see Lefebvre-Teillard 1976, 263. On Favre, see Bernard Barbiche, "Favre, Antoine," in *Dictionnaire historique des juristes français*, 322–3.

101 See Brillon, *Dictionnaire des arrests*, "Grossesse," which cites a 1696 decree of the Parlement de Tournay.

102 This remained true in 30 per cent of cases in Cambrai in the eighteenth century: see Demars-Sion 1991, 312.

103 On this dual prohibition, formulated by the Parlements of Rouen in 1723 and Dijon in 1732, see Lefebvre-Teillard 1990, 64–5.

Chapter 10

Mixed Marriages in Early Modern Europe

CECILIA CRISTELLON

Introduction

The subject of this chapter is mixed marriage understood primarily in the legal sense of marriage between members of different religious denominations.[1]

I will begin by setting out the legal background. In the twelfth and thirteenth centuries, Western legal scholars became increasingly concerned with the regulation of marriages between persons belonging to different confessions, religions, or rites, a concern that soon became a burning issue. While the Latin West was involved in ideological and doctrinal conflicts with various heretical movements, particularly the Cathars – conflicts that would become repression – in the East the Crusades had exacerbated the schism between the Latin and Byzantine worlds, which were forced to share territory and adherents while rejecting each other. The Western church found itself confronted with forms of day-to-day cohabitation that were still not effectively regulated ecclesiastically. It was no longer a matter of the marriage of Christians with Jews or with infidels, now well controlled by law, but of new types of marriages, those between Christians of different rites or between Catholics and "heretics." Concrete questions regarding this were submitted to the pope to decide. The resolutions of these questions would come to constitute a normative reference.[2]

It was in this context that the most innovative contribution regarding mixed marriages was conceived and elaborated. This contribution was initially not well recognized, but it had a great future ahead of it and serious social and political consequences. In the late twelfth century, Uguccione da Pisa explicitly connected marriage to baptism, a connection that would free Christian "heretics" from the diriment impediment of *disparitas cultus* – which thereafter remained limited to infidels and Jews.[3] This matter became pressing after the fall of Constantinople in 1453 and the re-conquest of the Iberian Peninsula.[4]

Following the Protestant Reformation, the process of confessionalization and the formation of nation-states in Europe rendered mixed marriages a political matter.[5] Various authorities – ecclesiastical, state, and local – fought each other for jurisdiction over the control and administration of interdenominational marriages, clashing, negotiating, and compromising. In this way, in early modern Europe through the medium of mixed marriages the foundations for religious coexistence and tolerance were laid, on the one hand, and on the other, interdenominational and interreligious boundaries were negotiated both internally (between Catholic, Protestant, and Jewish communities and territories) and externally (between Europe and the Muslims, the East, and the New World).

Marriage Becomes Mixed: Prohibitions, Reactions, Solutions, Jurisdictional Conflicts

After the unity of Christendom was broken and until the final decades of the sixteenth century, in places where Catholics and followers of the Reformation lived in contact with each other, marriages continued to be contracted according to criteria that for the most part did not take into account religious inclinations. Only when each church made access to a wedding celebration dependent upon participation in its own particular Eucharistic rite – the primary symbol of unity – did religious confession, now distinctly felt, become a potentially discriminating factor (albeit not an exclusive one) in the choice of a partner.[6] Sometimes to increase a daughter's matrimonial chances, parents avoided giving her an education in any particular denomination prior to marriage in order to promote her adherence to her eventual husband's religion.[7] And it was even possible for members of the Protestant nobility who desired alliance with the imperial house to raise a daughter and future empress as a Catholic, as happened in the case of Elisabeth Wilhelmine von Württemberg-Mömpelgard (1767–90), who was educated by the Salesians with a view towards her marriage to Emperor Franz I.[8]

All the Christian churches forbade and deplored mixed marriages. In discourse and even law they equated these marriages with sexual crimes like rape, fornication, and adultery.[9] On the part of Catholics at least, mixed marriage was moreover perceived as a sin graver than incest. In the requests made for dispensations in order to marry kin that came to the Apostolic Penitentiary from denominational border zones, a frequent argument made was the danger of the supplicants' marrying heretics if they did not receive the desired dispensations.[10]

The various churches implemented a variety of measures to impede bidenominational marriages or else to deny validity to the rites used to contract them. Marriages between Protestants and Catholics were likened by the Catholic Church to heresy and were censured in a bull issued by Clement VIII in 1596.[11] Beginning in the second half of the sixteenth century, Catholic synodal decrees forbade them, as did Protestant church regulations.[12] The Council of Trent's decree *Tametsi* (1563), while it did not explicitly mention mixed unions and confirmed the sacramental nature of marriage between the baptized, nonetheless became an instrument used to impede confessionally heterogeneous unions, since priests – whose presence was now required for a valid marriage – were forbidden to preside at bidenominational nuptial celebrations.[13] In canon law, moreover, marriage promises, which had already been delegitimized by the Council of Trent if contracted by adherents of different confessions, were deprived completely of validity. They could not even be used as an argument to obtain financial compensation for the seduced woman – to make up for her loss of reputation – because the law considered such promises fundamentally disgraceful.[14] A decision by the consistory of Coburg (1628), which influenced many Protestant theologians, established that a Lutheran was not required to keep a promise of marriage made to a Catholic because a Lutheran's consent was always implicitly conditional on the denomination of the other party: the declaration *desponso te mihi* ("I marry you") meant *si non es papista* ("if you are not a papist").[15]

Although their frequency varied according to the social and political context, cross-denominational marriages were nonetheless celebrated throughout the early modern period in both Protestant lands and in those of mixed denomination and, beginning at the end of the seventeenth century, even in uniformly Catholic areas.[16] While divided by confession, those who contracted mixed marriages shared values that evidently took precedence over matters of faith. A union could be driven by respect for a customary code of honour (as in seventeenth-century Geneva, when a man was compelled to marry a woman he had seduced despite their confessional differences);[17] by consideration of common social status (a mixed marriage was preferable to a *mésalliance*);[18] by political expediency (as in the case of the dynastic marriages of kings of England or German territorial princes); or by economic interests (in eighteenth-century Geneva a Catholic apprentice's career was furthered by his marriage to a coreligionist of his Calvinist master).[19] In a religiously homogeneous environment, mixed marriage could respond to the matrimonial aspirations of those who would otherwise be excluded from the marriage market, and for members of religious minorities it could be an approach to integration. In Livorno as well as in Genoa, a young Catholic woman without a dowry might be disposed to marry a wealthy Protestant. A union with a member of the denominational majority could be so attractive to a member of the minority that he would himself provide his wife's dowry.[20] Bidenominational marriage could also of course be driven by emotional impulses, factors that acquired contractual force in the eighteenth century in accord with a new sensibility: from Cambrai and Pisa, from Naples and Venice, the requests for dispensations forwarded to Rome tell of a Catholic and a Lutheran who burn with "such love," or of a Catholic and a Calvinist who "fell in love with one another" and were *invicem amore capti*, "inflamed by love."[21] Faithful to the ideals of romantic love, brides and grooms now declined more economically attractive and confessionally homogeneous marital prospects to pursue their own inclinations. Attempts by the groom's relatives to "dissuade him from this marriage ... by arranging that he take a world tour" would not succeed; "an honest prospect with a Catholic man" was consistently rejected by a bride, who was fruitlessly "placed in a convent in Livorno" so that she would renounce a bidenominational marriage of inclination.[22]

The formal celebration of mixed marriages was of course strongly conditioned by the legal context in which the contracting parties found themselves. In places where the decrees of the Council of Trent had not been published, mixed-confession couples could marry before a layman or a non-Catholic: the bond would be fully valid in the eyes of Rome, even though it held the union illegitimate.[23] In Protestant lands or in regions of mixed confession, such marriages were celebrated before a Protestant pastor with a dispensation from the relevant consistory,[24] but also by missionaries or by parish priests, despite the prohibition, or – given the frequent ineffectiveness of the prohibition – they were tolerated on the condition that the children would be raised as Catholics (even if it was not always observed).[25] Abbots, provosts, archdeacons, deans, and parish priests sometimes promoted these mixed unions, granting the couples a dispensation from the obligation of the reading of the banns required by the Council of Trent. They did so even though these particular officials did not have this power, which was generally reserved to the bishop and, in the case of mixed marriage, to an even higher authority.[26]

In places where Trent's decrees had already been published before the advent of the Reformation, such as Holland, marriages that were not celebrated before a parish priest had to be considered null and void for Catholics (prior to Pope Benedict XIV's Declaration of 1741).[27] This put Catholics in conflict with the secular authority, since in the United Provinces, in order to be valid, marriage had to be contracted in city hall before the civic official or in church by a Calvinist pastor; the latter method was also preferred by Catholics, both because marriages celebrated according to a religious rite were significantly less expensive[28] and because Catholics continued to consider the churches their own, despite the buildings' being used for Calvinist worship after the Reformation.[29] "From these invalid marriages," missionaries warned, "the gravest difficulties for offspring, for missionaries, for the Republic, for marriage" would follow: for children because they would be considered illegitimate; for missionaries because, accused "by the heretical side" of "preaching against these marriages," they would be forced "immediately into exile, and other grave evils"; for "the Republic because infinite disputes and confusion would take place" regarding inheritance; for marriage because the certainty of obtaining an annulment would encourage seduction by those Catholic men "who, living according to the flesh, would marry a heretic woman, and having enjoyed her and wasted her patrimony would abandon her and flee to Catholic territory, where they could easily contract a second marriage."[30] Cases like these, in fact, were denounced to the Congregation of the Council. And it was further considered that in those places where the Council of Trent decrees had been published, even Protestants could make use of *Tametsi* to obtain a divorce easily.[31]

Despite the prohibitions, up through the early decades of the seventeenth century, Catholic clergy at all levels continued to debate the licitness of mixed marriages. For example, in 1602 the nuncio of Cologne asked the Roman Holy Office "if marriages between Catholics and heretics might be permitted in countries where heresy flourishes with impunity," and in 1618 the bishop of Como asked "whether curates in Valtellina and Val Chiavenna could celebrate mixed marriages."[32] From the late seventeenth century forward, bishops and nuncios generally came to an awareness that these unions were illicit – in contrast to some missionaries and parish priests – but these higher churchmen acted as spokesmen for the practical needs of their clergy, who were confronted on a daily basis with the reality of mixed marriages. The bishop of Coira and the Swiss nuncio, for example, while prohibiting Capuchin friars from assisting at cross-denominational marriages, reminded Rome that these unions were "celebrated in all of Germany," where "Catholics [live] mixed with heretics," as well as in "Calvinist countries."[33] Catholic missionaries agreed to preside over mixed unions precisely because they wished to prevent the parties from resorting to a Protestant minister.[34]

Mixed marriages took place even in uniformly Catholic regions, such as the Italian peninsula, where the Tridentine decrees had been incorporated into secular law and where religious deviance seldom escaped the grasp of the Inquisition.[35] Rarely were they celebrated before willing parish priests:[36] generally they were contracted by catching the priest by surprise – his presence alone, not his assent to the union, being necessary for validity. In a church in Livorno, while the parish priest invited the faithful to prayer, "a heretic and a Catholic widow who had long been scandalously living together," addressed the priest with these words: "Signor curato, marry us, I want this woman for my wife" and "I want this man for my husband." They then retreated "to a villa where they lived as husband and wife."[37] Even in Catholic countries, moreover, bidenominational marriages were celebrated before Protestant pastors – irredeemably condemning them to invalidity and to the intervention of bishops and inquisitors. In such cases, as in those of surprise marriages, ecclesiastical authorities imposed separation on the couples.[38] This measure was effective in areas that were Catholic but was unenforceable in places where Catholics were only a tolerated minority, as, for example, the United Provinces or England.[39] In the Holy Roman Empire of the German Nation – even in the regions subject to Catholic authority – such disciplinary efforts were risky and counterproductive, because they could be interpreted as serious infringements of the freedom of religion that was guaranteed by the Peace of Westphalia and could destabilize fragile equilibria with the consistories that interpreted the marriage laws for their coreligionists.[40]

According to the Catholic Church, the only way to contract a mixed marriage legitimately was with a dispensation granted by the Holy Office in Rome.[41] Various theologians and canonists, however, were of the opinion that a dispensation was not necessary in areas where "Catholics [lived] mixed with heretics," that biconfessional marriages were permitted *ex tacita tolerantia*, and in fact Rome was seldom asked for such dispensations.[42] This type of dispensation, moreover, was granted only in exceptional cases, since Rome generally required the non-Catholic spouse's abjuration – at least in secret. The legal and theological debate over dispensations for mixed religion was driven by several important seventeenth-century political cases: the marriage of Catherine, the sister of Henry of France and Navarre, to the Duke of Bar; that of Henrietta Maria, sister of the king of France, to Charles I of England;[43] that of Maria d'Este to the Duke of York;[44] and the marriage of the Duke of Neuburg to Katharina Charlotte von Zweibrücken.[45]

The decisions made in these important cases crystallized into general principles: a dispensation would be granted rarely, for the protection of the Catholic public interest, and only if the Catholic party had no hope of finding a socially compatible Catholic spouse; moreover, there was to be no risk of the Catholic spouse being converted, freedom of worship was to be guaranteed, and all children born of the marriage were to be raised in the Catholic faith. Furthermore, it was necessary that the mixed marriage did not give rise to scandal. That is, it could be allowed only in Protestant lands or in those of mixed denomination – in the language of the Holy Office, in lands in which *hereses impune grassantur*, "heresies spread with impunity."[46] Lutheran and Calvinist consistories were also generally disposed to grant dispensations of mixed religion only after having been assured of the firmness in the faith of their coreligionist and on condition that the children of the union would be raised in the Lutheran or Calvinist faith.[47] Further, these bodies adopted measures that were similar to those taken by the Catholic authorities in order to ensure their own faithful had an orthodox environment, even by significantly limiting their geographical mobility.[48]

The requirements established by the Roman Inquisition for the granting of a dispensation were interpreted with varying degrees of strictness depending on the particular case. After having granted dispensations in several cases without demanding the non-Catholic spouse's abjuration, the Holy Office soon became uncompromising.[49] Having seen the failure of such exceptionally ambitious political projects as the reconquest of England for Catholicism (which would have been achieved with the marriage of Henrietta Maria to Charles I), as well as the failure of plans to convert to Catholicism a young bride who was considered particularly malleable – the Calvinist Katharina Charlotte von Zweibrücken, who had married the Duke of Neuburg[50] – Pope Innocent X ordered that dispensations no longer be granted based merely on the hope or promise of conversion. Prior to the marriage, abjuration would be required, declared before a notary and trustworthy witnesses.[51] Thus, the marriage that was being permitted was no longer mixed, at least legally, but between two Catholics. This hardening of attitude on the part of the Holy Office had an effect on the numbers of petitioners. Over the course of the eighteenth century, we see a progressive decline in the requests for dispensations from Protestant countries, where it was possible in practice to contract a mixed marriage despite Roman disapproval. The few requests coming from these countries, moreover, came to Rome's attention only when, in addition to the impediment of mixed confession, the marriage was also hindered by another impediment capable of rendering the bond void, such as the impediment of kinship, the most common reason for a dispensation request.[52] And even when a dispensation for a mixed marriage was requested from the Holy Office, it was requested to legitimize an existing situation – to confirm a marriage that had already taken place – rather than to permit the formation of a union.

Over the course of the eighteenth century, in parallel with the decline of dispensation requests coming out of zones of mixed religion, there came a significant increase in such requests from Catholic countries. Bishops and parish priests acted as advocates, driven for the most part by pastoral motives: the desire to confer the blessing of a marital union on a long-term concubinage relationship,[53] or to avoid the stigma of illegitimacy for an unborn child,[54] or to ward off the difficulties of re-entering the marriage market for a young woman who had married (with her family's approval) a non-Catholic,[55] but also in the hope of gaining for Catholicism the souls of Protestants who were well integrated into the religious majority. Local clergy, in fact, when confronted with communities of non-Catholics who were more or less officially tolerated and socially well integrated, at first reacted with decisive indignation to unions contracted despite clerical opposition. Later, however, after experiencing the reality of these marriages in the confessional, and after acting as mediators with the Apostolic Penitentiary for dispensation requests, the clergy learned to appreciate mixed marriage as a means of winning new members for the Catholic faith.[56]

In 1770, for example, the archbishop of Pisa sent the major Penitentiary a letter in which he said he had been "persuaded by many years of experience in the government of this church that the dispensations of marriages between non-Catholics and Catholic women [granted] by the four popes who have reigned in my time have not produced the least pernicious effect, but on the contrary have gained many families for our holy Catholic religion."[57] The Pisan prelate's appeal was in accord with that of other local church authorities, among them the nuncio of Cologne,[58] the archbishop of Lisbon,[59] the cardinal and prince-bishop of Wroclaw,[60] the patriarch and the nuncio of Venice,[61] and the archbishop of Genoa,[62] who had all learned that mixed marriages that took place within a Catholic environment, even when the conversion of the non-Catholic spouse was not required, ensured future generations for Catholicism. Emblematic of this is the case of George Jackson, a London bibliophile who married a Catholic noblewoman from Livorno with a dispensation granted by the Apostolic Penitentiary through the mediation of his friend Prospero Lambertini (the future Pope Benedict XIV). While Jackson remained loyal to his own religion until his death – he was buried in the non-Catholic cemetery in Livorno – he willingly accepted his children's Catholic upbringing: he named his firstborn Prospero in honour of his eminent friend and regularly visited his daughter who had chosen the cloister.[63] George Jackson's attitude was shared by many Protestants who married Catholics in Catholic-majority contexts. Accounts submitted to the Holy Office tell of how one non-Catholic, while he did not himself wish to convert, would accompany to church "an orphan boy whom he kept in his house" and not leave until he was sure that the orphan had taken communion,[64] while another non-Catholic, also resistant to abjuring his faith, nonetheless willingly accepted that the Calvinist children he had had with his first wife were taught the Catholic catechism.[65]

Of course, not all non-Catholics who married Catholics, particularly those belonging to the higher social classes, were willing to give up raising their children in accordance with their own religious beliefs, and they made use of domestic reading of the sacred Scripture and of the foreign literature available thanks to itinerant libraries. The portrait of the Calvinist Sara Sismondi reconstructed by Liana Funaro, for example, provides us with the image of a mother who played a pivotal role in the education of her children – in accordance with the recommendations of Genevan philosophers and educators – although with mixed success: while two of her children manifested sympathy for Calvinism from an early age, another became bishop of Pescia.[66] To the extent that her sensibilities would permit, Sara participated in the transmission of the Catholic education she had agreed should be provided for her children: for example, she attended with them the musical portions of Catholic ceremonies and sometimes heard Sunday sermons with them in Pescia. But she despaired when her daughter was put in a convent for several months to be educated by the nuns, and she refused to visit her. In her diary, furthermore, Sara Sismondi showed a persistent impatience with the superstition, roughness of manners, and lack of culture and of scriptural knowledge that she attributed both to the provincial context in which she found herself and to Catholicism itself, as well as to her husband, whom she now saw without the filter of romantic love that had induced her to write just after her wedding, "I have the best husband that can be wished for."[67]

"Frequent Conflict, and Domestic Discord": Patriarchal Authority, Sovereign Authority, and "Religious Freedom"

The case of Sara Sismondi casts light on some of the less harmonious aspects of mixed marriages. An authoritative tradition shared by the various Christian denominations held that confessional differences were "the source of frequent conflict, and domestic discord,"[68] which kept marriage from exercising its proper peacemaking function. Indeed, latent tensions and open conflict often accompanied mixed unions, in relation to both the free exercise of religion and, above all, children's education. Such conflicts could erupt at various phases of married life. A marriage was a dynamic relationship: the balance of faith, indeed, could shift with the birth of children or the deaths of family members, or when moving to a different religious environment. Conflicts of this sort have left traces in legal sources, in premarital contracts, and in spouses' letters; and they echo in pastors' sermons and the admonitions of missionaries, who were themselves often fomenters of discord.[69]

Within the context of mixed marriages, customary lay rules developed regarding the free exercise of worship and especially the education of children. Such rules were intended to regulate the irreconcilable desires of each church that the children of a mixed marriage follow its faith.[70] In some contexts, the children's religious upbringing was determined by their sex, with sons raised in the religion of the father and daughters in that of the mother; in others, the religion of the sovereign was determinative; in still others, the principle was birth order or the religion of the father, or whatever was laid out in legal agreements made prior to the marriage.[71]

This all, however, could come into conflict with the basic principles of patriarchal society, *patria potestas* and husbandly authority, when prenuptial agreements and local laws obstructed the operation of these principles. In the Holy Roman Empire, *patria potestas* could come into conflict with the freedom of religion guaranteed by the Peace of Westphalia, whenever a husband exercised his authority over his wife – sometimes even by resorting to violence – in questions of faith.[72] Such violence generally played out in the usual forms of domestic violence that served to stabilize patriarchal society, but it was sometimes justified by a sort of physical revulsion towards the non-Catholic and thus took on the traits of a purifying religious violence, as in the case of the husband who beat up his wife – guilty in his eyes of attending a "pigsty" church – saying that "it grieves me that I must sleep with a woman who is damned."[73]

Court records cast light on the conflicts that often accompanied mixed marriages. Not unrelated to the tensions was fear that children would be abducted, whether by the spouse, kin, guardians, or even authorities, above all Catholic ones.[74] In the case of widows, this was a particularly well-founded worry. Sometimes children were taken from them to be raised in an orphanage, where some of them would run away, some would be converted, and some would die.[75] In Hungary, these rulers were allowed to oversee parents' obligation to raise their children as Catholics. In cases of failure to comply, the children could be taken away to receive a Catholic education at the expense of the noncompliant party.[76] For redress in cases of abduction, in the Holy Roman Empire one could apply to increasingly higher courts – the Reichshofrat, the Reichskammergericht – and even to the emperor himself.[77] In the Netherlands, conflicts might arise such as to induce the secular authorities to retaliate by closing Catholic churches.[78] In the Calvinist Palatinate, which at the end of the eighteenth century was subject to a broad re-Catholicization policy by new rulers who promoted this type of abuse, these rulers were induced to modify their attitude by Brandenburg's threats to be equally aggressive towards Catholics living in that state.[79]

While mixed marriages between private persons threatened the familial unity that depended on respect for patriarchal authority, princely mixed marriages also threatened the cohesion of the body politic by undermining the authority of the sovereign. During the process of confessionalization in the German territories, for example, princes and their consorts had to cooperate in the religious homogenization within their territories, standing as the model and symbol of the unity of faith in the territory. The ruler who wanted to determine the religion of his kingdom without being able to impose it on his own wife was not credible.[80] Even if he gave her freedom of worship in private, he should not stop trying to convert her, nor cease exercising strict control over her, lest she proselytize.

Negotiating Spaces, Reconciling Differences

Those who entered into a mixed marriage knew that they were crossing confessional lines and they negotiated terms, often formalized in a contract. Such contracts are evidence of a certain degree of religious tolerance and at the same time recognition of that tolerance's fragility.

In the case of princely marriages, these contracts were the result of shrewd diplomatic activity that left room for secret agreements alongside the public ones and tended to define very clearly the spaces for and limits on the actions and movements granted to the spouses. For example, in the unprecedented case of a Catholic princess who came as a bride to a Protestant court – Henrietta Maria, sister of the king of France who became the wife of Charles, Prince of Wales, son of James I and destined to succeed him to the throne of England – the marital accords envisaged, among other things, the free exercise of the Catholic religion for herself and her court, the establishment of a chapel for the use of the bride and her retinue in every royal residence, where Mass could be celebrated, the sacraments administered, indulgences granted, and jubilees held. Henrietta Maria had in her retinue 28 priests and ecclesiastics who could officiate in the chapels at her disposal. All the bride's servants would be French and Catholic, chosen by the Most Christian King himself. If one died or the future queen wished a replacement, the new servant would meet the same requirements. Since it would be impossible to require the king of England to give his children a Catholic education, the demand was that until the age of 13 (i.e., the age of majority) they would be educated with their mother, certainly in order to assure that future English sovereigns would be Catholic.[81]

The details of the accords were revised and adapted many times. The marriage between Duke Wolfgang Wilhelm von Neuburg and Princess Katharina Charlotte von Zweibrücken, for example, was celebrated before the Roman Holy Office had granted the requested dispensation.[82] After lengthy consideration, it was granted on the condition that the children born of the union would be baptized and educated as Catholics, that Catholic guardians or tutors would be appointed for them, and that even their wet nurses would be Catholic, because according to the medical culture of the time it was believed that infants imbibed mental, physical, and moral characteristics along with their milk.[83] The bride had to submit to catechetical instruction and the duke had to do everything in his power to convert her to Catholicism. Prior to – and separately from – this, written accords had already been drawn up that, for the Calvinist side, were intended to guarantee Katharina Charlotte a certain freedom of worship, and for the Catholic side, to limit, even in a physical sense, the "heretical" element both in the family and at court. According to the contract, the duke would make available to his wife – in addition to a Calvinist lady-in-waiting and, if she wanted, her own cook and coachman – a Reformed preacher.[84] The duke condescended to have the preacher sent for whenever the princess asked for him so that she and her retinue could listen to him preach and receive the Lord's Supper, so long as he dwelt at least two miles from the couple's residence – the duke had at first proposed six – except in cases of war or pestilence.[85] In amendments demanded by the bride's grandmother, Princess Luise Juliane, in the winter the preacher had to be sent for the night before he was required, so long as – Wolfgang Wilhelm had specified – the preacher avoided spending time with people who did not follow the Reformed faith.[86]

The wedding ceremony itself was subject to negotiation. The marriage of Henrietta Maria of France and the prince of Wales, for example, was celebrated by proxy in Paris. While the bride and the Catholic guests entered the church of Notre Dame to attend the nuptial mass, the English ambassador and the Duke of Chevreuse, Prince Charles's proxy, remained at the door.[87] The accords for the marriage of the Duke of Neuburg to Katharina Charlotte von Zweibrücken, in contrast, envisaged that the wedding, which was to be celebrated according to the Catholic rite, take place in the evening in order to avoid the Mass – which was only celebrated in the morning – undoubtedly in consideration of the Calvinists' reluctance to participate.[88]

Marital accords to regulate the practice of different faiths and respective spheres of competence in the education of children, or else formally to confirm the pre-eminence of the husband's authority, were made at all levels of society. They were also sometimes imposed by the authorities, as happened, for example, in the Palatinate or from 1727 in Augsburg.[89] In the prince-bishopric of Osnabrück, one woman promised to convert to her husband's religion and to be faithful and obedient to him according to the holy commandment (1609). Another couple, in contrast, with the aim of "living in a good marriage," committed themselves to educating their sons in the father's religion and their daughters in the mother's, in keeping with the local practice; the newlyweds themselves promised not to impede the other's religious practice but rather to the extent possible to encourage each other in their religious observation (1766).[90] One highborn bride managed to induce her husband to sign a contract specifying that if she survived him, their children would be educated in her faith (1618);[91] but contracts were also made in which the mother was barred from the education of her children and would be deprived of support if, as a widow, she left the territory and educated her children in the Calvinist rather than the Lutheran faith, or if she entrusted them to Calvinist servants.[92]

A nuptial contract could also protect a wife and her role as mother in the case of her husband's conversion after the wedding. While Augustus II der Starke converted to Catholicism, his wife Christiane Eberhardine von Brandenburg-Bayreuth did not follow his example, and thanks to their marital accords (1693), she was able to have their son, who had been born the year before her husband's conversion, educated as a Lutheran.[93] A contract, further, could provide for a bride's disinheritance by her natal family if she abandoned her faith – certainly a deterrent to her husband's proselytizing impulses (1664).[94]

Such contracts were condemned by religious authorities, who were uncompromising on the subject of educating children in their own creed and united in demanding – or at least in hoping for – conversion of the "heretic." Nonetheless, similar agreements were concluded even in Catholic regions like Italy, in partial amelioration of the conditions imposed on the couple in order to obtain a dispensation for the mixed marriage. The long and intricate negotiations undertaken on the occasion of the marriage of Sara Sismondi of Geneva to the Tuscan nobleman Anton Cosimo Dante Forti, for example, were interrupted by the Holy Office's demand that the bride convert, which was unacceptable to her and to her family.[95] The negotiations resumed, however, after the groom committed himself in writing not to "disturb" the bride on the matter of religion but to guarantee her unlimited freedom of worship[96] – an act which did not conform to the usual conditions for a dispensation, under which a Catholic husband or wife was obliged to strive tirelessly for the conversion of his or her spouse.

Of course nuptial contracts by no means eliminated conflict associated with mixed-faith marriages. Indeed, it is often precisely because of this conflict that such marriages come to our notice. The variety of the contractual terms reveals how complex and potentially destabilizing the reality of mixed marriages was. The transgressive potential of these unions was linked, in particular, to the dynamism that they introduced into gender relations by constituting a threat to patriarchal authority, both when the husband belonged to a minority religion and in those parts of the Holy Roman Empire where the woman could oppose his authority by appealing to the principles of religious peace and the "freedom of conscience" that the empire upheld. To shore up the threatened patriarchal authority, the secular authorities found themselves intervening in the matter, sometimes by contravening the principle of the officially espoused faith. For example, in the Palatinate, children had to be educated according to the religion of the father, even if it was different from that of the prince. This tendency increased significantly in the nineteenth century, when in almost all the *Länder* of the empire legislation embraced the principle of paternal authority in determining the confession of children.[97]

Flexibility, "Human Respect," Divine Mercy

We have seen how religious differences could intensify marital conflict and how people sought to prevent this by negotiating spaces for and limits on the exercise of the different faiths – often without success, however. But we also have evidence of how a mixed union could constitute a cell of ecumenism, in which not only the husband and wife practised their own faiths freely, but their children were educated to respect both religions. For example, sometimes they would go to church with their Calvinist mother and sometimes with their Catholic father, as happened in the family of an eighteenth-century merchant working in the Indies. While he was away, the children were entrusted to the care of their Calvinist mother, but when he was home, they accompanied their father to Catholic church (Delft, 1737–38).[98] We have examples of Catholic fathers who presented their children to the Protestant pastor at baptism, as well as Protestant fathers who did the same for the Catholic priest (Vanzay, 1666).[99] At the beginning of the seventeenth century, Catholic godparents could be chosen for Protestant babies and Protestant godparents for Catholic babies.[100] It was not only a matter of adherents of the minority faith adapting to the religious practices of the majority. Missionary priests in Switzerland who were asked to celebrate the sacrament of matrimony did not immediately refuse to do so: they inquired of the Roman Inquisition if it were licit (1624).[101] The Inquisitor of Bergamo, having learned of such a practice, asked Rome if he should intervene to censure it (1618). In other cases, it was the nuncio who had to intervene to censure them.[102]

A mixed marriage could be one aspect of how an individual adapted to, and integrated himself into, a particular social and geographical context.[103] The case of Angelo Landini, a 38-year-old Sienese man recently settled in Vercelli, can be considered emblematic. Landini presented himself spontaneously to the Inquisition of that city in 1749. He had travelled in England, he told them, where he had tried to fulfil the Easter obligation "in the chapel of the king of France, Portugal, and Sardinia" but neglected to attend Sunday Mass and instead sometimes went to the "heretical" services. Then he had spent nine years in France, where he had been denied absolution because of his time in England. Having moved to Geneva, he worked at the "clock factory" of a "heretical merchant" who was willing to teach him the craft, and married a Calvinist[104] – a union that precluded his absolution when he confessed at Easter in the chapel of the "French emissary." From this marriage, celebrated by a Calvinist pastor, a son was born, who was baptized according to the Calvinist rite.[105] Although he had never repudiated Catholicism nor hidden his own faith, Angelo had "always dealt and spoken familiarly with heretics,"[106] adapted to their practices "in many external acts" (ca. 1778), attended "sermons of Protestant ministers many, many times," taking communion in both kinds, bread and wine, and attending the funerals of his wife's family members "by persuasion and out of human respect." Once back in Italy, he easily readapted to Catholic practices, and having been joined by his wife and son, he asked for a dispensation so that he could reunite with her,[107] whom he would try to convert, and promised to educate this and future children as Catholics.

Landini's mobility in Protestant territories and particularly his mixed marriage led him to *communicatio in sacris*, that is, to crossing the confessional boundaries as regards sacraments – a circumstance often documented in regions where different confessions and religions came into contact.[108] Mixed families brought into contact two religious groups whose members shared moments of sociability, above all ritual occasions associated with birth, marriage, and death – occasions on which, to use Landini's words, "human respect" prevailed over divisions of faith. These moments of confessional contact worried the churches more than the "frequent quarrels and domestic discords" that all the religions put forward as the reason for their rejection of mixed marriage. Rather, the churches seemed disturbed by the peaceful cohabitation of their members, as well as by the fear that their own faithful could consider heterodox rites and practices assimilable, or even equivalent, to those of their own faith.[109] The churches feared that their adherents would not consider it a sin to raise only their daughters but not their sons as Catholics and permit all their children to attend the Lutheran school, as Catholic missionaries in Denmark observed in 1686.[110] They feared that their members would refuse to believe that their own kin, in-laws, and friends were destined for damnation because they were "heretics," as the Catholic missionaries reported in the Diocese of Die in 1642.[111] They feared, in short, that their own adherents would come to believe – as one Catholic intending to marry a Protestant did – that "all those who invoked God's name would be saved, and God would choose the elect among every family" (Utrecht, 1703).[112]

NOTES

1 The following abbreviations are used in the citation of records held in archives:

ACDF: Archivio della Congregazione per la Dottrina della Fede, Città del Vaticano
Acta: *Acta Sacrae Congregationis*
APA: Archivio della Sacra Penitenzieria Apostolica, Città del Vaticano
APF: Archivio Storico de Propaganda Fide, Città del Vaticano
ASPV: Archivio Storico del Patriarcato di Venezia
ASV: Archivio Segreto Vaticano, Città del Vaticano
Congr. Concilio: Archivio della Sacra Congregazione del Concilio, Città del Vaticano
DM: *Dubia circa matrimonium*
Libri Decret.: *Libri Decretorum*
Libri Litterar.: *Libri Litterarum*
Misc. Cod. Ext.: *Miscellanea Codices Externi*
MM: *Matrimonia Mixta*
SC: Scritture riferite nei congressi
SO: *Sanctum Officium*
St. St.: *Stanza Storica*
Synopsis: *Synopsis Variarum Resolutionum ex selectioribus decretis Sacrae Congregationis Concilii collecta per materias ordine alphabetico disposita*

2 Maccarrone 1995.
3 Vaccari 1940, 340–1.
4 Orlando 2010, 173–237, esp. 173, 182. On the canonical foundations of mixed marriage, see Lang 2004, esp. 27–90; Ganster 2013.
5 See in this connection the studies of Freist 2001, 2002, 2011, 2016; Kaplan 2005, 2007, 2009, 2014; Luria 2005; Cristellon 2009, 2013a, 2013b, 2013c, 2014a; and Orlando 2010.

6 Lübcke, forthcoming.
7 For a German example see Knoop 1964, 167; Benedict 1991, 70. For French examples, see Dompnier 1985, 154, cited in Luria 2005, 163.
8 Hufschmidt 2004, 346 and bibliography in n62.
9 Cristellon 2014a.
10 See, for example, APA, *Matrimoniali*, b. 1, 12 March 1745; ibid., 26 November 1745.
11 *Bullarium Romanum*, vol. 10, CXXXVI, 280, § 2.
12 For examples of synodal decrees against mixed marriages, see Roskovány, *De matrimoniis mixtis*, 36. For examples of the early rules of the Protestant churches, see Lübcke, forthcoming.
13 *Conciliorum Oecumenicorum Decreta*, 753–9. For analysis of the various synodal decrees that prohibited parish priests from officiating at mixed marriages or that subjected their presence to detailed conditions, including the imperative that the children be raised as Catholics, see, for Germany, Geringer 1991, 27–54.
14 Petra, *Commentaria ad constitutiones apostolicas*, § 6, 74: "Improbavit igitur antiquitus ecclesia improbatque modo matrimonia catholicorum cum haereticis; unde est, ut sponsalia inter eosdem inita, utpote promissiones de re turpi, nedum illicita, sed prorsus irrita sint, et invalida, nullamque sponsalium obligationem inducant."
15 Roskovány, *De matrimoniis mixtis*, 36.
16 For the most recent bibliography on mixed marriages, see Freist, forthcoming. Scholars agree on the impossibility of determining the extent of the phenomenon because these unions were long not considered as mixed marriages, because of gaps in the records, and because these marriage were not always recorded as mixed, sometimes by the express desire of the religious authorities.
17 ASV, Congr. Concilio, *Synopsis*, fols. 78–9.
18 Religiously mixed marriages were generally socially homogeneous. See Kaplan 2005, which mentions the research of D.J. Noordam. Mésalliances were sometimes accepted by members of religious minorities who aspired to full integration into the context of the majority. For examples, see ACDF, *MM*, b. 4 (1766–77), IV, 1770 Genova; and ACDF, *SO*, *MM*, b. 5 (1778–83), I, 1778 Firenze.
19 ACDF, *SO*, *MM*, b. 3 (1723–67), 1749, Positio IV, Siena.
20 ACDF, *MM*, b. 4 (1766–77), IV, 1770 Genova.
21 ACDF, *SO*, *MM*, b. 5 (1778–85), respectively XXII, 1783 Cambray; II, 1779 Venezia; 1770, Positio VI, Pisa; XX, 1783 Napoli.
22 ACDF, *MM*, b. 4 (1766–77), 1770, Positio VI, Pisa.

23 The decrees of the Council of Trent were valid only in the countries in which they had been published and were binding starting 30 days after publication. On the Council of Trent and the debate over marriages, see Jedin 1973–81, 3:96–121, 4:140–63; Cozzi 1986; Jedin and Reinhardt 1985; Zarri 2000, 210–26.

24 Freist 2002.

25 The Holy Office explicitly prohibited parish priests from celebrating mixed marriages, so that, in uniformly Catholic countries, in granting dispensations *mixtae religionis* care was sometimes taken to notify the bishop sponsoring the dispensation request that "it is granted also to you, or to the person you designate, the power to attend the said wedding, without incurring any ecclesiastical sanction, so long as all of the conditions are fulfilled" that were required for the dispensation: see ACDF, *SO*, *MM*, b. 4 (1766–77), IV, 1770 Genova, f. 287. Examples of weddings celebrated by missionaries in APF, *SC*, Germania e Missioni Settentrionali, I (1622–80), f. 105, Lüneburg e Brunswick, 1682; for Danish, Dutch, and Swiss cases, see respectively ibid., f. 110, Danimarca, 1686; ACDF, *SO*, *St. St.*, UV 54, fasc. 10 (for Holland); ibid., *DM*, 1603–1722, fasc. 3, esp. fols. 58–9 (for Switzerland). For synodal prohibitions: *Concilia Germaniae ab anno MDCX ad MDCLXII*, IX, *Decretorum Synodalium pars quarta, De sacramento matrimonii (Colonia)*, § XXV, 1651, 775. For the difficulty applying the Roman and Tridentine directives, the case of Holland is particularly important, analysed, especially the period prior to the Declaration of 1741, in Kaplan 2005, 2007, 2009, 2014; Forclaz 2009.

26 This is lamented in *Concilia Germaniae*, § XV, 1651, 772.

27 On 4 November 1741 Benedict XIV declared that in the United Provinces marriages contracted without the formalities prescribed by the Council of Trent were valid. This was extended to the diocese of Breslau in 1765 by Clement XIII and later to other territories that had a strong Protestant presence. See Gaudemet 1987, 229.

28 Forclaz 2009, 260.

29 Frijhoff 2002, 20, 51, 119–23, 164, 169–70.

30 ACDF, *SO*, *St. St.*, UV 54, fasc. 10.

31 ASV, Congr. Concilio, *Libri Decret.*, II, (1575–81), fols. 32–3, no. 51, Daventrinensis, s.d. For Protestant use of the Tridentine decrees in this way, see ASV, Congr. Concilio, *Misc. Cod. Ext.*, I, fols. 402–3, s.d. (Augusta).

32 "An curati Vallistellinae, et valis Clavenne possint tuta conscientia celebrare matrimonia heretici cum catholica, seu catholicae cum heretico." See ACDF, *SO*, *DM*, 1663–1722, II, Lucerna seu Retia, f. 58.

33 Ibid., f. 59.

34 Ibid. It should be considered that, like the Church of Rome, Protestant consistories demanded the education of children of mixed marriages in their faith and the guarantee of freedom of worship for the Protestant spouse, if not the conversion of the other spouse, and that therefore encouraging recourse to a Protestant minister increased the risk of losing a church member. Essential in this regard are the studies of Freist 2001 and 2002. On the fear that excessive strictness might lead to recourse to a Protestant pastor, see also Dompnier 2009. For a paradigmatic example, ACDF, *SO*, *St. St.*, *MM*, 5g, fasc. 5.

35 The first mixed marriage celebrated in Italy that I have found documented took place in 1697. See ASV, *Synopsis*, f. 85. Taurin. matrimonii 28 September 1697.

36 See the example mentioned in Seidel Menchi 2004, 564 and n80.

37 ACDF, *MM*, b. 3 (1723–67), Positio XIX, 1725 and 1726 Pisa and Genova. For surprise marriages see, in this volume, Lombardi 103 and Seidel Menchi 321–3.

38 For a mixed marriage celebrated before the Protestant pastor in Livorno in 1680, Villani 2005, 385–6. This mixed marriage was declared null by the archbishop of Pisa. For other interventions by bishops and inquisitors, see Cristellon 2009 and 2013a.

39 See, for Holland, ACDF, *SO*, *St. St.*, UV 54, fasc. 10. For England, see the 1756 case mentioned in ACDF, *SO*, *St. St.*, *MM*, 5g, fasc. 9, Pro die iovis 2 sept. 1762 coram Sanctissimo.

40 Freist 2001; for the consistory's action following the Catholic authorities' imposition of separation on a couple that was religiously mixed as well as – according to canon law – incestuous, see ACDF, *SO*, *St. St.*, *MM*, 5g, fasc. 5, Hildesheim.

41 Marital impediments fall into one of two groups: diriment impediments, which render the marriage null, and nondiriment impediments, which render the union illicit but still valid and include the impediment *mixtae religionis*. See Plöchl 1959, 78–83.

42 This position, however, was not shared by the Holy Office, which continued to affirm the necessity of a papal dispensation for such unions to be legitimate and repeatedly specified that while the Holy See tolerated these marriages, it had never explicitly approved them. See, for example, the opinion of Vincenzo Petra (1662–1747), first a consultant to and then a member of the Sacred Congregation of the Holy Office, in his *Commentaria ad constitutiones apostolicas seu bullas singulas summorum pontificum in bullario romano contentas secundum collectionem Cherubini, incipientes a divo Leone Magno, tomus quartus*, Romae MDCCXI, Constitutio XII Johannis XII

incipiens *Cum nonnulli*, §§ 5–15, 74–7. On the question of whether a papal dispensation was necessary for a mixed marriage, see Connick 1960. For other positions taken in favour of the jurisdiction of the Holy Office over the matter, see, for example, the opinion expressed in ACDF, *SO*, *St. St.*, *MM*, 5g, fasc. 1, *Bispontina Dispensationis*, unpaginated, and ACDF, *SO*, *MM*, b. 3 (1723–67), Positio I, Germania.

43 The case has been analysed by Freist 2011. See further, Albion 1935, 49–77. On the negotiations regarding the marriage, see APF, *SC*, Anglia (1627–1707), esp. fols. 100–1. See also Cristellon 2013b.

44 In the historiographical literature this marriage is considered a union between Catholics: Lozano Navarro 2009. In the Vatican documents, it is treated as a mixed union – the Catholicism of the prince is the subject at issue in the debate over granting the dispensation. See ACDF, *SO*, *MM*, b. 1 (1630–73), 1659, Positio IV, Modena.

45 See, on this topic, Albizzi, *De inconstantia in iure*, and Petra, *Commentaria ad constitutiones apostolicas*. Another important debate about the appropriateness of granting a dispensation for political reasons is analysed by Villani 2009a. The Protestant doctrine on the matter was similarly influenced by actual, politically important cases: for example, in response to the planned marriage of the Lutheran Duke of Sachsen-Zeitz to the Calvinist sister of the Elector Friedrich III of Brandenburg, the Lutheran Christian Thomasius wrote the treatise *Rechtmäßige Erörterung der Ehe- und Gewissens Frage Ob zwei fürstliche personen im Römischen reich deren eine der Luterischen die andere der Reformierten Religion zugetan ist einander mit gutem gewissen heirathen können* (1689), in favour of the union. For the same occasion, Philip Müller wrote *Der Fang des edlen Lebens durch fremde Glaubens-Ehe* (1689), providing a vivid picture, in conformity with a widespread contemporary sensibility, of the quotidian problems associated with mixed marriage. See Freist 2001, 302–3.

46 ACDF, *SO*, *St. St.*, *MM*, 5g, fasc. 1, *Bispontina Dispensationis*. The possibility of granting dispensations in uniformly Catholic regions was considered only in the late eighteenth century: see Cristellon 2013a.

47 For example, Freist 2001, 305 (Dresden, seventeenth century).

48 Freist 2002, 295. For limitations on the mobility of mixed families living in Catholic regions, see Cristellon 2013b, esp. 86–8.

49 ACDF, *SO*, *St. St.*, *MM*, 5g, fasc. 1, *Bispontina Dispensationis*.

50 Cristellon 2013c.

51 Petra, *Commentaria ad constitutiones apostolicas*, § 14, 76.

52 A perfect example of this practice is the case of Andrea Achille, a Lutheran of Paderborn, who turned to the Holy Office for a dispensation *mixtae*

religionis in order to marry a Catholic woman to whom he was related in the first degree of kinship because she was the sister of his deceased wife. On the occasion of his marriage to his first wife, however, who was also Catholic, he had requested no dispensation because, beyond the religious difference, there existed no other impediment. ACDF, *SO*, *MM*, b. 7 (1791–9), fasc. 6, 1791, Paterbona, Federica Wichmann cattolica e Andrea Achille Luterano, 22 June 1791.

53 ACDF, *SO*, *MM*, b. 5 (1778–83), 1779, Positio II, Venezia; ACDF, *SO*, *MM*, b. 7 (1791–9), fasc. 5, Pisa, Carolina Scagliola cattolica e Giorgio Barbii protestante, 6 April 1791.

54 ACDF, *SO*, *MM*, b. 7 (1791–9), fasc. 36, Torino, Francesco Alessandro Bojvin cattolico e Francesca Brido protestante, 26 July 1794.

55 ACDF, *SO*, *MM*, b. 7 (1791–9), fasc. 8, Alicante, Cattarina Huzgibbons e Daniele Budd protestante, 6 July 1791.

56 Cristellon 2013b.

57 ACDF, *SO*, *MM*, b. 4 (1766–77), 1770, Positio VI, Pisa, f. 400.

58 ACDF, *SO*, *St. St.*, *MM*, 5g, fasc. 5, Pro die iovis 14. ianuarii 1762 coram Sanctissimo.

59 ACDF, *SO*, *MM*, b. 3 (1723–67), 1759, Positio VII, Lisbona.

60 Franz 1878, 29.

61 ACDF, *SO*, *MM*, b. 5 (1778–83), 1779, II, Venezia.

62 ACDF, *SO*, *MM*, b. 4 (1766–77), 1770, IV, Genova.

63 Sani 2006, 29. Jackson in fact died while visiting his daughter: Pissarello 1979, 6. For the file relating to the dispensation, see ACDF, *SO*, *MM*, b. 3 (1723–67), 1727, Positio XV, Pisa.

64 ACDF, *MM*, b. 6 (1786–90), 1788, Venezia.

65 ACDF, *MM*, b. 4 (1766–77), 1770, IV, Genova.

66 Funaro 2012, esp. 30–41.

67 Ibid., 58.

68 ACDF, *SO*, *St. St.*, *MM*, 5g, fasc. 5 (1762), unpaginated, opinion of Giambattista Colombini.

69 Luria 2005, 47–102; Freist 2001, 320–1. Regarding legal sources and pastors' sermons, see also Freist 1999 and 2002. For letters, an important example is the correspondence of the Duke of Neuburg and his wife Katharina Charlotte von Zweibrücken, edited in Marseille 1898, 95–111.

70 Lay customary laws regarding the education of children of mixed couples had been developing since the Middle Ages. See Orlando 2010, 173–237.

71 Freist 2001, 306–7. For an example of educating children according to their sex in the prince-bishopric of Osnabrück in the second half of the eighteenth century, see Freist 2002, 286. For a similar example in Antwerp,

see ACDF, *MM*, b. 7, fasc. 4 (1791); in Russia, Werth 2008, 307. In France in 1663 a law was enacted requiring all children with a Catholic father and Protestant mother to be educated as Catholics. See Luria 2005, 187. For the determination of children's religion according to birth order in Friesland and Utrecht, see Kaplan 2007, 288. See also Geringer 1991.

72 Freist 2001.

73 Cited by Kaplan 2009, 232. On purifying religious violence, the essential reference is Zemon Davis 1973, inspired by Douglas 1966.

74 Martin 1986, ch. 5; Quéniart 1985; Sauzet 1979, 305–10; Labrousse 1985, 307; Pittion 1983, esp. 222–9. B. Kaplan is currently engaged in research on the subject of the kidnapping of children of mixed marriages, which he discussed in the presentation "Child Kidnappings in the Dutch Republic: Struggles over the Religious Upbringing of the Children of Interfaith Couples," at the conference *Mixed Marriages in Europe: The Politics and Practices of Religious Plurality Between the Fourteenth and Nineteenth Centuries*, DHI Roma, 26–27 May 2011 (see Kaplan 2014).

75 Freist 1999.

76 For Hungary, see Foster, forthcoming.

77 Freist 2005.

78 Kaplan 2014.

79 Freist 2002, 292.

80 Seckendorff, *Teutscher Fürstenstaat*, 172–4. Hufschmidt 2004, 336–41, and the bibliography cited therein, 337n14.

81 On this case, see also the bibliography and sources cited in note 43.

82 ACDF, *SO*, *MM*, b. 1 (1630–73), 1630, Positio I, Germania. The dispensation was necessary for the degree of kinship, apart from the religious difference.

83 The topic of breastfeeding is a constant in the treatises artfully analysed by Prosperi 2015, for all that the author does not give it particular attention for the convincing reasons given in her introduction.

84 The preacher's wages were the responsibility of the bride.

85 Marseille 1898, 12–13.

86 Katharina Charlotte would have the right to send for him on her own initiative, if the duke refused to do so. In the case of his departure for whatever reason, the bride would be able to replace him. Protestant members of the court also could not be denied burial in a secure and honourable location. Marseille 1898, 12.

87 Hibbard 2004.

88 Marseille 1898, 24; Benedicti XIV, *De Synodo Diocesana*, VI, ch. V, 135–6.

89 Freist 2001, 298. For Augsburg, François 1991, 200.

90 Freist 2001, respectively 298 and 316.
91 Hufschmidt 2004, 351.
92 Ibid., 353.
93 Ibid., 354.
94 Wunder 2012, 314.
95 The Catholic hope was that the bride's conversion would lead her brother also to abjure Calvinism.
96 Funaro 2012.
97 Freist 2001, 322.
98 Kaplan 2009, 239.
99 See, respectively, Hanlon 1993, 218–19, and Luria 2005, 182–3.
100 ACDF, *SO*, *DM*, 1603–1722, fasc. III, Lucerna seu Retia 1624. In the document there is no explicit reference to the fact that this type of practice occurred particularly in the context of mixed marriages; however, the *dubia* on the matter were expressed in connection to *dubia* about mixed marriages.
101 Ibid.
102 Ibid.
103 ACDF, *SO*, *MM*, b. 3 (1723–67), 1749, Positio IV, Siena.
104 Ibid., f. 1178 for the quotations.
105 On the ordinances and practices related to baptism in Reformation Geneva, understood as the analytical keys to the relationships between families, church, and city, see Spierling 2005. For the quotations, see ACDF, *SO*, *MM*, b. 3 (1723–67), 1749, Positio IV, Siena, f. 1190.
106 Regarding, for example, Dutch missionaries, see Parker 2011. For the quotations, ACDF, *SO*, *MM*, b. 3 (1723–67), 1749, Positio IV, Siena, f. 1190.
107 Canon law considered religious difference a reason for a separation, which would end cohabitation while keeping the bond itself intact. At least in Catholic regions, the authorities imposed separation on mixed-faith couples. To improve the likelihood of receiving a dispensation, however, petitioners sometimes separated on their own initiative.
108 Windler 2013.
109 Stimulating in this regard, although not referring to mixed marriages, are the observations of Villani 2009b, 166 and n33.
110 APF, *SC*, Germania e Missioni Settentrionali (1622–80), f. 110, Danimarca (1686).
111 APF, *SC*, Francia (1621–1720), fols. 88–9, 1642.
112 Forclaz 2009, 265.

Chapter 11

Conjugal Experiments in Europe 1400–1800

SILVANA SEIDEL MENCHI

Traditional historiography drew a clear distinction between disciplined (legitimate) marriage and undisciplined (illegitimate) marriage.[1] The great historians of law whose works remain our reference points carried on an imaginary dialogue with the arbiters of marital disputes of the past. Their monographs reverberate with tones that recall the firm voice of the judge.

The historiographical developments of the past 20 years, however, have caused fissures in this edifice. Interest in the history of emotions, attention to the victims in history, and the imperative of giving voice to the silent ones have made scholars more attentive to day-to-day human dramas, more sensitive to the irrational dimension of experience, and more able to perceive the submerged voices of the past, including, but by no means only, those of women. The discovery of marital litigation and its recognition as an indispensable source for the history of marriage have coincided with these trends in historiography.

Scholars now understand that the border between legitimate and illegitimate unions was permeable, and they see the formation of a couple's bond as a process in a continuing state of readjustment.[2] My own conclusions go even further, presenting the formation of marriage in early modern Europe as an area of innovation and negotiation, the outcome of which was always open. The authors of this book have devoted a great deal of space to the variety of forms that a couple's union could take, as well as to experiments that ran parallel to institutionalized marriage. These experiments not only conflicted with formal marriage but also, through the process of conflict, modified its structure.[3]

In their search for alternatives to the rigid forms and times prescribed for contracting a proper formal marriage, men and women ventured into marital experiments with uncertain outcomes, which were generally disapproved of by the ecclesiastical and secular authorities: clandestine marriages, surprise marriages, secret marriages (or marriages of conscience), cicisbeo triangles, bigamous marriages, interdenominational or mixed marriages. In this chapter the reader will find five specific examples of such experiments, which elsewhere in the volume have been more often mentioned than described.

Clandestine Marriage

The concept of clandestine marriage appears frequently in the pages of this book (Lombardi 99–100, Lefebvre-Teillard 264–5). Sometimes the authors use synonyms for it, such as "secret marriage" or "informal marriage" (Donahue 35–7), and this recurrence of the idea suggests just how multiform, sometimes enigmatic or even contradictory, the phenomenon was. Legally, a "clandestine marriage" was one that did not observe one or more of the formalities required by secular or ecclesiastical authorities; socially, it was also a marriage that faced the opposition of one of the families involved.

The category of marriages that were potentially clandestine is thus very broad and not well defined. The *official* of Paris would have punished with a fine "clandestine" marriages that the patriarch of Venice encouraged and supported.[4] In England the endurance of the canon law rules made the category of clandestine marriage particularly broad and varied, as well as a phenomenon that lasted for centuries;[5] in Italy the label was later applied to those seventeenth- and eighteenth-century unions that will be defined in this chapter as "surprise marriages."

The suspicion of "clandestinity" was used against one of the marriages already encountered in this book, that of Gaston d'Orléans (Lefebvre-Teillard 262). I have chosen this union as representative of the category of marriages considered "clandestine" because it is one of the cornerstones of the chapter devoted to France.

The union between Gaston, Duke of Orléans (1608–60) and Marguerite of Lorraine (1615–72) was an emotional one. The term "love match" did not yet exist, but the experience was well recognized and had persuasive force (Lombardi 104, Cristellon 297). The rite binding Gaston and Marguerite had been celebrated on the night of 3 January 1632 at Nancy by a friar in a convent chapel. Only a few members of the Lorraine family witnessed the ceremony, which the duke managed to keep semi-secret for almost a year. The union seriously undermined the position of King Louis XIII, who had expressly prohibited the marriage. The groom was the king's only brother and, in the absence of any male issue from the king, the heir presumptive to the French throne; the bride was the sister of Charles, Duke of Lorraine, an insidious and deadly enemy of the king of France. Gaston d'Orléans had strong feelings for Marguerite of Lorraine, even if his choice was influenced by his rivalry with his brother the king and by his abhorrence of Cardinal Richelieu, the prime minister and architect of Louis XIII's policies. While continence (sexual or otherwise) and fidelity (marital or otherwise) were not among the duke's most pronounced virtues, he never repudiated Marguerite as his wife and considered himself bound to her in the forum of conscience throughout the duration of the controversy.

When Louis XIII and Richelieu became certain that the marriage had taken place, they decided that it had to be annulled. Jurisdiction over the sacraments belonged to the Catholic Church, and marriage was regarded as a sacrament. It was therefore necessary for them to identify valid reasons in their request to the pope for an annulment. In case of the pope's hesitation or opposition, however, the king and prime minister intended to turn to the French clergy, who had a deep loyalty to the crown because they owed their appointments to it. Thus, when the clergy of the Kingdom of France held one of its convocations in 1635–6, the most pressing matter on the table was the marriage of *Monsieur* (the title given to the king's brother). The marriage was also the most delicate question that troubled diplomatic relations between the crown of France and the Holy See, at that time ruled by Pope Urban VIII Barberini (1623–44).[6]

The two arguments that until 1634 the French king's representatives employed to obtain the annulment – the presumed "rapt" perpetrated on Gaston d'Orléans by the Duke of Lorraine, and the "clandestine" nature of the 1632 ceremony – carried no legal weight. For the first argument, Gaston d'Orléans was not disposed to think of himself as the victim of "rapt" and to ask Rome for the annulment of his marriage as a consequence of it. For the second argument, the decrees of the Council of Trent had not been proclaimed, and therefore had not acquired legal force, in the Kingdom of France (Donahue 37, Lefebvre-Teillard 265). On the basis of the pre-Tridentine canon law that remained in force in France, a marriage such as the one celebrated on 3 January 1632 in the chapel in Nancy was perfectly valid, and all the more so as it had been reiterated in Brussels before the archbishop of Malines at the request of Monsieur himself.

The final argument devised by the bishops, theologians, and jurists who were questioned by the crown in the attempt to have the undesired marriage annulled was that of custom. The ancient custom of the Kingdom of France required the consent of the king for the validity of the marriages contracted by princes of the blood, and particularly by the heir to the throne: so ruled the theologians and canonists gathered at the Assembly of the French clergy on 7 July 1635. As a result, the marriage of Monsieur would have been null and void.[7]

It was difficult to demonstrate that this ancient French custom actually existed, however, and therefore the proof of it was weak. What is more, the authoritative faculty of theology at Louvain pronounced in favour of the validity of Monsieur's marriage, a position that also had influential supporters in France itself. The controversy, in short, had the potential to cause a rift between Paris and Rome. However, neither Pope Urban VIII – who during the controversy had not failed to invoke the argument of the church's exclusive jurisdiction over the sacraments – nor Cardinal Richelieu had any intention of causing a conflict that might give rise to a schism. The precedent of Henry VIII was ever-present in everyone's mind. Paris and Rome alike avoided bellicose declarations and provocative actions. In particular, Louis XIII did not impose a new marriage upon his younger brother. The controversy remained in suspension.

In the end the solution was a dynastic one. In 1638, the French court celebrated the birth of a dauphin, the future Louis XIV. After 23 years of marriage, the queen Anne of Austria had given Louis XIII an heir. This birth changed the picture of the royal succession. The alliance of Gaston d'Orléans with a line inimical to the crown lost its potentially explosive effect. The death of Richelieu in 1642 rendered an act of royal clemency more feasible. Louis XIII gave his consent to his brother's marriage to Marguerite of Lorraine. The ceremony – following the advice of theologians – was solemnly reiterated in 1642. Five children were born of the union.

Surprise Marriage

In 1580, the following problem was submitted to the Congregation of the Council in Rome: "If a priest finds himself in attendance at the contracting of a marriage against his will or under constraint, is the marriage valid?" The response was affirmative: to contract a valid marriage the presence of the parish priest was required, but his consent was not.[8] The Congregation of the Council was an instrument of the Roman Curia set up in 1564 to oversee the enforcement of Trent's decrees and to settle doctrinal and other questions that might arise in the course of that enforcement. Its decisions were binding for the entire Catholic world.

The Roman decision of 1580 validated from that moment on a type of marriage called "surprise marriage" or "tumultuous marriage" (Lombardi 103, Cristellon 299).[9] The Catholic clergy were opposed to this expedient, the notaries and chancellors of the Curia condemned it by defining it as "clandestine marriage," and couples and their witnesses incurred excommunication by participating in it, yet marriage "by surprise" was nonetheless valid.[10]

The rite is described by a celebrated seventeenth-century jurist, Cardinal Giovanni Battista De Luca (1614–83). Among the many legal cases examined in his voluminous *Theatrum veritatis et iustitiae* (*Theatre of Truth and Justice*, 1669–73), De Luca narrated an event in which he had himself been professionally involved. He did not give the precise date, but indications point to 1648 or 1649.

The most opportune setting for a surprise marriage was the parish church during Mass, which ensured the presence of the right priest (the couple's "own parish priest" required by Trent), as well as the attention of numerous witnesses. In Casamassima in the Kingdom of Naples, the parish priest was standing to dismiss the faithful with the final *Dominus vobiscum* when one of them, Michele de Vaez, rose to his feet and, taking a young woman by the hand, declared to the priest in a loud and clear voice that he took the woman as his wife. "Signorsì, signorsì," said the woman, Giovanna Maria de Sciart, probably encouraged by her mother and other relatives who were also present in the church. Quickly grasping the situation, the priest rushed into the sacristy blocking his ears. The couple followed him, repeating the formula of reciprocal consent. Giving vent to his fury, the priest screamed, "You are excommunicated!" but this phrase itself demonstrated to those present that he had both seen and understood the sense of the scene before him. The act was irreversible.

This case is a valuable example. The canon law acceptance – however reluctant – of surprise marriage was a corrective adopted by the ecclesiastical authorities to attenuate the negative effects that the Tridentine nuptial ritual had on couples' freedom to marry. The publicity before and during the wedding, which the Council of Trent imposed on pain of invalidity, made it easy for a determined father or guardian to block a union that he opposed. The groom in question here, Michele de Vaez, was the Duke of Casamassima and the son of the Count of Mola, one of the great feudatories of the Kingdom of Naples. Giovanna Maria de Sciart, on the other hand, belonged to an impoverished noble family that could not provide her with a suitable dowry. Michele de Vaez had recourse to a surprise marriage to elude his father's opposition to their union.

The enamoured groom (*amore captus*, De Luca called him) did not persevere long in the purpose he had so loudly proclaimed, however. After only a few months of living with his "duchess," he put an end to their cohabitation and began legal proceedings to request an annulment of the marriage. Paternal authority – or the threat of disinheritance – carried more weight than the sentiment that had inspired his proclamation in the parish church.

Among the various judicial bodies that this controversy passed through, there was a general tendency to consider a "surprise" marriage to be fully valid. This was also the reasoned opinion of Giovanni Battista De Luca. The repudiated bride was not readmitted to the social status of duchess – this was outside the power of the ecclesiastical authority – but her right to financial support was recognized.[11]

Marriage of Conscience

In 1741, Pope Benedict XIV (1740–58) issued a vehement appeal to Catholic bishops in his encyclical *Satis vobis*. In it the pope denounced a practice that he called "secret marriage," clarifying that this was "commonly called marriage of conscience." The aim of the encyclical was to subject to episcopal control a practice that must have been so widespread that the pope – a great canonist – did not think it necessary to describe. We can easily reconstruct what it was like.[12]

At the request of the betrothed couple, their parish priest or bishop could dispense them from the obligation of publicity that had to precede a wedding according to the Council of Trent (Donahue 36 and 43, Lombardi 104). To obtain this dispensation, the couple had to show they had grave reasons for doing so, such as the opposition of one of their families or of an authority. But fear of incurring the wrath or vengeance of a powerful clan meant priests and bishops were not inclined to grant these dispensations, and some were even tempted when informed of the projected weddings to denounce the wayward children to their families (which might lead the children to have recourse to the expedient of surprise marriage, as we just saw).

A noticeable increase in marriages celebrated under such dispensation occurred around 1650. While the distinction between "surprise marriage" and "secret marriage" (or "marriage of conscience") was somewhat unclear to ecclesiastics, who often confused them, the difference is in fact plain: in the case of a "surprise marriage," the cleric was in attendance at the contract involuntarily or even by force; in the case of a "secret marriage" or "marriage of conscience," he was the couple's willing accomplice. An obliging priest or an indulgent friar would give a couple the nuptial blessing in the presence of the required two witnesses, dispensing the couple not only from the publication that should have preceded their wedding but also from resorting to their own parish priest and, above all, from the normally required process of formal certification that they were both in fact free to marry (i.e., were not already married to someone else). Weddings that were celebrated in this way were not recorded in parish marriage registers. This opened the door to all sorts of irregularity, from polygamy to the denial of rightful inheritance to legitimate children, whose parents' marriage had not been registered.

The motivation behind a marriage of conscience was usually status pride. A nobleman or patrician might be compelled by his conscience to marry a woman of a lower class, usually his mistress. The decision might be arrived at during illness or when there was danger of death, and it aimed to put an end to sin and to legitimate the children born of the relationship. But the party of higher social status – generally the man – felt such a marital bond was demeaning to him. Marrying a woman who was not noble – or did not have a large dowry – was for a nobleman tantamount to contaminating his bloodline, and the act therefore had to remain shrouded in secrecy. As the 1741 encyclical of Benedict XIV said, with such secrecy "even the memory of the act is to be erased and the act itself is to be relegated forever to the darkness of oblivion." The opportunity of putting an end to the state of sin in which the couple had been living, and of regularizing the status of their children, could induce the clergy to bless a marriage contracted in the strictest secrecy. As long as the secrecy persisted, however, the position of the woman and her children remained ambiguous. It was sometimes the man's intention that the existence of such a marriage would never come out.[13]

With his encyclical of 1741 Benedict XIV provided an administrative rather than a pastoral remedy. The pope ordered every diocese to set up a special register for secret marriages – a sealed book personally overseen by the bishop himself. After each entry, the register was to be closed up and was only to be reopened to record the next secret marriage. In cases of controversy, this register had obvious value.

Not even this measure, however, could protect the socially weakest parties – the women and their children – from the trickery and intrigues that status pride inspired in men of influence. Illustrative of this is a sequence of events that took place in the cities of Civitavecchia, Assisi, and Rome between 1781 and 1796. A careful investigation by the Holy Office of the Inquisition (1795–6) fully exposed the intricate deception of which it will be possible here to sketch only the barest outlines.[14]

In 1774, the orphanage of Civitavecchia received Margherita Svizzeri, the orphan of a soldier of the pontifical guard. The nuns who ran the orphanage where Margherita had found shelter had an assiduous visitor, Giovanni Battista Benzi, the commander of the city's military garrison. For the very young and beautiful Margherita, the nobleman conceived "a great passion." Later witnesses would describe Benzi, who was then almost 60 years old, as being in the grip of an amorous obsession. His original plan was to attach Margherita to his household by passing her off as the wife of one of his staff or of his illegitimate son and to then make her his concubine, but this idea was opposed by Margherita herself and probably also by the nuns of the orphanage. The noble Benzi, however, would not even consider a marriage with a completely destitute commoner: for a "gentleman such as he" it would have been a "degrading alliance." It was the girl's confessor, the parish priest Vittorio Gabrielli, who suggested a way out of the impasse: a secret marriage "of conscience."

Giovanni Battista Benzi married Margherita Svizzeri twice. The first wedding, in 1781, was an intricate deception. With the help of the priest Gabrielli, Benzi staged what Margherita believed was a marriage "of conscience" but was in fact just a bit of theatre. Although the groom solemnly promised to have the union registered in the book of secret marriages held by the bishop of Nocera, he broke this promise, which he had never intended to keep. First in Civitavecchia and later in Assisi at the Palazzo Benzi, Margherita passed for the wife of Giulio Cappelletti,

Benzi's personal servant. The palazzo was restructured to support this fiction.

In 1792, the deception was revealed. Alarmed by Benzi's grave illness, Margherita wanted to make sure of her own legitimate status and that of the four children she had borne Benzi. She discovered that not only did her marriage to the ex-governor of Civitavecchia appear nowhere in any register of secret marriages, but that instead Benzi had had the parish registers of the city falsified to make her appear to be the wife of his servant, Cappelletti. Furthermore, Margherita's children, who had been given a noble upbringing in the palazzo of their natural father, had been entered in the parish registers of Civitavecchia and Assisi as Cappelletti's children. Eleven years of living together had extinguished Benzi's passion for the beautiful fair-haired orphan. Margherita now had no influence on the nobleman, who only sought to free himself from her.

It was the most prominent religious authorities in Assisi, the Franciscan friars, who forced Benzi to yield. Appealing to his conscience and pointing out the danger to his soul, the friars convinced – and indeed constrained – the proud nobleman to marry Margherita Svizzeri in truth. He did so on 3 May 1794. This was another secret marriage, but this time a valid one, because the friars oversaw its actual registration in the sealed book of the bishop of Assisi, thus making Margherita Svizzeri into Margherita Benzi and her children into the legitimate heirs of the uncertain estate of their biological father. And although this was not the last legal battle that Margherita had to fight with her arrogant husband, she had won the war. In 1796 Pope Pius VI, the final judge of this complex marital controversy, granted her request to put all of Benzi's assets under the legal control of trustees.

Bigamy and Morganatic Marriage

Bigamy was not a rare phenomenon in the Western world. It was, however, illegal. The man or woman who took a second spouse during the life of the first, if discovered, would receive from a judge an order to leave the second spouse and rejoin the first. The second marriage was invalid, and the person who had illegally remarried was liable to penalties that could be severe.[15] Like many other crimes, bigamy was committed in secret. Landgrave Philip of Hesse (1504–67), however, legitimately married two women, openly lived with both of them as his legitimate wives (though in separate households), and with both had legitimate children.[16]

A marital experiment like this could only have taken place in Reformation Germany – in a nation that had modified the rules of social life, redefined the border between good and evil, and revolutionized the framework of constituted authority. The landgrave was an adherent of the Reformation and indeed one of its pillars in the Holy Roman Empire. His political and military importance decisively influenced the outcome of his family drama.

The origin of this experiment was a personal problem: the landgrave's disaffection with his wife, Christine of Saxony, whose place by his side from the time he was just 18 had been determined by a combination of the internal political situation of the empire and of his family's dynastic interests. His disaffection – which the landgrave himself described as outright repugnance – had not kept him from fathering seven children with Christine during their 16 years of marriage. Their conjugal life, therefore, had not been interrupted; but the absence of "desire" and "lust" in the marital bed had plunged the landgrave – to use his own words – into "whoring, unchastity and adultery." The virtue of continence, according to his own testimony, was incompatible with his nature.

The landgrave's awareness of living a sinful life disturbed his conscience and led him to abstain from participating in the Lord's Supper; the information circulating about his debaucheries undermined his authority as a ruler. Philip of Hesse was the head of the Lutheran Church in his landgraviate: in a society pervaded by calls to the Gospel, how could transgressions be credibly sanctioned by a ruler who claimed to be a follower of the Gospel but himself remained wallowing in sin?

This was the solution that the landgrave devised and managed to impose on the reluctant doctors at Wittenberg, Luther, and Melanchthon: he must take a second wife in order to have by his side a woman who met his requirements of attractiveness and fulfilled the promise of pleasure that the marital bed had thus far denied him. We cannot exclude that the Protestant ideal of marriage as a form of life of supreme perfection may have exercised a certain influence on the landgrave. What is certain is that he asked Luther and Melanchthon to authorize and bless a second legitimate marriage, concurrent with the first. Divorce from Christine of Saxony was not considered. Concubinage was excluded for two reasons: first, because it would not quiet the landgrave's conscience; second, because it did not fulfil the conditions set by the other party.

The other party was Margarethe von der Saale, a young woman from a family of minor Saxon nobility. Margarethe attended the court of Saxony, where one of Philip's sisters reigned as duchess. Naturally, it was not the inexperienced, 17-year-old Margarethe who negotiated the conditions of her union with the landgrave, but her mother, Anna von der Saale, who as a widow exercised legal authority over her daughter. Among the various conditions that Anna von der Saale initially placed on her daughter's union with the landgrave was the death of his first wife, Christine of Saxony; but waiting for this eventuality was not reconcilable with the impatient prince's desires. He exerted such pressure that Anna von der Saale in the end consented to giving him her daughter as his second wife, though on the condition that the union was deemed not contrary to the Law of God. Anna von der Saale wanted a marriage that was both blessed by a churchman and legally sealed by a contract.

Christine of Saxony gave written consent to Philip's second marriage on the condition that the new wife and their future children be relegated to an obviously inferior position. It does not appear to have been particularly difficult to obtain Christine's consent, once the landgrave guaranteed that she would maintain her privileged position at court, that their marital life – including its sexual component – would continue, and that the rights of inheritance of title and dignity would belong only to the children born of Landgrave Philip's first union.

More difficult was gaining the consent of the two doctrinal leaders of the Reformation. But in the end Luther and Melanchthon could not really oppose the landgrave's scheme because Philip wielded two powerful instruments of pressure. The first was the doctrinal authority of Martin Bucer, the reformer of Strasburg. He was at that time in Hesse, engaged in organizing the Lutheran Church in the principality, of which Philip was the institutional head, and Bucer supported the cause of his master. The second was the political and military importance of Hesse in the Schmalkaldic League, the alliance of Protestant rulers that had the task of protecting the Reformation militarily against the campaign of restoration pursued by the Catholic party, led by the Emperor Charles V.

The two reformers gave in and, on 4 March 1540, Philip of Hesse was joined in matrimony to Margarethe von der Saale. The presence of Melanchthon and Bucer at the celebration of the rite by the court chaplain gave the union an aura of ecclesiastical blessing, even though the event was kept very quiet. The condition that the reformers had placed on the ecclesiastical celebration – that it be kept in the strictest secrecy – was, however, immediately violated. The stakes were too high, the political climate too poisoned, the confessional conflict too violent for such an explosive piece of news to remain within a restricted circle. And the news did explode. It thrust itself into an existing pamphlet war, stirring up existing vehement hatreds and fuelling violent exchanges for years to come.

The onslaught of insult turned on the landgrave did not drive him to a contrite silence. Philip of Hesse and his publicists responded to the verbal violence with verbal violence: a flood of pamphlets, ever more impassioned in tone, covered Germany, as the exploits of the landgrave's principle opponent, the Duke Heinrich of Brunswick-Wolfenbüttel, the captain of the Catholic League for Northern Germany, furnished the landgrave with excellent subjects for a campaign of personal denigration. But we will not linger here.

More relevant for us are the doctrinal and legal arguments that the landgrave's publicists and allies mobilized in his favour. Taking two wives was not expressly forbidden in Scripture: this was the strong argument made in support of Philip of Hesse. In a culture that recognized the Bible as the ultimate source of authority, what the Bible did not prohibit was permitted. If this argument had been accepted, bigamy would have become legal in Protestant Germany, with no shortage of German princes eager to embrace Philip of Hesse's example.

But the argument was not accepted. Another German ruler attempted polygamy, but he was quickly taken to task by the clergy and had to fall into line. Philip of Hesse himself did not succeed in assuring his second wife the image of integrity and immaculate honour that she and her mother had been promised. On the contrary, Margarethe von der Saale knew the bitterest humiliation, spent part of her life in seclusion, and considered herself to have been deceived by her husband. Her children were generously provided for in a material sense – they were given a county – but the title of landgrave was denied them. The honour and prestige of the princely title was reserved for the children of the first marriage, the children of Christine of Saxony.

Philip of Hesse's experiment was nonetheless legally influential. The marriage model that Europe had inherited from Roman law elevated the wife to the status of her husband and gave the children of their union – especially the firstborn male – the father's dignities and titles. In the marriage of Philip of Hesse to Margarethe von der Saale, however, the property relations between the spouses and the inheritance status of their children were regulated by a legal contract that assured the wife and children specific rights and granted them notable benefits, but it expressly excluded them from the social status, full hereditary rights, and succession to the princely title. The status of landgravine, the ceremonial role of the wife, the inheritance of the title and of the principality were all guaranteed by contract to Christine of Saxony and the children she had borne – all this the price of Christine's consent to the second marriage.

The marriage of Philip of Hesse with Margarethe von der Saale gave new topicality to a type of marriage that had been present in ancient German law but had fallen into disuse centuries earlier. The ancient German law recognized a type of marriage that from the second half of the sixteenth century on was usually called either "left-hand marriage" or "morganatic marriage." The social-status inferiority of the wife was expressed ritually and symbolically during the wedding ceremony, when the bride stood on the groom's left side instead of the usual right. The designation "morganatic," which is usually used in scholarly literature, had its origin in a thirteenth-century compilation of Longobard feudal law customs. This collection defines as *ad morganaticam* the link that a widower of noble status who already had a legitimate heir from his first marriage contracted with a woman of lower status. On the basis of such an agreement, the lower-status wife and the children she bore the husband would after his death receive only the *Morgengabe*, or morning gift, granted her at the time of their marriage. In other words, the "morganatic" wife renounced for herself and her future children alike any claim to the status and property of her husband, which were reserved for his child or children from his first marriage.

The phrase "morganatic marriage" does not appear in the nuptial contract of Philip of Hesse and Margerethe von der Saale. But the legal precedent the landgrave of Hesse created in 1540 – and the attendant pamphlet campaign made the agreement widely known – found numerous emulators among the high nobility into the eighteenth century[17] and became one of the legal avenues open to the nobility of the empire and of the Kingdom of France in regard to marriage. This later practice of morganatic marriage, however, spared the wife of the prince or high aristocrat the derision and disdain that Margarethe von der Saale lamented, when she was reduced to living as a lower-status wife in the shadow of the "first and highest spouse," because German princes contracted morganatic marriages only after the death of their equal-status wives or following divorce. The morganatic wife was thus the only legitimate wife.

This regularization, however, locked a wife into her state of inferiority. It is clear, in fact, that only a woman of lower social status would have accepted a union that stressed so emphatically that she did not belong to the class into which she had wed. Whether the material and social benefits that these women were promised by marriage were adequate compensation for this humiliation, we do not know. In the case of Margarethe von der Saale they were not. And not all children born of such marriages quietly accepted their exclusion from their fathers' rank. In some cases notable conflict and turbulence arose from dynastic and inheritance claims advanced by these second-class descendants.

Marriage: A Human Rights Laboratory?

The five cases of marital experimentation treated in this chapter demonstrate the flexibility of the institution of marriage and also furnish concrete examples of the conflicts that flared up around it. In this volume, marriage appears as a far from peaceable event. The act of getting married in Europe was not fully under the control of the designated authorities – ecclesiastical, political, or familial. When the emotional dimension of marriage prevailed over the institutional dimension, it ignited tensions the outcome of which generally remained uncertain. The five cases examined here by no means cover the entire array of conjugal experimentation that took place in Europe between 1400 and 1800. Other experiments were attempted, ranging from widespread practices (such as cicisbeo triangles)[18] to isolated efforts (some cases of homosexual marriage).[19]

What interests us now, however, is not adding yet more types of marital experimentation to the list but signalling the historiographical decline of the conception of marriage as bastion of social conservatism and as stabilizer of gender relations. We have seen how a prospective couple could subvert the relationship between high and low, readjust gender roles, redistribute the social playing cards. The emotional component of the marital union strengthened the weaker party. The formation of the couple is thus to be regarded as one of those liminal phases, in the course of which everything is renegotiated: inheritance status, gender hierarchy, confessional boundaries.[20] These changes, at first bitterly resisted, gradually entered into social practice. As this volume's discourse draws to a close, it is difficult to avoid the conclusion that in Europe marriage was a workshop for the forging of human rights. And that workshop is still in operation.[21]

NOTES

1 The following abbreviations are used in the citation of records held in archives:

ASPVe: Archivio Storico del Patriarcato, Venice
ACDF: Archivio della Congregazione per la Dottrina della Fede, Città del Vaticano
St. St.: *Stanza Storica*

2 Parker 1990, 2.

3 Mazo Karras 2012, 7.

4 Donahue 2007, 345–71; Cristellon 2014b; Seidel Menchi 2014, 28–32.

5 Ingram 1987; Outhwaite 1995.

6 Blet 1959, 404–8.

7 Ibid., 410–29.

8 ASV, Congregazione del Concilio, *Synopsis Variarum Resolutionum ex selectioribus decretis Sacrae Congregationis Concilii collecta ac per materias ordine alphabetico disposita*, vol. 2, f. 88; *Canones et decreta Concilii Tridentini*, 224, 235.

9 For France, Le Bras 1927, 2248. For Spain, Cristellon 2009, 19. The notaries of the Holy Office of the Inquisition in Rome called this type of marriage *matrimonium praetensum clandestinum*. Seidel Menchi 2004, 560n69.

10 Plebani 2012, 221–58. The ASPVe holds two *filze* of *acta* pertaining to "clandestine" marriages celebrated between 1592 and 1758 (ASPVe, Matrimoni clandestini, 95, 96). The expedient of catching the parish priest by surprise in order to stipulate a marriage opposed by the social context was well known and widely practised: eight "clandestine," i.e. surprise, marriages were stipulated, and prosecuted as crimes, in the small diocese of Brugnato (northwest Italy) between 1588 and 1798. Cavarzere 2012, 125–315.

11 Moscarda 2001.

12 *Dictionnaire de droit canonique*, vol. 6, § XX, 782–3.

13 Plebani 2012, 265–80. The ASPVe holds 48 *filze* containing *acta* of secret marriages celebrated between 1633 and 1817 (ASPVe, Archivio Segreto, Matrimoni secreti, 1–48).

14 ACDF, *St. St. MM* b. 4, *Circa Margharitam Svizzeri Guildman, Dubium de matrimonio*. The affair of Margherita Svizzeri and Giovanni Battista Benzi fills four volumes held in the ACDF (*St. St. MM* b. 4, b, c, d, e).

15 Siebenhüner 2006. Different perspectives in McDougall 2012.

16 Sikora 2005; Sikora 2012.

17 A detailed analysis can be found in Sikora 2005, 26–8.

18 Bizzocchi 2008.

19 Alfieri 2011.

20 Turner 1969, ch. 3.

21 Hunt 2007.

Conclusion

SILVANA SEIDEL MENCHI

Under the three section headings of this book, let me recapitulate some of the features of our undertaking and attempt to draw up a balance.

Continuity and Change

If in 1480 an anthropologist *avant la lettre* had attempted to give an account of European marriage customs, he would have been disconcerted by the variety of forms that the rite assumed. Couples exchanged their consent in a stable or an inn, in a kitchen or an orchard, in a meadow or an attic, in a wood or blacksmith's shop, on the porch of a house or at a public fountain. One could get married sitting "beside the fire" or walking along the road returning from a party. If an innkeeper refused to provide lodging for an unmarried couple, they might exchange their consent on the spot, in his presence.[1] An alliance between patrician families shifted huge sums of money from one family to the other, employing notaries and mediators in negotiations that lasted for years.[2] A princely marriage was a major political event that could be staged in a cathedral and solemnized by the bishop, or even by the pope.[3] We know of peasants, however, who met women working in the fields, took them home, and "without any ceremony," "without the presence of a priest," installed them as spouses.[4] In perfect harmony with the Italian data, the London matrimonial causes of the fifteenth century yield descriptions of "about two hundred separate alleged contracts of marriage and three quarters of them were made in extra-ecclesiastical settings."[5]

For the vast majority of the contracting parties, the difference between espousals and marriage, between *verba de futuro* and *verba de presenti*, was by no means clear, nor did it have the importance that our modern historical analysis ascribes to it.[6] What counted was the reciprocal consent that was exchanged "without the slightest juridical formality," most often in a domestic context or at work.[7] The systematic study of matrimonial cases – the privileged sources that form the background to this volume – are gradually convincing us that, at least until the mid-sixteenth century, "lay people," men and women, "opposed their understanding and their practice of marriage – under the form of a reciprocal consent without any publicity – to the ... solemnization that the church sought to impose" and to the formalization that the secular authorities endeavoured unsuccessfully to prescribe.[8]

In the Franco-Belgian area, so far as we know, any espousals or marriages that evaded the publicity enjoined by the church, and so escaped the church's control, incurred pecuniary sanctions or even excommunication.[9] An entire network of ramified and efficient structures, the *officialités*, acted against transgressors (for the most part adopting the *ex officio* procedure), assessing and collecting fines.[10] In France these ecclesiastical courts showed themselves to be as zealous at assessing fines as they were flexible in negotiating the amounts. One man convicted of cohabitation (concubinage) and condemned to a fine of 40 *livres tournois* plus imprisonment managed to get off with a fine of 5 *livres*.[11]

In by far the greater part of Europe, however, the matrimonial plurality that I have sketched did not encounter any kind of sanction. From England to Venice, from Aragon to Regensburg, marriage based on the simple consent of the contracting parties was not penalized in any of its ritual variants (*toccamano*, verbal contract, the gift of the ring, bedding, *Morgengabe*), and indeed the traditional rituals were accepted as proof in court, so that a union thus stipulated might be upheld by the ecclesiastical judges.[12] In 1558 a frustrated groom presented in court a cross cut with a knife in a tree trunk, signalling the exchange of consent between him and his now recalcitrant bride, as evidence that their marriage had taken place.[13]

This extraordinary flexibility was the consequence of the uniformity that characterized the marriage rules. The pre-eminence of the church in civic society had had the effect of imposing canon law as the single normative framework throughout Europe. Normative uniformity gave rise to variegated phenomena because church law, by reducing to the minimum the requirements necessary for stipulating the marriage bond, had placed marriage into the hands of those most directly concerned, reserving to the local clergy a relatively marginal role, that of verification and control.[14] Since the parties most directly concerned might have extremely different interests, the range of possible variants was very broad. None of these variants was declared invalid per se; no type of marriage that respected the minimum requirements demanded by the canon law was subject to annulment. Throughout the Middle Ages, marriage was the dominion of continuity in multiplicity.

The liberality of the medieval papacy in the question of matrimonial regulations was, possibly, a remote effect of the marginal role assumed by the family in the New Testament. Christ's interlocutors are the sowers of the Word, ready to break the bonds of family affection and even to renounce the married state (Matthew 10:35–8, 19:12). For the most part, although elevating marriage to the dignity of a sacrament, theologians abstained from regulating in binding fashion – apart from a handful of basic rules of amazing brilliance – an eminently secular institution, one that involved renouncing celibacy, the highest form of Christian perfection.[15] But such a liberality of rules and multiplicity of forms could not last. When, for example, the prolonged absence of one spouse induced the other to contract a second union, concealing or denying the previous bond, the "astonishingly individualistic" marriage system delineated in this study favoured the families' instability.[16]

Even before the Reformation, the secular authorities tended to fill the normative gaps left by the church.[17] The Reformation leaders, and in rivalry with them the Catholic theologians assembled at Trent, decided to subordinate the validity of the conjugal bond to the fulfilment of rigorous conditions.[18] Thus the chapters in the first section of this volume focus on the turning point that transformed the procedure of marriage. Between 1525 and 1563, after more than three centuries of continuity, change was imposed on most of Europe.

Licit and Illicit

The convergence of intent among the churches is the main subject in the second section of this volume. In the period that runs from the turning point in the sixteenth century until the end of the seventeenth – and in some areas until the mid-eighteenth – the churches imposed a stringent discipline on potential couples, with the aim of putting an end to any uncertainty about the marriage bond and of sanctifying the conjugal state.

This reforming campaign was a complete success. By imposing a public rite, subjecting the stipulation of the bond to a considerable number of invalidating conditions, and specifying the length of time that had to pass between the betrothal and the wedding,[19] the churches removed marriage from the control of the contracting parties. The change created dismay, misunderstanding, and much suffering.[20] In most of Europe, however, precipitous marriage and improvised rites disappeared, for the consent of parents or guardians became a preliminary condition for marriage.[21] Unions formed solely by the principals' consent were judged to be invalid; *matrimonia clandestina* became crimes punishable in both ecclesiastical and secular forums. In Mediterranean countries, those who had attempted a "clandestine marriage" were permanently barred from marrying each other.[22] In the Kingdom of France, where Tridentine norms never came into effect, the crown energetically stamped out "clandestine" marriage, declaring it to be invalid and mandating severe punishments for the contracting parties and their "accomplices."[23] In England, where the medieval canonical norms remained in place, disputes arising from the ambiguity and volatility of the nuptial pact declined notably in the final decades of the sixteenth century, and in the seventeenth century were further reduced "from a fairly low incidence to the merest trickle."[24] Where clandestine marriage did not lose its legal basis, it lost its social credibility.[25]

The program of formalizing the nuptial process overlaps with efforts to regulate the sexual activity of the betrothed and even of married spouses.[26] In the course of the seventeenth century, the second objective prevailed over the first. The regulations imposed in certain parts of Europe erected a barrier between holy matrimony and every form of extra-conjugal *concubitus*, even if understood as a prelude to marriage. In England, the Netherlands, Geneva, Basel, Württemberg, and Sweden, the sin of "fornication" was persecuted by the church authorities in harmony with the civic authorities, with progressively systematic sanctions being mandated during the seventeenth century.[27] As regards the exercise of premarital sexuality, however, the campaign to regulate betrothed couples was, in the long term, an utter failure.[28]

In Mediterranean Europe the social tensions and legal disputes relating to the formation of marriage diminished rapidly in the later sixteenth century and to an even greater extent in the seventeenth; in the eighteenth century they disappeared almost entirely. The small diocese of Feltre in the Republic of Venice provides a particularly vivid example of this tendency. Here the controversies regarding the presence or absence of the conjugal bond, which prior to 1563 constituted 64 per cent of the cases dealt with by the bishop's tribunal, declined to 10.9 per cent in the seventeenth century and in the eighteenth shrank almost to nothing (0.5 per cent). The area of conflict had shifted from the stipulation of the marriage to the betrothal. In the diocese of Feltre, controversies regarding the betrothal, or *sponsalia*, represent 69.3 per cent of all the causes heard by the bishop's court in the course of the seventeenth century; in the diocese of Trent they amount to 91.5 per cent. The trend continued in the eighteenth century, when 69.8 per cent of the controversies debated in Feltre and 86.1 per cent of those debated in Trent concern the matrimonial promise.[29] In Spain we find the same tendency. In the diocese of Pamplona, for instance, conflicts regarding the promise to marry account for 57 per cent of all causes heard by the bishop's tribunal between 1511 and 1770.[30] In eighteenth-century France, the well-documented diocese of Cambrai registers 73 per cent of controversies regarding the matrimonial promise.[31]

Much more uncertain, in the Mediterranean area, are the results of the campaign to control sexuality. In principle, this campaign affected all the Catholic countries of Europe. Concubinage (cohabitation) – for centuries a widespread, socially well-integrated practice regulated by unwritten rules, occasionally even by a notarial contract – became a serious offence (*grave peccatum*) that bishops were obligated to prosecute *ex officio*.[32] Bigamy, sanctioned with imprisonment in some areas of Europe, but treated very mildly in others,[33] became a crime against the faith, prosecuted in Spain and Italy by tribunals of the Inquisition.[34] Reiterated efforts to eradicate prostitution were proclaimed. But how far were these norms put into practice? In Navarre, love letters of the seventeenth century allow us to hear the impassioned voices of young women who took the initiative in nocturnal encounters with their "spouses" without inhibitions or a sense of guilt.[35] In Vizcaya, criminal trials from the sixteenth to the eighteenth century describe for us engaged couples whose premarital sexual activity was observed with benevolent tolerance by their neighbours.[36] In Andalusia, criminal archives reveal the tenacious persistence of the principle of *matrimonium praesumptum*, legitimating sexual relations between the betrothed.[37] In central Italy too the cohabitation of engaged couples was sanctioned very unevenly: examination of those couples who were required to account for their premarital cohabitation in the episcopal court of Pisa between 1560 and 1660 has revealed, indeed, cases of repressive severity, but these are isolated and contradictory. Even the most severe interventions of the religious authorities coexist with wide margins of social toleration.[38]

An investigation of sexual transgressions in the city of Naples between about 1550 and 1650 reveals that the council's enactments regarding cohabitation remained a dead letter until the seventeenth century. Between 1613 and 1630, however, strict measures imposed separation on cohabiting couples – as appears from the 343 prosecutions for concubinage in the years 1613 and 1614 – and exposed the recalcitrant to public ignominy.[39] In the overwhelming majority of cases, however, the object of these severe measures was clerical concubinage. They hardly affected lay folk. Despite the establishment of a congregation devoted exclusively to combatting concubinage, the Neapolitan evidence suggests that around 1650 a large number of cohabitants continued to live unpunished in the populous Mediterranean capital, ignoring the archbishop's excommunications. In theory, a church funeral and burial in consecrated ground should have been denied to these impenitent sinners; in practice, as the pre-eminent historian of Neapolitan concubinage has found, no instances of the refusal of Christian burial occurred in the mid-seventeenth century.[40]

The study of a small diocese in north-west Italy shows us that the Neapolitan case was not an isolated one. The systematic documentation of *criminalia* in the episcopal archives of Brugnato speaks in the clearest tones. Out of 1,089 records distributed over three centuries – from 1588 to 1798 – those that involve cohabiting lay couples required to account for their crime in court amount to 11; in the same period, proceedings are recorded against 40 clerics for concubinage.[41] For the bishops of this peripheral diocese, evidently, concubinage was *par excellence* a clerical crime.[42]

Uniformity and Singularity

In 1780 an itinerant anthropologist would have had no difficulty recognizing the nuptial ceremony in all its variants. The preliminary conditions for the establishment of the marriage bond had been notably standardized across Europe, and the symbolic language of the wedding celebration had acquired common features in all European Christian cultures. Specific rituals such as the virginal crown, the bedding (*Bettsetzung*), and the churching of women crossed confessional and political frontiers, linking different traditions.

The standardization of the routes leading to the formation of a family was a product of the age of confessionalization. In the Enlightenment, the states took over from the churches the regulation of marriage. The Kingdom of France pioneered in this matter, claiming jurisdiction over the formation of the family from the sixteenth century and treating marriage as a contract from the seventeenth. In the eighteenth century the concept of marriage as a contract became established in several states in central Europe.[43] In the hereditary territories of Austria and in the Italian states ruled by the Habsburg princes as well, the concept of contract came to prevail, with the effect of entirely eliminating the binding force of the promise.[44]

The removal of marriage from the church's sphere of competence to that of the state is particularly evident in Prussia, where demographic concerns favoured the introduction of divorce. In the margraviate of Hesse-Kassel and in Bavaria, moreover, the right to marry was subjected to financial restrictions. Desire to prevent "beggars' weddings" and reluctance to burden the public purse with relief for the poor inspired laws that forbade marriage to those without the economic resources to found a family.[45]

The churches' loss of authority now manifested itself in the diminished presence of episcopal influence on the daily lives of the faithful. The court of first instance for a couple's problems was no longer that of the bishop. Between 1550 and 1599 the number of controversies submitted to the ecclesiastical tribunal in the small diocese of Feltre was more than 10 a year (a total of 546 in five decades); between 1600 and 1699 the number went down to 5 causes per annum (524 causes in the whole century); between 1700 and 1799 the tribunal dealt with only 2 causes each year (205 causes in the whole century).[46] Increasingly, couples in conflict approached the secular courts[47] and avoided ecclesiastical tribunals, where their chances of victory were now reduced.[48] There are tribunals, such as that of Florence, in which suits for broken promises to marry multiplied astonishingly in the later eighteenth century after having virtually disappeared in the seventeenth. But these turn out to have been not so much suits aimed at validating a marriage as expedients for obtaining financial compensation, often a small one, from ex-lovers, who if there was a claim against them were prevented from entering into marriage with third parties.[49] Such expedients were thus tantamount to blackmail.[50]

The process of standardization that imposed uniformity on marriage was paralleled by experiments with alternative conjugal models. Emotions and affections challenged the dominance of institutions – state, church, family – and opened up other possibilities. Many aspirant spouses claimed marriage as a right. Refusing ambiguous solutions, they tried instead to follow their own itineraries – and sometimes they succeeded.[51]

The area of the most audacious experimentation is the so-called mixed marriage, the union that crosses confessional and religious frontiers.[52] The eighteenth century also saw the multiplication of unions that challenged class homogamy. These found legitimation in a principle that possessed an enormous power of conviction in the age of the Enlightenment: the right to happiness.[53] Another principle of singular efficacy in promoting individual conjugal experiments was the imperative of conscience. It was appealed to not only by Catholic clerics seeking to convince and tranquilize their "wives of conscience"[54] but also by a great canonist, Pope Benedict XIV. In formalizing the "marriage of conscience," he inaugurated a canonical procedure, not without its dangers, for the use of lay persons reluctant to bind themselves by formal public unions.[55] Conjugal experimentation is the area in which singularity prevails.

The Lessons of Experience

In the decade 1996–2006, together with my colleague Diego Quaglioni and a small team of young scholars, I took the initiative of investigating 4,345 matrimonial cases, ranging in date from 1420 to 1803, preserved in five Italian ecclesiastical archives: Venice, Verona, Naples, Trent, and the small but surprisingly rich archive of Feltre. We examined fully the documentation only in the two smaller archives of Trent (1632–1803) and Feltre (1550–1799). In the other three archives, our team was not able to analyse all the matrimonial cases because of the vast quantity of material (Venice) and the difficulty of accessing the documents (Naples and Verona).[56] This Italian experience impelled me to seek information about and compare other scholars' findings on similar experiences in the rest of Europe.

Comparing the results of research on matrimonial cases in eight European countries has taught me some basic lessons of historiographical practice. For the benefit of readers, I should like to outline the most important of them.

The Italian project focused on the life stories that emerged from matrimonial cases. Bishops' chanceries had in their service notaries well versed in high humanist culture, who recorded in these archival fascicles thousands upon thousands of biographical and autobiographical stories – stories of men and women, even adolescents and children. Moreover, in the cases that affect the strongest interests – most often immaterial values, and in particular honour – the individual stories ramify: small rural communities, or urban business networks, take form through the depositions of witnesses, who are not only those called to confirm one or another version of the facts presented to the judge, but are also representatives of that "public voice and fame" (*publica vox et fama*) by which the Northern Italian judge of the pre-Tridentine period often oriented his judgment.

Richard Helmholz, citing the *Codex Iustinianus*, calls the life stories emerging from the matrimonial causes *exempla*, and contrasts them with the *leges*, the norms.[57] In Italy, these *exempla* speak a language – the vernacular – of extraordinary efficacy and freshness. Dazzled by them, I initially failed to take into due account the institution that had produced our *exempla* and the filters through which the *exempla* have reached us. However, as Charles Donahue reminds us, "we need to understand the institutional filters through which the law flowed."[58] Certain results of our investigation that puzzle us today would have been less mysterious if we had subjected to preliminary analysis the structure, activity, and documentary tradition of the ecclesiastical courts whose output we were studying. I will mention just a few unanswered questions arising from our belated awareness.

Ecclesiastical courts exercised civil and criminal jurisdiction. The most frequent civil cases involving laypeople of the centuries before 1563 – verbal contracts of marriage – became criminal cases thereafter. We historians cannot rigidly separate the two jurisdictions; our task is to connect them. But how did civil and criminal spheres of jurisdiction interact? In the documentation pertaining to the patriarchal tribunal of Venice we find a superabundance of civil matrimonial cases, while criminal cases are almost entirely lacking. What is the relation between "instance cases" and "office cases," that is, proceedings initiated by an individual litigant (*ad instantiam*) and proceedings initiated by the court (*ex officio*)?[59] Between 1420 and 1500 the tribunal of Venice handled 706 matrimonial suits. Why is only one of these an *ex officio* case?[60] Since the Council Fathers of Trent had expressly recommended that bishops proceed *ex officio* in cases of cohabitation (concubinage), why did certain Italian ecclesiastical courts show themselves so reluctant to do so, that is, to exercise disciplinary jurisdiction?[61] Out of 546 matrimonial suits heard by the tribunal of Feltre in half a century (1550–99), only 57 were *ex officio* cases, despite the fact that all instances of cohabitation (including clerical cohabitation) and fornication (those that until 1563 had been legitimate *matrimonia praesumpta*) were liable to disciplinary jurisdiction.[62]

From the research carried out by Charles Donahue both in the English and in the Franco-Belgian area and by Richard Helmholz, Martin Ingram, and R.B. Outhwaite in England,[63] we have in the meanwhile learned not only to study the ecclesiastical courts in the round – even though matrimonial cases remain the most conspicuous and fascinating part of their activity.[64] We have also learned to consider with the closest attention, and not without a degree of suspicion, the information supplied to us by ecclesiastical archivists.

In effect, a troubling doubt has emerged from the comparative experience that has given rise to this book. Our work as historians is based on the archivists' labours of ordering and conserving. What have been the ruling imperatives of the ecclesiastical archivists who – especially between the eighteenth and the twentieth century – have ordered, parcelled out, selected, and catalogued the documentation that lies at the base of our investigation? The criminal jurisdiction of the bishops left uncomfortable memories in the ecclesiastical archives. The custodians of these memories took irreversible decisions that condition forever our work as historians. For reasons unknown to us – internal censorship? – entire sets of documents on which we depend for a reconstruction of the past were destroyed.[65]

This humbling lesson, however, does not diminish our confidence in the approach to marriage through the examination of single, concrete cases in various times and places. Indeed, a recent conference, "Norms and Exceptions: A Comparative Approach to Casuistry," enhances it.[66] Convinced that we are on the right hermeneutic track, we accept the challenge of pressing forward.

NOTES

1 Seidel Menchi 2001, 18–19.

2 Klapisch-Zuber 1985a.

3 A single example: Heinig 1997, 2:825–6.

4 Paolin 1984, 203: "Molti … andavano a tuor le donne nelli campi per sua moglie, et le conducevano a casa"; "se sposavano et se andavano a dormir con loro senza che pretti fussero presenti"; "si tollevano fra loro et andavano a casa tra loro senza quelle cerimonie che si costumano adesso."

5 McSheffrey 2006, 21, 27–8.

6 Seidel Menchi 2001, 35–8; Deutsch 2005, 263–99; Outhwaite 1995, xix–xx; Charageat 2011, 30–1, 37–43.

7 Oïffer-Bomsel 2014, 264. An analogous judgment in Outhwaite 1995, 21–2, and McSheffrey 2006, 29.

8 Charageat 2011, 29, in connection with marriage in Aragon in the fifteenth and sixteenth centuries; the same conclusion, for Andalusia, is reached by Oïffer-Bomsel 2014, 264.

9 Donahue 2007, 376–7, 598–603, esp. 602; Donahue 2014, 334–7.

10 Donahue 2007, 486–7, 518–19, 598–9; Beaulande-Barraud and Charageat 2014.

11 Beaulande-Barraud 2014, 201.

12 For England Helmholz 1974; for Venice Cristellon 2010; for Aragon Charageat 2011; for Regensburg Deutsch 2005, 268–88, esp. 278–82; for the Holy Roman Empire, Wunder, in this volume, 63–7. The presence in Germany of the marriage of pure consent, subtracted from ecclesiastical control, appears also in Schmugge 2008, 185–247, 250–1. For the judges' solidarity with women who had stipulated a verbal contract of marriage, Seidel Menchi and Cristellon 2011, 276–8, and Seidel Menchi 2014, 31–4.

13 Paolin 1984, 204.

14 See, in this volume, Donahue 35.

15 *Conciliorum Oecumenicorum Decreta*, Concilium Tridentinum, sess. 24, *Canones de sacramento matrimonii*, Canon 10.

16 Scaramella 2004, 447–57; McDougall 2012. An "astonishingly individualistic" marriage system is spoken of by McSheffrey 2006, 21, citing Sheehan 1996.

17 Lombardi 2001, 42–68; Lombardi 2008, 42–5; see, in this volume, Usunáriz 202, 206–7, and Lefebvre-Teillard 264–5.

18 See Donahue 36–8.

19 Luperini 2001, 381–2.

20 Ibid., 384–90; Lombardi, in this volume, 109–10.

21 See Wunder 72–3, van der Heijden 160, 163, 167, and Korpiola 231–2, 245–6.

22 *Conciliorum Oecumenicorum Decreta*, Concilium Tridentinum, sess. 24, *Canones super reformatione circa matrimonium*, caput 1.

23 See Lefebvre-Teillard 262–8.

24 Ingram 1987, 191–4 (cit. 192), 205–9; Outhwaite 2006, 49–50.

25 See Helmholz 136–7; Ingram 2014, 93.

26 Alfieri 2010, 161–6; Avignon 2014, 233 (distinction between the *affectus fornicarius* and the *affectus coniugalis*).

27 See van der Heijden 163–5, Burghartz 179–80, 187–8, and Korpiola 248–50. For England, Ingram 1987, 219–37, 243–5.

28 Lombardi 110–11, van der Heijden 169–70, Burghartz 188–9, 190, and Korpiola 250.

29 The quantitative data given here derive from a survey of 4,345 Italian matrimonial causes carried out in five ecclesiastical archives between 1996 and 2006; see this volume, 340. For the data regarding Feltre and Trento in particular, see Ciappelli 2006, 82–90, and Poian 2006, 159–61.

30 See Usunáriz 211.

31 Donahue 2014, 330.

32 Lombardi 2001, 165–6; Eisenach 2004a; Ferrante 2004; *Conciliorum Oecumenicorum Decreta*, Concilium Tridentinum, sess. 24, *Canones super reformatione circa matrimonium*, caput 8.

33 McDougall 2012, esp. 71–94; Scaramella 2004; Cristellon 2010, 205. Where women were convicted of bigamy, Italian ecclesiastical judges – in the majority of cases so far known – limited themselves to imposing cohabitation with the first husband, without further sanctions: Scaramella 2004, esp. 448–55.

34 Tanco 2002; Loi 2006; Siebenhüner 2006.

35 See Usunáriz 207–16.

36 Barahona 2003.

37 Oïffer-Bomsel 2014, 279.

38 Luperini 2001 and Luperini 2004a.

39 Romeo 2008, 112–49.

40 Ibid., 150–82, 196–7, 220.

41 Cavarzere 2012, esp. his inventory of the *Criminalia* of Brugnato, 125–315. In the adjacent diocese of Sarzana, out of 125 proceedings for concubinage in the same period, no fewer than 115 regarded members of the clergy (ibid., 30).

42 The attitude of the Catholic clergy towards sexuality (or to use the preferred term in moral theology, "love") is currently the object of debate on new doctrinal bases (see Angenendt 2015). This debate opens the prospect of Catholic priests' access to marriage, analogous with Protestant clergy.

43 See Lefebvre-Teillard 268–9 and Wunder 87–8.

44 See Lombardi 116–17.

45 See Wunder 79 and 91nn105, 106, Burghartz 181 and 197nn22, 23. For England, Ingram 1987, 214–15, and Outhwaite 1995, 58–9.

46 Poian 2006, 159–61.

47 Arrivo 2006.

48 Ciappelli 2006, 83–6.

49 This kind of suit was a survival of the action known in England as "jactitation of marriage" (very frequent in pre-Tridentine Italy too); see Helmholz 146 and, for Italy, Cristellon 2010, 54–5.

50 Lombardi 2001, 167–77.

51 See Seidel Menchi 322 and 332n10; Plebani 2012.

52 See chapter 10.
53 Trampus 2008, 190–5, 203–10.
54 ACDF, *St. St. M* b. 5 q, *Alatri 1768, Matrimonium clandestinum factum absque praesentia Parochi et Testium.*
55 See Seidel Menchi 323–6.
56 Seidel Menchi and Quaglioni 2000, 2001, 2004, 2006.
57 See Helmholz 124 and 148n11.
58 Donahue 2014, 327.
59 See Helmholz 131–2, 144–6; Seidel Menchi 2014, 28–31.
60 Cristellon 2006, 122.
61 See, in this volume, 337–8.
62 Poian 2006, 159.
63 Helmholz 1974; Ingram 1987; Outhwaite 1995; Outhwaite 2006; Donahue 2007.
64 Cavarzere 2012 and Pia 2014 are among the very first studies in the round of Italian episcopal courts.
65 The two series of *Criminalia monialium* and *Criminalia presbyterorum* in the Archivio Storico del Patriarcato of Venice were largely or totally destroyed in the eighteenth century as the result of an internal decision. In some Italian ecclesiastical archives, moreover, I was denied access to the *matrimonialia* of the fifteenth, sixteenth, and seventeenth centuries – for reasons of privacy, as the archivists in charge explained.
66 The conference "Norms and Exceptions: A Comparative Approach to Casuistry," Florence, 11–13 December 2014, was devised and directed by Carlo Ginzburg. The proceedings are to be published.

Bibliography and Abbreviations

NB: All the titles of the primary sources, cited in the notes in abbreviated form, are given in full in the following bibliography. In those cases where the abbreviation has so altered the title as to make it less easy to recognise, the abbreviated title appears in the list, immediately followed by the full title of the cited source.

Primary Sources

Acta van de Nederlandsche synoden der zestiende eeuw, edited by Frederik Lodewijk. Dordrecht: Rutgers University Press, 1980.

Agricola, Mikael (1549), *Käsikiria Castesta ia muista Christikunnan Menoista* (Manual on baptism and other Christian rites), in *Mikael Agricolan teokset*, vol. 3. Porvoo: WSOY, 1931.

Albizzi, Francesco, *De inconstantia in iure admittenda vel non: Opus in varios tractatus divisum*. Amsterdam, 1683.

Anglican Canons: *The Anglican Canons 1529–1947*, edited by Gerald Bray. Woodbridge, UK: Boydell Press, 1998.

Arboga stads tänkebok, edited by Erik Noreen and Torsten Wennström. 4 vols. Samlingar utgivna av Svenska fornskrift-sällskapet. Uppsala: Almqvist & Wiksell, 1935–50.

Ärkebiskop Abrahams räfst, edited by Otto Holmström. Skrifter utgifna af Kyrkohistoriska Föreningen, Ser. 4, Vol. 1. Uppsala: Wretman, 1901.

Bardet, Pierre, *Recueil d'arrests du Parlement de Paris pris des Mémoires de feu M. Pierre Bardet*. 2 tomes. Avignon, P.-J. Roberty, 1773.

Beiträge zur Geschichte des Buss- und Beichtwesens in der Schwedischen Kirche des Mittelalters, edited by Jaakko Gummerus. Uppsala, 1900.

Benedicti XIV Pont. Max. olim Prospero Lambertini, *De Synodo Diocesana libri tredecim*. Rome, 1767.

Beust, Joachim von, *De sponsalibus, de matrimoniis et de dotibus*. Leipzig, 1597.

"Bidrag till Svenska kyrkans historia i sextonde århundradet," edited by Otto Ahnfelt. *Lunds universitets årsskrift* 31 (1895): 1–46.

Biskop Hans Brasks registratur: Textutgåva med inledning, edited by Hedda Gunneng. Samlingar utgivna av Svenska fornskriftsällskapet. Serie 1. Svenska skrifter 85. Uppsala: H. Gunneng, 2003.

Biskop Hans Brasks släktbok, edited by Hans Gillingstam and Göran Setterkrans. Stockholm: Personhistoriska samfundet, 1970.

Bodin, Jean, *Les six livres de la République*. Paris, 1576.

Boerius, Nicolaus, *Decisiones Supremi Senatus Burdegalensis*. Lyon, 1559.

Boileau, Jacques, *Traité des empêchemens du mariage*. Cologne, 1691.

Bouchel, Laurent, *Bibliothèque ou trésor du droit français où sont traitées les matières civiles, criminelles et bénéficiales*. Paris, 1667.

Brandis, Henning, *Diarium: Hildesheimische Geschichten aus den Jahren 1471–1528*, edited by Ludwig Hänselmann. Hildesheim, 1896.

Brillon, Pierre-Jacques, *Dictionnaire des arrests ou Jurisprudence universelle des Parlemens de France et autres tribunaux*, 3 vols. Lyon, 1711.

Brisson, Barnabé, *Code du roy Henri III, roy de France et de Pologne*. Paris, 1587.

Bullarium Romanum : Magnum Bullarium Romanum, 24 vols., edited by L. Tomassetti. Augustae Taurinorum, 1857–72.

C. [*Causa*], q. [*quaestio*], c. [chapter] = *Decretum Magistri Gratiani*, in *Corpus Iuris Canonici*, part 1.

Cajetanus (see De Vio, Tommaso).

Canones et decreta Concilii Tridentini ex editione romana A. MDCCCXXXIV. repetiti, edited by Johann Friedrich von Schulte and Ludwig Aemilius Richter. Leipzig, 1853.

Canons and Decrees of the Council of Trent, edited by H.J. Schroeder. St Louis: B. Herder, 1941.

Cardwell, Edward, *Documentary Annals of the Reformed Church of England*, 2 vols. Oxford, 1844.

Catecismo Romano compuesto por decreto del sagrado Concilio tridentino para los párrocos de toda la Iglesia y publicado por San Pío V, 2 vols., edited by Lorenzo Agustín Manterola. Pamplona, 1780 (English translation: *The Catechism of the Council of Trent Published by Command of Pope Pius the Fifth*, edited by Jeremy Donovan, Baltimore, MD, 1829).

Claro, Giulio, *Volumen, alias Liber quintus*. Venice, 1583 (1st ed. Venice, 1568).

Cocceji, Samuel von, *Project des Corporis Juris Fridericiani*, 2nd ed. Halle, 1750.

Cod. [followed by book, title, and paragraph] = *Codex Iustinianus,* see *Corpus Iuris Civilis,* vol. 2.

Concilia Germaniae ab anno MDCX ad MDCLXII, edited by Johann Friedrich Schannat. Coloniae Augustae Agrippinensium, 1771.

Conciliorum Oecumenicorum Decreta, edited by Giuseppe Alberigo, Giuseppe L. Dossetti, Pericles P. Joannou, Claudio Leonardi, and Paolo Prodi. Bologna: Istituto per le Scienze Religiose, 1991.

Conset, Henry, *Practice of the Spiritual or Ecclesiastical Courts.* London, 1695.

Consistorii ecclesiastici aboënsis protokoller I–II. *SKHS:n toimituksia* 2–3 (1899–1902). Borgå.

Coras, Jean de, *Arrest mémorable du Parlement de Tolose contenant une histoire prodigieuse de nostre temps.* Lyon, 1561.

Corpus Iuris Canonici, edited by Emil Ludwig Richer and Emil Friedberg, 2 vols., Leipzig: Bernhard Taucnitz, 1879–81 (reprint, Graz: Akademische Druck- und Verlagsanstalt, 1959).

Corpus Iuris Civilis, edited by Teodor Mommsen, Paul Krüger, Rudolf Schöll, and Wilhelm Kroll, 3 vols. Berlin, 1967–73.

Cortes de los antiguos reinos de León y de Castilla, 5 vols., edited by Real Academia de la Historia. Madrid, 1861–1903.

Costanus, Antonius Guibertus, *De sponsalibus et matrimoniis* (1st ed. Lyon, 1578), in *Tractatus universi iuris* IX (1584), fols. 46va–61vb.

Covarrubias y Leyva, Diego de, *De sponsalibus et matrimoniis,* Salamanca (1st ed. 1545), in *Opera omnia,* 2 vols. Antwerp, 1614.

D [followed by title, fragment, and section number] = *Digesta seu Pandectae;* see *Corpus Iuris Civilis,* vol. 1.

Dal Portico, Girolamo, *Love between persons of different sexes examined according to the principles of moral theology for the edification of new confessors (Gli amori tra le persone di sesso diverso disaminati co' principi della morale teologia per istruzione de' novelli confessori).* Lucca, 1751.

Decrees of the Ecumenical Councils, 2 vols., edited by Norman P. Tanner. London: Sheed and Ward, 1990.

Decretum Magistri Gratiani, see *Corpus Iuris Canonici,* part 1.

Den svenska kyrkoordningen 1571 jämte studier kring tillkomst, innehåll och användning, edited by Sven Kjöllerström. Lund: H. Ohlsson, 1971.

De Vio, Tommaso (Cajetanus), *Summula Cajetani.* Venice, 1565 (1st ed. Rome, 1525).

Diplomatarium Dalekarlicum, 3 vols. and 1 suppl., edited by C.G. Kröningssvärd and J. Lidén. Stockholm and Falun, 1842–55.

Diplomatarium Suecanum, 11 vols. Kungl. vitterhets historie och antikvitetsakademien och Riksarkivet. Stockholm, 1829–.

Du Fail, Noël, *Mémoires des plus notables et solemnels arrêts du Parlement de Bretagne.* Rennes, 1652.

Dupuy, Pierre, *Preuves des Libertés de l'Église gallicane*. Paris, 1651.

Ecclesiastique Samlingar, vols. 1–4, edited by Olof Wallquist. Wexjö, 1789–90.

Ecclesiastique Samlingar, vols. 5–8, edited by Olof Wallquist. Stockholm and Linköping, 1791–5.

Eyb, Albrecht von, *Ob einem manne sey zunehmen ein eelichs weyb oder nicht*, edited by Helmut Weihnacht. Darmstadt: Wissenschaftliche Buchgesellschaft, 1982.

Fevret, Charles, *Traité de l'abus, et du vray sujet des appellations qualifiées de ce nom d'abus*. 2 vols. Lyon: Duplain, 1736.

Fontana, Giovanni, *La santità e la pietà trionfante in ogni dignità, conditione, e stato*. Venice, 1716.

Förarbetena till Sveriges rikes lag 1686–1736, vol. 4, edited by Wilhelm Sjögren. Uppsala, 1902.

Fournel, Jean-François, *Traité de la séduction, considérée dans l'ordre judiciaire*. Paris, 1781.

Fréminville, de La Poix, Edme de, *Dictionnaire ou traité de la police générale des villes, bourgs, paroisses et seigneuries de la campagne*. Paris, 1758.

Gl. ord.: *Glossa ordinaria*, consulted in *Decretales D. Gregorii papae IX. suae integritati una cum glossis restitutae*, Rome: In aedibus populi Romani, 1584.

Gómez, Antonio, *Ad leges Tauri commentarium absolutissimum*. Lugduni, 1733 (1st ed. Salamanca, 1555).

Grotius, *Inleiding tot de Hollandsche rechts-geleertheyd*: Groot, Hugo de [Grotius], *Inleiding tot de Hollandsche rechts-geleertheyd*, edited by F. Dovring, H.F.W.D. Fischer, and E.M. Meijers. Leiden: Leiden University, 1952.

Handlingar till Sverges reformations- och kyrkohistoria under Konung Gustaf I, vols. 1–2. Handlingar rörande Sverges inre förhållanden under Konung Gustaf I, I. Stockholm, 1841–5.

Hippel, Theodor Gottlieb von, *Über die bürgerliche Verbesserung der Weiber*. Berlin, 1792.

Hippel, Theodor Gottlieb von, *Über die Ehe*. Mit Illustrationen von Daniel Chodowiecki. Berlin, 1774.

Hostiensis (Henry of Susa), *Summa aurea*. Paris, 1512.

Inst. [followed by book, title, and paragraph] = *Institutiones Iustiniani*, see *Corpus Iuris Civilis*, vol. 1.

Isambert, Jourdan, and Decrusy, *Recueil des anciennes lois françaises*: *Recueil général des anciennes lois françaises, depuis l'an 420 jusqu'à la Révolution de 1789*, 29 vols., edited by François-André Isambert, Alfred Jourdan, and Decrusy. Paris, 1821–33.

Johan Skyttes kommentar till den svenska stadsrätten 1608, vol. 1, edited by Jan Eric Almquist. Skrifter utgivna av rättsgenetiska institutet vid Stockholms Universitet 4. Stockholm: Norstedt, 1962.

Journal des audiences: Journal des principales audiences du Parlement [de Paris], avec les arrêts qui y ont été rendus et plusieurs questions et règlemens (1622–1722), 7 vols., edited by Jean Dufresne, François Jamet De la Guessière, Nicolas Nupied, and Michel Duchemin. Paris, 1754.

"Kinder-Zucht": see *Universallexikon*.

Kircko-Laki Ja Ordningi 1686, edited by Lahja-Irene Hellemaa, Anja Jussila, and Martti Parvio. SKS:n toimituksia 444. Helsinki: Suomalaisen kirjallisuuden Seura, 1986.

Kongl. Stadgar, Förordningar, Bref och Resolutioner 1528–1701, edited by Johan Schmedeman. Stockholm, 1706.

Kulturella interiörer från storhetstidens uppryckningsarbete, edited by Bror Rudolf Hall. Stockholm, 1915.

Kuningas Kristoferin maanlaki 1442, edited by Martti Ulkuniemi. SKS:n toimituksia 340. Vaasa, 1978.

Lagförslag i Carl den Niondes tid. Handlingar rörande Sveriges historia 2:1. Stockholm, 1864.

Lambertini, Prospero Lorenzo (Benedetto XIV), *Raccolta di alcune notificazioni, editti, ed istruzioni [...] pel buon governo della sua diocesi*, 4 vols. Bologna, 1733–8.

La Roche-Flavin, Bernard de, *Arrests notables du Parlement de Tolose donnés et prononcés sur diverses matières civiles, criminelles, bénéficiales et feudales*. Toulouse, 1617.

Le Ridant, Pierre, *Code matrimonial, ou Recueil des édits, ordonnances et déclarations sur le mariage*. 2 vols. Paris, 1770.

Magnus Erikssons landslag i nusvensk tolkning, edited by Åke Holmbäck and Elias Wessén. Rättshistoriskt bibliotek 6. Lund: Nordiska bokhandel, 1962.

Magnus Erikssons stadslag i nusvensk tolkning, edited by Åke Holmbäck and Elias Wessén. Rättshistoriskt bibliotek 7. Lund: Nordiska bokhandel, 1966.

Maitland, Frederic William, *The Letters*, edited by P.N.R. Zutshi. London: Selden Society, 1995.

Mascardus, Josephus, *Conclusiones probationum omnium*. Frankfurt am Main, 1593.

Milow, Margarethe E., *Ich will aber nicht murren*, edited by Rita Bake and Birgit Kiupel. Hamburg: Dölling und Galitz, 1993.

Montesquieu, Charles de Secondat, baron de, *De l'esprit des lois*, 2 vols., edited by Gonzague Truc. Paris: Editions Garnier frères, 1962.

Müller, Philip, *Der Fang des edlen Leben durch fremde Glaubens-Ehe*. Halle, 1689.

Nueva Recopilación (Recopilación de las leyes destos reynos hecha por mandado de la Magestad Católica del rey D. Felipe Segundo). Valladolid: Lex Nova, 1982.

Pandectae Justinianeae in novum ordinem digestae, cum legibus codicis et novellis quae jus pandectarum confirmant aut abrogant, edited by Robert Joseph Pothier. Paris and Chartres, 1748–52.

Petra, Vincenzo, *Commentaria ad constitutiones apostolicas seu bullas singulas summorum pontificum in bullario romano contentas secondum collectionem Cherubini, incipientes a divo Leone Magno*, vol. 4. Rome: Prope templum S. Mariae Pacis, 1711.

Petri, Olaus, *Kommentar till Stadslagen*, in *Samlade skrifter af Olavus Petri*, 4. Uppsala, 1917.

Platter, Felix, *Tagebuch (Lebensbeschreibung) 1536–1567*, edited by Valentin Lötscher for the Historische und antiquarische Gesellschaft zu Basel, Basler Chroniken 10. Basel, 1976.

Pothier, *Contrat de mariage*: Pothier, Robert Joseph, *Traité du contrat de mariage*. 2 vols. Paris, 1768.

Precedents and Proceedings in Criminal Causes: *A Series of Precedents and Proceedings in Criminal Causes, 1475–1640*, edited by William Hale. Edinburgh, 1847 (reprinted 1973).

Proceedings in Connection with the Parliaments called in 1640: *Proceedings, principally in the County of Kent, in Connection with the Parliaments called in 1640*, edited by Lambert B. Larking. London, 1862.

"Provinsialkonsiliet i Söderköping år 1436," edited by Sigurd Kroon, *Scania* 17 (1946): 271–82.

Pufendorf, Samuel von, *De iure naturae et gentium libri octo*. Amsterdam, 1688 (English translation by Charles Henry Oldfather and William Abbott Oldfather, 2 vols., Oxford: Clarendon Press, 1934).

Recueil des ordonnances des rois de France: *Recueil des grandes ordonnances, édits et déclarations des rois de France, concernant l'ordre judiciaire, et les matières publiques les plus importantes. Depuis 1536 jusques en 1681 inclusivement*, edited by Jean-Armand-Honoré-Marie-Bernard Pijon. Toulouse, 1786.

Riksrådet Johan Skyttes kommentar till stadslagen, edited by Emil Wolff. Gothenburg, 1905.

Rinaldi, Giovanni Domenico, *Observationes criminales, civiles, et mixtae*, 2 vols. Rome: 1688–90.

Rituel de la province de Reims. Paris, 1677.

Rituel de la province de Sens. Sens, 1694.

Rituel du diocèse de Bourges. Bourges, 1666.

Roskovány, Agoston, *De matrimoniis mixtis inter catholicos et protestantes*. Quinque-Ecclesiis, 1842.

Royal Proclamations of King James I: *Stuart Royal Proclamations*, Vol. I: *Royal Proclamations of King James I 1603–1625*, edited by James Larkin and Paul Hughes. Oxford: Clarendon Press, 1973.

Sammlung der württembergischen Gesetze: *Vollständige, historisch und kritisch bearbeitete Sammlung der württembergischen Gesetze*, 19 vols., edited by August Ludwig Reyscher. Stuttgart and Tübingen, 1828–41.

Sánchez, *De sancto matrimonii sacramento*: Sánchez, Tomás, *Disputationum de sancto matrimonii sacramento tomi tres*. Antwerp: Apud Haeredes Martini Nuti & Ioannem Meursium, 1626.

Seckendorff, Veit Ludwig von, *Teutscher Fürstenstaat*. Frankfurt am Main: Götz, 1665.

Seckendorff, Veit Ludwig von, *Teutscher Fürsten-Stat. nebst Additiones*. Frankfurt am Main, 1678.

Siete Partidas: *Las Siete Partidas*. Madrid, 1985 (English translation from *Las Siete Partidas*, 4 vols., translated by Samuel Parsons Scott, edited by Robert I. Burns, Philadelphia: University of Pennsylvania Press, 2001).

Sörmländska häradsdomböcker från 1500-talet, edited by Magnus Collmar. Sörmländska handlingar 16. Eskilstuna, 1953.

SR: *Statutes of the Realm*, 10 vols. London, 1810–27.

Stockholms stads (och Norrmalms stads) tänkeböcker från år 1592, VIII, edited by Nils Staf. Stockholm, 1966.

Stryk, *Usus modernus*: Stryk, Samuel, *Specimen usus moderni pandectarum*. Halle and Magdeburg, 1713.

Svenskt Diplomatarium, vols. 1–3, edited by Carl Silfverstolpe. Stockholm, 1879–87.

Svenska landskapslagar, vols. 1–4, edited and translated by Åke Holmbäck and Elias Wessén. Uppsala, 1933–46.

Svenska riksdagsakter jämte andra handlingar som höra till statsförfattningens historia under tidehvarfvet 1521–1718, 4 vols., edited by Emil Hildebrand. Stockholm, 1888.

Svenska Synodalakter 1: *Svenska Synodalakter efter 1500-talets ingång*. 1. serien, Uppsala ärkestift, edited by Herman Lundström. Skrifter utgifna af kyrkohistoriska föreningen II:3. Uppsala, 1903–8.

Svenska Synodalakter 2: *Svenska Synodalakter efter 1500-talets ingång*. 2. serien, Strängnäs stift, edited by Herman Lundström. Skrifter utgifna af kyrkohistoriska föreningen II:4. Uppsala, 1909–11.

Sveriges Rikes Lag, Gillad och Antagen på Riksdagen Åhr 1734. Rättshistoriskt bibliotek 37. Lund: Nordiska Bokhandel, 1984.

Swinburne, Henry, *Treatise of Spousals or Matrimonial Contracts*. London, 1686.

Synodalstatuter och andra kyrkohistoriska aktstycken från den svenska medeltidskyrkan, edited by Jaakko Gummerus. Uppsala, 1902.

Synodicon Hispanum, 10 vols., directed by Antonio García y García. Madrid: Biblioteca de Autores Cristianos, 1981–2011.

Thomasius, Christian, *Rechtmäßige Erörterung der Ehe-und Gewissens Frage Ob zwei fürstliche personen im Römischen reich deren eine der Luterischen die andere der Reformierten Religion zugetan ist einander mit gutem gewissen heirathen können*. Halle: Salfeld, 1689.

Tractatus universi iuris, 25 vols., edited by Francesco Ziletti. Venice, 1584–6.

Undersökningar och aktstycken: Bidrag till svenska kyrkans historia, edited by Herman Lundström. Uppsala, 1898.

Upplands lagmansdombok 1581 och 1586, edited by Nils Edling and Olof Svenonius. Uppländska domböcker utgivna av Kungliga humanistiska vetenskapssamfundet i Uppsala 8. Uppsala, 1950.

Utdrag ur Åbo stads dombok 1626–1632, edited by Carl von Bonsdorff. Bidrag till Åbo stads historia IV. Helsingfors, 1887.

Vår äldsta kommentar till landslagen: Juris professor B. Crusius' föreläsningar vid Uppsala universitet hösten 1630, edited by Jan Eric Almquist. Uppsala universitets årsskrift, Juridik 2. Uppsala: Almqvist & Wiksells, 1927.

X [followed by book, title, and chapter] = *Decretales Gregorii Noni*, see *Corpus Iuris Canonici*, part 2.

Zink, Burkart, *Chronik: Buch III*. In *Die Chroniken der deutschen Städte vom 14. bis ins 16. Jahrhundert*, vol. 5, *Die Chroniken der schwäbischen Städte: Augsburg*, 2, edited by Carl Hegel, 122–43. Leipzig, 1866.

Zurk, Eduard van, *Codex Batavus, waar in het algemeen kerk-, publyk en burgerlijk recht van Holland en het ressort der Generaliteyt kortelyk is begrepen*. Rotterdam, 1728.

Works of Reference

Dictionnaire de droit canonique, 7 vols., directed by Raoul Naz. Paris: Letouzey et Ané, 1935–65.

Dictionnaire historique des juristes français (XIIe–XXe siècle), edited by Patrick Arabeyre, Jean-Louis Halpérin, and Jacques Krynen. Paris: Presses universitaires de France, 2007.

Diocese of Chichester: A Catalogue of the Records of the Bishop, Archdeacons and Former Exempt Jurisdictions, edited by Francis Steer and Isabel Kirby. Chichester, UK: West Sussex Record Office, 1966.

DTC: *Dictionnaire de théologie catholique*, 15 vols. Paris: Letouzey et Ané, 1899–1950.

Handwörterbuch zur deutschen Rechtsgeschichte, 2nd ed., edited by Albrecht Cordes, Hans-Peter Haferkamp, Heiner Lück, Dieter Werkmüller, Ruth Schmidt-Wiegand, and Christa Bertelsmeier-Kierst. Berlin: Erich Schmidt, 2004.

Historisches Lexikon der Schweiz, 13 vols., edited by Marco Jorio, Stiftung Historisches Lexikon der Schweiz. Basel: Schwabe, 1988–2014.

Merlin, Philippe-Antoine. *Répertoire universel et raisonné de jurisprudence*, 17 vols. 4th ed. Paris, 1812–25.

Records of the Medieval Ecclesiastical Courts: The Records of the Medieval Ecclesiastical Courts, Part 2, edited by Charles Donahue Jr. Berlin: Duncker & Humblot, 1994.

Universallexikon: Großes vollständiges Universallexikon aller Wissenschaften und Künste, 64 vols. Halle and Leipzig, 1732–54.

Secondary Literature

Aalto, Seppo. 1996. *Kirkko ja kruunu siveellisyyden vartijoina: Seksuaalirikollisuus, esivalta ja yhteisö Porvoon kihlakunnassa 1621–1700*. Bibliotheca Historica 12. Helsinki: Suomen Historiallinen Seura.

Addy, John. 1989. *Sin and Society in the Seventeenth Century*. London and New York: Routledge.

Agostini, Grazia, ed. 1978. *Tiziano nelle gallerie fiorentine*. Florence: Centro Di.

Ågren, Maria. 2009. *Domestic Secrets: Women and Property in Sweden 1600–1857*. Chapel Hill: University of North Carolina Press.

Albion, Gordon. 1935. *Charles I and the Court of Rome: A Study in Seventeenth Century Diplomacy*. London: Burns, Oates & Washbourne.

Alessi, Giorgia. 1989. "L'onore riparato: Il riformismo del Settecento e le 'ridicole leggi' contro lo stupro." In *Onore e storia nelle società mediterranee*, edited by Giovanna Fiume, 129–42. Palermo: La Luna.

Alessi, Giorgia. 1990. "Il gioco degli scambi: Seduzione e risarcimento nella casistica cattolica del XVI e XVII secolo." *Quaderni Storici* 25: 805–31.

Alessi, Giorgia. 2006. "Stupro non violento e matrimonio riparatore: Le inquiete peregrinazioni dogmatiche della seduzione." In Seidel Menchi and Quaglioni 2006, 609–40.

Alfani, Guido. 2009. *Fathers and Godfathers: Spiritual Kinship in Early-Modern Italy*. Aldershot, UK: Ashgate.

Alfieri, Fernanda. 2010. *Nella camera degli sposi: Tomás Sánchez, il matrimonio, la sessualità (secoli XVI–XVII)*. Bologna: Il Mulino.

Alfieri, Fernanda. 2011. "'Sub ficto habitu virili': Identità, finzione e matrimonio fra le carte del Sant'Uffizio." In *Famiglia e religione nell'Europa moderna, Studi in onore di Silvana Seidel Menchi*, edited by Giovanni Ciappelli, Serena Luzzi, and Massimo Rospocher, 161–74. Rome: Edizioni di storia e letteratura.

Allegra, Luciano. 1981. "Il parroco: Un mediatore fra alta e bassa cultura." In *Storia d'Italia, Annali 4, Intellettuali e potere*, 897–947. Turin: Einaudi.

Angenendt, Arnold. 2015. *Ehe, Liebe und Sexualität im Christentum: Von den Anfängen bis heute*. Münster: Aschendorff.

Ankum, Hans. 1978. "Études sur le statut juridique des enfants mineurs dans l'histoire du droit privé néerlandais à partir du treizième siècle." *Legal History Review* 46: 204–49.

Arellano, Ignacio, and Jesús M. Usunáriz, eds. 2005. *El matrimonio en Europa y el mundo hispánico: Siglos XVI y XVII*. Madrid: Visor Libros.

Arrivo, Georgia. 2006. *Seduzioni, promesse, matrimoni: Il processo per stupro nella Toscana del Settecento*. Rome: Edizioni di storia e letteratura.

Avignon, Carole. 2014. "Les officialités normandes et la lutte contre les mariages clandestins à la fin du Moyen Âge." In Beaulande-Barraud and Charageat 2014, 227–44.

d'Avray, David. 2005. *Medieval Marriage: Symbolism and Society*. Oxford: Oxford University Press. http://dx.doi.org/10.1093/acprof:oso/9780198208211.001.0001.

Aznar Gil, Federico Rafael. 1989. *La Institución matrimonial en la Hispania cristiana bajomedieval (1215–1563)*. Salamanca: Publicaciones Universidad Pontificia Salamanca.

Bachorski, Hans-Jürgen, ed. 1991. *Ordnung und Lust: Bilder von Liebe, Ehe und Sexualität in Spätmittelalter und Früher Neuzeit*. Trier: Wissenschaftlicher Verlag Trier.

Bänninger, Hans. 1948. "Untersuchungen über den Einfluss des Polizeistaates im 17. und 18. Jahrhundert auf das Recht der Eheschliessung in Stadt und Landschaft Zürich." PhD diss., University of Zurich.

Barahona, Renato. 2003. *Sex Crimes, Honour, and the Law in Early Modern Spain: Vizcaya, 1528–1735*. Toronto: University of Toronto Press.

Barbiche, Bernard. 1999. *Les institutions de la monarchie française à l'époque moderne: XVIe–XVIIIe siècles*. Paris: Presses universitaires de France.

Bartsch, Robert. 1903. *Die Rechtsstellung der Frau als Gattin und Mutter: Geschichtliche Entwicklung ihrer persönlichen Stellung im Privatrecht bis in das 18. Jahrhundert*. Leipzig: Veit.

Bastl, Beatrix. 2000. *Tugend, Liebe, Ehre: Die adelige Frau in der Frühen Neuzeit*. Vienna: Böhlau.

Battafarano, Italo Michele. 1991. "Hardörffers italianisierender Versuch, durch die Integration der Frau das literarische Leben zu verfeinern." In *Georg Philipp Harsdörffer: Ein deutscher Dichter und europäischer Gelehrter*, edited by Italo Michele Battafarano, 267–86. Berne: P. Lang.

Bayer, Andrea. 2008. "From Cassone to Poesia: Paintings of Love and Marriage." In *Art and Love in Renaissance Italy*, edited by Andrea Bayer, 230–7. New York: Metropolitan Museum of Art.

Beaulande-Barraud, Véronique. 2014. "Peines et coercition dans la pratique judiciaire des officialités champenoises (Troyes, Châlons, XVe siècle)." In Beaulande-Barraud and Charageat 2014, 189–203.

Beaulande-Barraud, Véronique, and Martine Charageat, eds. 2014. *Les officialités dans l'Europe médiévale et moderne: Des tribunaux pour une société chrétienne.* Turnhout: Brepols.

Beck, Rainer. 1983. "Illegitimität und voreheliche Sexualität auf dem Land: Unterfinning, 1671–1770." In *Kultur der einfachen Leute*, edited by Richard van Dülmen, 112–50. Munich: Beck.

Beck, Rainer. 1992. "Frauen in Krise: Eheleben und Ehescheidung in der ländlichen Gesellschaft Bayerns während des Ancien régime." In *Studien zur historischen Kulturforschung 4, Dynamik der Tradition*, edited by Richard van Dülmen, 137–212. Frankfurt am Main: Fischer.

Becker, Hans-Jürgen. 1978. "Die nichteheliche Lebensgemeinschaft (Konkubinat) in der Rechtsgeschichte." In *Die nichteheliche Lebensgemeinschaft*, edited by Götz Landwehr, 13–38. Göttingen: Vandenhoeck and Ruprecht.

Becker-Cantarino, Barbara. 1997. "Frauenzimmer Gesprächspiele: Geselligkeit, Frauen und Literatur im Barockzeitalter." In *Geselligkeit und Gesellschaft im Barockzeitalter*, Wolfenbütteler Arbeiten zur Barockforschung 28, part 1, edited by Wolfgang Adam, 17–42. Wiesbaden: Harrassowitz.

Beer, Mathias. 2001. "Private Correspondence in Germany in the Reformation Era: A Forgotten Source for the History of the Burgher Family." *Sixteenth Century Journal* 32 (4): 931–51. http://dx.doi.org/10.2307/3648985.

Bel Bravo, María Antonia. 2000. *La familia en la historia: Propuestas para su estudio desde la "nueva" historia cultural.* Madrid: Encuentro.

Bellavitis, Anna. 2001. *Identité, mariage, mobilité sociale: Citoyennes et citoyens à Venise au XVIe siècle.* Rome: École française de Rome.

Bels, Pierre. 1968. *Le mariage des protestants français jusqu'en 1685.* Paris: Librairie générale de droit et de jurisprudence.

Benedict, Philip. 1991. *The Huguenot Population of France, 1600–1685: The Demographic Fate and Customs of a Religious Minority.* Philadelphia, PA: American Philosophical Society.

Benker, Gitta. 1986. "'Ehre und Schande' – Voreheliche Sexualität auf dem Lande im ausgehenden 18. Jahrhundert." In *Frauenkörper – Medizin – Sexualität*, edited by Johanna Geyer-Kordesch and Anette Kuhn, 10–27. Düsseldorf: Schwann.

Bertling Biaggini, Claudia. 2002–3. "Die unglückliche Braut: Zur Deutung eines mythischen Hochzeitsbildes aus der Zeit zwischen 1520 und 1530." *Georges-Bloch-Jahrbuch des Kunsthistorischen Instituts der Universität Zürich* 9–10: 94–111.

Bizzarri, Dina. 1937. "Per la storia dei riti nuziali in Italia." In *Studi di storia del diritto italiano*, edited by Federico Patetta and Mario Chiudano, 611–29. Turin: Lattes.

Bizzocchi, Roberto. 2008. *Cicisbei: Morale privata e identità nazionale in Italia.* Rome and Bari: Laterza.

Blasius, Dirk. 1987. *Ehescheidung in Deutschland 1794–1945. Scheidung und Scheidungsrecht in historischer Perspektive.* Kritische Studien zur Geschichtswissenschaft 74. Göttingen: Vandenhoeck and Ruprecht.

Blauert, Andreas. 1993. "Kriminaljustiz und Sittenreform als Krisenmanagement? Das Hochstift Speyer im 16. und 17. Jahrhundert." In *Mit den Waffen der Justiz: Zur Kriminalitätsgeschichte des späten Mittelalters und der Frühen Neuzeit*, edited by Andreas Blauert and Gerd Schwerhoff, 115–136. Frankfurt am Main: Fischer Taschenbuch.

Blet, Pierre. 1959. *Le clergé de France et la monarchie: Étude sur les assemblées générales du clergé de 1615 à 1666.* 2 vols. Rome: Librairie éditrice de l'Université grégorienne.

Bonfield, Lloyd. 2001. "Developments in European Family Law." In Kertzer and Barbagli 2001, 87–124.

Borgolte, Michael. 2004a. *Die mittelalterliche Kirche.* Enzyklopädie deutscher Geschichte 17. 2nd ed. Munich: Oldenbourg.

Borgolte, Michael. 2004b. "Kulturelle Einheit und religiöse Differenz: Zur Verbreitung der Polygynie im mittelalterlichen Europa." *Zeitschrift fur Geschichtswissenschaft* 31: 1–36.

Bors, Marc. 1998. *Bescholtene Frauen vor Gericht: Zur Rechtsprechung des Preußischen Obertribunals und des Zürcher Obergerichts auf dem Gebiet des Nichtehelichenrechts.* Veröffentlichungen des Max-Planck-Instituts für Europäische Rechtsgeschichte 11. Frankfurt am Main: Klostermann.

Bossy, John. 1985. *Christianity in the West, 1400–1700.* Oxford: Oxford University Press.

Brackett, John K. 1992. *Criminal Justice and Crime in Late Renaissance Florence, 1537–1609.* Cambridge and New York: Cambridge University Press.

Brambilla, Elena. 2000. *Alle origini del Sant'Uffizio: Penitenza, confessione e giustizia spirituale dal Medioevo al XVI secolo.* Bologna: Il Mulino.

Brambilla, Elena. 2006. *La giustizia intollerante: Inquisizione e tribunali confessionali in Europa (secoli IV–XVIII).* Rome: Carocci.

Breit, Stefan. 1991. *"Leichtfertigkeit" und ländliche Gesellschaft: Voreheliche Sexualität in der Frühen Neuzeit.* Munich: Oldenbourg.

Brink, Leendert. 1977. *De taak van de kerk bij de huwelijkssluiting.* Nieuwkoop: Heuff.

Brinkworth, Edwin Robert Courtney. 1972. *Shakespeare and the Bawdy Court of Stratford.* London and Chichester, UK: Phillimore.

Brooke, C.N.L. 1989. *The Medieval Idea of Marriage.* Oxford: Oxford University Press.

Brooks, Christopher W., Richard H. Helmholz, and Peter G. Stein. 1991. *Notaries Public in England since the Reformation*. London: Erskine Press.
Brucker, Gene A. 1986. *Giovanni and Lusanna: Love and Marriage in Renaissance Florence*. Berkeley: University of California Press.
Brundage, James A. 1987. *Law, Sex, and Christian Society in Medieval Europe*. Chicago: University of Chicago Press.
Bryson, W. Hamilton, and Serge Dauchy, eds. 2006. *Ratio decidendi: Guiding Principles of Judicial Decisions*. Berlin: Duncker & Humblot.
Buchholz, Stefan. 1988. *Recht, Religion und Ehe: Orientierungswandel und gelehrte Kontroversen im Übergang vom 17. zum 18. Jahrhundert*. Frankfurt am Main: Klostermann.
Buchholz, Stefan. 1991. "Philippus Bigamus." *Rechtshistorisches Journal* 10: 145–59.
Burghartz, Susanna. 1999. *Zeiten der Reinheit, Orte der Unzucht: Ehe und Sexualität in Basel während der Frühen Neuzeit*. Munich: Paderhorn.
Burghartz, Susanna. 2004. "Ordering Discourse and Society: Moral Politics, Marriage and Fornication during the Reformation and the Confessionalisation Process in Germany and Switzerland." In *Social Control in Europe, 1500–1800*, vol. 1, edited by Herman Roodenburg and Pieter Spierenburg, 78–98. Columbus: Ohio State University Press.
Burguière, André. 1987. "The Formation of the Couple." *Journal of Family History* 12 (1): 39–53. http://dx.doi.org/10.1177/036319908701200103.
Calabrese, Omar. 2003. "La *Venere di Urbino* di Tiziano Vecellio." In *Venere svelata: La Venere di Urbino di Tiziano*, edited by Omar Calabrese, 29–45. Cisinello Balsamo, Milan: Silvana Editoriale.
Campo Guinea, María del Juncal. 1998. *Comportamientos matrimoniales en Navarra: Siglos XVI–XVII*. Pamplona: Gobierno de Navarra.
Candau Chacón, María Luisa. 2004. "Mujer y deseo: La pasión contrariada de una viuda andaluza de fines del Seiscientos." In *Mujer y deseo: Representaciones y prácticas de vida*, edited by M. Gloria Espigado Tocino, María José de la Pascua Sánchez, and María del Rosario García-Doncel Hernández, 405–18. Cádiz: Universidad de Cádiz.
Carbasse, Jean-Marie. 2000. *Histoire du droit pénal et de la justice criminelle*. Paris: Presses universitaires de France.
Carlsson, Lizzie. 1965. *"Jag giver dig min dotter": Trolovning och äktenskap i den svenska kvinnans äldre historia*. Vol. 1. Rättshistoriskt bibliotek 8. Lund: Nordiska Bokhandeln.
Carlson, Eric. 1994. *Marriage and the English Reformation*. Oxford: Blackwell.
Casanova, Cesarina. 2007. *Crimini nascosti: La sanzione penale dei reati "senza vittima" e nelle relazioni private (Bologna, XVII secolo)*. Bologna: CLUEB.

Casey, James. 2007. *Family and Community in Early Modern Spain: The Citizens of Granada, 1570–1739*. Cambridge and New York: Cambridge University Press.

Cavallar, Osvaldo, and Julius Kirshner. 2004. "Making and Breaking Betrothal Contracts ('Sponsalia') in Late Trecento Florence." In *"Panta rei": Studi dedicati a Manlio Bellomo*, edited by Orazio Condorelli, 5 vols., 1:395–452. Rome: Il Cigno.

Cavallo, Sandra. 1995. *Charity and Power in Early Modern Italy: Benefactors and Their Motives in Turin, 1541–1789*. Cambridge and New York: Cambridge University Press.

Cavallo, Sandra, and Simona Cerutti. 1990. "Female Honor and the Social Control of Reproduction in Piedmont between 1600 and 1800." In Muir and Ruggiero 1990, 73–109.

Cavarzere, Marco. 2012. *La giustizia del vescovo: I tribunali ecclesiastici della Liguria orientale*. Pisa: Pisa University Press.

Cavina, Marco. 2011. *Nozze di sangue: Storia della violenza coniugale*. Rome and Bari: Laterza.

Chabot, Isabelle. 2011. *La dette des familles: Femmes, lignage et patrimoine à Florence aux XIVe et XVe siècles*. Rome: École Française de Rome.

Charageat, Martine. 2011. *La délinquance matrimoniale: Couples en conflit et justice en Aragon au Moyen Âge (XVe–XVIe siècle)*. Paris: Publications de la Sorbonne.

Chavarría Múgica, Fernando. 2001. "Mentalidad moral y Contrarreforma en la España Moderna (Fornicarios, confesores e inquisidores: El Tribunal de Logroño, 1571–1623)." *Hispania Sacra* 53: 725–59.

Cheney, Christopher Robert. 1972. *Notaries Public in England in the Thirteenth and Fourteenth Centuries*. Oxford: Clarendon Press.

Chojnacki, Stanley. 2000. *Women and Men in Renaissance Venice: Twelve Essays on Patrician Society*. Baltimore, MD: Johns Hopkins University Press.

Christ-von Wedel, Christine. 1995. "*Praecipua coniugii pars est animorum coniunctio*: Die Stellung der Frau nach der 'Eheanweisung' des Erasmus von Rotterdam." In Wunder 1995, 125–49.

Ciappelli, Giovanni. 2006. "I processi matrimoniali: Quadro di raccordo dei risultati della schedatura (Venezia, Verona, Napoli, Feltre e Trento, 1420–1803)." In Seidel Menchi and Quaglioni 2006, 67–100.

Cohen, Sherrill. 1992. *The Evolution of Women's Asylums Since 1500: From Refuge for Ex-Prostitutes to Shelters for Battered Women*. New York: Oxford University Press.

Connick, Alfred J. 1960. "Canonical Doctrine Concerning Mixed Marriages: Before Trent and During the Seventeenth and Early Eighteenth Centuries." *Jurist (Washington, D.C.)* 20: 295–326, 398–418.

Conrad, Anne, ed. 1999a. *"In Christo ist weder man noch weyb"*: Frauen in der Reformation und der katholischen Reform. Katholisches Leben und Kirchenreform im Zeitalter der Glaubensspaltung 59. Münster: Aschendorff.

Conrad, Anne. 1999b. "Aufbruch der Laien – Aufbruch der Frauen: Überlegungen zu einer Geschlechtergeschichte der Reformation und katholischen Reform." In Conrad 1999a, 7–22.

Coontz, Stephanie. 2006. *Marriage, a History: How Love Conquered Marriage.* New York: Penguin Books.

Cowan, Alexander. 2007. *Marriage, Manners, and Mobility in Early Modern Venice.* Aldershot, UK: Ashgate.

Cozzi, Gaetano. 1976. "Padri, figli e matrimoni clandestini (metà sec. XVI–metà sec. XVIII)." *La cultura: Rivista di filosofia, letteratura e storia* 14: 169–213.

Cozzi, Gaetano. 1986. *Il dibattito sui matrimoni clandestini: Vicende giuridiche, sociali, religiose dell'istituzione matrimoniale tra Medioevo ed Età moderna.* Venice: Cooperativa Universitaria Studio Lavoro.

Cressy, David. 1997. *Birth, Marriage, and Death: Ritual, Religion and the Life-Cycle in Tudor and Stuart England.* Oxford: Oxford University Press. http://dx.doi.org/10.1093/acprof:oso/9780198201687.001.0001.

Cressy, David, and Lori Anne Ferrell, eds. 1996. *Religion and Society in Early Modern England.* London and New York: Routledge.

Cristellon, Cecilia. 2003. "L'ufficio del giudice: Mediazione, inquisizione e confessione nei processi matrimoniali veneziani (1420–1532)." *Rivista storica italiana* 115: 851–98.

Cristellon, Cecilia. 2006. "'Io voleva tuor quello che mio padre me daria': Autorità parentale e scelte matrimoniali dei figli: Venezia XV e XVI secolo." In *Generazioni: Legami di parentela tra passato e presente*, edited by Daniela Lombardi and Ida Fazio, 205–21. Rome: Viella.

Cristellon, Cecilia. 2008. "Marriage and Consent in Pre-Tridentine Venice: Between Lay Conception and Ecclesiastical Conception, 1420–1545." *Sixteenth Century Journal* 39 (2): 389–418. http://dx.doi.org/10.2307/20478893.

Cristellon, Cecilia. 2009. "Does the Priest Have to Be There? Contested Marriages before Roman Tribunals, Italy, Sixteenth to Eighteenth Centuries." Translated by Emlyn Eisenach. *Österreichische Zeitschrift für Geschichtswissenschaften* 20 (3): 10–30.

Cristellon, Cecilia. 2010. *La carità e l'eros: Il matrimonio, la Chiesa, i suoi giudici nella Venezia del Rinascimento (1420–1545).* Bologna: Il Mulino.

Cristellon, Cecilia. 2013a. "Sposare (o non sposare) 'l'eretico': Matrimoni misti e politica del Santo Uffizio: Venezia nel contesto europeo." In *Protestanten zwischen Venedig und Rom in der Frühen Neuzeit*, edited by Michael Matheus and Uwe Israel, 159–77. Venice: Akademie Verlag. http://dx.doi.org/10.1524/9783050063263.159.

Cristellon, Cecilia. 2013b. "'Unstable and Weak-Minded' or a Missionary? Catholic Woman in Mixed Marriages (1563–1798)." In *Gender Difference in European Legal Cultures: Historical Perspectives*, Festschrift für Heide Wunder, edited by Karin Gottschalk, 83–93. Stuttgart: Steiner.

Cristellon, Cecilia. 2013c. "L'inquisizione, il duca di Neoburgo e i matrimoni misti in Germania in età moderna." *Rivista storica italiana* 125 (1): 76–108.

Cristellon, Cecilia. 2014a. "Due fedi in un corpo: Matrimoni misti fra *delicta carnis*, scandalo, seduzione e sacramento nell'Europa di età moderna." *Quaderni Storici* 145: 1–29.

Cristellon, Cecilia. 2014b. "Il giudice come confessore." In Beaulande-Barraud and Charageat 2014, 311–24.

Cristellon, Cecilia, ed. Forthcoming. *Mixed Marriages in Europe: The Politics and Practices of Religious Plurality Between the Fourteenth and Nineteenth Centuries.* Farnham and Burlington: Ashgate.

Dean, Trevor. 1998. "Fathers and Daughters: Marriage Laws and Marriage Disputes in Bologna and Italy, 1200–1500." In *Marriage in Italy, 1300–1650*, edited by Trevor Dean and Kate J.P. Lowe, 85–106. Cambridge: Cambridge University Press.

Dean, Trevor, and Kate J. P. Lowe, eds. 1998. *Marriage in Italy, 1300–1650.* Cambridge: Cambridge University Press.

De Boer, Wietse. 2001. *The Conquest of the Soul.* Leiden: Brill.

Delille, Gérard. 1985. *Famille et propriété dans le Royaume de Naples (XVe–XIXe siècle).* Rome: École française de Rome.

Demars-Sion, Véronique. 1983. "Illégitimité et l'abandon de l'enfant: La position des provinces du Nord (XVIe–XVIIIe siècles)." *Revue du Nord* 65: 481–506.

Demars-Sion, Véronique. 1988. "Un épisode peu connu de l'histoire du rapt de séduction: L'utilisation de la législation royale au profit des femmes déshonorées dans la jurisprudence du XVIIe siècle." *Revue de science criminelle et de droit pénal comparé* 4: 713–50.

Demars-Sion, Véronique. 1991. *Femmes séduites et abandonnées au XVIIIe siècle: L'exemple du Cambrésis*. Hellemmes, France: Ester.

Demoulin-Auzary, Florence. 2004. *Les actions d'État en droit romano-canonique: Mariage et filiation (XIIe–XVe siècles).* Paris: LGDJ.

Dettlaff, Susanne. 1989. "Sittliche Verstöße und niedergerichtliche Straftätigkeit: Aufschlüsse aus Brücheregistern in schleswig-holsteinischen Amtsrechnungen." In *Volksleben, Kirche und Obrigkeit in Schleswig-Holstein von der Reformation bis ins 19. Jahrhundert*, edited by Karl S. Kramer, Frauke Rehder, Annelie Stobinsky, and Susanne Dettlaff, Studien zur Volkskunde und Kulturgeschichte Schleswig-Holsteins 21, 309–452. Neumünster: K. Wachholtz.

Deutsch, Christina. 2005. *Ehegerichtsbarkeit im Bistum Regensburg (1480–1538).* Forschungen zur kirchlichen Rechtsgeschichte und zum Kirchenrecht 29. Cologne: Böhlau.

Diefendorf, Barbara B. 1983. *Paris City Councillors in the Sixteenth Century.* Princeton, NJ: Princeton University Press. http://dx.doi.org/10.1515/9781400853779.

Dieterich, Hartwig. 1970. *Das protestantische Eherecht in Deutschland bis zur Mitte des 17. Jahrhunderts.* Jus Ecclesiasticum 10. Munich: Claudius Verlag.

Di Renzo Villata, Gigliola. 1989. "Separazione personale dei coniugi (Storia)." In *Enciclopedia del diritto*, 41:1350–76. Milan: Giuffrè.

Di Simplicio, Oscar. 1994. *Peccato penitenza perdono, Siena 1575–1800: La formazione della coscienza nell'Italia moderna.* Milan: Franco Angeli.

Döhlemeyer, Barbara. 1997. "Frau und Familie im Privatrecht des 19. Jahrhunderts." In Gerhard 1997, 633–58.

Dompnier, Bernard. 1985. *Le venin de l'hérésie: Image du protestantisme et combat catholique au XVIIe siècle.* Paris: Le Centurion.

Dompnier, Bernard. 2009. "L'administration des sacrements en terre protestante à la lumière des *facultates* et des *dubia* des missionaires (XVII–XVIII siècle)." In "Administrer les sacrements en Europe et au Nouveau Monde: la Curie romaine et les *dubia circa sacramenta*," edited by Paolo Broggio, Charlotte de Castelnau-L'Estoile, and Giovanni Pizzorusso. *MEFRIM* 121 (1): 23–38.

Donahue, Charles, Jr. 1976. "The Policy of Alexander the Third's Consent Theory of Marriage." In *Proceedings of the Fourth International Congress of Medieval Canon Law*, edited by Stephan Kuttner, Monumenta Iuris Canonici, C:5, 251–81. Vatican City.

Donahue, Charles, Jr. 1978. "The Case of the Man Who Fell into the Tiber: The Roman Law of Marriage at the Time of the Glossators." *American Journal of Legal History* 22 (1): 1–53. http://dx.doi.org/10.2307/845232.

Donahue, Charles, Jr. 1981. "Proof by Witnesses in the Church Courts of Medieval England: An Imperfect Reception of the Learned Law." In *On the Laws and Customs of England: Essays in Honor of Samuel E. Thorne*, edited by Morris S. Arnold, Thomas A. Green, Sally A. Scully, and Stephen D. White, 127–58. Chapel Hill: University of North Carolina Press.

Donahue, Charles, Jr. 1995. "Was There a Change in Marriage Law in the Late Middle Ages?" *Rivista internazionale di diritto comune* 6: 49–80.

Donahue, Charles, Jr. 2006. "Historical Introduction: Comparative Law Before the *Code Napoléon*." In *The Oxford Handbook of Comparative Law*, edited by Mathias Reimann and Reinhard Zimmermann, 3–32. Oxford: Oxford University Press.

Donahue, Charles, Jr. 2007. *Law, Marriage, and Society in the Later Middle Ages*. New York: Cambridge University Press.

Donahue, Charles, Jr. 2008a. "Private Law Without the State and During Its Formation." *American Journal of Comparative Law* 56 (3): 541–66 (repr. in *Beyond the State: Rethinking Private Law*, edited by Nils Jansen, Tübingen: Mohr Siebeck, 2008).

Donahue, Charles, Jr. 2008b. "The Western Canon Law of Marriage: A Doctrinal Introduction." In *The Islamic Marriage Contract: Case Studies in Islamic Family Law*, edited by Asifa Quraishi and Frank E. Vogel, 46–56. Cambridge, MA: Harvard University Press.

Donahue, Charles, Jr. 2014. "By Way of a Conclusion." In Beaulande-Barraud and Charageat 2014, 325–38.

Douglas, Mary. 1966. *Purity and Danger: An Analysis of the Concepts of Pollution and Taboo*. London and New York: Praeger. http://dx.doi.org/10.4324/9780203361832.

Duguit, Léon. 1886. "Étude historique sur le rapt de séduction." *Nouvelle revue historique de droit français et étranger* 10: 586–685.

van Dülmen, Richard. 1988. "Fest der Liebe: Heirat und Ehe in der Frühen Neuzeit." In *Armut, Liebe, Ehre*, edited by Richard van Dülmen, 67–106. Frankfurt am Main: Fischer Taschenbuch.

van Dülmen, Richard. 1990. "Heirat und Eheleben in der Frühen Neuzeit: Autobiographische Zeugnisse." *Archiv für Kulturgeschichte* 72 (1): 153–71.

Derrett, Duncan, and John Martin. 1973. *Henry Swinburne (?1551–1624): Civil Lawyer of York*. York: St Anthony's Press.

Duncker, Arne. 2004. *Gleichheit und Ungleichheit in der Ehe: Persönliche Stellung von Frau und Mann im Recht der ehelichen Lebensgemeinschaft 1700–1914*. Cologne: Böhlau.

Durand, Bernard. 1974. "'Aut nubere aut dotare.'" *Recueil de mémoires et travaux publiés par la Société d'histoire du droit et des institutions des anciens pays de droit écrit* 9: 295–9.

Dürr, Renate. 1995. *Mägde in der Stadt: Das Beispiel Schwäbisch Hall in der Frühen Neuzeit*. Geschichte und Geschlechter 13. Frankfurt am Main and New York: Campus.

Durston, Christopher. 1996. "Puritan Rule and the Failure of Cultural Revolution, 1645–1660." In *The Culture of English Puritanism, 1560–1700*, edited by Christopher Durston and Jacqueline Eales, 211–33. New York: St Martin's Press.

Eisenach, Emlyn. 2004a. *Husbands, Wives, and Concubines: Marriage, Family, and Social Order in Sixteenth-Century Verona*. Kirksville, MO: Truman State University Press.

Eisenach, Emlyn. 2004b. "'Femine e zentilhomini': Concubinato d'élite nella Verona del Cinquecento." In Seidel Menchi and Quaglioni 2004, 269–303.

Elton, G.R. 1969. *England, 1200–1640*. Ithaca, NY, and London: Cornell University Press.

Eming, Jutta, and Ulrike Gaebel. 1988. "Wie man zwei Rinder in ein Joch spannt: Zu Heinrich Bullingers "Der Christliche Ehestand." In *Eheglück und Liebesjoch: Bilder von Liebe, Ehe und Familie in der Literatur des 15. und 16. Jahrhunderts*, Ergebnisse der Frauenforschung 14, edited by Maria E. Müller, 125–54. Berlin: Beltz.

Enderle, Wilfried. 1993. "Ulm und die evangelischen Reichsstädte im Südwesten." In *Die Territorien des Reichs im Zeitalter der Reformation und Konfessionalisierung, Land und Konfession 1500–1650*, vol. 5, *Der Südwesten*, edited by Anton Schindling and Walter Ziegler, 194–212. Münster: Aschendorff.

Enfance abandonnée et société en Europe: XIVe–XXe siècle. 1991. Actes du colloque de Rome (30–31 janvier 1987). Rome: Publications de l'École française de Rome, 140.

Erickson, Amy Louise. 2005. "The Marital Economy in Comparative Perspective." In *The Marital Economy in Scandinavia and Britain 1400–1900*, edited by Amy Louise Erickson and Maria Ågren, 3–37. Aldershot, UK: Ashgate.

Esmein, Adhémar. 1891. *Études sur l'histoire du droit canonique privé: Le mariage en droit canonique*. 2 vols. 1st ed. Paris: Larose et Forcel

Esmein, Adhémar. 1929–35. *Le mariage en droit canonique*. 2 vols. Edited by Robert Génestal and Jean Dauvillier. 2nd ed. Paris: Libr. du Recueil Sirey.

Esmyol, Andrea. 2002. *Geliebte oder Ehefrau? Konkubinen im Frühen Mittelalter*. Cologne: Böhlau.

Esposito, Anna. 2004. "Adulterio, concubinato, bigamia: Testimonianze dalla normativa statutaria dello Stato pontificio (secoli XIII–XVI)." In Seidel Menchi and Quaglioni 2004, 21–42.

Essegern, Ute. 2003. "Kursächsische Eheverträge in der ersten Hälfte des 17. Jahrhunderts." In Schattkowsky 2003, 115–35.

Fabbri, Lorenzo. 1991. *Alleanza matrimoniale e patriziato nella Firenze del '400: Studio sulla famiglia Strozzi*. Florence: L.S. Olschki.

Fazio, Ida. 2009. "Matrimoni, conflitti, istituzioni giudiziarie: La specificità italiana di un percorso di ricerca." *Rivista storica italiana* 121: 639–66.

Ferrante, Lucia. 2000. "Honor Regained: Women in the Casa del Soccorso in San Paolo in Sixteenth-Century Bologna." In Muir and Ruggiero 1990, 46–72.

Ferrante, Lucia. 2004. "'Consensus concubinarius': Un'invenzione giuridica per il principe?" In Seidel Menchi and Quaglioni 2004, 107–32.

Ferraro, Joanne M. 2001. *Marriage Wars in Late Renaissance Venice*. Oxford: Oxford University Press.

Fietze, Katharina. 1996. "Frauenbildungskonzepte im Renaissance-Humanismus." In *Geschichte der Mädchen- und Frauenbildung*, edited by Elke Kleinau and Claudia Opitz, 1:121–34. Frankfurt am Main and New York: Campus.

Flandrin, Jean-Louis. 1984. *Familles: Parenté, maison, sexualité dans l'ancienne société*. Paris: Editions du Seuil.

Forclaz, Bertrand. 2009. "The Emergence of Confessional Identities: Family Relationships and Religious Coexistence in Seventeenth-Century Utrecht." In *Living with Religious Diversity in Early-Modern Europe*, edited by C. Scott Dixon, Dagmar Freist, and Mark Greengrass, 250–66. Farnham, UK: Ashgate.

Fossaluzza, Giorgio. 2012. "Vittore Belliniano: Un consuntivo, novità e problemi di attribuzione." *Bulletin du Musée Hongrois des Beaux-Arts* 116–17: 69–102.

Foster, Ellinor. Forthcoming. "Marriage Between Catholics, Protestants and Juifs in Austria: Politics and Practices." In Cristellon, forthcoming.

Foster, Marc R., and Benjamin J. Kaplan, eds. 2005. *Piety and Family in Early Modern Europe: Essays in Honour of Steven Ozment*. Aldershot, UK: Ashgate.

François, Étienne. 1991. *Die unsichtbare Grenze: Protestanten und Katholiken in Augsburg 1648–1806*. Sigmaringen: Thorbecke.

Franz, Adolph. 1878. *Die gemischten Ehen in Schlesien*. Breslau: Aderholz.

Frassek, Ralf. 2005. *Eherecht und Ehegerichtsbarkeit in der Reformationszeit: Der Aufbau neuer Rechtsstrukturen im sächsischen Raum unter besonderer Berücksichtigung der Wirkungsgeschichte des Wittenberger Konsistoriums*. Jus Ecclesiasticum 78. Tübingen: Mohr Siebeck.

Freist, Dagmar. 1999. "Religious Difference and the Experience of Widowhood in Early Modern Germany." In *Widows in Medieval and Early Modern Europe*, edited by Sandra Cavallo and Lyndan Warner, 164–78. New York: Longman.

Freist, Dagmar. 2001. "Zwischen Glaubensfreiheit und Gewissenszwang." In *Frieden und Krieg in der Frühen Neuzeit: Die europäische Staatenordnung und die außereuropäische Welt*, edited by Ronald G. Asch, Wulf Eckart Voß, and Martin Wrede, 293–322. Munich: Fink.

Freist, Dagmar. 2002. "One Body, Two Confessions: Mixed Marriages in Germany." In *Gender in Early Modern German History*, edited by Ulinka Rublack, 275–305. Cambridge: Cambridge University Press.

Freist, Dagmar. 2005. "Der Fall von Albini: Rechtsstreitigkeiten um die väterliche Gewalt in konfessionell gemischten Ehen." In *In eigener Sache: Frauen vor den höchsten Gerichten des Alten Reiches*, edited by Siegried Westphal, 245–70. Cologne and Vienna: Böhlau.

Freist, Dagmar. 2011. "Popery in Perfection? The Experience of Catholicism – Henrietta Maria Between Private Practice and Public Discourse." In *The Experience of Revolution in Stuart Britain: Essays Presented to John Morrill to Mark His 65th Birthday*, edited by Michael Braddick and David Smith, 33–51. Cambridge: Cambridge University Press. http://dx.doi.org/10.1017/CBO9780511975745.005.

Freist, Dagmar. Forthcoming. *Glaube – Liebe – Zwietracht: Konfessionell gemischte Ehen in Deutschland in der Frühen Neuzeit*. Munich: Oldenbourg.

Frijhoff, Willem. 2002. *Embodied Belief: Ten Essays on Religious Culture in Dutch History*. Hilversum: Uitgeverij Verloren.

Fuhrmann, Inken. 1998. "Die Diskussion über die Einführung der fakultativen Zivilehe in Deutschland und Österreich seit Mitte des 19. Jahrhunderts." PhD diss., Universität Kiel, Frankfurt am Main.

Funaro, Liana Elda. 2012. "'Orgoglio e pregiudizio': Il matrimonio di Sara Sismondi." In *Andare sposa: Usi e tradizioni matrimoniali nella documentazione archivistica dal Quattrocento all'Ottocento*, edited by Vincenza Papini, 43–66. Lucca: Buggiano Castello.

Ganster, Susanne. 2013. *Religionsverschiedenheit als Ehehindernis: Eine rechtshistorische und kirchenrechtliche Untersuchung*. Paderborn: Schöningh.

Gaudemet, Jean. 1987. *Le mariage en Occident: Les moeurs et le droit*. Paris: Cerf.

Gaunt, David. 1996. *Familjeliv i Norden*. Södertälje, Sweden: Gidlund.

Gerhard, Ute, ed. 1997. *Frauen in der Geschichte des Rechts: Von der Frühen Neuzeit bis zur Gegenwart*. Munich: Beck.

Geringer, Karl-Theodor. 1991. "Die Konfessionsbestimmung bei Kindern aus gemischten Ehen in der Zeit seit dem Ende der Glaubenskriege (1648) bis Benedikt XIV (1758)." In *Scientia canonum*, edited by Hans Paarhammer and Alfred Rinnerthaler, 27–54. Munich: R. Kovar.

Ghestin, Jacques. 1956. "L'action des parlements contre les 'mésalliances' aux XVIIe et XVIIIe siècles." *Revue historique de droit français et étranger* 34: 74–110.

Giesen, Dieter. 1973. *Grundlagen und Entwicklung des englischen Eherechts in der Neuzeit bis zum Beginn des 19. Jahrhunderts vor dem Hintergrund der englischen Geschichte: Rechts- und Kirchengeschichte*. Schriften zum deutschen und europäischen Zivil-, Handels- und Prozessrecht 74. Bielefeld: Gieseking.

Gleixner, Ulrike. 1994. *"Das Mensch" und "der Kerl": Die Konstruktion von Geschlecht in Unzuchtsverfahren der Frühen Neuzeit (1700–1760)*. Geschichte und Geschlechter 8. Frankfurt am Main and New York: Campus.

Gleixner, Ulrike. 2003. "Zwischen göttlicher und weltlicher Ordnung: Die Ehe im lutherischen Pietismus." *Pietismus und Neuzeit* 28: 147–84.

Goldberg, P.J.P. 1992. *Women, Work, and Life Cycle in a Medieval Economy*. Oxford: Oxford University Press.

Gottlieb, Beatrice. 1974. "Getting Married in Pre-Reformation Europe." PhD diss., Columbia University, Ann Arbor, MI.

Gottlieb, Beatrice. 1980. "The Meaning of Clandestine Marriage." In *Family and Sexuality in French History*, edited by Robert Wheaton and Tamara K. Hareven, 49–83. Philadelphia: University of Pennsylvania Press.

Gottlieb, Beatrice. 1993. *The Family in the Western World from the Black Death to the Industrial Age*. Oxford: Oxford University Press.

Göttsch, Silke. 1996. "'... sie trüge ihre Kleider mit Ehren ...': Frauen und traditionelle Ordnung im 17. und 18. Jahrhundert." In *Weiber, Menscher, Frauenzimmer: Frauen in der ländlichen Gesellschaft 1500–1800*, edited by Heide Wunder and Christina Vanja, 199–213. Göttingen: Vandenhoeck and Ruprecht.

Gritschke, Caroline. 2006. *Via Media: Spiritualistische Lebenswelten und Konfessionalisierung. Das süddeutsche Schwenckfeldertum im 16. und 17. Jahrhundert*. Berlin: Akademie Verlag. http://dx.doi.org/10.1524/9783050055862.

Grochowina, Nicole. 1999. "Zwischen Gleichheit im Martyrium und Unterordnung in der Ehe: Aktionsräume von Frauen in der täuferischen Bewegung." In Conrad 1999a, 95–113.

Groppi, Angela. 1994. *I conservatori della virtù: Donne recluse nella Roma dei papi*. Rome and Bari: Laterza.

Grosse, Christian. 2008. *Les rituels de la cène: Le culte eucharistique réformé à Genève (XVIe–XVIIe siècle)*. Geneva: Droz.

Günther, Bettina. 2000. "Sittlichkeitsdelikte in den Policeyordnungen der Reichsstädte Frankfurt am Main und Nürnberg (15.–17. Jahrhundert)." In *Policey und frühneuzeitliche Gesellschaft*, edited by Karl Härter, 121–48. Frankfurt am Main: Klostermann.

Habermas, Rebekka, and Tanja Hommen, eds. 1999. *Das Frankfurter Gretchen: Der Prozeß gegen die Kindsmörderin Susanna Margaretha Brandt*. Munich: Beck.

Hacke, Daniela. 2004. *Women, Sex, and Marriage in Early Modern Venice*. Aldershot, UK: Ashgate.

Hagemann, Rudolf, and Heide Wunder. 1995. "Heiraten und Erben: Das Basler Ehegüterrecht und Ehegattenerbrecht." In Wunder 1995, 150–66.

Haks, Donald. 1982. *Huwelijk en gezin in Holland in de 17de en 18de eeuw: Processtukken en moralisten over aspecten van het 17de en 18de-eeuwse gezinsleven*. Utrecht: HES.

Haliczer, Stephen. 1996. *Sexuality in the Confessional*. New York and Oxford: Oxford University Press.

Hamm, Berndt. 1996. *Bürgertum und Glaube: Konturen der städtischen Reformation*. Göttingen: Vandenhoeck and Ruprecht.

Hanawalt, Barbara. 1986. *The Ties that Bound: Peasant Families in Medieval England*. New York: Oxford University Press.

Hanlon, Gregory. 1993. *Confession and Community in Seventeenth Century France: Catholic and Protestant Coexistence in Aquitaine*. Philadelphia: University of Pennsylvania Press.

Hansen, Lars Ivar, ed. 2000. *Family, Marriage, and Property Devolution in the Middle Ages*. Tromsø: University of Tromsø.

Harrington, Joel F. 1995. *Reordering Marriage and Society in Reformation Germany*. Cambridge: Cambridge University Press.

Haverkamp, Alfred, ed. 1984. *Haus und Familie in der spätmittelalterlichen Stadt*. Städteforschung A 18. Cologne: Böhlau.

Head-König, Anna-Lise. 2003. "Les politiques étatiques coercitives et leur influence sur la formation du mariage en Suisse au XVIIIe siècle." In *Eheschließungen im Europa des 18. und 19. Jahrhunderts*, Veröffentlichungen des Max-Planck-Instituts für Geschichte 197, edited by Christophe Duhamelle and Jürgen Schlumbohm, 89–214. Göttingen: Vandenhoeck and Ruprecht.

Heckel, Martin. 1973. *Lex charitatis: Eine juristische Untersuchung über das Recht in der Theologie Martin Luthers*. 2nd ed. Cologne: Böhlau.

Heijden, Manon, van der. 1996. "Secular and Ecclesiastical Marriage Control: Rotterdam 1550–1700." In *Private Domain, Public Inquiry: Families and Life-styles in the Netherlands and Europe, 1550 to Present*, edited by Anton Schuurman and Pieter Spierenburg, 39–60. Hilversum: Verloren.

Heijden, Manon, van der. 1998. *Huwelijk in Holland: Stedelijke rechtspraak en kerkelijke tucht 1550–1700*. Amsterdam: Bakker.

Heijden, Manon, van der. 1999. "Op de grens van spel en overtreding: Een bruiloftsritueel in de 16e en 17e eeuw." *Historisch Tijdschrift Holland* 31 (2): 63–73.

Heijden, Manon, van der. 2000. "Women as Victims of Sexual and Domestic Violence in Seventeenth-Century Holland: Criminal Cases of Rape, Incest, and Maltreatment in Rotterdam and Delft." *Journal of Social History* 33 (3): 623–44. http://dx.doi.org/10.1353/jsh.2000.0017.

Heijden, Manon, van der. 2004. "Punishment versus Reconciliation: Marriage Control in 16th- and 17th-Century Holland." In *Social Control in Europe*, vol. 1, *1500–1800*, edited by Herman Roodenburg and Pieter Spierenburg, 55–77. Columbus: Ohio State University Press.

Heinig, Paul-Joachim. 1997. *Kaiser Friedrich III (1440–1493): Hof, Regierung und Politik*. 3 vols. Cologne: Böhlau.

Heinig, Paul-Joachim. 2006. "Fürstenkonkubinat um 1500 zwischen Usus und Devianz." In *"Wir wollen der Liebe Raum geben": Konkubinate geistlicher und weltlicher Fürsten um 1500*, edited by Andreas Tacke, 11–37. Göttingen Wallstein.

Helbig, Herbert. 1980. *Die Vertrauten 1680–1980: Eine Vereinigung Leipziger Kaufleute*. Stuttgart.

Helmholz, Richard H. 1974. *Marriage Litigation in Medieval England*. Cambridge: Cambridge University Press.

Helmholz, Richard H. 1990. *Roman Canon Law in Reformation England*. Cambridge: Cambridge University Press. http://dx.doi.org/10.1017/CBO9780511522574.

Helmholz, Richard H. 1998. "Harboring Sexual Offenders: Ecclesiastical Courts and Controlling Misbehavior." *Journal of British Studies* 37 (3): 258–68. http://dx.doi.org/10.1086/386163.

Helmholz, Richard H. 2004. *Oxford History of the Laws of England: The Canon Law and Ecclesiastical Jurisdiction from 597 to the 1640s*. Oxford: Oxford University Press.

Helmholz, Richard H. 2007. "Marriage Contracts in Medieval England." In Reynolds and Witte 2007, 260–86. http://dx.doi.org/10.1017/CBO9780511511769.008.

Hemmer, Ragnar. 1954. *Suomen oikeushistorian oppikirja II: Perheoikeuden, perintöoikeuden ja testamenttioikeuden historia*. Hyvinkää: Akateeminen kirjakauppa.

Henderson, John, and Richard Wall, eds. 2004. *Poor Women and Children in the European Past*. London: Routledge.

Henze, Barbara. 1999. "Kontinuität und Wandel des Eheverständnisses im Gefolge von Reformation und Katholischer Reform." In Conrad 1999a, 129–51.

Hering, Robert. 1932. "Das Elternhaus Goethes und das Leben in der Familie." In *Die Stadt Goethes: Frankfurt am Main im 18. Jahrhundert*, edited by Heinrich Voelcker, 363–446. Frankfurt am Main: Blazek & Bergmann.

Herrmann, Ulrich. 2005. "Familie, Kindheit, Jugend." In *Handbuch der deutschen Bildungsgeschichte*, vol. 2, edited by Notker Hammerstein and Ulrich Herrmann, 67–96. Munich: Beck.

Hess, Ursula. 1988. "Lateinischer Dialog und gelehrte Partnerschaft: Frauen als humanistische Leitbilder in Deutschland (1500–1550)." In *Deutsche Literatur von Frauen*, vol. 1, edited by Gisela Brinker-Gabler, 113–48. Munich: Beck.

Hibbard, Caroline M. 2004. "Caroline Henrietta Maria (1609–1669)." In *Oxford Dictionary of National Biography*, edited by H.C.G. Matthew and Brian Harrison. Oxford: Oxford University Press.

Hildesheimer, Françoise. 2004. *Richelieu*. Paris: Flammarion.

Hill, Christopher. 1956. *Economic Problems of the Church: From Archbishop Whitgift to the Long Parliament*. Oxford: Clarendon Press.

Hintze, Otto. 1892. *Die Preußische Seidenindustrie im 18. Jahrhundert und ihre Begründung durch Friedrich den Großen*, vol. 3. Acta Borussica V:IX. Berlin: Parey.

Hoffmann, Gabriele. 1984. *Constantia von Cosel und August der Starke: Die Geschichte einer Mätresse*. Bergisch-Gladbach, Germany: G. Lubbe.

Hoffmann, Barbara. 1996. *Radikalpietismus um 1700: Der Streit um das Recht auf eine neue Gesellschaft*. Geschichte und Geschlechter 15. Frankfurt am Main and New York: Campus.

Holzem, Andreas. 2000. *Religion und Lebensform: Katholische Konfessionalisierung im Sendgericht des Fürstentums Münster 1570–1800*. Forschungen zur Regionalgeschichte 33. Paderborn: F. Schöningh.

Hooper, Wilfrid. 1910. "The Court of Faculties." *English Historical Review* 25 (C): 670–86. http://dx.doi.org/10.1093/ehr/XXV.C.670.

Houlbrooke, Ralph. 1979. *Church Courts and the People During the English Reformation: 1520–1570*. Oxford: Oxford University Press.

Hufschmidt, Anke. 2000. "Ilse von Saldern (1539–1607)." In Merkel and Wunder 2000, 49–63.

Hufschmidt, Anke. 2001. *Adelige Frauen im Weserraum zwischen 1570 und 1700: Status, Rollen, Lebenspraxis*. Münster: Veröffentlichungen der Historischen Kommission für Westfalen 22, A 15.

Hufschmidt, Anke. 2004. "'Den Krieg im Braut-Bette schlichten': Zu konfessionsverschiedenen Ehen in fürstlichen Familien der Frühen Neuzeit." In *Lesarten der Geschichte: Ländliche Ordnungen und Geschlechterverhältnisse*, edited by Jens Flemming, Pauline Puppel, Werner Troßbach, Christina Vanja, and Ortrud Wörner-Heil. Kasseler Semesterbücher, Studia Cassellana 14, 333–55. Kassel: Kassel University Press.

Hull, Felix, ed. 1958. *Guide to the Kent County Archives Office*. Maidstone: Kent County Council.

Hull, Isabel V. 1996. *Sexuality, State, and Civil Society in Germany, 1700–1815*. Ithaca, NY, and London: Cornell University Press.

Hunecke, Volker. 1987. *Die Findelkinder von Mailand: Kindaussetzung und aussetzende Eltern vom 17. bis zum 19. Jahrhundert*. Stuttgart: Klett-Cotta.

Hunt, Lynn. 2007. *Inventing Human Rights: A History*. New York and London: Norton & Company.

Ingendahl, Gesa. 2006. *Witwen in der Frühen Neuzeit: Eine kulturhistorische Studie*. Geschichte und Geschlechter 54. Frankfurt am Main and New York: Campus.

Ingram, Martin. 1987. *Church Courts, Sex, and Marriage in England, 1570–1640*. Cambridge: Cambridge University Press.

Ingram, Martin. 2014. "Church Courts in Tudor England (1485–1603): Continuity, Changes, Transformations." In Beaulande-Barraud and Charageat 2014, 91–105.

Israël, Jonathan. 1995. *The Dutch Republic: Its Rise, Greatness, and Fall 1477–1806*. Oxford: Clarendon Press.

Jancke, Gabriele. 2002. *Autobiographie als soziale Praxis: Beziehungskonzepte in Selbstzeugnissen des 15. und 16. Jahrhunderts im deutschsprachigen Raum*. Selbstzeugnisse der Neuzeit 10. Cologne: Böhlau.

Jedin, Hubert. 1951–75. *Geschichte des Konzils von Trient*. 4 vols. Freiburg: Herder.

Jedin, Hubert. 1973–81. *Storia del Concilio di Trento*. 4 vols. Brescia: Morcelliana.

Jedin, Hubert, and Klaus Reinhardt. 1985. *Il matrimonio: Una ricerca storica e teologica*. Brescia: Morcelliana.

Jemolo, Arturo Carlo. 1914. *Stato e Chiesa negli scrittori politici italiani del Seicento e del Settecento*. Turin: Bocca.

Kaplan, Benjamin J. 2005. "The Practice and Peril of Mixed Marriages in the Dutch Golden Age." In *Piety and Family in Early Modern Europe: Essays in Honour of Steven Ozment*, edited by Benjamin J. Kaplan and Marc R. Forster, 115–33. Aldershot, UK: Ashgate.

Kaplan, Benjamin J. 2007. *Divided by Faith: Religious Conflict and the Practice of Toleration in Early Modern Europe*. Cambridge, MA: Harvard University Press. http://dx.doi.org/10.4159/9780674039308.

Kaplan, Benjamin J. 2009. "Intimate Negotiations: Husbands and Wives of Opposing Faiths in Eighteenth-Century Holland." In *Living with Religious Diversity in Early Modern Europe*, edited by C. Scott Dixon, Dagmar Freist, and Mark Greengrass, 225–48. Farnham, UK: Ashgate.

Kaplan, Benjamin J. 2014. *Cunegonde's Kidnapping: A Story of Religious Conflict in the Age of Enlightenment*. New Haven, CT, and London: Yale University Press.

Karant-Nunn, Susan C. 1997. *The Reformation of Ritual: An Interpretation of Early Modern Germany*. London: Routledge.

Kartschoke, Erika, ed. 1996. *Repertorium deutschsprachiger Ehelehren der Frühen Neuzeit*, vol. 1. Berlin: Akademie Verlag.

Kertzer, David I., and Marzio Barbagli, eds. 2001. *The History of the European Family*, vol. 1, *Family Life in Early Modern Times 1500–1789*. New Haven, CT, and London: Yale University Press.

Kingdon, Robert M. 1972. "The Control of Morals in Calvin's Geneva." In *The Social History of the Reformation*, edited by Lawrence P. Buck and Jonathan W. Zophy, 3–16. Columbus: Ohio State University Press.

Klapisch-Zuber, Christiane. 1979. "Zacharie, ou le père évincé: Les rites nuptiaux toscans entre Giotto et le concile de Trente." *Annales E.S.C.* 34 (6): 1216–43.

Klapisch-Zuber, Christiane. 1985a. "Zacharias, or the Ousted Father: Nuptial Rites in Tuscany Between Giotto and the Council of Trent." In *Women, Family, and Ritual in Renaissance Italy*, by Christiane Klapisch-Zuber, 178–212. Chicago: University of Chicago Press.

Klapisch-Zuber, Christiane. 1985b. "The 'Mattinata' in Medieval Italy." In *Women, Family, and Ritual in Renaissance Italy*, by Christiane Klapisch-Zuber, 261–82. Chicago: University of Chicago Press.

Kluge, Dietrich. 1977. "Die 'Kirchenbuße' als staatliches Zuchtmittel im 15.–18. Jahrhundert." *Jahrbuch für westfälische Kirchengeschichte* 70: 51–62.

Klusmeyer, Douglas Benjamin. 1989. "Between Church and State: Prussian Marriage Law from the German Enlightenment through the Foundation of the Second Empire." PhD diss., Stanford University, Palo Alto, CA.

Knoop, Mathilde. 1964. *Kurfürstin Sophie von Hannover*. Hildesheim: A. Lax.

Koch, Elisabeth. 1991. *Maior dignitas est in sexu virili: Das weibliche Geschlecht im Normensystem des 16. Jahrhunderts*. Frankfurt am Main: V. Klostermann.

Köbler, Gerhard. 1984. "Familienrecht in der spätmittelalterlichen Stadt." In Haverkamp 1984, 136–60.

Kohl, Thomas. 1985. *Familie und soziale Schichtung: Zur historischen Demographie Triers 1730–1860*. Stuttgart: Klett-Cotta.

Köhler, Walther. 1932. *Zürcher Ehegericht und Genfer Konsistorium*. Vol. 1. Leipzig: M. Heinsius Nachfolger.

Köhler, Walther. 1942. *Zürcher Ehegericht und Genfer Konsistorium*. Vol. 2. Leipzig: M. Heinsius Nachfolger.

Kopitzsch, Franklin. 1982. *Grundzüge einer Sozialgeschichte der Aufklärung in Hamburg und Altona*. Beiträge zur Geschichte Hamburgs 21. Hamburg: Christians.

Korpiola, Mia. 2005. "Marrying Off Sons and Daughters: Attitudes to the Consent of Parents and Guardians in Early Modern Sweden." In *Less Favored – More Favored: Proceedings from a Conference on Gender in European Legal History, 12th–19th Centuries, September 2004*, edited by Grethe Jacobsen et al. Copenhagen: The Royal Library.

Korpiola, Mia. 2006. "Lutheran Marriage Norms in Action: The Example of Post-Reformation Sweden, 1520–1600." In *Lutheran Reformation and the Law*, edited by Virpi Mäkinen, 131–69. Leiden: Brill.

Korpiola, Mia. 2007. "'The Fall and Restoration of Elin Tönnesdotter': Land, Noble Property Strategies, and the Law in Early Seventeenth-Century Sweden." In *The Trouble with Ribs: Women, Men and Gender in Early Modern Europe*, edited by Anu Korhonen and Kate J.P. Lowe, 153–79. COLLeGIUM 2. Available online (accessed 19 December 2014): http://www.helsinki.fi/collegium/e-series/volumes/volume_2/index.htm.

Korpiola, Mia. 2009. *Between Betrothal and Bedding: Marriage Formation in Sweden, 1200–1600*. Leiden: Brill.

Korpiola, Mia. 2011. "Kerstin Oxenstierna's Lost Maidenhead: Honour, Sin, and Matrimonial Law in Late Sixteenth-Century Sweden." In *Inter amicos: Liber amicorum Monique Vleeschouwers-van Melkebeek*, edited by Michiel Decaluwe, Véronique Lambert, and Dirk Heirbaut, 243–68. Iuris scripta historica 26. Brussels: Koninklijke Vlaamse Academie van België voor Wetenschappen en Kunsten.

Korpiola, Mia. 2012. "The Deathbed Marriage of Karl Knutsson Bonde: Legitimization by Subsequent Marriage, Property, and Family Strategies in Late Medieval Sweden." *Tijdschrift voor Rechtsgeschiedenis* 80 (1–2): 129–55. http://dx.doi.org/10.1163/157181912X626948.

Korpiola, Mia. 2014. "Lutheran Marriage Law in Sixteenth- and Early Seventeenth-Century Sweden: Authorities and Sources of Law." In *Law and Religion: The Legal Teachings of the Catholic and Protestant Reformations*, edited by Wim Decock, Jordan J. Ballor, Michael Germann, and Laurent Waelkens, 107–32. Refo500 Academic Studies 20. Göttingen: Vandenhoeck and Ruprecht.

Koselleck, Reinhart. 1975. *Preußen zwischen Reform und Revolution: Allgemeines Landrecht, Verwaltung und soziale Bewegung von 1791 bis 1848*. 2nd ed. Industrielle Welt. Stuttgart: Klett.

Kruse, Britta-Juliane. 2007. *Witwen: Kulturgeschichte eines Standes in Spätmittelalter und Früher Neuzeit*. Berlin: De Gruyter.

Labouvie, Eva. 2000. "Geistliche Konkubinate auf dem Land: Zum Wandel von Ökonomie, Spiritualität und religiöse Vermittlung." *Geschichte und Gesellschaft* 26: 105–27.

Labrousse, Elisabeth. 1985. "Calvinism in France, 1598–1685." In *International Calvinism 1541–1715*, edited by Menna Prestwich, 285–314. Oxford: Clarendon Press.

Lacey, Thomas Alexander. 1912. *Marriage in Church and State*. London: R. Scott.

Lahtinen, Anu. 2011. "The Marriage Process in the Light of Family Correspondence: Swedish Evidence in a Comparative Perspective." In *Regional Variations in Matrimonial Law and Custom in Europe 1150–1600*, edited by Mia Korpiola, 251–73. Leiden: Brill. http://dx.doi.org/10.1163/9789004211438_012.

Lang, Markus. 2004. *Das Eheverbot wegen Glaubensverschiedenheit: Die Entwiklung von den jüdisch-alttestamentlichen Rechtsgrundlage bis in das Zweite Deutsche Kaiserreich*. Münster: Lit.

Langer-Ostrawsky, Gertrude, and Margareth Lanzinger. 2005. "More Favored – Less Favored? Women and Men in Different Marital Property Right

Systems: A Comparative Study of Marital Property Rights in the Habsburg Empire During the 18th Century." In *Less Favored – More Favored: Proceedings from a Conference on Gender in European Legal History, 12th–19th Centuries, September 2004*, edited by Grethe Jacobsen, Helle Vogt, Inger Dübeck, and Heide Wunder, 4 A. Copenhagen.

Lanzinger, Margareth, Gunda Barth-Scalmani, Ellinor Forster, and Gertrude Langer-Ostrawsky. 2010. *Aushandeln von Ehe: Heiratsverträge der Neuzeit im europäischen Vergleich*. Vienna: Böhlau. http://dx.doi.org/10.7788/boehlau.9783412212940.

La Rocca, Chiara. 2009. *Tra moglie e marito: Matrimoni e separazioni nel Settecento a Livorno*. Bologna: Il Mulino.

Le Bras, Gabriel. 1927. "Mariage." In *DTC*, IX, 2, 2123–317 (see *DTC* in Works of reference).

Lefebvre-Teillard, Anne. 1973. *Recherches sur les officialités à la veille du Concile de Trente*. Paris: Librairie générale de droit et de jurisprudence.

Lefebvre-Teillard, Anne. 1976. "L'enfant naturel dans l'ancien droit français." *Recueil de la Société Jean Bodin pour l'histoire comparative des institutions*, 36 (2): 251–69; reprinted in Lefebvre-Teillard 2008, 259–73.

Lefebvre-Teillard, Anne. 1978. "Ad matrimonium contrahere compellitur." *Revue de droit canonique* 28: 210–17.

Lefebvre-Teillard, Anne. 1990. *Le nom: Droit et histoire*. Paris: PUF.

Lefebvre-Teillard, Anne. 1996. *Introduction historique au droit des personnes et de la famille*. Paris: PUF.

Lefebvre-Teillard, Anne. 1997. "'Mulieri asserenti se ex operibus alicujus praegnantem an credi debeat etiamsi hoc affirmet juramento?' Les origines d'une célèbre 'decisio' de N. Boerius." In *Proceedings of the IX Congress of Medieval Canon Law* (Munich, 1992), edited by Peter Landau and Jörg Müller, 575–90. Vatican City: Biblioteca Apostolica Vaticana; reprinted in Lefebvre-Teillard 2008, 221–39.

Lefebvre-Teillard, Anne. 2002. "L'effet rétroactif de la légitimation en droit canonique." In *Le temps et le droit*, Acts of the Journées Internationales d'Histoire du Droit (Nice, 25–8 Mai 2000), 25–35. Nice; reprinted in Lefebvre-Teillard 2008, 329–41.

Lefebvre-Teillard, Anne. 2003. "Naissance du droit français: L'apport de la jurisprudence des arrêts." *Droits: Revue française de théorie, de philosophie et de culture juridiques* 38: 69–82.

Lefebvre-Teillard, Anne. 2008. *Autour de l'enfant: Du droit canonique et romain médiéval au Code Civil de 1804*. Leiden and Boston: Brill. http://dx.doi.org/10.1163/ej.9789004169371.i-381.

Lempiäinen, Pentti. 1965. *Kastekäytäntö Suomen kirkossa 1500- ja 1600-luvulla*. SKHS:n toimituksia 60. Helsinki: SKHS.

Lennartsson, Malin. 1999. *I säng och säte: Relationer mellan kvinnor och män i 1600-talets Småland*. Bibliotheca historica lundensis 92. Lund: Lund University Press.

Lenz, Rudolf. 1986. "'Ehestand, Wehestand, Süßbitter Standt'? Betrachtung zur Familie der Frühen Neuzeit." *Archiv für Kulturgeschichte* 68: 371–405.

Lischka, Marion. 2006. *Liebe als Ritual: Eheanbahnung und Brautwerbung in der frühneuzeitlichen Grafschaft Lippe*. Paderborn: Schöningh.

Lizarraga Artola, Alejandro. 1991. "La praxis acerca del matrimonio en la diócesis de Pamplona antes del Concilio de Trento (1501–1560)." *Cuadernos doctorales* 9: 331–92.

Loi, Salvatore. 2006. *Inquisizione, sessualità e matrimonio: Sardegna, secoli XVI–XVII*. Cagliari: AM&D.

Lombardi, Daniela. 1988. *Povertà maschile, povertà femminile: L'ospedale dei Mendicanti nella Firenze dei Medici*. Bologna: Il Mulino.

Lombardi, Daniela. 2001. *Matrimoni di antico regime*. Bologna: Il Mulino.

Lombardi, Daniela. 2008. *Storia del matrimonio: Dal Medioevo a oggi*. Bologna: Il Mulino.

Lombardi, Daniela. 2016. "Women's Reputation and Marriage Disputes in Protestant and Catholic Europe, 1500–1800." In *The History of Families and Households: Comparative European Dimensions*, edited by Silvia Sovic, Pat Thane, and Pier Paolo Viazzo, 119–41. Leiden: Brill.

Lozano Navarro, Julián José. 2009. "Beatrice Maria d'Este: Il rapporto tra una sovrana del Seicento e la Compagnia di Gesù." In *I linguaggi del potere nell'età barocca*, vol. 2, *Donne e sfera pubblica*, edited by Francesca Cantù, 125–41. Rome: Viella.

Lübcke, David. Forthcoming. "Making Marriages Mixed: Religious Pluralization, Ritual, and the Formation of Intra-Christian Marriage Barriers in Late Sixteenth- and Early Seventeenth-Century Germany." In Cristellon, forthcoming.

Luperini, Sara. 2001. "La promessa sotto accusa (Pisa 1584)." In Seidel Menchi and Quaglioni 2001, 363–94.

Luperini, Sara. 2004a. "Il gioco dello scandalo: Concubinato, tribunali e comunità nella diocesi di Pisa (1597)." In Seidel Menchi and Quaglioni 2004, 383–415.

Luperini, Sara. 2004b. "Chi fugge e chi resta: La separazione di fatto fra tribunale ecclesiastico e relazioni di vicinato (Pisa, 1560–1660)." *Genesis: Rivista della Società Italiana delle Storiche* 3: 115–45.

Luria, Keith P. 2005. *Sacred Boundaries: Religious Coexistence and Conflict in Early Modern France*. Washington, D.C.: Catholic University of America Press.

Lutz, Alexandra. 2006. *Ehepaare vor Gericht: Konflikte und Lebenswelten in der Frühen Neuzeit*. Geschichte und Geschlechter 51. Frankfurt am Main and New York: Campus.

Maccarrone, Michele. 1995. "Sacramentalità e indissolubilità del matrimonio nella dottrina di Innocenzo III." In *Nuovi studi su Innocenzo III*, edited by Roberto Lambertini, 47–110. Rome: Istituto storico italiano per il Medio Evo.

Maier, Heidi-Melanie, ed. 2004. *"Gestern Abend schlief er auf dem Sofa ein": Alltägliches Leben um 1800*. Quellen zur Geschichte Thüringens 21. Erfurt: Landeszentrale für politische Bildung Thüringen.

Maitland, Frederic William. 1898. *Roman Canon Law in the Church of England*. London: Methuen.

Makower, Felix. 1895. *The Constitutional History and Constitution of the Church of England*. London: S. Sonnenschein & Co.

Manetsch, Scott. 2006. "Pastoral Care East of Eden: The Consistory of Geneva, 1568–1582." *Church History* 75 (2): 274–313. http://dx.doi.org/10.1017/S0009640700111321.

Manetsch, Scott. 2010. "Holy Terror or Pastoral Care? Church Discipline in Calvin's Geneva, 1542–1596." In *Calvin – Saint or Sinner?* ed. Herman J. Selderhuis, 283–306. Tübingen: Mohr.

Manning, Roger. 1969. *Religion and Society in Elizabethan Sussex*. Leicester: Leicester University Press.

Marongiu, Antonio. 1963. "La forma religiosa del matrimonio nel diritto bizantino, normanno e svevo." In *Raccolta di scritti in onore di Arturo Carlo Jemolo*, 2 vols., 1:851–77. Milan: Giuffrè.

Marseille, Gustav. 1898. "Studien zur kirchlichen Politik des Pfalzgrafen Wolfgang Wilhelm von Neuburg." *Beiträge zur Geschichte des Niederrheins* 13: 1–111.

Martens, Wolfgang. 1968. *Die Botschaft der Tugend: Die Aufklärung im Spiegel der deutschen moralischen Wochenschriften*. Zeitschrift für Historische Forschung, Beiheft 28. Stuttgart: Metzler.

Martin, Victor. 1975. *Le Gallicanisme et la réforme catholique*. 1919. Geneva: Slatkine-Megariotis Reprints.

Martin, Odile. 1986. *La Conversion protestante à Lyon (1659–1687)*. Geneva: Droz.

Martines, Lauro. 1974. "A Way of Looking at Women in Renaissance Florence." *Journal of Medieval and Renaissance Studies* 4: 15–28.

Maschke, Erich. 1980. *Die Familie in der deutschen Stadt des späten Mittelalters* (Sitzungsberichte der Heidelberger Akademie der Wissenschaften, Philosophisch-historische Klasse)." Abhandlung 4. Heidelberg: Winter.

Matheeussen, Constant, and Charles Fantazzi, eds. 2002. *Juan Luis Vives: De subventione pauperum sive de humanis necessitatibus*. Leiden and Boston: Brill.

Mazo Karras, Ruth. 2012. *Unmarriages: Women, Men, and Sexual Unions in the Middle Ages*. Philadelphia: University of Pennsylvania Press.

McCarthy, Conor. 2004. *Marriage in Medieval England: Law, Literature, and Practice*. Woodbridge, UK: Boydell.

McDougall, Sara. 2012. *Bigamy and Christian Identity in Late Medieval Champagne*. Philadelphia: University of Pennsylvania Press.

McIntosh, Marjorie Keniston. 1998. *Controlling Misbehavior in England, 1370–1600*. Cambridge: Cambridge University Press.

McSheffrey, Shannon. 2006. *Marriage, Sex, and Civic Culture in Late Medieval London*. Philadelphia: University of Pennsylvania Press.

Meckseper, Cord. 1985. *Stadt im Wandel: Kunst und Kultur des Bürgertums in Norddeutschland 1150–1650,* Ausstellungskatalog I. Stuttgart: Bad Cannstatt.

Medick, Hans. 1980. "Spinnstuben auf dem Dorf: Jugendliche Sexualkultur und ländlicher Feierabendbrauch in der ländlichen Gesellschaft der frühen Neuzeit." In *Sozialgeschichte der Freizeit*, edited by Gerhard Huck, 19–48. Wuppertal: Hammer.

Medick, Hans, and David Warren Sabean, eds. 1984. *Interest and Emotion: Essays on the Study of Family and Kinship*. Cambridge and New York: Cambridge University Press.

Meise, Helga. 1988. "Der Frauenroman: Erprobungen der 'Weiblichkeit.'" In *Deutsche Literatur von Frauen*, edited by Gisela Brinker-Gabler, 434–52. Munich: Beck.

Merkel, Kerstin, and Heide Wunder, eds. 2000. *Deutsche Frauen der Frühen Neuzeit: Dichterinnen, Malerinnen, Mäzeninnen*. Darmstadt: WBG.

Michalik, Kerstin. 2006. "The Development of the Discourse on Infanticide in the Late Eighteenth Century and the New Legal Standardization of the Offense in the Nineteenth Century." In *Gender in Transition: Discourse and Practice in German-Speaking Europe, 1750–1830,* edited by Ulrike Gleixner and Marion W. Gray, 51–71. Ann Arbor: University of Michigan Press.

Mikat, Paul. 1988. *Die Polygamiefrage in der Frühen Neuzeit*. Rheinisch-Westfälische Akademie der Wissenschaften, Geisteswissenschaften, Vorträge G 294. Opladen: Westdeutscher Verlag.

Mitterauer, Michael. 1983. *Ledige Mütter: Zur Geschichte illegitimer Geburten in Europa*. Munich: Beck.

Moeller, Bernd. 1987. "Die Brautwerbung Martin Bucers für Wolfgang Capito: Zur Sozialgeschichte des evangelischen Pfarrerstandes." In *Philologie als Kulturwissenschaft: Studien zur Literatur und Geschichte des Mittelalters: Festschrift für K. Stackmann zum 65. Geburtstag*, edited by L. Grenzmann, 306–25. Göttingen: Vandenhoeck and Ruprecht.

Möhle, Sylvia. 1997. *Ehekonflikte und sozialer Wandel: Göttingen 1740–1840.* Geschichte und Geschlechter 18. Frankfurt am Main and New York: Campus.

Molho, Anthony. 1994. *Marriage Alliance in Late Medieval Florence.* Cambridge, MA: Harvard University Press.

Monter, E. William. 1976. "The Consistory of Geneva, 1559–1569." *Bibliothèque d'Humanisme et Renaissance* 38: 467–84.

Morant Deusa, Isabel. 1991. "Familia, amor y matrimonio: Un ensayo sobre historiografía." In *Los estudios sobre la mujer: De la investigación a la docencia,* edited by Cristina Bernis et al., 573–95. Madrid: Instituto Universitario de Estudios de la Mujer.

Morel, Henri. 1979. "Le mariage clandestin de Jeanne de Piennes et de François de Montmorency." In *Mélanges offerts à Jean Dauvillier,* edited by Université des sciences sociales, 555–76. Toulouse: Centre d'histoire juridique méridionale.

Moscarda, Dea. 2001. "Il cardinale Giovanni Battista De Luca giudice rotale e la causa matrimoniale tra Michele De Vaez e Giovanna Maria De Sciart (Napoli 1650)." In Seidel Menchi and Quaglioni 2001, 415–29.

Muir, Edward, and Guido Ruggiero, eds. 1990. *Sex and Gender in Historical Perspective: Selections from Quaderni Storici.* Baltimore, MD: Johns Hopkins University Press.

Müller, Daniela. 1994. "*Vir caput mulieris*: Zur Stellung der Frau im Kirchenrecht unter besonderer Berücksichtigung des 12. und 13. Jahrhunderts." In *Vom mittelalterlichen Recht zur neuzeitlichen Rechtswissenschaft,* Bedingungen, Wege und Probleme der europäischen Rechtsgeschichte: Rechts- und staatswissenschaftliche Veröffentlichungen der Görres-Gesellschaft Neue Reihe 22, edited by Norbert Brieskorn, Paul Mikat, Daniela Müller, and Dietmar Willoweit, 224–46. Paderborn: Schöningh.

Nalle, Sara T. 1992. *God in La Mancha: Religious Reform and the People of Cuenca, 1500–1650.* Baltimore, MD: Johns Hopkins University Press.

Nolte, Cordula. 2000. "Bey eytler finster in einem weichen pet geschrieben: Eigenhändige Briefe in der Familienkorrespondenz der Markgrafen von Brandenburg (1470–1530)." In *Adelige Welt und familiäre Beziehung: Aspekte der "privaten Welt" des Adels in böhmischen, polnischen und deutschen Beispielen vom 14. bis zum 16. Jahrhundert,* edited by Heinz-Dieter Heimann, 177–202. Potsdam: Verlag für Berlin-Brandenburg.

Noodt, Birgit. 2000. *Religion und Familie in der Hansestadt Lübeck anhand der Bürgertestamente des 14. Jahrhunderts.* Veröffentlichungen zur Geschichte der Hansestadt Lübeck B 33. Lübeck: Schmidt-Römhild.

Nylander, Ivar. 1961. *Studier rörande den svenska äktenskapsrättens historia.* Studia juridica Stockholmiensia 12. Stockholm: Acta Universitatis Stockholmiensis.

O'Hara, Diana. 2000. *Courtship and Constraint: Rethinking the Making of Marriage in Tudor England*. Manchester: Manchester University Press.

Oïffer-Bomsel, Alicia. 2014. "Les officialités andalouses et leur activité judiciaire en matière matrimoniale à l'époque moderne (XVIe–XVIIe siècles)." In Beaulande-Barraud and Charageat 2014, 259–80.

Orlando, Ermanno. 2010. *Sposarsi nel Medioevo: Percorsi coniugali tra Venezia, mare e continente*. Rome: Viella.

Oßwald-Bargende, Sybille. 2000. *Die Mätresse, der Fürst und die Macht: Christina Wilhelmina von Grävenitz und die höfische Gesellschaft*. Frankfurt am Main: Campus.

Ourliac, Paul, and Jehan de Malafosse. 1961–8. *Histoire du droit privé*. 3 vols. Paris: Presses Universitaires de France.

Outhwaite, R.B. 1995. *Clandestine Marriage in England, 1500–1850*. London: Hambledon Press.

Outhwaite, R.B. 2006. *The Rise and Fall of the English Ecclesiastical Courts, 1500–1860*. Cambridge: Cambridge University Press.

Ozment, Steven. 1983. *When Fathers Ruled: Family Life in Reformation Europe*. Cambridge, MA: Harvard University Press.

Panke-Kochinke, Birgit. 1993. *Göttinger Professorenfamilien: Strukturmerkmale weiblichen Lebenszusammenhangs im 18. und 19. Jahrhundert*. Pfaffenweiler: Centaurus.

Panter-Brick, Catherine, and Malcolm T. Smith, eds. 2000. *Abandoned Children*. Cambridge: Cambridge University Press.

Paolin, Giovanna. 1984. "Monache e donne nel Friuli del Cinquecento." In *Società e cultura del Cinquecento nel Friuli occidentale*, edited by Andrea Del Col, 201–28. Pordenone: Edizioni della Provincia di Pordenone.

Paolucci, Antonio. 2003. "La 'donna nuda' e altre storie sulla commessa della *Venere di Urbino*." In *Venere svelata: La Venere di Urbino di Tiziano*, edited by Omar Calabrese, 59–73. Cisinello Balsamo, Milan: Silvana Editoriale.

Papagna, Elena. 2006. "Storie comuni di sposi promessi: I processi della curia arcivescovile di Trani nel tardo Settecento." In Seidel Menchi and Quaglioni 2006, 459–95.

Parish, Helen. 2000. *Clerical Marriage and the English Reformation*. Aldershot, UK: Ashgate.

Parker, Stephen. 1990. *Informal Marriage, Cohabitation, and the Law 1750–1989*. New York: St Martin's Press.

Parker, Charles H. 2011. *Faith on the Margins: Catholics and Catholicism in the Dutch Golden Age*. Cambridge, MA: Harvard University Press.

Passeron, Jean-Claude, and Jacques Revel, eds. 2005. *Penser par cas*. Paris: Éditions de l'École des Hautes Études en Sciences Sociales.

Pedersen, Frederik. 2000. *Marriage Disputes in Medieval England*. London and Rio Grande, OH: Hambledon.

Pelaja, Margherita. 1994. *Matrimonio e sessualità a Roma nell'Ottocento*. Rome and Bari: Laterza.

Petersson, Hans. 1973. *Morgongåvoinstitutet i Sverige under tiden fram till omkring 1734 års lag*. Rättshistoriskt bibliotek 21. Lund: Nordiska Bokhandeln.

Phan, Marie-Claude. 1975. "Les déclarations de grossesse en France (XVIe–XVIIIe siècles): Essai institutionnel." *Revue d'Histoire Moderne et Contemporaine* 22: 61–88.

Phan, Marie-Claude. 1986. *Les amours illégitimes: Histoires de séduction en Languedoc (1676–1786)*. Paris: Editions du Centre national de la recherche scientifique.

Philips, Roderick. 1988. *Putting Asunder: A History of Divorce in Western Society*. Cambridge: Cambridge University Press.

Pia, E. Claudio. 2014. *La giustizia del vescovo: Società, economia e chiesa cittadina ad Asti tra XIII e XIV secolo*. Rome: Viella.

Pietilä, Antti J. 1903–4. "Kirkon tuomiovalta kihlaus- ja avioliittoasioissa Ruotsissa ja Suomessa uskonpuhdistuksesta 1686:n kirkkolakiin saakka." In *Suomen kirkkohistoriallisen seuran pöytäkirjat liitteineen* vol. 4: *1903–1904*, 77–161. Porvoo: WSOY.

Pissarello, Giulia. 1979. "Note sulla biblioteca jacksoniana." *Quaderni ETS* 6. Pisa: ETS.

Pittion, Jean Paul. 1983. "L'affaire Paulet (Montpellier 1680–83) et les conversions forcées d'enfants." In *La conversion au XVIIe siècle: Actes du XIIe Colloque de Marseille (Janvier 1982)*, 209–29. Marseille.

Plebani, Tiziana. 2012. *Un secolo di sentimenti: Amori e conflitti generazionali nella Venezia del Settecento*. Venice: Istituto veneto di scienze, lettere ed arti.

Plöchl, Willibald M. 1959. *Geschichte des Kirchenrechts*, vol. 3. Vienna: Herold.

Plummer, Marjorie Elizabeth. 2012. *From Priest's Whore to Pastor's Wife: Clerical Marriage and the Process of Reform in the Early German Reformation*. Farnham, UK: Ashgate.

Poian, Marina. 2006. "I processi matrimoniali dell'Archivio Vescovile di Feltre (secoli XVI–XVIII)." In Seidel Menchi and Quaglioni 2006, 141–61.

Pollock, Frederick, and Frederic William Maitland. 1898 (rev. ed. 1968). *The History of English Law Before the Time of Edward I*. 2 vols. Cambridge: Cambridge University Press.

Pommeray, Léon. 1933. *L'officialité archidiaconale de Paris aux XVe et XVIe siècles: Sa composition et sa compétence criminelle*. Paris: Libr. du Recueil Sirey.

Poos, Lawrence R., ed. 2001. *Lower Ecclesiastical Jurisdiction in Late-Medieval England: The Courts of the Dean and Chapter of Lincoln, 1336–1349, and the Deanery of Wisbech, 1458–1484*. Oxford: Oxford University Press.

Poudret, Jean-François. 1992. "Procès matrimoniaux à la fin du XIVe siècle selon le plus ancien registre de l'officialité de Lausanne." *Zeitschrift für schweizerische Kirchengeschichte* 86: 7–46.

Price, F. Douglas. 1942. "The Abuses of Excommunication and the Decline of Ecclesiastical Discipline under Queen Elizabeth." *English Historical Review* 57 (225): 106–15. http://dx.doi.org/10.1093/ehr/LVII.CCXXV.106.

Prosperi, Adriano. 1996. *Tribunali della coscienza: Inquisitori, confessori, missionari*. Turin: Einaudi.

Prosperi, Adriano. 2005. *Dare l'anima: Storia di un infanticidio*. Turin: Einaudi.

Prosperi, Laura. 2015. *Nascere sotto il cavolo: Dietetica e procreazione in antico regime*. Milan: Franco Angeli.

Puppel, Pauline. 2003. "Formen von Witwenherrschaft: Landgräfin Anna von Hessen (1485–1525)." In Schattkowsky 2003, 139–61.

Pylkkänen, Anu. 1990. *Puoli vuodetta, lukot ja avaimet: Nainen ja maalaistalous oikeuskäytännön valossa 1660–1710*. Helsinki: Lakimiesliiton Kustannus.

Quéniart, Jean. 1985. *La Révocation de l'Édit de Nantes: Protestants et catholiques en France de 1598 à 1685*. Paris: Desclée de Brouwer.

Rasi, Piero. 1941. "L'applicazione delle norme del Concilio di Trento in materia matrimoniale." In *Studi di storia e diritto in onore di A. Solmi*, 2 vols., 1:235–81. Milan: A. Giuffrè.

Reggiani, Flores. 2014. *Sotto le ali della colomba: Famiglie assistenziali e relazioni di genere a Milano dall'età moderna alla Restaurazione*. Rome: Viella.

Reynolds, Philip L., and John Witte Jr., eds. 2007. *To Have and To Hold: Marrying and Its Documentation in Western Christendom, 400–1600*. Cambridge: Cambridge University Press.

Ritchie, Carson. 1956. *The Ecclesiastical Courts of York*. Arbroath: Harold Press.

Rockwell, William Walker. 1904. *Die Doppelehe des Landgrafen Philipp von Hessen*. Marburg: N.G. Elwert.

Rodes, Robert, Jr. 1991. *Law and Modernization in the Church of England: Charles II to the Welfare State*. Notre Dame, IN: University of Notre Dame Press.

Rodríguez Arango, Crisanto. 1955. "El matrimonio clandestino en la novela cervantina." *Anuario de Historia del Derecho Español* 25: 731–74.

Rodríguez Sánchez, Ángel. 1990. "El poder familiar: La patria potestad en el Antiguo Régimen." *Chronica nova: Revista de historia moderna de la Universidad de Granada* 18: 365–80.

Rogge, Roswitha. 1998. *Zwischen Moral und Handelsgeist: Weibliche Handlungsräume und Geschlechterbeziehungen im Spiegel des hamburgischen Stadtrechts vom 13. bis zum 16. Jahrhundert*. Ius Commune, Sonderhefte 109. Frankfurt am Main: Klostermann.

Romeo, Giovanni. 1998. *Esorcisti, confessori e sessualità femminile nell'Italia della Controriforma*. Florence: Le Lettere.

Romeo, Giovanni. 2008. *Amori proibiti: I concubini tra Chiesa e Inquisizione, Napoli 1563–1656*. Rome and Bari: Laterza.

Roper, Lyndal. 1987. "The 'Common Man,' the 'Common Good,' 'Common Women': Gender and Meaning in the German Reformation Commune." *Social History* 12 (1): 1–21. http://dx.doi.org/10.1080/03071028708567669.

Roper, Lyndal. 1989. *The Holy Household: Women and Morals in Reformation Augsburg*. Oxford: Clarendon Press.

Roper, Lyndal. 1994. *Oedipus and the Devil: Witchcraft, Sexuality, and Religion in Early Modern Europe*. London and New York: Routledge. http://dx.doi.org/10.4324/9780203426296.

Rosa, Mario. 1969. *Riformatori e ribelli nel '700 religioso italiano*. Bari: Dedalo.

Rothe, Arnold. 1978. "Padre y familia en el Siglo de Oro." *Iberoromania* 7: 120–67.

Rougemont, Denis de. 1962. *L'amour et l'Occident*. Paris: Plon.

Rublack, Hans-Christoph. 1977. "Zur Sozialstruktur der protestantischen Minderheit in der geistlichen Residenz Bamberg am Ende des 16. Jahrhunderts." In *Stadtbürgertum und Adel in der Reformation. Studien zur Sozialgeschichte der Reformation in England und Deutschland*, edited by Wolfgang J. Mommsen, 130–48. Stuttgart: Klett-Cotta.

Rublack, Ulinka. 1998. *Magd, Metz' oder Mörderin: Frauen vor frühneuzeitlichen Gerichten*. Frankfurt am Main: Fischer Taschenbuch Verlag.

Rublack, Ulinka. 1999. *The Crimes of Women in Early Modern Germany*. Oxford Studies in Social History. Oxford: Clarendon Press.

Ruggiero, Guido. 1985. *The Boundaries of Eros: Sex Crime and Sexuality in Renaissance Venice*. New York: Oxford University Press.

Sabean, David Warren. 1990. *Property, Production, and Family in Neckarhausen, 1700–1870*. Cambridge: Cambridge University Press.

Safley, Thomas Max. 1984. *Let No Man Put Asunder: The Control of Marriage in the German Southwest: A Comparative Study, 1550–1600*. Kirksville, MO: Sixteenth Century Journal Publishers.

Salonen, Kirsi, and Ludwig Schmugge. 2009. *A Sip from the "Well of Grace": Medieval Texts from the Apostolic Penitentiary*. Washington, DC: Catholic University of America Press.

Sani, Filippo. 2006. "Il Settecento." In *La massoneria a Livorno: Dal Settecento alla Repubblica*, edited by Fulvio Conti, 27–98. Bologna: Il Mulino.

Sarti, Raffaella. 2006. "Nubili e celibi tra scelta e costrizione: I percorsi di Clio (Europa occidentale, secoli XVI–XX)." In *Nubili e celibi tra scelta e costrizione (secoli XVI–XX)*, edited by Margareth Lanzinger and Raffaella Sarti, 145–318. Udine: Forum.

Sauzet, Robert. 1979. *Contre-Réforme et Réforme catholique en Bas-Languedoc: Le diocèse de Nîmes au XVIIe siècle*. Paris: Diffusion Vander-Oyez.

Scaramella, Pierroberto. 2004. "Controllo e repressione ecclesiastica della poligamia a Napoli in età moderna: Dalle cause matrimoniali al crimine di fede (1514–1799)." In Seidel Menchi and Quaglioni 2004, 443–501.

Scharffenorth, Gerta. 1982. "Geist Freunde werden: Die Beziehungen von Mann und Frau bei Luther." In *Den Glauben ins Leben ziehen. Studien zu Luthers Theologie*, edited by Gerta Scharffenorth, 122–202. Munich: Kaiser.

Schattkowsky, Martina, ed. 2003. *Witwenschaft in der Frühen Neuzeit: Fürstliche und adelige Witwen zwischen Fremd- und Selbstbestimmung*. Schriften zur Sächsischen Geschichte und Volkskunde 6. Leipzig: Leipziger Universitätsverlag.

Schild, Maurice E. 1989. "Ehe/Eherecht/Ehescheidung, VII: Reformationszeit." In *Theologische Realenzyklopädie*, vol. 9, 336–46. Berlin: De Gruyter.

Schilling, Heinz. 1989. "Sündenzucht und Frühneuzeitliche Sozialdisziplinierung: Die Calvinistische presbyteriale Kirchenzucht in Emden vom 16. bis 19. Jahrhundert." In *Stände und Gesellschaft im Alten Reich*, edited by Georg Schmidt, 265–302. Stuttgart: Veröffentlichungen des Instituts für Europäische Geschicihte Mainz, 29.

Schilling, Heinz. 1994. "Reform and Supervision of Family Life in Germany and the Netherlands." In *Sin and the Calvinists: Morals Control and the Consistory in the Reformed Tradition*, Sixteenth Century Essays and Studies 32, edited by Raymond A. Mentzer, 199–236. Kirksville, MO: Sixteenth Century Journal Publishers.

Schindler, Norbert. 1996. "Die Hüter der Unordnung: Rituale der Jugendkultur in der Frühen Neuzeit." In *Geschichte der Jugend*, edited by Giovanni Levi and Jean-Claude Schmitt, vol. 1, 319–82. Frankfurt: Fischer.

Schmidt, Heinrich Richard. 1992. *Konfessionalisierung im 16. Jahrhundert*. Enzyklopädie deutscher Geschichte 12. Munich: Oldenbourg.

Schmidt, Heinrich Richard. 1995. *Dorf und Religion: Reformierte Sittenzucht in Berner Landgemeinden der Frühen Neuzeit*. Quellen und Forschungen zur Agrargeschichte 41. Stuttgart: G. Fischer.

Schmidt, Heinrich Richard. 1998. "Hausväter vor Gericht: Der Patriarchalismus als zweischneidiges Schwert." In *Hausväter, Priester, Kastraten: Zur Konstruktion von Männlichkeit in Spätmittelalter und Früher Neuzeit*, edited by Martin Dinges, 213–36. Göttingen: Vandenhoeck and Ruprecht.

Schmidt-Voges, Inken. 2013. "The Ambivalence of Order: Gender and Peace in Domestic Litigation in 18th-Century Germany." In *Gender Difference in European Legal Cultures: Historical Perspectives*, edited by Karin Gottschalk, 71–82. Wiesbaden: Franz Steiner Verlag.

Schmugge, Ludwig. 2008. *Ehen vor Gericht: Paare der Renaissance vor dem Papst.* Berlin: Berlin University (published in English translation as *Marriage on Trial: Late Medieval German Couples at the Papal Court*, translated by Atria Larson, Washington, DC: Catholic University of America Press, 2012).

Schnabel-Schüle, Helga. 1997. *Überwachen und Strafen im Territorialstaat.* Cologne: Böhlau.

Schneider, Susanne. 2000. "Christiana Marina von Ziegler (1695–1760)." In Merkel and Wunder 2000, 139–52.

Schnell, Rüdiger. 2002. *Sexualität und Emotionalität in der vormodernen Ehe.* Cologne: Böhlau.

Schnyder, Albert. 1996. "Lichtstuben im alten Basel: Zu einer von Frauen geprägten Form frühneuzeitlicher Geselligkeit." *Schweizerisches Archiv fur Volkskunde* 92 (1): 1–13.

Schnyder Burghartz, Albert. 1992. *Alltag und Lebensformen auf der Basler Landschaft um 1700: Vorindustrielle, ländliche Kultur und Gesellschaft aus mikrohistorischer Perspektive – Bretzwil und das obere Waldenburger Amt von 1690 bis 1750.* Liestal: Verlag des Kantons Basel-Landschaft.

Schorn-Schütte, Luise. 1991. "'Gefährtin' und 'Mitregentin': Zur Sozialgeschichte der evangelischen Pfarrfrau in der Frühen Neuzeit." In *Wandel der Geschlechterbeziehungen*, edited by Heide Wunder and Christina Vanja, 109–53. Frankfurt am Main: Suhrkamp.

Schreiner, Klaus. 1984. "Laienbildung als Herausforderung für Kirche und Gesellschaft: Religiöse Vorbehalte und soziale Widerstände gegen die Verbreitung von Wissen im späten Mittelalter und in der Reformation." *Zeitschrift fur Historische Forschung* 11: 257–354.

Schröter, Michael. 1984. "Staatsbildung und Triebkontrolle: Zur gesellschaftlichen Regulierung des Sexualverhaltens vom 13. bis 16. Jahrhundert." In *Macht und Zivilisation*, edited by Peter Gleichmann, Johan Goudsblom, and Hermann Korte, Materialien zu Norbert Elisas' Zivilisationstheorie 2, 148–92. Frankfurt am Main: Suhrkamp.

Schröter, Michael. 1991. "Zur Intimisierung der Hochzeitsnacht im 16. Jahrhundert: Eine zivilisationstheoretische Studie." In *Ordnung und Lust: Bilder von Liebe, Ehe und Sexualität in Spätmittelalter und Früher Neuzeit*, edited by Hans-Jürgen Bachorski, 359–414. Trier: Wissenschaftlicher Verlag Trier.

Schuster, Beate. 1995. *Die freien Frauen: Dirnen und Frauenhäuser im 15. und 16. Jahrhundert.* Geschichte und Geschlechter 12. Frankfurt am Main and New York: Campus.

Schuster, Peter. 1992. *Das Frauenhaus: Städtische Bordelle in Deutschland 1350 bis 1600.* Paderborn: Schöningh.

Schwab, Dieter. 1967. *Grundlagen und Gestalt der staatlichen Ehegesetzgebung in der Neuzeit bis zum Beginn des 19. Jahrhunderts*. Bielefeld: Gieseking.

Schwab, Dieter. 1997. "Gleichberechtigung und Familienrecht im 20. Jahrhundert." In Gerhard 1997, 790–827.

Schwerhoff, Gerd. 1991. *Köln im Kreuzverhör: Kriminalität, Herrschaft und Gesellschaft in einer frühneuzeitlichen Stadt*. Bonn: Bouvier.

Seidel, Max. 2003. "Studies of Nuptial Iconography in the Fourteenth Century." In Max Seidel, *Italian Art of the Middle Ages and the Renaissance*, vol. 1: *Painting*, 409–42. Venice: Marsilio.

Seidel Menchi, Silvana. 2001. "Percorsi variegati, percorsi obbligati: Elogio del matrimonio pre-tridentino." In Seidel Menchi and Quaglioni 2001, 17–60.

Seidel Menchi, Silvana. 2004. "Il matrimonio finto: Clero e fedeli post-tridentini fra sperimentazione liturgica e registrazione di stato civile." In Seidel Menchi and Quaglioni 2004, 535–72.

Seidel Menchi, Silvana. 2006. "Cause matrimoniali e iconografia nuziale: Annotazioni in margine a una ricerca d'archivio." In Seidel Menchi and Quaglioni 2006, 663–703.

Seidel Menchi, Silvana. 2009. "Ritratto di famiglia in un interno: I Dandolo di San Moisè (1514–1526)." In *Ritratti: La dimensione individuale nella storia (secoli XV–XX)*, Studi in onore di Anne Jacobson Schutte, edited by Robert A. Pierce and Silvana Seidel Menchi, 99–125. Rome: Edizioni di Storia e Letteratura.

Seidel Menchi, Silvana. 2014. "Notes introductives: Les officialités françaises et italiennes: Comparaisons et contrastes." In Beaulande-Barraud and Charageat 2014, 25–34.

Seidel Menchi, Silvana, and Cecilia Cristellon. 2011. "Words or Gestures? Marriage Rituals before Tribunals in Renaissance Italy: Continuity and Change, 1400–1600." In *Regional Variations in Matrimonial Law and Custom in Europe, 1150–1600*, edited by Mia Korpiola, 275–87. Leiden: Brill.

Seidel Menchi, Silvana, and Diego Quaglioni, eds. 2000. *Coniugi nemici: La separazione in Italia dal XII al XVIII secolo*. Bologna: Il Mulino.

Seidel Menchi, Silvana, and Diego Quaglioni, eds. 2001. *Matrimoni in dubbio: Unioni controverse e nozze clandestine in Italia dal XIV al XVIII secolo*. Bologna: Il Mulino.

Seidel Menchi, Silvana, and Diego Quaglioni, eds. 2004. *Trasgressioni: Seduzione, concubinato, adulterio, bigamia (XIV–XVIII secolo)*. Bologna: Il Mulino.

Seidel Menchi, Silvana, and Diego Quaglioni, eds. 2006. *I tribunali del matrimonio (secoli XV–XVIII)*. Bologna: Il Mulino.

Sellar, W. David H. 1992. "Marriage by Cohabitation with Habit and Repute: Review and Requiem?" In *Comparative and Historical Essays in Scots Law: A*

Tribute to Professor Sir Thomas Smith, Q.C., edited by Carey D.L. Miller and David W. Meyers, 117–36. Edinburgh: Butterworths.

Sheehan, Michael M. 1971. "The Formation and Stability of Marriage in Fourteenth-Century England: Evidence of an Ely Register." *Mediaeval Studies* 33: 228–63.

Sheehan, Michael. 1996. *Marriage, Family, and Law in Medieval Europe: Collected Studies*. Ed. James Farge. Toronto: University of Toronto Press.

Shorter, Edward. 1971. "Illegitimacy, Sexual Revolution, and Social Change in Modern Europe." *Journal of Interdisciplinary History* 2 (2): 237–72. http://dx.doi.org/10.2307/202844.

Shorter, Edward. 1975. *The Making of the Modern Family*. New York: Basic Books.

Sibeth, Uwe. 1994. *Eherecht und Staatsbildung: Ehegesetzgebung und Eherechtssprechung in der Landgrafschaft Hessen (-Kassel) in der Frühen Neuzeit*. Quellen und Forschungen zur hessischen Geschichte 98. Darmstadt and Marburg: Hessische Historische Kommission.

Sibeth, Uwe. 1997. "Zur Bedeutung von Güteverfahren und Vergleichen in der protestantischen Eherechtssprechung, dargestellt am Beispiel Hessen (-Kassels)." *Archiv für Reformationsgeschichte* 88: 217–57. http://dx.doi.org/10.14315/arg-1997-jg08.

Siebenhüner, Kim. 2006. *Bigamie und Inquisition in Italien, 1600–1750*. Paderborn: Schöningh.

Signori, Gabriela. 2011. *Von der Paradiesehe zur Gütergemeinschaft: Die Ehe in der mittelalterlichen Lebens- und Vorstellungswelt*. Geschichte und Geschlechter 60. Frankfurt am Main and New York: Campus.

Sikora, Michael. 2005. "Ungleiche Verbindlichkeiten: Gestaltungsspielräume standesverschiedener Partnerschaften im deutschen Hochadel der Frühen Neuzeit." *zeitenblicke* 4, no. 3 (13 Dec.): 1–48. http://www.zeitenblicke.de/2005/3/Sikora/index_html, URN: urn:nbn:de:0009-9-2301.

Sikora, Michael. 2007. "Über den Umgang mit Ungleichheit: Bewältigungsstrategien für Mesalliancen im deutschen Hochadel der Frühen Neuzeit – Das Haus Anhalt als Beispiel." In *Zwischen Schande und Ehre: Erinnerungsbrüche und die Kontinuität des Hauses. Legitimationsmuster und Traditionsverständnis des frühneuzeitlichen Adels in Umbruch und Krise*, Veröffentlichungen des Instituts für Europäische Geschichte Mainz, Abteilung für Universalgeschichte, Beiheft 73, edited by Martin Wrede and Horst Carl, 97–124. Mainz: Vandenhoeck and Ruprecht.

Sikora, Michael. 2012. "As Long As It's Marriage: The Hessian Bigamy Case of 1540 within the Competing Interests of Dynasty, Desire and New Moral Demands." *Dimensioni e problemi della ricerca storica* 25 (2): 33–60.

Simon, Christian. 1981. "Untertanenverhalten und obrigkeitliche Moralpolitik." PhD diss., University of Basel.

Smith, Richard Michael. 1986. "Marriage Processes in the English Past: Some Continuities." In *The World We Have Gained: Histories of Population and Social Structure*, edited by Lloyd Bonfield, Richard Michael Smith, Keith Wrightson, and Peter Laslett, 43–99. Oxford and New York: Blackwell.

Smout, T. Christopher. 1982. "Scottish Marriage, Regular and Irregular, 1550–1940." In *Marriage and Society: Studies in the Social History of Marriage*, edited by R.B. Outhwaite, 204–36. New York: St Martin's Press.

Söderlind, Nils. 1950. "Svenska prästerskapet och folkliga bröllopsseder under 1600-talet." *Kyrkohistorisk Årsskrift* 50: 1–52.

Söderlind, Nils. 1967. "'Lagha' ålder och 'olika': Ett bidrag till äktenskapsålderns historia." *Kyrkohistorisk Årsskrift* 67: 69–86.

Söderlind, Nils. 1969. "Error personæ. Svensk domkapitelspraxis under 1600-talet." *Kyrkohistorisk Årsskrift* 69: 97–116.

Spierenburg, Pieter. 2004. "Social Control and History: An Introduction." In *Social Control in Europe*, vol. 1, *1500–1800*, edited by Herman Roodenburg and Pieter Spierenburg, 1–21. Columbus: Ohio State University Press.

Spierling, Karen E. 2005. *Infant Baptism in Reformation Geneva: The Shaping of a Community, 1536–1564*. Aldershot, UK, and Burlington, VT: Ashgate.

Spiess, Karl-Heinz. 1993. *Familie und Verwandtschaft im deutschen Hochadel des Spätmittelalters: 13. bis Anfang des 16. Jahrhunderts*, VSWG Beihefte 111. Stuttgart: Steiner.

Spieß, Karl-Heinz. 2003. "Witwenversorgung im Hochadel: Rechtlicher Rahmen und praktische Gestaltung im Spätmittelalter und zu Beginn der Frühen Neuzeit." In Schattkowsky 2003, 87–114.

Spitzer, Elke. 2002. *Emanzipationsansprüche zwischen der Querelle des Femmes und der modernen Frauenbewegung: Der Wandel des Gleichheitsbegriffs am Ausgang des 18. Jahrhunderts*. Kassel: Kassel University Press.

Sprengler-Ruppenthal, Anneliese. 1982. "Zur Rezeption des Römischen Rechts im Eherecht der Reformatoren." *Zeitschrift der Savigny-Stiftung fur Rechtsgeschichte. Kanonistische Abteilung* 99: 363–418.

Sprengler-Ruppenthal, Anneliese. 1992. "Das kanonische Recht in Kirchenordnungen des 16. Jahrhunderts." In *Canon Law in Protestant Lands*, Comparative Studies in Continental and Anglo-American Legal History 11, edited by Richard Helmholz, 49–121. Berlin: Duncker & Humblot.

Spurr, John. 1991. *The Restoration Church of England, 1646–1689*. New Haven, CT, and London: Yale University Press.

Stambaugh, Rita, ed. 1972–80. *Teufelbücher in Auswahl*, vols. 2–5. Berlin: De Gruyter.

Stollberg-Rilinger, Barbara. 2000. *Europa im Jahrhundert der Aufklärung*. Stuttgart: Reclam.
Stone, Lawrence. 1990. *The Road to Divorce: England 1530–1987*. Oxford: Oxford University Press.
Stone, Lawrence. 1992. *Uncertain Unions: Marriage in England 1660–1753*. Oxford: Oxford University Press.
Stone, Lawrence. 1993. *Broken Lives: Separation and Divorce in England, 1660–1857*. Oxford: Oxford University Press.
Storme, Hans. 1992. *Die trouwen wilt voorsichtelijck: Predikanten en moralisten over de voorbereiding op het huwelijk in de Vlaamse bisdommen (17e–18e eeuw)*. Leuven: Leuven University Press.
Strasser, Ulrike. 2004. *State of Virginity: Gender, Religion, and Politics in an Early Modern Catholic State*. Ann Arbor: University of Michigan Press.
Straussman-Pflanzer, Eve. 2008. "Allegorical Wedding Picture" [Exhibition Number 147]. In *Art and Love in Renaissance Italy*, edited by Andrea Bayer, 319–21. New York: Metropolitan Museum of Art.
Strype, John. 1822. *Life and Acts of John Whitgift*. Oxford: Clarendon Press.
Sutter, Eva. 1995. *"Ein Act des Leichtsinns und der Sünde": Illegitimität im Kanton Zürich: Recht, Moral und Lebensrealität (1800–1860)*. Zurich: Chronos.
Tacke, Andreas, ed. 2006. *"… wir wollen der Liebe Raum geben": Konkubinate geistlicher und weltlicher Fürsten um 1500*. Schriftenreihe der Stiftung Moritzburg 3. Göttingen: Wallstein.
Tanco, Beatriz. 2002. "La bigamia en el Tribunal Inquisitorial de Logroño: Siglos XVI y XVII." In *Grupos sociales en la historia de Navarra, relaciones y derechos*, Actas del V Congreso de Historia de Navarra, edited by Carmen Erro Gasca et al., 1:333–42. Pamplona: Eunate.
Testón, Isabel. 1985. *Amor, sexo y matrimonio en Extremadura*. Badajoz, Spain: Universitas.
Thompson, E.P. 1991. *Customs in Common*. London: New Press.
Thomson, Arthur. 1966. *Otidigt sängelag: En rättshistorisk studie*. Rättshistoriskt bibliotek 9. Lund: Nordiska Bokhandeln.
Thum, Veronika. 2006. *Die Zehn Gebote für die ungelehrten Leut': Der Dekalog in der Graphik des späten Mittelalters und der Frühen Neuzeit*. Kunstwissenschaftliche Studien 136. Munich: Deutscher Kunstverlag.
Thunander, Rudolf. 1993. *Hovrätt i funktion*. Rättshistoriskt bibliotek 49. Lund: Nordiska Bokhandeln.
Tineo, Primitivo. 1996. "La recepción de Trento en España (1565): Disposiciones sobre la actividad episcopal." *Anuario de Historia de la Iglesia* 5: 241–96.
Tolkemitt, Brigitte. 1998. "Knotenpunkte im Beziehungsnetz der Gebildeten: Die gemischte Geselligkeit in den offenen Häusern der Hamburger Familien

Reimarus und Sieveking." In *Ordnung, Politik und Geselligkeit der Geschlechter im 18. Jahrhundert*, Das achtzehnte Jahrhundert, Supplementa 6, edited by Ulrike Weckel, Claudia Opitz, Olivia Hochstrasser, and Brigitte Tolkemitt, 167–202. Göttingen: Wallstein.

Toppe, Sabina. 1999. *Polizey und Geschlecht: Der obrigkeitsstaatliche Mutterschafts-Diskurs in der Aufklärung*. Frauen- und Geschlechterforschung in der Historischen Pädagogik 3. Weinheim: Deutscher Studien Verlag.

Tosi, Claudio. 1990. "Giuseppinismo e legislazione matrimoniale in Lombardia: La Costituzione del 1784." *Critica Storica* 27: 235–301.

Trampus, Antonio. 2008. *Il diritto alla felicità: Storia di un'idea*. Rome and Bari: Laterza.

Turner, Victor Witter. 1969. *The Ritual Process: Structure and Anti-Structure*. Chicago: Aldine.

Ulbricht, Otto. 1990. *Kindsmord und Aufklärung in Deutschland*. Ancien Régime, Aufklärung und Revolution 18. Munich: R. Oldenbourg.

Usunáriz, Jesús M. 2004. "El matrimonio y su reforma en el mundo hispánico durante el siglo de Oro: La promesa matrimonial." In *Temas del Barroco Hispánico*, edited by Ignacio Arellano and Eduardo Godoy, 293–312. Madrid: Iberoamericana.

Usunáriz, Jesús M. 2005. "El matrimonio como ejercicio de libertad en la España del Siglo de Oro." In *El matrimonio en Europa y el mundo hispánico: Siglos XVI y XVII*, edited by Ignacio Arellano and Jesús M. Usunáriz, 167–95. Madrid: Visor Libros.

Usunáriz, Jesús M. 2012. "Palabras de amor en el mundo hispánico: Emociones y sentimientos en la correspondencia privada del Siglo de Oro." In *Por seso e por maestría: Homenaje a la profesora Carmen Saralegui*, edited by Concepción Martínez Pasamar and Cristina Tabernero Sala, 555–97. Pamplona: Eunsa.

Usunáriz, Jesús M. 2014. "Sentimientos e Historia: La correspondencia amorosa en los siglos XVI–XVIII." In *Cinco Siglos de Cartas: Historia y prácticas epistolares en las épocas moderna y contemporánea*, edited by Antonio Castillo and Verónica Sierra Blas, 251–73. Huelva: Universidad de Huelva.

Usunáriz, Jesús M., and Rocío García Bourrellier. 2012. *Amar y convivir: Matrimonio y familia en Navarra (siglos XIII–XVI)*. Pamplona: Gobierno de Navarra.

Vaccari, Pietro. 1940. "Dalla 'Summa de matrimonio' alla 'Summa decretalis' di Bernardo da Pavia." In *Studi di storia e diritto in onore di Carlo Calisse*, 2: 337–54. Milan: Giuffrè.

Valsecchi, Chiara. 1999. "Causa matrimonialis est gravis et ardua: 'Consiliatores' e matrimonio fino al Concilio di Trento." In *Studi di storia del diritto*, 2:408–580. Milan: Giuffrè.

Vanja, Christina. 1996. "Das 'Weibergericht' in Breitenbach: Verkehrte Welt in einem hessischen Dorf des 17. Jahrhunderts." In *Weiber, Menscher, Frauenzimmer: Frauen in der ländlichen Gesellschaft 1500–1800*, edited by Heide Wunder and Christina Vanja, 214–22. Göttingen: Vandenhoeck and Ruprecht.

Velten, Hans-Rudolf. 1995. *Das selbst geschriebene Leben: Eine Studie zur deutschen Autobiographie im 16. Jahrhundert*. Frankfurter Beiträge zur Germanistik 29. Heidelberg: Winter.

Viazzo, Pier Paolo. 2001. "Mortality, Fertility, and Family." In Kertzer and Barbagli 2001, 157–87.

Villani, Stefano. 2005. "Donne inglesi a Livorno nella prima età moderna." In *Sul filo della scrittura: Fonti e temi per la storia delle donne a Livorno*, edited by Lucia Frattarelli Fischer and Olimpia Vaccari, 377–99. Pisa: Plus-Pisa University Press.

Villani, Stefano. 2009a. "Il matrimonio di una principessa: Le trattative per le nozze di Caterina di Ferdinando Medici con il principe Enrico d'Inghilterra." In *Nobildonne, monache e cavaliere dell'ordine di Santo Stefano: Modelli e strategie femminili nella vita pubblica della Toscana granducale*, edited by Manuela Aglietti, 215–34. Pisa: ETS.

Villani, Stefano. 2009b. "Una finestra mediterranea sull'Europa: I 'nordici' nella Livorno della prima età moderna." In *Livorno 1606–1806: Luogo di incontro tra popoli e culture*, edited by Adriano Prosperi, 158–77. Livorno: Allemandi.

Vogel, Ursula. 1997. "Gleichheit und Herrschaft in der ehelichen Vertragsgesellschaft – Widersprüche der Aufklärung." In Gerhard 1997, 265–92.

Völker-Rasor, Anette. 1993. *Bilderpaare, Paarbilder: Die Ehe in Autobiographien des 16. Jahrhunderts*. Freiburg: Rombach.

Wagner, Wolfgang Eric. 2007. Uxorati – conjugati – bigami*: Die Verheirateten an der spätmittelalterlichen Universität*. Rostocker Universitätsreden Neue Folge 16. Rostock: Historisches Institut.

Walsham, Alexandra. 2006. *Charitable Hatred: Tolerance and Intolerance in England, 1500–1700*. Manchester: Manchester University Press.

Watt, Jeffrey R. 1992. *The Making of Modern Marriage: Matrimonial Control and the Rise of Sentiment in Neuchâtel, 1550–1800*. Ithaca, NY, and London: Cornell University Press.

Watt, Jeffrey R. 2001. "The Impact of Reformation and Counter-Reformation." In Kertzer and Barbagli 2001, 125–56.

Weckel, Ulrike. 1998. *Zwischen Häuslichkeit und Öffentlichkeit: Die ersten deutschen Frauenzeitschriften im späten 18. Jahrhundert und ihr Publikum*. Studien und Texte zur Sozialgeschichte der Literatur 61. Tübingen: M. Niemeyer.

Wedberg, Birger. 1944. *Karl XII på justitietronen*. Stockholm: P.A. Norstedt & Söner.

Weigand, Rudolf. 1984. "Ehe- und Familienrecht in der mittelalterlichen Stadt." In Haverkamp 1984, 161–94.

Weigand, Rudolf. 1993. "Zur mittelalterlichen kirchlichen Ehegerichtsbarkeit." In *Liebe und Ehe im Mittelalter*, edited by Rudolf Weigand, 307–41. Goldbach: Keip.

Weinstein, Roni. 2004. *Marriage Rituals Italian Style: A Historical Anthropological Perspective on Early Modern Italian Jews*. Leiden: Brill.

Werkstetter, Christine. 2001. *Frauen im Augsburger Zunfthandwerk: Arbeit, Arbeitsbeziehungen und Geschlechterverhältnisse im 18. Jahrhundert*. Colloquia Augustana 14. Berlin: Akademie Verlag.

Werth, Paul. 2008. "Empire, Religious Freedom, and the Legal Regulation of 'Mixed' Marriages in Russia." *Journal of Modern History* 80 (2): 296–331. http://dx.doi.org/10.1086/588853.

Westphal, Siegrid. 2008. *Ehen vor Gericht – Scheidungen und ihre Folgen am Reichskammergericht*. Schriftenreihe der Gesellschaft für Reichskammergerichtforschung 35. Wetzlar: Gesellschaft für Reichskammergerichtsforschung.

Whitman, James Q. 2008. *The Origins of Reasonable Doubt: Theological Roots of the Criminal Trial*. New Haven, CT: Yale University Press.

Windler, Christian. 2013. "Uneindeutige Zugehörigkeiten: Katholische Missionare und die Kurie im Umgang mit 'communicatio in sacris.'" In *Konfessionelle Ambiguität: Uneindeutigkeit und Verstellung als religiöse Praxis in der Frühen Neuzeit*, edited by Andreas Pietsch and Barbara Stollberg-Rilinger, 314–45. Gütersloh, Germany: Gütersloher Verlagshaus.

Witte, John, Jr. 1997. *From Sacrament to Contract: Marriage, Religion, and Law in the Western Tradition*. 1st ed. Louisville, KY: Westminster John Knox Press.

Witte, John, Jr. 2012. *From Sacrament to Contract: Marriage, Religion, and Law in the Western Tradition*. 2nd ed. Louisville, KY: Westminster John Knox Press.

Witte, John, Jr. 1998. "Between Sacrament and Contract: Marriage in John Calvin's Geneva." *Calvin Theological Journal* 33: 9–75.

Witte, John, Jr., and Robert M. Kingdon. 2005. *Sex, Marriage, and Family in John Calvin's Geneva*. Grand Rapids, MI: W.B. Eerdmans.

Woodcock, Brian. 1952. *Medieval Ecclesiastical Courts in the Diocese of Canterbury*. Oxford: Oxford University Press.

Wunder, Gerd. 1980. *Die Bürger von Hall: Sozialgeschichte einer Reichsstadt 1216–1802*. Sigmaringen: Thorbecke.

Wunder, Heide. 1992. *"Er ist die Sonn, sie ist der Mond": Frauen in der Frühen Neuzeit*. Munich: Beck (English translation: *"He Is the Sun, She Is the Moon": Women in Early Modern Germany*, translated by Thomas Dunlap, Cambridge, MA: Harvard University Press, 2006).

Wunder, Heide, ed. 1995. *Eine Stadt der Frauen: Studien und Quellen zur Geschichte der Baslerinnen im späten Mittelalter und zu Beginn der Neuzeit (13.–17. Jh.)*. Basel: Helbing & Lichtenhahn.

Wunder, Heide. 1998. "'Iustitia, Teutonice Fromkeyt': Theologische Rechtfertigung und bürgerliche Rechtschaffenheit: Ein Beitrag zur Sozialgeschichte eines theologischen Konzepts." In *Die frühe Reformation in Deutschland als Umbruch*, Schriften des Vereins für Reformationsgeschichte 199, edited by Bernd Moeller in cooperation with Stephen E. Buckwalter, 307–32. Gütersloh: Gütersloher Verlagshaus.

Wunder, Heide. 2001. "Construction of Masculinity and Male Identity in Personal Testimonies: Hans von Schweinichen (1552–1616) in His *Memorial*." In *Time, Space, and Women's Lives in Early Modern Europe*, edited by Anne Jacobson Schutte, Thomas Kuehn, and Silvana Seidel Menchi, 305–24. Kirksville, MO: Truman State University Press.

Wunder, Heide. 2002. "'What Made a Man a Man?' Sixteenth- and Seventeenth Century Findings." In *Gender in Early Modern German History*, edited by Ulinka Rublack, 21–48. Cambridge: Cambridge University Press.

Wunder, Heide. 2009. "Matrimonio e formazione del patrimonio nella prima età moderna: Un contributo sulla relazione tra la storia di genere e la storia economica." *Studi Storici* 50: 747–78.

Wunder, Heide. 2012. "Herrendienst, Konfession und in Stande bleiben: Die österreichischen Freiherren von Hohenfeld im Reich und im Vatterland." *Nassauische Annalen: Jahrbuch des Vereins für Nassauische Altertumsurkunde und Geschichtsforschung* 123: 305–48.

Wunderli, Richard M. 1981. *London Church Courts and Society on the Eve of the Reformation*. Cambridge, MA: Medieval Academy of America.

Ylikangas, Heikki. 1967. *Suomalaisen Sven Leijonmarckin osuus vuoden 1734 lain naimiskaaren laadinnassa*. Historiallisia tutkimuksia 71. Helsinki: Forssan Kirjapaino.

Ylikangas, Heikki. 1988. *Valta ja väkivalta keski- ja uuden ajan taitteen Suomessa*. Porvoo, Finland: Söderström.

Zarri, Gabriella. 2000. *Recinti: Donne, clausura e matrimonio nella prima età moderna*. Bologna: Il Mulino.

Zemon Davis, Natalie. 1973. "The Rites of Violence: Religious Riot in Sixteenth-Century France." *Past & Present* 59 (1): 51–91. http://dx.doi.org/10.1093/past/59.1.51.

Zemon Davis, Natalie. 1975. *Society and Culture in Early Modern France*. Stanford, CA: Stanford University Press.

Zimmermann, Clemens. 1991. "'Behörigen Orthen angezeigt': Kindsmörderinnen in der ländlichen Gesellschaft Württembergs, 1581–1792." *Medizin, Gesellschaft und Geschichte* 10: 67–102.

Zimmermann, Reinhard. 1996. *The Law of Obligations: Roman Foundations of the Civilian Tradition*. Oxford: Clarendon Press.

Index

www.ingramcontent.com/pod-product-compliance
Lightning Source LLC
LaVergne TN
LVHW090146080826
844660LV00013B/692/J

* 9 7 8 1 4 4 2 6 3 7 5 0 4 *